TAKING SIDES

Clashing Views in

Family and Personal Relationships

TAKING SIDES

Clashing Views in

Family and Personal Relationships

NINTH EDITION

Selected, Edited, and with Introductions by

David M. Hall, Ed.D
Professional Trainer/Consultant

Mc Graw Hill

*Connect
Learn
Succeed*™

TAKING SIDES: CLASHING VIEWS IN FAMILY AND PERSONAL RELATIONSHIPS,
NINTH EDITION

Published by McGraw-Hill, a business unit of The McGraw-Hill Companies, Inc., 1221 Avenue of
the Americas, New York, NY 10020. Copyright © 2013 by The McGraw-Hill Companies, Inc. All
rights reserved. Printed in the United States of America. Previous editions © 2010, 2008, and
2006. No part of this publication may be reproduced or distributed in any form or by any means,
or stored in a database or retrieval system, without the prior written consent of The McGraw-Hill
Companies, Inc., including, but not limited to, in any network or other electronic storage or
transmission, or broadcast for distance learning.

Some ancillaries, including electronic and print components, may not be available to customers
outside the United States.

This book is printed on acid-free paper.

Taking Sides® is a registered trademark of the McGraw-Hill Companies, Inc.
Taking Sides is published by the **Contemporary Learning Series** group within the McGraw-Hill
Higher Education division.

1 2 3 4 5 6 7 8 9 0 DOC/DOC 1 0 9 8 7 6 5 4 3 2

MHID: 0-07-805038-3
ISBN: 978-0-07-805038-1
ISSN: 96-85806 (print)
ISSN: Pending (online)

Managing Editor: *Larry Loeppke*
Senior Developmental Editor: *Jill Meloy*
Senior Permissions Coordinator: *Shirley Lanners*
Senior Marketing Communications Specialist: *Mary Klein*
Project Manager: *Erin Melloy*
Design Coordinator: *Brenda A. Rolwes*
Cover Graphics: *Rick D. Noel*
Buyer: *Nicole Baumgartner*
Media Project Manager: *Sridevi Palani*

Compositor: MPS Limited, a Macmillan Company
Cover Image: © Design Pics RF

www.mhhe.com

Editors/Academic Advisory Board

Members of the Academic Advisory Board are instrumental in the final selection of articles for each edition of TAKING SIDES. Their review of articles for content, level, and appropriateness provides critical direction to the editors and staff. We think that you will find their careful consideration well reflected in this volume.

TAKING SIDES: Clashing Views in FAMILY AND PERSONAL RELATIONSHIPS
Ninth Edition

EDITOR
David M. Hall
Professional Trainer/Consultant

ACADEMIC ADVISORY BOARD MEMBERS

Bill Anderson
Illinois State University

David Ayers
Grove City College

Laurence Basirico
Elon University

Timothy Baylor
Lock Haven University of Pennsylvania

Zsuzsa Berend
University of California—Los Angeles

Amy Blackstone
University of Maine

John Bodinger de Uriarte
Susquehanna University

Kathryn Bonach
Indiana University of Pennsylvania

Carolyn Bradley
Monmouth University

Corby Caffrey-Dobosh
Waynesburg University

Stanley Clawar
Rosemont College

Theodore Cohen
Ohio Wesleyan University

John Conahan
Kutztown University of Pennsylvania

Jason Lee Crockett
Kutztown University of Pennsylvania

Regina Davis-Sowers
Santa Clara University

Nancy DeCesare
Chestnut Hill College

Eli DeHope
West Chester University of Pennsylvania

Cynthia Drenovsky
Shippensburg University

John Durst
Ohio Wesleyan University

Monica Faulkner
University of Texas—Austin

Julie Fennell
Gallaudet University

Diane Ferrero-Paluzzi
Iona College

Laci Fiala Ades
Walsh University

Sheila Fox
Immaculata University

Cynthia Franklin
University of Texas—Austin

Anita Garey
University of Connecticut

Craig Goforth
Mars Hill College

Melissa Gosdin
Ohio University

Ruby Gourdine
Howard University

Laura Groves
Cabrini College

C. Margaret Hall
Georgetown University

Brent Harger
Albright College

Joann Haws
DeSales University

Terrell Hayes
High Point University

Susan Herrick
West Liberty University

Gary Jones
Cabrini College

Eric Jorrey
Ohio University—Athens

Kara Joyner
Bowling Green State University

Antonia Keane
Loyola University

Editors/Academic Advisory Board continued

Preface

Human beings naturally seek out relationships. While these relationships vary depending on whether they are among family, coworkers, friends, acquaintances, or significant others, relationships with intimate others can be the most rewarding and challenging. From a public policy and social interaction perspective, they can also be the most controversial. The ways in which our personal and family relationships are understood and respected can influence not just our intimate relationships but also our social relationships and livelihood. Too often in the national media, our family and relationship diversity is approached from a controversial perspective that can foster division and animosity. *Taking Sides: Family and Personal Relationships* is intended to provide thoughtful discourse, standing in sharp contrast with the divisive portrayals and rhetoric too often found in the national media.

The ninth edition of *Taking Sides: Family and Personal Relationships* provides thoughtful discourse from diverse perspectives on some of the most controversial issues in American society today. This volume contains 20 questions, with 40 thoughtful and engaging viewpoints that are designed for readers not just to reinforce but also to challenge their existing perspectives and values. Each chapter includes an *introduction* from the editor, which provides a context for this debate. The *introduction* may cite important statistics, pertinent history, and an overview of the debate. The *introduction* is followed by two competing views on the controversial question. Following the competing viewpoints are *critical questions* and *common ground* from the editor, which will examine suggestions for further thought, research, or action to the topic posed in the chapter. The section *Additional Resources* provides a list of sources that will help further the reader's understanding about the topics in this volume.

Taking Sides: Family and Personal Relationships will challenge readers to examine contrary viewpoints regarding contemporary issues. Topics relate to parenting, cyberspace, infidelity, sexual orientation, sexual decision making, and many other issues that are sensitive and often difficult to discuss openly. Each chapter will provide the reader with an opportunity to reinforce what they already believe, while also challenging some of their already held beliefs and convictions.

A word to the instructor An *Instructor's Resource Guide with Test Questions* provides multiple-choice and essay questions related to this text for help with assessment of student reading. While the *Instructor's Resource Guide with Test Questions* is tailor-made for this specific volume, educators can also reference *Using Taking Sides in the Classroom*, which provides an overview of ways in which instructors can manage discussions about divergent viewpoints within their classroom. For an online version of *Using Taking Sides in the Classroom* and a correspondence service for *Taking Sides* adopters, please visit http://www.mhcls.com/usingts.

McGraw-Hill provides a dynamic list of titles in this series in addition to *Taking Sides: Family and Personal Relationships* that can be used in a wide variety of courses, ranging from titles that relate to specific course content to using any of the volumes in teaching students how to write and debate persuasively. If interested in reviewing other thought-provoking editions, please visit the Taking Sides Web site at http://www.mhcls.com/takingsides.

Acknowledgments First and foremost, let me thank McGraw-Hill's Jill Meloy and Jade Benedict. Writing and editing can be so very personal, and therefore challenging. However, Jill and Jade could not have been more thoughtful and collaborative throughout this process. Their feedback and support would almost instantaneously follow my emails and phone calls. They have been an invaluable resource in creating this edition. Jill and Jade's timely, thoughtful feedback, combined with their support for my goal to create the best edition possible, have been critical to the creation of this volume. Had it not been for Jill and Jade, this edition would never have reached publication with this level of quality.

I would also like to thank:

- William J. Taverner, Editor-in-Chief of the *American Journal for Sexuality Education* and editor of *Taking Sides: Human Sexuality*, for his generous spirit of collaboration and mentorship. I have learned so very much from Bill's intellect and creativity. It is unlikely that I would be editor of this volume had it not been for Bill.
- David Trevaskis, Esq., an extraordinarily talented attorney and educator. David provided an outstanding contribution on grandparents' rights. He also provided a draft introduction for the chapter on grandparents' rights that I was free to edit for this edition.
- Lauren Ewaniuk, a gifted educator and curriculum author, for serving as Contributing Editor to the Instructor's Manual that accompanies this book. Lauren was also invaluable for help in researching potential articles for this book, and she has put extensive work into significantly expanding the book's Advisory Board to help ensure that the chapters meet the needs and objectives of those who are assigning it. Lauren has been an invaluable partner in this edition. That is evident throughout this edition. Her work on expanding the Advisory Board will have a lasting impact not just on this edition, but also on future editions to this text.
- My dear spouse, Annie Hall. With three young children, there were days when much more was asked of her as a mother so that this book could be completed with the necessary quality. She never complained and always provided our kids with exciting enrichment each and every time.
- The authors featured in this edition. I am fortunate to have had the opportunity to collaborate with bright and talented scholars who have framed a powerful debate that will enhance not only learning but also public discourse.

Remember that while reading this volume, you may very well find viewpoints that you find challenging and even offensive. This is why I want to end by acknowledging you, the reader, for the courage to challenge your deeply held convictions in reading these chapters. It is difficult to entertain positions that one finds morally wrong, but doing so leads to stronger moral and intellectual growth. Thank you for taking the time to read and interact with this book.

David M. Hall, Ph.D.
Professional Trainer and Consultant
Doylestown, PA

This book is dedicated in loving memory to
Winfield A. Hall, my loving father,
for teaching me so very much
about love and understanding.

Contents in Brief

Contents

Tony Dokoupil is a staff writer at *Newsweek* and *The Daily Beast.* Dokoupil writes about different issues affecting national life, often related to diversity. In this chapter, he writes about the increasing number of transracial adoptions in the United States in recent years but notes that we are seeing limited examples of African American families adopting white babies. When an African American family adopts a white baby, a unique set of challenges is created, he argues, due to deep-seated views about race in American society today. Dokoupil explores questions related to what this reveals about contemporary views on race in American society. Ezra Griffith and Rachel Bergeron, both faculty members of the Yale University School of Medicine's psychiatry department, argue that requiring racial and ethnic matching, although an appropriate effort, would leave too many children of color languishing in the foster and adoption systems. By maintaining that only in-race adoption is the best and ideal situation, they ask rhetorically, does our society actually do more to reinforce cultural stereotypes or to truly serve children needing homes?

Sarah Werthan Buttenwieser is a writer and lives in Northampton. She earned her BA at Hampshire College and her MFA from Warren Wilson

College. Contributor to many magazines, newspapers, and online publications, she has a blog called "Standing in the Shadows," which can be found at http://www.valleyadvocate.com. Jane Johnson Struck and Angela Thomas are the authors of *My Single-Mom Life*, published by Thomas Nealson. Thomas, a mother of four, possesses a Masters degree from the Dallas Theological Seminary. Thomas writes that being a single mom was not God's design for parenting. She believes in children being raised by a man and a woman in love. Despite her beliefs and the challenges she has faced through divorce, her belief is that God and Jesus protect her and her children when they are in need. She argues that faith in God is what people need to protect them from the challenges of being a single mother and a child of a divorced family.

Chris Jeub, writer and president of Training Minds Ministries, is a former public school teacher with 11 children, all of whom he and his wife have home-schooled. Naming several famous home-schooled individuals, such as Winston Churchill, Benjamin Franklin, and Florence Nightingale, he argues that the home is the best environment in which to teach children, for social, academic, family strengthening, and religious reasons. Home-schooling, he maintains, frees parents to impart their own values to their children without concern for how these beliefs might clash with what is presented in the public school system. Carole Moore, a freelance writer, discusses how she weighed the options of home-schooling versus public schooling and argues that even though home-schooling might offer some benefits to children, in the end, home-schooling provides children a distorted view of the world at large. Children will, she writes, make good decisions and bad decisions as a part of growing up, and whether they are home-schooled or public schooled is not the determining factor in whether they grow up healthy and well adjusted.

Child developmentalists Jeanne Brooks-Gunn, Wen-Jui Han, and Jane Waldfogel assert that their findings show many types of negative effects from maternal employment on the later cognitive and educational outcomes of children. Professor of sociology and anthropology Thomas M. Vander Ven and his colleagues argue that their studies show that a working mother will have relatively little or no negative influence on the social, emotional, and behavioral functioning of her children.

William Brennan is regarded as one of the greatest intellectual leaders of the twentieth-century Supreme Court. He was regarded for writing extraordinarily forward-thinking opinions, especially regarding civil rights and civil liberties. This case proves no exception, as he captures an issue that seems even more pertinent today than when the Supreme Court addressed it. Brennan believes that children who are in the country and undocumented have a constitutional right to a public education. Warren Burger was the Chief Justice of the Supreme Court during a time in which it was slowly moving in a more conservative direction. He was an instrumental voice in many cases before the Supreme Court that had a more conservative outcome. Burger believes that undocumented immigrant children have no constitutional right to an education.

Professor John A. Robertson of the University of Texas at Austin's School of Law argues that preconception Gender selection of infants in utero for medical purposes should be allowed, and that insufficient data exist to demonstrate that any clear harm exists in allowing parents to do so. Norman Daniels and contributors argue that one aspect of allowing such a procedure as preconception gender selection, introduces socioeconomic status inequality since the procedure would likely not be covered by health insurance.

Jennifer Russell is an attorney at SeniorLAW Center. She provides legal services to grandparents and other seniors raising relative children. Russell contends that grandparent custody and visitation statutes should be upheld, and argues that grandparents often play an essential role in their grandchildren's lives, especially during times of family turmoil. Sandra Day O'Connor was the first woman appointed to the United States Supreme Court. For much of her time on the court, she was the justice most likely to wind up in the majority opinion. O'Connor argues that the rights of parents trumps grandparents. As a result, grandparents would not have the right to see their grandchildren.

Neal Kumar Katyal served as Acting Solicitor General in the Obama administration at the time of this case. Katyal argues that Congress created legislation with a different standard of citizenship for biological fathers versus biological mothers and that this different standard served a rational interest and should be upheld. Steven Hubachek is the Counsel of Record for the Federal Defenders of San Diego, Inc. Hubachek argues that this law discriminates against men because it makes it more difficult for immigrant fathers to pass on their citizenship to their children than for immigrant mothers.

Calvin P. Johnson, Esq., is the attorney for the parents, Colleen and Anthony Hauser. Johnson argues that the government forcing medical care for the Hauser child violates his religious liberty and is abusive to this child. Judge John R. Rodenberg is the District Court judge in this case. Rodenberg argues that all parties are acting out of convictions for the best interest of the child. He also argues that the state has a compelling interest to act against Hauser's religious views for medical care since the child is only thirteen years old.

UNIT 3   NONTRADITIONAL FAMILIES AND RELATIONSHIPS   179

The Human Rights Campaign (HRC), America's largest lesbian and gay organization, outlines the disparities American lesbian and gay couples experience when they are not allowed to marry legally, as well as the logistical considerations involved in granting same-sex couples the right to marry. Peter Sprigg, director of the Center for Marriage and Family Studies at the Family Research Council, outlines why nonheterosexual relationships do not carry with them the same validity as heterosexual relationships, and therefore gays and lesbians should not be allowed to marry legally.

Issue 11.   Should Private Sexual Acts Between Gay Couples Be Illegal?   199

Anthony Kennedy, Associate Justice of the Supreme Court of the United States, was appointed to the Court by President Reagan in 1988. In this case, Kennedy is writing for a six-member majority that overturns a previous case, *Bowers v. Hardwick*. *Bowers* is overturned by Kennedy's opinion, therefore striking down state antisodomy laws. Antonin Scalia, Associate Justice of the Supreme Court of the United States, was appointed to the Court by President Reagan in 1986. Scalia writes that there are no constitutional protections from discrimination based on sexual orientation and that state sodomy laws should be upheld.

Issue 12.   Are Traditional Families Better for Children?   219

Allan Carlson is president of the Howard Center for Family, Religion & Society and Distinguished Fellow in Family Policy Studies at the Family Research Council in Washington, D.C. Paul Mero is president of the Sutherland Institute and a trustee of the ALS Foundation. Carlson and Mero argue that America needs to return to a traditional family headed by a man and woman. Mark Good is a professor of counselor education at West Chester University and the president of Opn-Wyd, a diversity and communication company. Good argues that diversity in traditional and nontraditional families is healthy. In fact, he argues that it can be damaging to hold up the traditional family as the ideal familial structure.

Issue 13.   Should Lesbian and Gay Individuals Be Able to Adopt Children?   244

Joan Biskupic, legal affairs correspondent for *USA Today*, discusses the
personal challenges for same-gender couples attempting to adopt in
states that are not friendly to them and provides an update of legal issues
and options available to lesbian and gay couples; these indicate a
changing tide of acceptance toward couples of the same gender, as well
as lesbian and gay individuals, adopting children. Timothy J. Dailey, senior
research fellow at the Center for Marriage and Family Studies, provides
an overview of state laws pertaining to adoption by lesbian or gay parents.
He points to studies showing that children do much better in family settings
that include both a mother and a father, and that the sexual behaviors
same-sex parents engage in make them, by definition, inappropriate role
models for children.

The National Campaign to Prevent Teen and Unplanned Pregnancy is
dedicated to reducing teenage pregnancy. Their research argues that
teens face significant consequences if they have unplanned pregnancy.
Simon Duncan, Claire Alexander, and Rosaline Edwards have written a
chapter in a book about teen pregnancy and parenting. This chapter,
which takes a global perspective by looking at another Western society,
England, argues that teenage pregnancy and parenting is not a problem.

UNIT 4   TWENTY-FIRST-CENTURY FAMILY AND RELATIONSHIP ISSUES   285

Susan Milstein is a certified health education specialist and a certified
sexuality educator. She is an associate professor in the Department of
Health Enhancement at Montgomery College in Maryland, as well as the
lead consultant for Milstein Health Consulting. Milstein contends that
while it is diffcult to create a universal definition of cheating, the majority
of people feel that cybersex outside of a primary relationship is cheating.
Crystal Bedley argues that the anonymous nature of cybersex means that
it is not cheating.

Wayne Grinwis has been a sexual health educator for Planned Parenthood for 15 years. He is also adjunct professor in the Department of Health at West Chester University. Grinwis credits Andrea Daniels for help with this article. Grinwis argues that pornography is all right for adults, but for teenagers, it can create unrealistic expectations about sex, provide a negative and inaccurate sexuality education, and increase sexual violence against women. Justin Sitron is an assistant professor of education at Widener University. Sitron argues that pornography has no negative impact on teenagers and, in fact, has potential benefits. Sitron contends that Internet pornography can be helpful in providing teens an opportunity to see real bodies, a chance to learn about sex from seeing rather than doing, and an open door for communication with parents.

Sherry F. Colb, columnist and law professor, uses a case study involving a statutory rape case to raise concerns about whether rape and assault cases would be prosecuted sufficiently without statutory rape laws. Although not perfect, statutory rape laws can be assets in such rape cases as when the older partner denies the rape occurred or denies responsibility for a resulting pregnancy or infection. Marc Tunzi, a family physician, believes that statutory rape laws are ineffective because people can get around them too easily. These laws, he argues, require that an otherwise healthy relationship between two people of different ages be criminalized solely because there is some kind of sexual activity involved. As a result, medical and other licensed professionals do not want to break up these relationships that, in their professional opinion, are not problematic based on just the age difference between the two partners.

Jessiva Isner, Annie Koval, and Lisa Paul wrote this article for *NWI Parent,* which advertises that their publication provides "Real Solutions for Real Families." The authors are concerned that MTV's episodes related to teenage parenthood fail to capture accurately the true challenges of teenage parenthood. The National Campaign to Prevent Teen and Unplanned Pregnancy is dedicated to reducing teenage pregnancy. Their research reveals that teenagers who watch *16 and Pregnant* are more likely to express a negative view about the ways in which parenthood affects a teen's life.

Lisa E. Soronen, Nicole Vitale, and Karen A. Haase are writing on legal issues for the National School Boards Association. This article encourages administrators to hand over cell phone sexting cases to the appropriate law enforcement agencies. Julie Hilden is a graduate of Harvard College and Yale Law School. A former clerk for Supreme Court Justice Stephen Breyer, she has more recently appeared on *Good Morning America,* Court TV, CNN, and NPR. Hilden argues that harsh penalties are extreme and unjust.

Donald Dyson is assistant professor of human sexuality education at Widener University and the national co-chair of the conference for the American Association of Sexuality Educators, Counselors, and Therapists. Dyson argues that there are essential qualities of a healthy relationship and that an open relationship can be successful. Stanley Kurtz, a writer and senior fellow at the Ethics and Public Policy Center, argues that allowing same-sex marriage will create a slippery slope, eventually leading to plural marriages. Kurtz contends that such marriages prove destructive to the institution of marriage itself.

Correlation Guide

The *Taking Sides* series presents current issues in a debate-style format designed to stimulate student interest and develop critical thinking skills. Each issue is thoughtfully framed with an issue summary, an issue introduction, learning outcomes, and critical thinking and reflection questions. The pro and con essays—selected for their liveliness and substance—represent the arguments of leading scholars and commentators in their fields.

Taking Sides: Clashing Views in Family and Personal Relationships, 9/e is an easy-to-use reader that presents issues on important topics such as *parental decision-making, children's rights, nontraditional families,* and *relationship issues*. For more information on *Taking Sides* and other *McGraw-Hill Contemporary Learning Series* titles, visit http://www.mhhe.com/cls.

This convenient guide matches the issues in **Taking Sides: Family and Personal Relationships, 9/e** with the corresponding chapters in two of our best-selling McGraw-Hill Sociology textbooks by DeGenova et al. and Lauer/Lauer.

Taking Sides: Family and Personal Relationships, 9/e	Intimate Relationships, Marriages, and Families, 8/e by DeGenova et al:	Marriage and Family: The Quest for Intimacy, 8/e by Lauer/Lauer
Issue 1: Is It Beneficial if Adoptive Parents Adopt Only Within Their Own Racial/Ethnic Group?	**Chapter 11:** Family Planning and Parenting **Chapter 13:** Parent-Child Relationships	**Chapter 2:** Diversity in Families **Chapter 12:** Becoming a Parent
Issue 2: Does Divorce Have a Negative Impact on Children?	**Chapter 16:** The Family and Divorce	**Chapter 14:** Separation and Divorce
Issue 3: Should Parents Home-school Their Children?	**Chapter 9:** Power, Decision Making, and Communication	**Chapter 11:** Work and Home
Issue 4: Do Mothers Who Work Outside the Home Have a Negative Impact on Their Children?	**Chapter 8:** Work, Family Roles, and Material Resources **Chapter 13:** Parent-Child Relationships	**Chapter 11:** Work and Home
Issue 5: Should Illegal Immigrant Families Be Able to Send Their Children to Public Schools?		**Chapter 1:** Marriage and Family in America: Needs, Myths, and Dreams **Chapter 2:** Diversity in Families
Issue 6: Should Parents Be Able to Select the Biological Sex of Their Children?	**Chapter 11:** Family Planning and Parenting **Chapter 12:** Pregnancy and Childbirth	**Chapter 12:** Becoming a Parent
Issue 7: Should Grandparents Have Visitation Rights for Their Grandchildren?	**Chapter 14:** Parents and Extended Family Relationships **Chapter 15:** Conflict, Family Crises, and Crisis Management	**Chapter 13:** Family Crises

Taking Sides: Family and Personal Relationships, 9/e	Intimate Relationships, Marriages, and Families, 8/e by DeGenova et al:	Marriage and Family: The Quest for Intimacy, 8/e by Lauer/Lauer
Issue 8: Should Courts Be Able to Discriminate Against Immigrant Fathers?		
Issue 9: Do Parents Have the Right to Deny Their Children Lifesaving Medical Care Due to Their Religious Convictions?	**Chapter 9:** Power, Decision Making, and Communication	
Issue 10: Should Same-Sex Couples Be Able to Legally Marry?	**Chapter 1:** Intimate Relationships, Marriages, and Families in the Twenty-First Century **Chapter 2:** Gender: Identity and Roles **Chapter 10:** Sexual Relationships	**Chapter 4:** Sexuality **Chapter 8:** Getting Married
Issue 11: Should Private Sexual Acts Between Gay Couples Be Illegal?	**Chapter 10:** Sexual Relationships	**Chapter 4:** Sexuality
Issue 12: Are Traditional Families Better for Children?	**Chapter 1:** Intimate Relationships, Marriages, and Families in the Twenty-First Century **Chapter 11:** Family Planning and Parenting **Chapter 13:** Parent-Child Relationships	**Chapter 1:** Marriage and Family in America: Needs, Myths, and Dreams **Chapter 2:** Diversity in Families
Issue 13: Should Lesbian and Gay Individuals Be Able to Adopt Children?	**Chapter 1:** Intimate Relationships, Marriages, and Families in the Twenty-First Century **Chapter 11:** Family Planning and Parenting **Chapter 13:** Parent-Child Relationships	**Chapter 1:** Marriage and Family in America: Needs, Myths, and Dreams **Chapter 2:** Diversity in Families **Chapter 12:** Becoming a Parent
Issue 14: Are Teenagers Too Young to Become Parents?	**Chapter 11:** Family Planning and Parenting **Chapter 13:** Parent-Child Relationships	**Chapter 12:** Becoming a Parent
Issue 15: Is Cybersex "Cheating"?		
Issue 16: Is Internet Pornography Harmful to Teenagers?		
Issue 17: Are Statutory Rape Laws Effective at Protecting Minors?		
Issue 18: Do Reality Television Shows Have a Negative Influence on Teenage Pregnancy and Parenting?	**Chapter 11:** Family Planning and Parenting **Chapter 13:** Parent-Child Relationships	**Chapter 9:** The Challenge of Communication

(Continued)

Taking Sides: Family and Personal Relationships, 9/e	Intimate Relationships, Marriages, and Families, 8/e by DeGenova et al:	Marriage and Family: The Quest for Intimacy, 8/e by Lauer/Lauer
Issue 19: Should There Be Harsh Penalties for Teens Sexting?		
Issue 20: Are Open Relationships Healthy?	**Chapter 1:** Intimate Relationships, Marriages, and Families in the Twenty-First Century **Chapter 9:** Power, Decision Making, and Communication **Chapter 10:** Sexual Relationships	**Chapter 1:** Marriage and Family in America: Needs, Myths, and Dreams **Chapter 9:** The Challenge of Communication

Topic Guide

This topic guide suggests how the selections in this book relate to the subjects covered in your course. You may want to use the topics listed on these pages to search the Web more easily. On the following pages a number of Web sites have been gathered specifically for this book. They are arranged to reflect the units of this Taking Sides reader. You can link to these sites by going to http://www.mhhe.com/cls. All issues, and their articles that relate to each topic are listed below the bold-faced term.

Attraction and Dating

11. Should Private Sexual Acts Between Gay Couples Be Illegal?
15. Is Cybersex "Cheating"?
19. Should There Be Harsh Penalties for Teens Sexting?
20. Are Open Relationships Healthy?

Conflict, Family Crises, and Crisis Management

5. Should Illegal Immigrant Families Be Able to Send Their Children to Public Schools?
7. Should Grandparents Have Visitation Rights for Their Grandchildren?

Divorce

2. Does Divorce Have a Negative Impact on Children?
7. Should Grandparents Have Visitation Rights for Their Grandchildren?

Family Planning and Parenting

14. Are Teenagers Too Young to Become Parents?
18. Do Reality Television Shows Have a Negative Influence on Teenage Pregnancy and Parenting?

Gender Identity and Roles

4. Do Mothers Who Work Outside the Home Have a Negative Impact on Their Children?
6. Should Parents Be Able to Select the Biological Sex of Their Children?
12. Are Traditional Families Better for Children?

Love and Mate Selection

10. Should Same-Sex Couples Be Able to Legally Marry?
11. Should Private Sexual Acts Between Gay Couples Be Illegal?
12. Are Traditional Families Better for Children?
14. Are Teenagers Too Young to Become Parents?
15. Is Cybersex "Cheating"?
20. Are Open Relationships Healthy?

Marital Relationships

10. Should Same-Sex Couples Be Able to Legally Marry?
12. Are Traditional Families Better for Children?
15. Is Cybersex "Cheating"?

Parent-Child Relationships

1. Is It Beneficial if Adoptive Parents Adopt Only Within Their Own Racial/Ethnic Group?
3. Should Parents Home-school Their Children?
6. Should Parents Be Able to Select the Biological Sex of Their Children?
7. Should Grandparents Have Visitation Rights for Their Grandchildren?
9. Do Parents Have the Right to Deny Their Children Lifesaving Medical Care Due to Their Religious Convictions?
12. Are Traditional Families Better for Children?
13. Should Lesbian and Gay Individuals Be Able to Adopt Children?
14. Are Teenagers Too Young to Become Parents?

Parents and Extended Family Relationships

2. Does Divorce Have a Negative Impact on Children?
7. Should Grandparents Have Visitation Rights for Their Grandchildren?

Power, Decision Making, and Communication

3. Should Parents Home-school Their Children?
5. Should Illegal Immigrant Families Be Able to Send Their Children to Public Schools?
6. Should Parents Be Able to Select the Biological Sex of Their Children?
7. Should Grandparents Have Visitation Rights for Their Grandchildren?
8. Should Courts Be Able to Discriminate Against Immigrant Fathers?
9. Do Parents Have the Right to Deny Their Children Lifesaving Medical Care Due to Their Religious Convictions?
10. Should Same-Sex Couples Be Able to Legally Marry?
11. Should Private Sexual Acts Between Gay Couples Be Illegal?
13. Should Lesbian and Gay Individuals Be Able to Adopt Children?
19. Should There Be Harsh Penalties for Teens Sexting?

Pregnancy and Childbirth

14. Are Teenagers Too Young to Become Parents?
18. Do Reality Television Shows Have a Negative Influence on Teenage Pregnancy and Parenting?

Racial Diversity and Families

1. Is It Beneficial if Adoptive Parents Adopt Only Within Their Own Racial/Ethnic Group?
5. Should Illegal Immigrant Families Be Able to Send Their Children to Public Schools?
8. Should Courts Be Able to Discriminate Against Immigrant Fathers?

Religion and Family Relationships

2. Does Divorce Have a Negative Impact on Children?

3. Should Parents Home-school Their Children?
9. Do Parents Have the Right to Deny Their Children Lifesaving Medical Care Due to Their Religious Convictions?
12. Are Traditional Families Better for Children?

Sexuality and Relationships

6. Should Parents Be Able to Select the Biological Sex of Their Children?
10. Should Same-Sex Couples Be Able to Legally Marry?
11. Should Private Sexual Acts Between Gay Couples Be Illegal?
12. Are Traditional Families Better for Children?
13. Should Lesbian and Gay Individuals Be Able to Adopt Children?
14. Are Teenagers Too Young to Become Parents?
15. Is Cybersex "Cheating"?
16. Is Internet Pornography Harmful to Teenagers?
17. Are Statutory Rape Laws Effective at Protecting Minors?
18. Do Reality Television Shows Have a Negative Influence on Teenage Pregnancy and Parenting?
19. Should There Be Harsh Penalties for Teens Sexting?
20. Are Open Relationships Healthy?

Single

2. Does Divorce Have a Negative Impact on Children?

Technology, Media and Relationships

15. Is Cybersex "Cheating"?
16. Is Internet Pornography Harmful to Teenagers?
18. Do Reality Television Shows Have a Negative Influence on Teenage Pregnancy and Parenting?
19. Should There Be Harsh Penalties for Teens Sexting?

Work, Family Roles, and Material Resources

4. Do Mothers Who Work Outside the Home Have a Negative Impact on Their Children?
12. Are Traditional Families Better for Children?

Introduction

Frameworks for Examining Debate

David M. Hall

Taking Sides: Family and Personal Relationships is released at a time when American society is reconstructing its concept of families and relationships. More children are growing up in nontraditional homes than ever before. In fact, concepts of the traditional family that were once considered universal norms are not reflective of the diverse families that exist. These changes can be a source of societal conflict. Conversely, these changes can also be a source of societal strength and growth.

Pluralistic nations thrive by demonstrating a willingness to cooperate despite existing differences. For this to occur, the citizenry must engage in thoughtful and respectful discourse. In that spirit, this volume examines the diversity of views in American society as they relate to family and personal relationships to provide a context for weighing more carefully not just one's own values, but also opposing values. Most readers will find that their responses to issues raised in this volume are anchored in a moral or intellectual foundation. Four such frameworks are identified in this introduction to assist the reader in providing a larger context for the issues debated in this volume.

Many readers will find themselves conducting further research on the topics raised in each chapter. Today, issues in this volume often permeate discourse in society, families, the law, and education. *Taking Sides: Family and Personal Relationships* is designed to provide an intellectual foundation for much of this discourse.

Carefully evaluate the arguments made throughout this book. Readers should be able to identify statements of fact, statements of value, and the credibility of research used to support each author's thesis. While such evaluation is important when reading persuasive essays, higher-level thinking skills can be used to examine each chapter through a variety of frameworks.

This introduction outlines four potential frameworks: political ideology, religion, linguistics, and legal theory. Try applying one or more frameworks to the issues addressed in this book. How would you compare and contrast your conclusions for each chapter in this book? Are there areas in which competing frameworks create a conflict for you? If so, how would you reconcile these differences?

Let us now examine the four frameworks that can be used for analysis throughout this volume.

Political Ideology Framework

Many of the topics raised in this book are political and can sometimes be significant issues in campaigns and elections. The political ideology continuum contains the following stages: Reactionary, Conservative, Liberal, and Radical (see Table 1). Reactionary ideology supports going back to a previous way of doing things. Reactionaries believe that most social problems are the result of democratic excesses that favor the masses at the expense of proven traditions. Conservative ideology believes in defending the status quo and making only small changes. Liberal ideology believes in change that guarantees greater individual rights. Radical ideology, typically the antithesis of reactionary, favors fundamental restructuring of society to ensure equality.

Table 1
Political Ideology Continuum

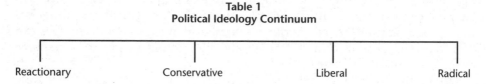

| Reactionary | Conservative | Liberal | Radical |

If the reader chooses, for example, to examine the issue of whether or not open relationships are healthy, a reactionary view would oppose open relationships, as well as support changing marriage laws to make divorce more difficult. In fact, they would probably argue that cultural acceptance of divorce will ultimately lead to polygamy. A conservative perspective would likely oppose open relationships and same-sex marriage, but support leaving divorce laws as they are. A liberal view would likely support allowing same-sex marriage, but voice opposition for polyamory. A radical perspective would favor fundamentally reconstructing the culture of marriage so that polyamory is as much the expected norm as monogamy.

The political ideology framework can be used for any topic within this book. Is your political ideology the same for adoption as it is for marriage? How about with other topics in this book? What does this comparison and contrast reveal about your overall political ideology?

Religious Framework

Many people have views about sexual orientation and gender identity that are the result of their religious upbringing. However, religious views vary not just from one religion to the next, but also within certain faiths themselves. Debate over acceptance, tolerance, and rejection based on sexual orientation is dividing many places of worship. Dr. James Nelson, a Christian minister, created a continuum for religious responses to lesbian, gay, and bisexual individuals, which consists of Rejecting Punitive, Rejecting Non-Punitive, Qualified Acceptance, and Full Acceptance (see Table 2). Readers who come from a strong religious background may want to consider where their faith falls along this continuum and whether their personal views correspond with their faith. When reading each chapter, consider how religious values may affect your views on particular issues.

Table 2
Nelson Continuum

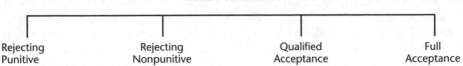

| Rejecting Punitive | Rejecting Nonpunitive | Qualified Acceptance | Full Acceptance |

A rejecting punitive place of worship would expel anyone who identifies as lesbian, gay, bisexual, or transgender. Rejecting nonpunitive values are found in places of worship where lesbian, gay, bisexual, and transgender individuals are welcome to attend but will regularly hear sermons about the immorality of their identity. Qualified acceptance is found in a place of worship in which one will never hear hatred from the pulpit and generally feel accepted. However, if one day a gay attendee offers to teach his child's Bible study group, a committee at the church might meet and decide that gay members of the church may not teach children. Full acceptance is featured in a place of worship that holds same-sex weddings and allows for the full inclusion of all lesbian, gay, bisexual, and transgender members, including serving as clergy.

When reading the sections involving LGBT issues and definitions of family, try and identify if your response has a religious foundation. Where does your school community fall on this continuum? Where does your home community fall on this continuum? What do you believe is the most ethical response on this continuum and why?

While Nelson uses this framework in the context of religious faith and sexual orientation, it can be applied to any of the topics found in this book.

Linguistics Framework

George Lakoff, a leading professor of linguistics, uses a Nation as Family framework for examining political rhetoric. Lakoff argues that Americans view the nation as a family, which is evidenced by metaphors such as "founding fathers," "daughters of the American revolution," and "sending our sons off to war." Using the Nation as Family model, Lakoff contends that Republicans tend to support what he calls Strict Father Morality and that Democrats tend to support what he calls Nurturant Parent Morality. A Lakoffian framework is pertinent to this particular volume in the *Taking Sides* series, as it demonstrates that our concept of family applies not just to our personal lives, but also to our sense of patriotism and national psyche.

Strict Father Morality rests upon a patriarchal system that values adherence to past moral standards to ensure future success. Strict Father Morality would not only support defining marriage as between a man and a woman but also argue that a nation's success comes from such a traditional family structure. Conversely, Nurturant Parent Morality values independent thinking that will strengthen the family. Nurturant Parent Morality would support marriage being reconstructed to include same-sex couples as an issue of fairness and equality for all members of the familial society. Nurturant Parent Morality argues that such a change will strengthen American society.

Few people fit entirely into either Strict Father or Nurturant Parent Morality. For example, a person can adhere to Strict Father Morality about social welfare programs but Nurturant Parent Morality about funding for education. Are your Nation as Family views regarding family and personal relationship issues consistent across chapters in this volume? How do your Nation as Family views on topics raised within this volume compare and contrast with your views on other issues within American society?

Legal Framework

The two primary competing legal philosophies are Orignialism and Living Constitution. This framework can be applied to any article involving law and policy. Originalism is the belief that judges should base their decisions on the original meaning of the text of the Constitution. Their understanding of the intent is based on the writings of the framers and the debates at the Constitutional Convention. In the case of constitutional amendments, advocates of Originalism would consider the writings and discussions at the time of the amendment's adoption. In contrast, Living Constitution is the belief that the Constitution was written with the intent that its interpretation would evolve in response to an ever-changing society. Those who believe in Living Constitution believe it is against the spirit and intent of the Constitution to interpret contemporary legal issues with a nineteenth-century mindset.

The Fourteenth Amendment guarantees equal protection under the law. Sexual orientation was not debated during passage of this amendment. As a result, an Originalist would argue that such protection refers only to race because the intent was to protect newly freed slaves, and that it therefore categorically denies protection based on sexual orientation. However, adherents of a Living Constitution perspective argue that the equal protection guarantee was written without mention of any identity, including race, so applications of this right could be applied differently for successive generations. Supporters of the Living Constitution perspective would support extending equal protection rights based on biological sex as well as sexual orientation.

Conclusion

During early American history, someone caught having sex outside of marriage was likely to be severely punished. Within marriage, sex for procreation was typically the expected norm. In fact, married couples lacked a defined, constitutional right to contraception until the 1960s. Over the past 50 years, accepted norms of family and personal relationships have been fundamentally reconstructed. Today, Americans are living in an era in which society is openly grappling with a wide variety of changes related to family and personal relationships.

The debate over rights for non-traditional families is sometimes referred to as part of a "culture war." While there is no protracted physical battle, the passion associated with many people's deeply held beliefs is at stake in the issues addressed in this volume. In some cases, individual livelihoods and even lives are threatened. The use of such a violent metaphor as "culture war" reflects the strong feelings and deep divisions that exist within American society when people discuss many of the issues addressed in this volume.

Each chapter provides an engaging examination of both sides of each issue. Readers may find that they will be challenged in some of their beliefs, and that they need to conduct further research. It is important not only to read about these issues, but also to work for better understanding of the diversity of views that are expressed in this volume. A willingness to consider diverse views will allow for growth and mutual collaboration, thereby strengthening America's pluralistic society.

Internet References . . .

National Adoption Center

The National Adoption Center works to expand adoption opportunities for children living in foster care throughout the United States and to be a resource to families and to agencies who seek permanent, caring homes for children.

http://www.adopt.org

National Association of Black Social Workers

The National Association of Black Social Workers was established in 1968 to "advocate and address important social issues that impact the health and welfare of the Black community." Their affiliate chapters, including student chapters, are spread throughout the United States.

http://www.nabsw.org

National Home Education Network

The National Home Education Network (NHEN) works to encourage and facilitate the grassroots efforts of state and local home-schooling organizations and individuals by providing information, fostering networking, and promoting public relations on a national level. NHEN supports "the freedom of all individual families to choose home education and to direct such education."

http://www.nhen.org/

National Association of Social Workers

The National Association of Social Workers (NASW) is the largest membership organization of professional social workers in the world. NASW works to enhance the professional growth and development of its members, create and maintain professional standards, and advance sound social policies.

http://www.naswdc.org

Parental Decision Making: Parents Know Best . . . Or Do They?

*U*se of the oft-quoted "it takes a village to raise a child" is still met with understanding, thoughtful nods as we appreciate the concept that many people beyond the family structure play key roles in raising children. There are, however, numerous factors that contribute to, interfere with, detract from, and otherwise affect how parents raise their children. Parenting styles vary. The so-called village includes the government, which is met with open arms by some and skepticism and mistrust by others. This section examines five questions that society often asks relating to parenting issues:

- Is It Beneficial if Adoptive Parents Adopt Only Within Their Own Racial/ Ethnic Group?
- Does Divorce Have a Negative Impact on Children?
- Should Parents Home-school Their Children?
- Do Mothers Who Work Outside the Home Have a Negative Impact on Their Children?

ISSUE 1

Is It Beneficial if Adoptive Parents Adopt Only Within Their Own Racial/Ethnic Group?

YES: Tony Dokoupil, from "Raising Katie: What Adopting a White Girl Taught a Black Family About Race in the Obama Era," *The Daily Beast* (April 22, 2009)

NO: Ezra E. H. Griffith and Rachel L. Bergeron, from "Cultural Stereotypes Die Hard: The Case of Transracial Adoption," *Journal of the American Academy of Psychiatry Law* (vol. 34, pp. 303–14, 2006)

Learning Outcomes

As a result of this issue, readers will be able to:

- Identify the major arguments made for and against transracial adoption.
- Compare and contrast the competing challenges caused by transracial adoption depending on the race of the parents and children.
- Evaluate the implications of contemporary views about race in the United States and how that informs the controversy related to transracial adoption.

ISSUE SUMMARY

YES: Tony Dokoupil is a staff writer at *Newsweek* and *The Daily Beast*. Dokoupil writes about different issues affecting national life, often related to diversity. In this chapter, he writes about the increasing number of transracial adoptions in the United States in recent years but notes that we are seeing limited examples of African American families adopting white babies. When an African American family adopts a white baby, a unique set of challenges is created, he argues, due to deep-seated views about race in American society today. Dokoupil explores questions related to what this reveals about contemporary views on race in American society.

NO: Ezra Griffith and Rachel Bergeron, both faculty members of the Yale University School of Medicine's psychiatry department, argue that requiring racial and ethnic matching, although an appropriate effort, would leave too many children of color languishing in the foster and adoption systems. By maintaining that only in-race adoption is the best and ideal situation, they ask rhetorically, does our society actually do more to reinforce cultural stereotypes or to truly serve children needing homes?

The practice of adopting children is nothing new; adoptions have been documented in the United States going back to the late nineteenth century. In the twentieth century, international adoptions in the United States increased at the end of World War II, a logical response to the number of children orphaned when families were uprooted or eradicated by the war's violence. This increase was also documented after the Korean and Vietnam wars, and more recently as violence continues to mar various countries worldwide and the number of children needing homes grows.

This means that many of the adults who have adopted and are currently adopting children are from a different racial or ethnic group than their adoptive children. In the most recent U.S. census, just over 17 percent of adopted children under age 18 had adoptive parents of a different racial background than theirs. One thing that we are learning is that the public has different views depending on which race(s) are involved in transracial adoption.

Although adoption as a practice is much less stigmatized today, adopting children outside one's own racial or ethnic group remains controversial in some circles. Some believe that raising a child in a family outside the child's racial group impedes the child from forming a healthy identity and from coping effectively in the world. In 1972, in response to the increase in transracial adoptions, the National Association of Black Social Workers (NABSW) produced a resolution stating, in part, that "black children belong physically and psychologically and culturally in black families where they can receive the total sense of themselves and develop a sound projection of their future. Only a black family can transmit the emotional and sensitive subtleties of perceptions and reactions essential for a black child's survival in a racist society." Although this statement is specifically about black and African American children, the 2003 position statement of the National Association of Social Workers (NASW) about foster care and adoption includes all racial and ethnic backgrounds.

Others argue that love is the most important component of any family, that parents of any racial or ethnic background can invest time and resources to teach their children about their racial or ethnic heritage and history and connect them with social supports to ensure that their children integrate whatever identity best fits them. It is better, these individuals argue, to give a child a home, regardless of the different racial or ethnic backgrounds of the family members, than to let a child languish in foster care. Another controversial aspect of this debate is that these same individuals argue that there is an implicit bias in the NABSW and NASW guidelines, that they assume an adoptive family that is white; there are no guidelines or discussions around placing white children with families of color.

Indeed, the controversy over transracial adoption has typically focused on Caucasian families adopting children of color. These positions have been made in the larger context of a growing number of transracial adoptions. However, transracial adoptions have historically been discussed involving white couples adopting children of color. What role does race play in public perception when the adoptive parents are African American? What about when the African American couple is adopting a white child?

In the following selections, one side reflects on African American parents raising an adopted white child. How does race and power interject in public views and interactions regarding such families? The opposing side cites research demonstrating, they assert, that children of transracial adoptions can develop strong identities and high self-esteem, the difference between their and their family's backgrounds notwithstanding.

As with any discussion of race, culture, or ethnicity, presumptions, perceptions, and biases can all affect how a person forms her or his opinion about this sensitive topic.

Consider your reactions to the readings—would your views change at all if the discussion were not about two parents of the same racial or ethnic background adopting a child from a different background, but rather about a man and a woman of two different racial or ethnic background choosing to procreate together? Why or why not? In doing so, the couple is intentionally creating a child who will have a race or ethnicity that is different from—albeit a combination of—their own. If adopting outside one's own group is okay—or not okay—with you, what about planned procreation, done within the context of a long-term, committed relationship?

What makes good parents? Think about this for a moment, then make a list. Many people will begin their list with characteristics (e.g., patience) that are not related to race, religion, ethnicity, or other forms of identity. If you were in charge of an adoption agency, what criteria would you look for in finding suitable parents for adoption? Does race play a role? Is income important? What about religion? Would you apply the same criteria to Christians, Muslims, Scientologists, and atheists? What role does marital status play? What about sexual orientation or gender identity or expression? If these identities are on your list, how important are they? Are they a primary or a secondary concern?

The compelling question in this case, for most people, is: What is in the best interest of the child? What role does racism play in American society that affects the ways in which people see this topic? How does it change a child's sense of self-involving their own race?

Also, consider your own racial or ethnic makeup—how, do you think, does this come into play as you think about your position for or against transracial adoption? What role does our own identity play in how we might view issues such as this?

4

Later in this edition, we will discuss adoption by same-sex parents. Keep the thoughts you had in response to this topic in mind as you read the later issue, and see whether your arguments can be applied to a same-sex couple adopting a child who may be heterosexual.

YES

Tony Dokoupil

Raising Katie: What Adopting a White Girl Taught a Black Family About Race in the Obama Era

Several pairs of eyes follow the girl as she pedals around the playground in an affluent suburb of Baltimore. But it isn't the redheaded fourth grader who seems to have moms and dads of the jungle gym nervous on this recent Saturday morning. It's the African-American man—six feet tall, bearded and wearing a gray hooded sweatshirt—watching the girl's every move. Approaching from behind, he grabs the back of her bicycle seat as she wobbles to a stop. "Nice riding," he says, as the fair-skinned girl turns to him, beaming. "Thanks, Daddy," she replies. The onlookers are clearly flummoxed.

As a black father and adopted white daughter, Mark Riding and Katie O'Dea-Smith are a sight at best surprising, and at worst so perplexing that people feel compelled to respond. Like the time at a Pocono Mountains flea market when Riding scolded Katie, attracting so many sharp glares that he and his wife, Terri, 37, and also African-American, thought "we might be lynched." And the time when well-intentioned shoppers followed Mark and Katie out of the mall to make sure she wasn't being kidnapped. Or when would-be heroes come up to Katie in the cereal aisle and ask, "Are you OK?"—even though Terri is standing right there.

Is it racism? The Ridings tend to think so, and it's hard to blame them. To shadow them for a day, as I recently did, is to feel the unease, notice the negative attention, and realize that the same note of fear isn't in the air when they attend to their two biological children, who are 2 and 5 years old. It's fashionable to say that the election of Barack Obama has brought the dawn of a post-racial America. In the past few months alone, *The Atlantic Monthly* has declared "the end of white America," *The Washington Post* has profiled the National Association for the Advancement of Colored People's struggle for relevance in a changing world, and National Public Radio has led discussions questioning the necessity of the annual Black History Month. Perhaps not surprising, most white and black Americans no longer cite racism as a major social problem, according to recent polls.

But the Ridings' experience runs counter to these popular notions of harmony. And adoption between races is particularly fraught. So-called transracial adoptions have surged since 1994, when the Multiethnic Placement Act reversed decades of outright racial matching by banning discrimination against adoptive families on the basis of race. But the growth has been all one-sided. The number of white families adopting outside their race is growing and is now in the thousands, while cases like Katie's—of a black family adopting a nonblack child—remain frozen at near zero.

Decades after the racial integration of offices, buses, and water fountains, persistent double standards mean that African-American parents are still largely viewed with unease as caretakers of any children other than their own—or those they are paid to look after. As Yale historian Matthew Frye Jacobson has asked: "Why is it that in the United States, a white woman can have black children but a black woman cannot have white children?"

That question hit home for the Ridings in 2003, when Terri's mother, Phyllis Smith, agreed to take in Katie, then 3, on a temporary basis. A retired social worker, Phyllis had long been giving needy children a home—and Katie was one of the hardest cases. The child of a local prostitute, her toddler tantrums were so disturbing that foster families simply refused to keep her. Twelve homes later, Katie was still being passed around. Phyllis was in many ways an unlikely savior. The former president of the Baltimore chapter of the National Association of Black Social Workers, she joined her colleagues in condemning the adoption of black children by white families as "cultural genocide"—a position she still holds in theory, if not in practice. She couldn't say no to the "charming, energetic" girl who ended up on her front doorstep.

Last November, after a grueling adoption process—"[adoption officials] pushed the envelope on every issue," says Mark—little Irish-Catholic Katie O'Dea, as pale as a communion wafer, became Katie O'Dea-Smith: a formally adopted member of the African-American Riding-Smith family. (Phyllis is her legal guardian, but Mark and Terri were also vetted as legal surrogates for Phyllis.)

To be sure, it's an unconventional arrangement. Katie spends weekdays with Phyllis, her legal guardian. But Mark and Terri, who live around the corner, are her de facto parents, too. They help out during the week, and welcome Katie over on weekends and holidays. As for titles: Katie calls Phyllis "Mommy" and Terri "Sister," since technically it's true. Mark has always been "Daddy" or "Mark."

"Let me just put it out there," says Mark, a 38-year-old private-school admissions director with an appealing blend of megaphone voice and fearless opinion, especially when it comes to his family. "I've never felt more self-consciously black than while holding our little white girl's hand in public." He used to write off the negative attention as innocent curiosity. But after a half-decade of rude comments and revealing faux pas—like the time his school's guidance counselor called Katie a "foster child" in her presence—he now fights the ignorance with a question of his own: why didn't a white family step up to take Katie?

Riding's challenge hints at a persistent social problem. "No country in the world has made more progress toward combating overt racism than [the

United States]," says David Schneider, a Rice University psychologist and the author of "The Psychology of Stereotyping." "But the most popular stereotype of black people is still that they're violent. And for a lot of people, not even racist people, the sight of a white child with a black parent just sets off alarm signals."

Part of the reason for the adoptive imbalance comes down to numbers, and the fact that people tend to want children of their own race. African-Americans represent almost one third of the 510,000 children in foster care, so black parents have a relatively high chance of ending up with a same-race child. (Not so for would-be adoptive white parents who prefer the rarest thing of all in the foster-care system: a healthy white baby.) But the dearth of black families with nonblack children also has painful historical roots. Economic hardship and centuries of poisonous belief in the so-called civilizing effects of white culture upon other races have familiarized Americans with the concept of white stewardship of other ethnicities, rather than the reverse.

The result is not only discomfort among whites at the thought of non-whites raising their offspring; African-Americans can also be wary when one of their own is a parent to a child outside their race. Just ask Dallas Cowboys All-Pro linebacker DeMarcus Ware and his wife, Taniqua, who faced a barrage of criticism after adopting a nonblack baby last February. When *The New York Times* sports page ran a photo of the shirtless new father with what appeared to be a white baby in his arms (and didn't mention race in the accompanying story), it sent a slow shock wave through the African-American community, pitting supporters who celebrated the couple's joy after three painful miscarriages against critics who branded the Wares "self-race-hating individuals" for ignoring the disproportionate number of blacks in foster care. The baby, now their daughter, Marley, is in fact Hispanic. "Do you mean to tell me that the Wares couldn't have found a little black baby to adopt?" snarled one blogger on the *Daily Voice,* an online African-American newspaper.

For the relatively few black families that do adopt non-African-American children, and the adoptive children themselves, the experience can be confusing. "I hadn't realized how often we talked about white people at home," says Mark. "I hadn't realized that dinnertime stories were often told with reference to the race of the players, or that I often used racial stereotypes, as in the news only cares about some missing spring-break girl because she is blonde."

Katie, too, has sometimes struggled with her unusual situation, and how outsiders perceive it. When she's not drawing, swimming, or pining after teen heartthrob Zac Efron, she's often dealing with normal kid teasing with a nasty edge. "They'll ignore me or yell at me because I have a black family," she says. Most of her friends are black, although her school is primarily white. And Terri has noticed something else: Katie is uncomfortable identifying people by their race.

Is she racially confused? Should her parents be worried? Opinions vary in the larger debate about whether race is a legitimate consideration in adoption. At present, agencies that receive public funding are forbidden from taking race into account when screening potential parents. They are also banned from asking parents to reflect on their readiness to deal with race-related issues, or from requiring them to undergo sensitivity training. But a well-meaning policy intended to ensure colorblindness appears to be backfiring. According to a study published last year by the Evan B. Donaldson Adoption Institute, transracial parents are often ill equipped to raise children who are themselves unprepared for the world's racial realities.

Now lawmakers may rejoin the charged race-adoption debate. Later this year the U.S. Commission on Civil Rights, an independent federal think tank, is expected to publish a summary of expert testimony on adoption law—much of which will ask Congress to reinstate race as a salient consideration in all cases. The testimony, from the Evan B. Donaldson Institute and others, will also suggest initiatives currently banned or poorly executed under existing policies, including racial training for parents and intensifying efforts to recruit more black adoptive families.

Would such measures be a step back for Obama's post-racial America? It's hard to tell. The Ridings, for their part, are taking Katie's racial training into their own hands. They send her to a mixed-race school and mixed-race summer camps, celebrate St. Patrick's Day with gusto and buy Irish knickknacks, like a "Kiss Me I'm Irish" T shirt and a mug with Katie's O'Dea family crest emblazoned on it. But they worry it won't be enough. "All else being equal, I think she should be with people who look like her," says Mark. "It's not fair that she's got to grow up feeling different when she's going to feel different anyway. She wears glasses, her voice is a bit squeaky, and on top of that she has to deal with the fact that her mother is 70 and black."

But even if Katie feels different now, the Riding-Smiths have given her both a stable home and a familiarity with two ethnic worlds that will surely serve her well as she grows up in a country that is increasingly blended. And it may be that hers will be the first truly post-racial generation.

Ezra E. H. Griffith
and Rachel L. Bergeron

 **NO**

Cultural Stereotypes Die Hard: The Case of Transracial Adoption

The adoption of black children by white families, commonly referred to as transracial adoption in the lay and professional literature, is the subject of a debate that has persisted in American society for a long time.[1] On one side of the divide are those who believe that black children are best raised by black families. On the other are the supporters of the idea that race-matching in adoption does not necessarily serve the best interests of the child and that it promotes racial discrimination.[2]

Coming as it does in the midst of myriad other discussions in this country about black-white interactions, transracial adoption has occupied an important place in any debate about adoption policy. But in addition, as can be seen in language utilized by the Fifth Circuit Court in a 1977 case,[3] there is a long-held belief that since family members resemble one another, it follows that members of constructed families should also look like each other so as to facilitate successful adoption outcomes.

> [A]doption agencies quite frequently try to place a child where he can most easily become a normal family member. The duplication of his natural biological environment is part of that program. Such factors as age, hair color, eye color, and facial features of parents and child are considered in reaching a decision. This flows from the belief that a child and adoptive parents can best adjust to a normal family relationship if the child is placed with adoptive parents who could have actually parented him. To permit consideration of physical characteristics necessarily carries with it permission to consider racial characteristics [Ref. 3, pp 1205–6].

In utilizing this language, the court acknowledged that transracial adoption ran counter to the cultural beliefs that many people held about the construction of families. Still, the court concluded that while the difficulties attending transracial adoption justified the consideration of race as a relevant factor in adoption proceedings, race could not be the sole factor considered. With a bow to both sides in the transracial adoption debate, the argument could only continue.

As the debate marches on, mental health professionals are being asked to provide expert opinions about whether it would be preferable for a particular

From *The Journal of the American Academy of Psychiatry and the Law*, vol. 34, no. 3, 2006, pp. 303–12 (excerpts). Copyright © 2006 by American Academy of Psychiatry and the Law. Reprinted by permission via S&S Management Services, Inc.

black child to be raised by a black family or by a family or adult of a different ethnic or racial group. There are, of course, different scenarios that may lead to the unfolding of these adoption disputes. For example, the question may arise when a black child is put up for adoption after having spent a number of months or years in an out-of-home placement. The lengthy wait of black children for an adoptive black family may understandably increase the likelihood of a transracial adoption. In another situation, the death of a biracial child's parents, one of whom was white and the other black, may lead to competition between the white and black grandparents for the right to raise the child. In a third possible context, the divorce of an interracial couple may result in a legal struggle for custody of the biracial child, with race trumpeted at least as an important factor if not the crucial factor to be considered in the decision about who should raise the child. Mental health professionals should therefore make an effort to stay abreast of the latest developments around this national debate if they intend to provide an informed opinion about the merits or problems of a potential transracial adoption.

We have already alluded to two significant factors that have played a role in the evolution of adoption policy concerning black children, particularly with respect to the question of whether race-neutral approaches make sense and whether transracial adoption is good practice. One factor has been judicial decision-making. In a relatively recent review, Hollinger[4] reminded us that, in general, racial classifications are invalidated unless they can survive the "strict scrutiny" test, which requires meeting a compelling governmental interest. Hollinger suggested that the "best-interest-of-the-child" standard commonly used in adoption practice would serve a substantial governmental interest. Such argumentation would allow the consideration of race as one element in an adoption evaluation. Following this reasoning, while race-neutral adoption may be a lofty objective, the specific needs of a particular child could legally allow the consideration of race.

The second factor to influence the evolution of adoption policy in this arena has been the academic research on transracial adoption.[5-9] This work has cumulatively demonstrated that black children can thrive and develop strong racial identities when nurtured in families with white parents. Transracially adopted children also do well on standard measures of self-esteem, cognitive development, and educational achievement. However, neither judicial decision-making nor scholarly research has settled the debate on transracial adoption policy.

In this article, we focus on a third factor that emerged as another mechanism meant to deal with transracial adoptions and the influential race-matching principle. These statutory efforts started with the Multiethnic Placement Act, which Hollinger stated "was enacted in 1994 amid spirited and sometimes contentious debate about transracial adoption and same-race placement policies."[4] We will point out that even though the statutory attempts were meant to eliminate race as a controlling factor in the adoption process, their implementation has left room for ambiguity regarding the role that race should play in adoption proceedings. Consequently, even though the statutes were intended to eliminate adoption delays and denials because of race-matching, they may have allowed the continued existence of a cultural stereotype—that black children belong with black families—and may have facilitated its continued existence. This article is therefore principally about statutory attempts in the past decade to influence public policy concerning transracial adoption. Secondarily, we shall comment on potential implications of these developments for the practice of adoption evaluations.

We emphasize once again that in referring to transracial adoption, we mean the adoption of black children by white parents. This is the focus of the statutes we consider. The adoption by Americans of children from other countries (international adoptions) and other transcultural adoptions (such as the adoption of Native American children by Anglos) are explicitly outside the parameters of this article. We also do not wish to suggest that although transracial adoption has been the subject of a significant national debate, it is a numerically common phenomenon. Later in this article, we review the available data on transracial adoption.

Brief Review of Race-Matching in Adoption

Feelings about who should raise a black child have run high in the United States for a long time. These feelings come from different groups for different reasons. Kennedy[1] presented a number of historical cases to illustrate this. Among the cases he described, Kennedy told the early 1900s story of a white girl who was found residing with a black family (Ref. 1, p 368). The authorities concluded that the child had been kidnapped and rescued her. They then placed her with a white family. When it was learned later that the child was black, she was returned to the black family because it was not proper for the black child to be living with a white family. This case, along with others described by Kennedy, is part of the fabric of American racism and racial separatist practices. Kennedy also pointed to the practice during slavery of considering "the human products of interracial sexual unions" as unambiguously black and the mandate that they be reared within the black slave community as an attempt to undermine any possibility of interracial parenting (Ref. 1, pp 367–8).

Whites have not been the only ones to support the stance of race-matching—the belief that black or white children belong with their own group. In 1972, the National Association of Black Social Workers (NABSW) stated unambiguously that white families should never be allowed to adopt black children.[10] The NABSW opposed transracial adoption for two main reasons: the Association claimed that transracial adoption prevents black children from forming a strong racial identity, and it prevents them from developing survival skills necessary to deal with a racist society.

Since its 1972 statement, the NABSW has remained steadfast in its opposition to transracial adoption. In testimony before the Senate Committee on Labor and Human Resources in 1985, the President of the NABSW reiterated the Association's position and stated that the NABSW viewed the placement of black children in white homes as a hostile act against the black community, considering it a blatant form of race and cultural genocide.[11]

In 1991, the NABSW reaffirmed its position that black children should not be placed with white parents under any circumstances, stating that even the most loving and skilled white parent could not avoid doing irreparable harm to an African-American child.[12] In its 1994 position paper on the preservation of African-American families, the NABSW indicated that, in placement decisions regarding a black child, priority should be given to adoption by biological relatives and then to black families.[13] Transracial adoption "should only be considered after documented evidence of unsuccessful same race placements has been reviewed and supported by appropriate representatives of the African American community" (Ref. 13, p 1).

The NABSW's position was reflected in the 1981 New York case of *Farmer v. Farmer*.[14] Mr. Farmer, a black man, sought custody of his six-year-old daughter after he and his white wife divorced. He argued that his daughter, who looked black, would do better being raised by him than by her white mother and that her best interests could be achieved only by awarding custody to him, the parent with whom she would be racially identified by a racially conscious society. Three experts testified on his behalf. Each addressed the importance of racial identity problems that the child would face and the importance of her identification with her black heritage, but none would state categorically that custody of the child should be determined by her dominant racial characteristic. The judge rejected Mr. Farmer's race-based argument, finding that "between two natural parents of different races who have opted to have a child, neither gains priority for custody by reason of race alone. Nor can race disqualify a natural parent for custody" (Ref. 14, pp 589–90). He awarded custody to the mother based on the determination of the best interests of the child. In this determination race was not a dominant, controlling, or crucial factor, but was weighed along with all other material elements of the lives of the family.

Race-matching has been and remains an influential and controversial concept regarding how best to construct adoptive families. Matching, in general, has been a classic principle of adoption practice, governing non-relative adoptions for much of the 20th century. Its goal was to create families in which the adoptive parents looked as though they could be the adopted child's biological parents. Matching potential adoptive parents and children on as many physical, emotional, and cultural characteristics as possible was seen as a way of insuring against adoptive failure.[5] It was not uncommon for potential adoptive parents to be denied the possibility of adoption if their hair and eye color did not match those of a child in need of adoption.[5] Differences among family members in constructed families were seen as threats to the integration of an adopted child and the child's identification with the adoptive parents. Race, along with religion, was considered the most important characteristic to be matched, and it continued to be important even as the matching concept regarding other characteristics began to shift.[5] For example, in 1959, in its *Standards for Adoption Service* (SAS), the Child Welfare League of America (CWLA) recommended that

> . . . similarities of background or characteristics should not be a major consideration in the selection of a family, except where integration of

the child into the family and his identification with them may be facilitated by likeness, as in the case of some older children or some children with distinctive physical traits, such as race [Ref. 5, pp 3–4].

The CWLA reiterated its view in its discussion of the role of physical characteristics: "Physical resemblances should not be a determining factor in the selection of a home, with the possible exception of such racial characteristics as color" (Ref. 5, p 4). It was not until 1968 that the CWLA omitted any reference to color as a criterion for adoption: "Physical resemblances of the adoptive parents, the child or his natural parents should not be a determining factor in the selection of a home" (Ref. 5, p 6). By 1971, the CWLA considered characteristics that had been encompassed in the matching concept to be broad guidelines rather than specific criteria and the weight afforded them depended on the potential adoptive parents (i.e., their desire for a child similar to them in particular ways should be taken into consideration).[5] While not identified as a strict criterion of adoption, matching continued to be a broad principle in adoption practices. For example, the CWLA's 1988 *Standards for Adoption Service* and its 1993 statement of its children's legislative agenda reflected its belief that the developmental needs of black adopted children could best be met by black adoptive parents.[5,6]

> Children in need of adoption have a right to be placed into a family that reflects their ethnicity or race. Children should not have their adoption denied or significantly delayed, however, when adoptive parents of other ethnic or racial groups are available. . . . In any adoption plan, however, the best interests of the child should be paramount. If aggressive, ongoing recruitment efforts are unsuccessful in finding families of the same ethnicity or culture, other families should be considered [Ref. 5, p 32].

Matching, of course, continued to influence child placement decisions outside of adoption agencies, as evidenced by the comments of the Drummond court. Following that court's decision, the general rule has been that trial courts may consider race as a factor in adoption proceedings as long as race is not the sole determinant.[15,16]

Statutory Attempts at Remedies

As we previously noted, in 1972 the National Association of Black Social Workers (NABSW) issued a position paper in which the Association vehemently opposed the adoption of black children by white families.[10] The Black Social Workers had a quick and striking effect on transracial adoption policy. Following the appearance of the paper, adoption agencies, both public and private, either implemented race-matching approaches or used the NABSW position to justify already existing race-matching policies. As a result, the number of transracial adoptions were estimated to drop significantly—39 percent within one year of the publication of the NABSW statement.[17] Although robust data were lacking, it was thought that the number and length of stay of black children in out-of-home placements increased as social workers and other foster care and adoption professionals, believing that same-race placements were in the best interest of the child, searched for same-race foster and adoptive parents. Agencies and their workers had considerable discretion in deciding the role race played in placement decisions. States, while generally requiring that foster care and adoption decisions be made in the best interest of the child, varied in their directions regarding the extent to which race, culture, and ethnicity should be taken into account in making the best-interest determination.[18]

While race-matching policies were not the sole determinant of increasing numbers of black children in institutions and out-of-home placements, there was growing concern that such policies, with their focus on same-race placement and their exclusion of consideration of loving, permanent interracial homes, kept black children from being adopted.[19] Because he was concerned that race had become the determining factor in adoption placements and that children were languishing in foster care homes and institutions, Senator Howard Metzenbaum introduced legislation to prohibit the use of race as the sole determinant of placement.[19] Senator Metzenbaum believed that same-race adoption was the preferable option for a child, but he also believed that transracial placement was far preferable to a child's remaining in foster care when an appropriate same-race placement was not available.[19]

Multiethnic Placement Act

Congress passed the Howard Metzenbaum Multiethnic Placement Act (MEPA) and President Clinton signed it into law on October 20, 1994.[20] MEPA's main goals were to decrease the length of time children had to wait to be adopted; to prevent discrimination based on race in the placement of children into adoptive or foster homes; and to recruit culturally diverse and minority adoptive and foster families who could meet the needs of children needing placement.[18] In passing MEPA, Congress was concerned that many children, especially those from minority groups, were spending lengthy periods in foster care awaiting adoption placements.[19] Congress found, within the parameters of available data, that nearly 500,000 children were in foster care in the United States; tens of thousands of these children were waiting for adoption; two years and eight months was the median length of time children waited to be adopted; and minority children often waited twice as long as other children to be adopted.[21]

Under MEPA, an agency or entity receiving federal funds could not use race as the sole factor in denying any person the opportunity to become an adoptive or foster parent. Furthermore, an agency could not use race as a single factor to delay or deny the placement of a child in an adoptive or foster care family or to otherwise discriminate in making a placement decision. However, an agency could consider a child's racial, cultural, and ethnic background as one of several factors—not the sole factor—used to determine the best interests of the child.[22] MEPA stated:

> An agency, or entity, that receives Federal assistance and is involved in adoption or foster care placements may not—(A) categorically deny to any person the opportunity to become an adoptive or a foster parent, solely on the basis of the race, color or national origin of the adoptive or foster parent, or the child involved; or (B) delay or deny the placement of a child for adoption or into foster care, or otherwise discriminate in making a placement decision, solely on the basis of the race, color, or national origin of the adoptive or foster parent, or the child involved.[23]

However, MEPA also contained the following permissible consideration:

> An agency or entity . . . may consider the cultural, ethnic, or racial background of the child and the capacity of the prospective foster or adoptive parents to meet the needs of a child of this background as one of a number of factors used to determine the best interests of a child.[24]

So, under MEPA, agencies could consider a child's race, ethnicity, or culture as one of a number of factors used to determine the best interests of the child, as long as it was not the sole factor considered, and they could consider the ability of prospective parents to meet the needs of a child of a given race, ethnicity, or culture.[22]

Following the passage of MEPA, the Department of Health and Human Services (DHHS), Office of Civil Rights, provided policy guidance to assist agencies receiving federal financial assistance in complying with MEPA.[25] The guidance permitted agencies receiving federal assistance to consider race, culture, or ethnicity as factors in making placement decisions to the extent allowed by MEPA, the U.S. Constitution and Title VI of the Civil Rights Act of 1964.[25]

Under the Equal Protection Clause of the Fourteenth Amendment, laws or practices drawing distinctions on the basis of race are inherently suspect and subject to strict scrutiny analysis.[26] To pass such analysis, classifications or practices based on race have to be narrowly tailored to meet a compelling state interest.[26] The Supreme Court has not specifically addressed the question of transracial adoption. It has considered race as a factor in a child placement decision in the context of a custody dispute between two white biological parents when the mother, who had custody of the child, began living with a black man, whom she later married. The Court found the goal of granting custody on the basis of the best interests of the child to be "indisputably a substantial government interest for purposes of the Equal Protection Clause" (Ref. 27, p 433). The DHHS guidance on the use of race, color, or national origin as factors in adoption and foster care placements addressed the relevant constitutional issues and indicated that the only compelling state interest in the context of child placement decisions is protecting the best interests of the child who is to be placed.[25] So, under MEPA, consideration of race or ethnicity was permitted as long as it was narrowly tailored to advance a specific child's best interests.[25] Agencies receiving federal funds could consider race and ethnicity when making placement decisions only if the agency made a narrowly tailored, individualized determination that the facts and circumstances of a particular case required the contemplation of race or ethnicity to advance the best interests of the child in need of placement.[18,25] Agencies could not assume that race, ethnicity, or culture was at issue in every case and make general policies that applied to all children.[18] The guidance also specifically prohibited policies that established periods during which same-race searches were conducted, created placement preference hierarchies based on race, ethnicity, or culture, required social workers to justify transracial placement decisions or resulted in delayed placements to find a family of a particular race, ethnicity, or culture.[18]

The DHHS policy guidance did address MEPA's permissible consideration of the racial, cultural, or ethnic background of a child and the capacity of the prospective foster or adoptive parents to meet the needs of a child of this background as one of a number of factors in the best-interest-of-the-child determination. The guidance allowed agencies to assess the ability of a specific potential adoptive family to meet a specific child's needs related to his or her racial, ethnic, or cultural background, as long as the assessment was done in the context of an individualized assessment[18,25]:

> As part of this assessment, the agency may examine the attitudes of the prospective family that affect their ability to nurture a child of a particular background and consider the family's ability to promote development of the child's positive sense of self. The agency may assess the family's ability to nurture, support, and reinforce the racial, ethnic, or cultural identity of the child, the family's capacity to cope with the particular consequences of the child's developmental history, and the family's ability to help the child deal with any forms of discrimination the child may encounter [Ref. 18, pp 9–10].

However, agencies were not allowed to make decisions based on general assumptions regarding the needs of children of a specific race, ethnicity, or culture or about the ability of prospective parents of a specific race, ethnicity, or culture to care or nurture the identity of a child of a different race, ethnicity, or culture.[18]

To increase the pool of potential foster or adoptive parents, MEPA also required states to develop plans for the recruitment of potential foster and adoptive families that reflected the ethnic and racial diversity of the children needing placement.[28] The recruitment efforts had to be focused on providing all eligible children with the opportunity for placement and on providing all qualified members of the community with an opportunity to become an adoptive or foster parent.[18] As a result, while MEPA sought in a reasonable way to recruit a broad racial and cultural spectrum of adoptive families, the law was at the same time underlining the idea that there was something special about a black child's being raised by a black family.

Those who objected to the permissive consideration of race in MEPA asserted that it allowed agencies to continue to delay adoptions of minority children based on race concerns.[21] They also argued that race-matching policies could and did continue under MEPA. Social workers could, for example, use race as a factor to support a finding that a transracial adoption was not in a given child's best interest. Supporters of MEPA reached their own conclusion that it did not accomplish its goal of speeding up the adoption process and moving greater numbers of minority children into foster care or adoption placements and that the permissive consideration of race allowed agencies legitimately to continue race-matching to deny or delay the placement of minority children with white adoptive parents.[22] Senator Metzenbaum himself agreed with this conclusion about MEPA and worked for its repeal.[29] As we shall see later, the arguments and counterarguments about the effectiveness of MEPA were being made in the absence of robust data.

The Interethnic Adoption Provisions

MEPA was repealed when on August 20, 1996, President Clinton signed the Small Business Job Protection Act of 1996. Section 1808 of the Act was entitled "Removal of Barriers to Interethnic Adoption" (The Interethnic Adoption Provisions; IEP).[30] MEPA's permissible consideration provision was removed and its language changed. (The words in brackets were part of MEPA and do not appear in the IEP.)

> A person or government that is involved in adoption or foster care placements may not—(a) [categorically] deny to any individual the opportunity to become an adoptive or a foster parent, [solely] on the basis of race, color, or national origin of the individual, or the child involved; or (b) delay or deny the placement of a child for adoption or into foster care [or otherwise discriminate in making a placement decision, solely] on the basis of race, color, or national origin of the adoptive or foster parent, or the child, involved [Ref. 22, pp 1616–17].

Under the IEP, states were still required to "provide for the diligent recruitment of potential foster and adoptive families that reflect the ethnic and racial diversity of children in the State for whom foster and adoptive homes are needed."[28]

Failure to comply with MEPA was a violation of Title VI of the Civil Rights Act of 1964[17]; failure to comply with the IEP is also a violation of Title VI.[31] Under MEPA, an agency receiving federal assistance that discriminated in its child placement decisions on the basis of race and failed to comply with the Act could forfeit its federal assistance[17] and an aggrieved individual had the right to bring an action seeking equitable relief in federal court[32] or could file a complaint with the Office of Civil Rights. The IEP added enforcement provisions that specified graduated fiscal sanctions to be imposed by DHHS against states found to be in violation of the law and gave any individual aggrieved by a violation the right to bring an action against the state or other entity in federal court.[33]

The Department of Health and Human Services issued two documents to provide practical guidance for complying with the IEP: a memorandum[34] and a document in question-and-answer format.[35] According to the guidance,

Congress, in passing the IEP, clarified its intent to eliminate delays in adoption or foster care placements when they were in any way avoidable. Race and ethnicity could not be used as the basis for any denial of placement nor used as a reason to delay a foster care or adoptive placement.[34] The repeal of MEPA's "permissible consideration" provision was seen as confirming that strict scrutiny was the appropriate standard for consideration of race or ethnicity in adoption and foster care placements.[34] DHHS argued that it had never taken the position that MEPA's permissible consideration language allowed agencies to take race into account routinely in making placement decisions because such a view would be inconsistent with a strict scrutiny standard.[34] It reaffirmed that any decision to consider race as a necessary element in a placement decision has to be based on concerns arising out of the circumstances of the particular situation:

> The primary message of the strict scrutiny standard in this context is that only the most compelling reasons may serve to justify consideration of race and ethnicity as part of a placement decision. Such reasons are likely to emerge only in unique and individual circumstances. Accordingly, occasions where race or ethnicity lawfully may be considered in a placement decision will be correspondingly rare [Ref. 34, p 4].

The guidance again made clear that the best interest of the child is the standard to be used in making placement decisions. So, according to the guidance, the IEP prohibits the routine practice of taking race and ethnicity into consideration ("Public agencies may not routinely consider race, national origin, and ethnicity in making placement decisions" (Ref. 35, p 2)), but it allows for the consideration of race, national origin, and ethnicity in certain specific situations ("Any consideration of these factors must be done on an individualized basis where special circumstances indicate that their consideration is warranted" (Ref. 35, p 2)). Once again, such language seems to suggest that, in certain contexts, the adoptive child may well benefit from placement in a same-race family.

The DHHS guidance seemed to frame the possibility for adoption agencies to continue the practice of race-matching.[22] For example, while warning that assessment of a prospective parent's ability to serve as a foster or adoptive parent must not act as a racial or ethnic screen and indicating that considerations of race must not be routine in the assessment function, the guidance conceded that an important aspect of good social work is an individualized assessment of a prospective parent's ability to be an adoptive or foster parent.

Thus, it allows for discussions with prospective adoptive or foster care parents about their feelings, preferences, and capacities regarding caring for a child of a particular race or ethnicity.[22,35]

Data Collection

Hansen and Simon[36] have pointed out that the Adoption and Safe Families Act (ASFA) of 1995 created an adoption incentive program that paid bonuses to states that increased the number of adoptions of children from foster care. The incentive program also provided an incentive for data collection, using a system known as the Adoption and Foster Care Analysis and Reporting System (AFCARS). States must submit data to AFCARS on each adoption in which a public child welfare agency was involved in any fashion. AFCARS issues periodic reports, and others (such as the Child Welfare League of America) use the AFCARS data to publish analytic reports from time to time. AFCARS reports may be preliminary, interim, or final as data continue to be submitted by states over many months.

Tables 1 and 2 show that in fiscal year (FY) 2002 and in FY 2003, more whites were adopted than blacks in the public foster care system. The two fiscal years show some difference between whites and blacks in terms of the comparative number of whites and blacks waiting for adoption. The data for FY 2003 show that more whites than blacks were in the foster care system. Of course, these numbers of children in the foster care system must be viewed in light of their representation in the general population. Data from the 2000

Table 1

Children Waiting to Be Adopted from the Public Foster Care System, by Race, by Fiscal Year

	On Sept. 30, 2002*		On Sept. 30, 2003[†]	
	Number	%	Number	%
Black/non-Hispanic	54,832	43	47,630	40
White/non-Hispanic	58,975	46	43,820	37
Total	127,942	100	119,000	100

*Reference 37.
[†]Reference 38.

Table 2

Children Adopted from the Public Foster Care System, by Race, by Fiscal Year

	Fiscal Year 2002*		Fiscal Year 2003[†]	
	Number	%	Number	%
Black/non-Hispanic	18,957	36	16,570	33
White/non-Hispanic	27,272	52	20,940	42
Total	52,138	100	50,000	100

*Reference 37.
[†]Reference 38.

U.S. Census . . . show that of the total population under age 18 years, 68.6 percent (49,598,289) are white and 15.1 percent (10,885,696) are black. Consequently, a substantially greater proportion of blacks (.4%), in comparison to whites (.09%), were awaiting adoption in September 2003. Still, of the children awaiting adoption in September 2002, 30 percent of black children were adopted in FY 2003 in comparison to 36 percent of white children.

The AFCARS data from FY 2001 have been the subject of greater analysis, which has led to the following conclusions.[36,39] In FY 2001, mean time for adoption of black children was 18 months compared with 15 months for white children. It was also estimated that about 17 percent of black children adopted in FY 2001 were adopted transracially by white, non-Hispanic parents. This figure of transracial adoptions (about 2,500) provided for the public foster care system is not significantly above estimates given for earlier years— about 2,574 in 1971. However, the FY 2001 data do not include private sector adoptions. This has led Hansen and Simon[36] to conclude that there has been no clear increase in transracial adoptions, at least in the arena of public child welfare agency adoptions. In 2003, McFarland[40] published a report pointing out that while AFCARS is now producing robust data about public sector adoptions, information about private sector adoptions is scant.

Nevertheless, it has been estimated that in 2001, about 127,000 children were adopted in the United States,[41] including public, private, and intercountry adoptions. These adoptions arise out of the estimated 500,000 children in out-of-home placements in the United States.

Discussion

The IEP addresses individual cultural elements such as race, color, or national origin and does not address the broad role of culture in placement decisions. The DHHS guidance notes:

> There are situations where cultural needs may be important in placement decisions, such as where a child has specific language needs. However, a public agency's consideration of culture would raise Section 1808 [IEP] issues if the agency used culture as a proxy for race, color, or national origin. Thus, while nothing in Section 1808 directly prohibits a public agency from assessing the cultural needs of all children in foster care, Section 1808 would prohibit an agency from using routine cultural assessments in a manner that would circumvent the law's prohibition against the routine consideration of race, color, or national origin [Ref. 35, p 2].

This raises questions about the role of cultural capacity or cultural competence of parents in adoption and foster care decisions. In response to a question regarding whether public agencies may assess the cultural capacity of all foster parents, the DHHS responded in the negative, but seemed to open the door to such assessment, at least of particular parents:

> Race, color, and national origin may not routinely be considered in assessing the capacity of particular prospective foster parents to care

for specific children. However, assessment by an agency of the capacity of particular adults to serve as foster parents for specific children is the heart of the placement process, and essential to determining what would be in the best interests of a particular child [Ref. 35, p 2].

The DHHS guidance makes a similar statement regarding cultural competency:

The term "cultural competency," as we understand it, is not one that would fit in a discussion of adoption and foster placement. However, agencies should, as a matter of good social work practice, examine all the factors that may bear on determining whether a particular placement is in the best interest of a particular child. That may in rare instances involve the consideration of the abilities of prospective parents of one race or ethnicity to care for a child of another race or ethnicity [Ref. 35, p 5].

Such language is obviously far from being lucid and specific. It grants the potential importance of considering race and cultural competence, but cautions against general and routine use of these factors, while contemplating their utility in particular situations.

In considering the best interests of a child who is being placed for adoption, DHHS is suggesting that there could be special circumstances uniquely individualized to the child that require consideration of ethnicity and race of the potential adoptive parents. Presumably this should not be done routinely and should not be seen as serving as a proxy for a consistent and mundane contemplation of ethnicity or race in the adoption context. Undoubtedly, what constitutes special circumstances in the practices of any given adoption agency is likely to be a matter of interpretation. While agencies can readily assert what their routine practices are, much may turn on how vigorously supervised are the claims that special circumstances exist with respect to a particular black child that dictate consideration of ethnicity and race in that child's case. As a practical result, while it appears no one is now allowed to claim that every black child needs a black family, it may still be reasonable and practicable to claim that a black child requires adoption by a black family, as dictated by consideration of the best interests of that child. For example, Kennedy (Ref. 1, p 416) has raised the possibility that an older child might say he or she wanted to be adopted only by a black family. Such a context could indeed make it difficult for the child's wish to be refused outright, without any consideration whatsoever.

Such reasoning is articulated starting from the point of view of the child. Giving consideration to the interests of the potential adoptive parent is another matter. In other words, what should we consider about the adoptive parent's interest in raising black children and the parent's ability to do so? The opinions about this matter remain divided. Kennedy (Ref. 1, pp 416, 434) and Bartholet[42] have proposed that prospective adoptive parents be allowed to state a preference for adopting a child from a particular ethnic group. This is, in their view, permissible race-matching that ultimately serves the best interests of the child. After all, what would be the use of forcing a family to adopt a child they really did not want? In addition, both authors also have argued that state intervention in such racial selectivity in the formation of families would be akin to imposing race-based rules on the creation of married couples. However, Banks[43] has opposed this accommodationist stance, where in practice adoption agencies would simply show prospective adoptive parents only the class of ethnic children the adoptive parent was interested in adopting. Banks thought this merely perpetuated the status quo, as white adoptive parents had little interest in black children. This would result in black children's continuing to languish in out-of-home placements, and their time spent awaiting adoption would remain prolonged.

Kennedy and Bartholet were permissive in their attitude toward the racial selectivity of prospective adoptive parents, respecting parents' choice to construct families as they wish.

There has been and continues to be strong support for the belief that black children belong with black adoptive parents. It is not only the NABSW, which has called for the repeal of the IEP,[13] that has taken this position. For example, in a 1998 letter to the Secretary of the Department of Health and Human Services, a former executive director of the Child Welfare League of America strongly disagreed with the DHHS's interpretation of MEPA/IEP, stating that prohibiting any consideration of race in adoptive and foster care placement decisions contradicts best-practice standards in child welfare:

> CWLA standards for adoption and foster care services clearly state that the best practice requires consideration of race. . . . Children in need of adoption have a right to be placed into a family that reflects their ethnicity or race. . . . These standards—calling for the explicit consideration of race in adoption and foster care placement decisions—reflect the best thinking of child welfare experts from across the country [Ref. 44, p 2].

The CWLA, in its most recent *Standards of Excellence for Adoption Services* (2000), reiterated its belief that race is to be considered in all adoptions and that placement with parents of the same race is the first choice for any child. Other placements should be considered only after a vigorous search for parents of the same race has failed:

> All children deserve to be raised in a family that respects their cultural heritage. . . . If aggressive, ongoing recruitment efforts are unsuccessful in finding families of the same race or culture as the child, other families should be considered to ensure that the child's adoptive placement is not delayed [Ref. 45, p 68].

In its most recent policy statement on foster care and adoption (2003), the National Association of Social Workers also reiterated its position that consideration of race should play a central role in placement decisions:

> Placement decisions should reflect a child's need for continuity, safeguarding the child's right to consistent care and to service arrangements. Agencies must recognize each child's need to retain a significant engagement

with his or her parents and extended family and respect the integrity of each child's ethnicity and cultural heritage [Ref. 46, p 147].

The social work profession stresses the importance of ethnic and cultural sensitivity. An effort to maintain a child's identity and his or her ethnic heritage should prevail in all services and placement actions that involve children in foster care and adoption programs [Ref. 46, p 148].

The placement of choice should be within the child's family of origin, among relatives (kinship placement) who can provide a more stable environment for the child during the period of family crisis. If no such relatives are available, every effort should be made to place a child in the home of foster parents who are similar in racial and ethnic background to the child's own family. The recruitment of foster parents from each relevant racial and ethnic group should be pursued vigorously to meet the needs of children who require placement [Ref. 46, p 150].

Others[47–49] have espoused the view that inracial adoption is the preferred option for a black child because black families inherently possess the competence to raise children with strong black identities and the ability to cope with racism. While questions of cultural competence to raise a black child often arise about prospective white adoptive parents, no such questions are posed about prospective black adoptive parents.[1] The competence of black families to raise black children is regularly referred to as though black families are culturally identical or homogeneous and all are equally competent to raise black children and equip them to live in our society.[1,50] We may all think about black cultural competence as though it is a one-dimensional concept. Indeed, we may all be referring simply to stereotypical indicators of what we think it means to be black. We may be referring to our own personal preferences for the stereotypic activities of black people: involvement in a black church; participation in a community center where black-focused programs are operating; viewing movies with a clearly black theme; reading literature authored by blacks. What is rarely considered is that some black families are drawn to rap music, others to jazz greats, and still others to traditional classical music. Indeed, some families obviously manage to exhibit an interest in all these genres of music. With respect, therefore, to even these stereotyped indicators of what it means to be black, black families vary in the degree of their attachment to the indicators. This is to say that blacks differ in their level of commitment to the salience of black-oriented culture in their individual and family lives. As a result, there is considerable cultural heterogeneity among black families. Such variability may well lead to differences in black families' ways of coping with racism.[50]

To date, the statutory attempts to deal with transracial adoptions have not been considered as spectacularly successful, especially in the case of MEPA. Nevertheless, efforts have been made to limit the routine consideration of race and ethnicity in adoption, with the result that black children may be remaining for shorter periods in undesirable out-of-home placements. (National data are not yet able to demonstrate clear trends.[36,40]) However, DHHS guidance still permits consideration of race and ethnicity in specific cases, with the apparent concession that some black children may need a black family for the realization of the child's best interests.

The burden is on forensic psychiatrists and other mental health professionals who perform adoption evaluations to point out cogently and logically two points: first, whether race is a factor that is relevant in the adoption evaluation; and second, whether there is something unique or particular about that adoption context that requires race to be considered. It will require special argumentation for the evaluator to claim that a particular black child could benefit more from placement with a black family than with a non-black family. As stated earlier, the evidence is clear that black children can do well in transracial placements. The pointed objective, therefore, in future evaluations will be to show that a particular black child has such unique and special needs that he or she deserves particular consideration for placement in a black family. It will be interesting to see whether our forensic colleagues, in striving for objectivity, will consider the factor of race in their evaluations only when something unique about that particular adoption context cries out for race to be considered so that the best-interest-of-the-child standard can be met. It seems clear that forensic professionals must be careful not to state that they routinely consider race in their adoption evaluations unless they intend to argue clinically that race is always relevant. And even then, they should be cautious about not articulating a general preference for inracial over transracial adoptions.

Despite federal statutory attempts to remove race as a controlling factor in adoption and foster care placement decisions, the debate over transracial adoption is not over. Indeed, strains of the debate are evidenced in the statutes and their implementation guidelines and the argument continues among our mental health colleagues. For example, following passage of MEPA and the IEP, a group of adoption experts from different disciplines was assembled by the Stuart Foundation to reconsider the controversies surrounding racial matching and transracial adoption. The Adoption and Race Work Group concluded that "race should not be ignored when making placement decisions and that children's best interests are served—all else being equal—when they are placed with families of the same racial, ethnic, and cultural background as their own" (Ref. 51, p 169). The Work Group decided that the research to date was insufficient, even though research has supported transracial adoption.

The ultimate outcome of the group's deliberations is perhaps the clearest indication of how difficult it is in this debate to meld passion and scholarship. The ongoing debate exemplifies Courtney's conclusion that "those with strongly held views are likely to maintain their convictions: advocates of TRA will continue to believe that the research supports their beliefs, while opponents will contend that TRA is harmful, or that the jury is still out" (Ref. 52, p 753). After two years of work analyzing racial matching and transracial adoption, the Stuart work group acknowledged that thinking about the debate in terms of those who oppose or support transracial or inracial adoptions may get us nowhere. "It may be more productive to regard the issue in terms of assessing, deciding, and documenting when the law allows us to place more or less emphasis on race and racial matching and when good social work practice calls for it" (Ref. 52, p 177). This may be a concession to the notion that, with respect to transracial adoption, cultural stereotypes die hard.

References

1. Kennedy R: Interracial Intimacies: Sex, Marriage, Identity and Adoption. New York: Pantheon Books, 2003

2. For further commentary on the debate, see: Griffith EEH, Duby JL: Recent developments in the transracial adoption debate. Bull Am Acad Psychiatry Law 19:339–50, 1991. Griffith EEH: Forensic and policy implications of the transracial adoption debate. Bull Am Acad Psychiatry Law 23:501–12, 1995

3. Drummond v. Fulton County Department of Family and Children's Services, 563 F.2d 1200 (5th Cir. 1977)

4. Hollinger JH: A Guide to the Multiethnic Placement Act of 1994 as Amended by the Interethnic Adoption Provisions of 1996. National Resource Center on Children and the Law. . . .

5. Simon RJ, Alstein H: Adoption, Race and Identity: From Infancy to Young Adulthood. New Brunswick, NJ: Transaction Publishers, 2002

6. Vroegh KS: Transracial adoptees: developmental status after 17 years. Am J Orthopsychiatry 67:568–75, 1997

7. Griffith EEH, Adams AK: Public policy and transracial adoptions of black children, in Family, Culture and Psychobiology Edited by Sorel E. Ottawa, ON, Canada: Legas Press, 1990, pp 211–33

8. Griffith EEH, Silverman IL: Transracial adoptions and the continuing debate on the racial identity of families, in Racial and Ethnic Identity: Psychological Development and Creative Expression. Edited by Harris HW, Blue HC, Griffith EEH. New York: Routledge, 1995, pp 95–114

9. Burrow AL, Finley GE: Transracial, same-race adoptions, and the need for multiple measures of adolescent adjustment. Am J Orthopsychiatry 74:577–83, 2004

10. National Association of Black Social Workers: Position Statement on Transracial Adoptions. September 1972. . . .

11. Testimony of William T Merritt, President of the National Association of Black Social Workers, Hearings Before the Committee on Labor and Human Resources, United States Senate, 99th Congress, June 25, 1985

12. Institute for Justice: Separate is not equal: striking down state-sanctioned barriers to interracial adoption. . . .

13. National Association of Black Social Workers: Preserving Families of African Ancestry. Washington, DC: NABSW, 2003

14. Farmer v. Farmer, 439 N.YS.2d 584 (N.Y Sup. Ct. 1981)

15. Farrell T, Gregor R, Payne A, *et al:* Adoption § 138 Interethnic Adoption. Am Jur 2d: 138, 2004

16. Zitter JM: Race as a factor in adoption proceedings. ALR 4th 34:167, 2004

17. Marby CR: "Love alone is not enough!" in transracial adoptions: scrutinizing recent statutes, agency policies, and prospective adoptive parents. Wayne Law Rev 42:1347–23, 1996

18. Bussiere A: A Guide to the Multiethnic Placement Act of 1994. ABA Center on Children and the Law. . . .

19. Metzenbaum HM: S. 1224—In Support of the Multiethnic Placement Act of 1993. Duke J Gender Law Policy 2:165–71, 1995

20. 42 U.S.C. § 5115a (1994)

21. Varan R: Desegregating the adoptive family: in support of the Adoption Antidiscrimination Act of 1995. J Marshall Law Rev 30:593–625, 1997

22. Campbell SB: Taking race out of the equation: transracial adoption in 2000. SMU Law Rev 53:1599–626, 2000

23. 42 U.S.C. § 5115a (a) (1)(A)-(B) (1994)

24. 42 U.S.C. § 5115a(a) (2) (1994)

25. Hayashi D: Policy Guidance on the Use of Race, Color or National Origin as Considerations in Adoption and Foster Care Placements. Washington, DC: Office of Civil Rights, Department of Health and Human Services. . . .

26. Adarand Constructors, Inc. v. Pena, 515 U.S. 200 (1995)

27. Palmore v. Sidoti, 466 U.S. 429 (1984)

28. 42 U.S.C. § 622(b)(9)

29. Statement of the Honorable Howard Metzenbaum: Testimony Before the Subcommittee on Human Resources of the House Committee on Ways and Means. Hearing on Interethnic Adoptions, September 15, 1998. . . .

30. 42 U.S.C.S. § 1996 b(l) (2003)

31. 42 U.S.C.S. § 1996 b(2) (2003)

32. 42 U.S.C.S. § 5115a(b) (1994)

33. 42 U.S.C.S. § 674(d) (2003)

34. Hayashi D: Interethnic Adoption Provisions of the Small Business Job Protection Act of 1996. Memorandum, Office for Civil Rights, Department of Health and Human Services. June 4, 1997. . . .

35. Questions and Answers Regarding the Multiethnic Placement Act of 1994 and Section 1808 of the Small Business and Job Protection Act of 1996. Office for Civil Rights, Department of Health and Human Services. . . .

36. Hansen ME, Simon RJ: Transracial Placement in Adoptions With Public Agency Involvement: What Can We Learn From the AFCARS Data? . . .

37. National Data Analysis System. . . .

38. U.S. Department of Health and Human Services, Administration for Children and Families: The AFCARS Report 10. . . .

39. The Multiethnic Placement Act. National Data Analysis System. . . .

40. McFarland MC: Adoption Trends in 2003: A Deficiency of Information. National Center for State Courts, 2003. . . .

41. National Adoption Information Clearinghouse: How Many Children Were Adopted in 2000 and 2001? . . .

42. Bartholet E: Private race preferences in family formation. Yale Law J 107:2351–6, 1998

43. Banks RR: The color of desire: fulfilling adoptive parents' racial preferences through discriminatory state action. Yale Law J 107: 875–964, 1998

44. Letter from David Liederman, Former CWLA Executive Director to Donna Shalala, HHS Secretary, December 21, 1998. . . .

45. Child Welfare League of America: Standards of Excellence: Standards of Excellence for Adoption Services (revised edition). Washington, DC: Child Welfare League of America, Inc., 2000

46. National Association of Social Workers: Foster care and adoption, in Social Work Speaks: National Association of Social Workers Policy Statements, 2003–2006 (ed 6). Washington, DC: NASW Press, 2003, pp 144–51

47. Chimezie A: Transracial adoption of black children. Social Work 20:296–301, 1975

48. Jones E: On transracial adoption of black children. Child Welfare 51:156–64, 1972

49. Bowen JS: Cultural convergences and divergences: the nexus between putative Afro-American family values and the best interests of the child. J Family Law 26:487–531, 1987–88

50. Griffith EEH: Culture and the debate on adoption of black children by white families, in American Psychiatric Press Review of Psychiatry (vol 14). Edited by Oldham JM, Riba MB. Washington, DC: American Psychiatric Press, 1995, pp 543–64

51. Brooks D, Barth RP, Bussiere A, *et al:* Adoption and race: implementing the Multiethnic Placement Act and the Interethnic Adoption Provisions. Social Work 44:167–78, 1999

52. Courtney ME: The politics and realities of transracial adoption. Child Welfare 76:749–79, 1997

EXPLORING THE ISSUE

Is It Beneficial if Adoptive Parents Adopt Only Within Their Own Racial/Ethnic Group?

Critical Thinking and Reflection

- What are some of the arguments made by each side with which you agree or disagree?
- What are the strengths and weaknesses of the two positions argued in this chapter?
- Pick the side with which you most agree. What are some additional arguments you would make to strengthen the case for or against transracial adoption?
- Think more broadly of the issue of transracial adoption. What are the benefits of homogeneous family structures and what are the benefits of heterogeneous family structures? What are the weaknesses or limitations?

Is There Common Ground?

Everyone wants children to have the best childhood possible, and everyone knows that parents' loving a child is the most important factor. At the same time, our nation has a long and complicated history related to race, and that history cannot be easily separated or removed from the subject of transracial adoption. Why is transracial adoption more controversial with some races than with others? How does this affect children when they learn about attitudes regarding race and traditional families? Are there certain situations that would be more ideal for transracial adoption than others?

Additional Resources

H. M. Dalmadge, *Tripping on the Color Line: Black-White Multiracial Families in a Racially Divided World* (Piscataway, NJ: Rutgers University Press, 2000).

H. Fogg-Davis, *Ethics of Transracial Adoption* (Ithaca, NY: Cornell University Press, 2001).

J. Lang, *Transracial Adoptions: An Adoptive Mother's Documentary of Racism, Injustice, & Joy* (Universe, Incorporated, 2002).

S. Patton, *Birthmarks: Transracial Adoption in Contemporary America* (New York: New York University Press, 2000).

R. J. Simon and H. Altstein, *Adoption Across Borders: Serving the Children in Transracial and Intercountry Adoption* (Lanham, MD: Rowman & Littlefield Publishers, Inc., 2000).

R. J. Simon and R. Roorda, In *Their Own Voices: Transracial Adoptees Tell Their Stories* (New York: Columbia University Press, 2000).

G. Steinberg and B. Hall, *Inside Transracial Adoption* (Indianapolis, IN: Perspectives Press, Inc., 2000).

J. J. J. Trenka, S. Y. Shin, J. C. Oparah, and S. Y. Shin, eds., *Outsiders Within: Writing on Transracial Adoption* (Cambridge, MA: South End Press, 2006).

ISSUE 2

Does Divorce Have a Negative Impact on Children?

YES: Sarah Werthan Buttenwieser, from "Does Divorce Have a Negative Impact on Children? Yes," revised from *Taking Sides: Family and Personal Relationships* (2009)

NO: Jane Johnson Struck and Angela Thomas, from "Solo Act: Single Mom Angela Thomas Reflects on Raising Kids Alone," *Today's Christian Woman* (May/June 2008)

Learning Outcomes

As a result of this issue, readers will be able to:

- Identify the major challenges that divorce causes parents and children.
- Compare and contrast the competing arguments made for and against divorce in this issue.
- Evaluate issues that authors raise about how they will help create a more peaceful divorce (e.g., communication and collaboration, religious faith).

ISSUE SUMMARY

YES: Sarah Werthan Buttenwieser is a writer and lives in Northampton. She earned her BA at Hampshire College and her MFA from Warren Wilson College. Contributor to many magazines, newspapers, and online publications, she has a blog called "Standing in the Shadows," which can be found at http://www.valleyadvocate.com.

NO: Jane Johnson Struck and Angela Thomas are the authors of *My Single-Mom Life*, published by Thomas Nealson. Thomas, a mother of four, possesses a Masters degree from the Dallas Theological Seminary. Thomas writes that being a single mom was not God's design for parenting. She believes in children being raised by a man and a woman in love. Despite her beliefs and the challenges she has faced through divorce, her belief is that God and Jesus protect her and her children when they are in need. She argues that faith in God is what people need to protect them from the challenges of being a single mother and a child of a divorced family.

In the United States today, 63 percent of children grow up with both biological parents. The highest divorce rates in the United States are found in Nevada and Arkansas, while the lowest divorce rates are found in Washington, DC, Massachusetts; and Pennsylvania. Divorces lead to a division of parenting responsibility as well as finances. Almost 7.8 million Americans pay approximately $40 billion each year in child and spousal support. While there has been a slight decline in divorces over recent years, there has been a corresponding decrease in marriage as well.

Couples today are often focused on the well-being of the children in the family. How, then, do we assess the impact of separation on children? Marriage and cohabitation laws vary across the states. These laws are often based on the belief that marriage will provide greater family and societal stability by keeping couples together. Over the last 50 years, American values related to marriage and cohabitation have changed significantly. It was not until 1967, in the case of *Loving v. Virginia*, that the U.S. Supreme Court ruled to strike down state laws forbidding interracial marriages. During more recent times, some courts have struck down state laws prohibiting cohabitation, policies intended to discourage living together out of wedlock.

The history of marriage is diverse and fluid. It can be a story of extraordinary love and joy. It can also be a story of great pain and even abuse. Across time, the meaning of marriage and love has been reconstructed. What was once often a financial arrangement is today something that is much more likely to have a foundation in love. In the United States today, the economic necessity to remain married, or even to get married in the first place, is less than it ever has been in this nation's history.

Considering the decrease in marriage, the challenges of separation now extend well beyond the martial relationship. Many unmarried couples with children choose to cohabitate. In fact, the frequency of cohabitation with children is four times higher today than it was in 1970. With a sizable number of children born out of wedlock, the concept of parents staying together extends well beyond marriage and divorce.

Clearly, concepts of family and matrimony are being reconstructed in American society. Virtually every reader has experience with these changes. It is difficult to grow up in American society today without having personal experiences or knowing someone well who comes from a divorced family. Additionally, there are many families today where two parents, whether married or not, are raising a child. The same challenges and questions for staying together face them as those challenges that face married couples.

The focus of debate in this chapter is whether or not couples should stay together for the sake of their children. If the reader refers to the Political Ideology Continuum featured in the Introduction to this book, reactionaries or conservatives would be more likely to support staying together for the sake of the children. In contrast, liberals and radicals tend to support ending the relationship if they think that is best. However, those labels tend to stop at the level of political theory and are limited in translating it into affecting personal lives. Indeed, many conservatives have their marriages end in divorce while their children are young. Meanwhile, a significant number of liberals stay in their relationships for the sake of their children. In fact, the writers in this chapter prove that there are limitations when applying the Political Ideology Continuum too rigidly. Specifically, when taking a close look at Buttenwieser's article, readers will notice a sometimes liberal but often nonpolitical framework for a position that is traditionally associated with conservative values. In contrast, the opposing article is written through a traditionally Christian framework.

When reading, give consideration to how these views shared fit into the Political Ideology Continuum. Apply these views to experiences in your own world, either in your own family or the relationships of others you know well.

One of the ways to avoid becoming an unhappy married couple is to work on entering healthy relationships and work on ensuring that a relationship remains healthy. However, this is a challenging goal, and unhealthy relationships, or even relationships that are just not right, are inevitable. Despite this fact, little time is invested in helping teenagers identify the qualities of a healthy relationship and to further develop the skills of making relationships work.

While an equal relationship does not guarantee a happy relationship, it is a critical component. Dating and domestic violence organizations will often cite the following qualities in a healthy relationship: negotiation and fairness, nonthreatening behavior, respect, trust and support, honesty and accountability, responsible parenting, shared responsibility, and economic partnership. In all relationships, including happy ones, it is typically necessary to work on ensuring that both individuals are treated equally and feel valued and respected within their relationship.

If separation is inevitable for a couple, it is critical to examine what can make this experience work as well as possible for the children involved. WebMD lists nine do's and don'ts in helping children with divorce. This advice can also be applied to non-marital cohabitation as well:

Don't confide in your children about adult concerns like your disagreements with your spouse or your money worries. Find a friend or counselor to confide in instead.

Don't criticize your ex. If you have a dispute with your ex-spouse, don't expose your children to your conflicts and frustration.

Don't quiz your child about the other parent or what goes on at the other parent's house. It's fine to ask general questions about your child's time there, but don't snoop.

Don't introduce major changes in your child's life if you can help it. Try to keep to your usual family routines and community ties.

Do continue to parent as you always have. You may feel guilty that your children have to cope with divorce, but it won't help to give them special presents or let them stay up late. They'll feel more secure if you're firm and consistent.

Do encourage children to call the other parent when they have news or just to talk. Keep the other parent informed about school events and other activities.

Do learn more about how to help your child cope with divorce.

Do get help for a child having trouble coping with divorce. A young child may show regressive behavior like excessive clinginess or bedwetting, while an older child may become angry, aggressive, withdrawn, or depressed, or have problems in school. A therapist can provide a safe place for your child to express his or her feelings.

Do seek help if you and your ex can't interact without hostility. A family therapist or professional mediator can help you develop a more friendly communication style—one with fewer negative effects on your children.

How would you assess WebMD's list? What advice is most important to adhere to? What advice is most challenging to adhere to?

Although there are differences regarding whether unhappy couples should separate for the sake of their children, there are good and bad ways to go about separation, not only for the children but also for the former couple. Adhering to these guidelines can help limit the struggles associated with divorce or separation.

YES

Sarah Werthan Buttenwieser

Does Divorce Have a Negative Impact on Children?

We all know that Tolstoy was right: "Happy families are all alike; every unhappy family is unhappy in its own way." And so often, unhappy couples decide that their ticket to happiness, their shot at it, begins with divorce.

From divorce, there is possibility—of freedom and of a love relationship working out the next time around.

What about the couple's children? Does divorce have a negative impact on them?

Yes, divorce probably does have a negative impact on children.

Why? Because divorce creates a fissure in a family's life and for the child or children: divorce assumes a great deal of disruption—two households rather than one. Contact with both parents becomes chopped up or the contact with one parent is lost, simultaneously shifting all responsibility onto one parent's shoulders.

That doesn't mean divorce can't have many positive effects, too. It definitely can—and often does. But a happier outcome doesn't happen magically; it takes work.

Divorce can ultimately turn out well for the children *if* the parents decide that a healthy divorce—one that benefits the children—is worth the hard work that it entails. This so-called ideal divorce could be dubbed a peaceful divorce, a friendly divorce, or even a loving divorce. I'd like to share some ideas about how to make divorce work well for the children.

Before I begin, let me make an exception. This is critical: Safety is the top priority. If anyone in a family—spouse or child—is being abused, physically or emotionally, that person's safety is a stand-alone and nonnegotiable consideration.

The premise of a divorce that has a positive impact upon children begins with a commitment from both parents—and any future partners—to work hard for the sake of a peaceful coexistence, and to forge a family that works for the kids—even if it occurs in two places. Some people use the phrase "a family apart" to ensure the child envisions family as a complete entity, even if divided by geography and other life changes. Whatever it's called, a positive divorce scenario for the kids almost inevitably requires a lot of work on the part of the adults. It's harder to have a positive divorce than a happy, uninterrupted marriage.

While marriage is a contract with a legal route to dissolution in its makeup, children come with no equally simple and clear documentation. That's why children do not resemble finances or even custody; they cannot be divvied up like furniture or real estate and remain emotionally intact. And unlike even marriage, children are *the* lifelong commitment parents make. Far more than roof over head and food in bellies, parents owe children a version of a happy family, even if it's post-divorce and a family-apart model rather than a family-together one.

I believe that any couple contemplating divorce should think long and hard about whether they could really commit to a good divorce. I don't think sticking it out until the kids leave is a great alternative. Whether a couple chooses to stay together or separate, children benefit from their parents honestly and earnestly working through either choice toward what is essentially a happy ending. A marriage that vanishes as soon as the child leaves for college, and any sense of goodwill with it, that's like an illusion: a thing that seemed real crumbling into dust.

Once kids appear, whether in a solid, happy marriage, a primarily disappointing marriage, or a divorce, parents need to remain focused on their children's best interests. In order to do so, they need to remain flexible in thought and in action in order to accommodate their children's needs. That's really the main message here. And it's a different message than neglecting your own needs because you are focused upon your children; it's more of a plea to remember what a huge responsibility you've assumed by becoming a parent.

Ideally, everyone's happiness lines up like stars on a perfect evening, like ducks in a row, like that equation we hope is true, that "happy parent equals happy child." However, by choosing one's own adult happiness, one's child's happiness does not inevitably follow. Parents cannot protect children from all unhappiness (nor should they; learning to deal with disappointment and unhappiness is an essential part of life, indeed of a happy life). But parents should try to protect their children, and in so doing, should—I believe—place their children's happiness, if not on a pedestal, in a safe place.

That's why I'm advocating that if parents are divorcing, they should: (1) remain focused on the child or children, (2) remain flexible, and (3) remain willing to put their child's happiness above their own sometimes.

Full disclosure: I'm a (grown) child of divorce contemplating this issue from within a very happy marriage (with four kids). In the case of my parents' divorce, obviously I had no say in whether it happened. Although I cannot rewrite history, I do think all of our lives were better for their choosing to part ways. My parents' was a protracted and ambivalent and messy split. Once it was finally finished, what came next was an improvement upon the uneasy marriage or the mercurial uncertainty that endured for a few more years.

Even though divorce turned out to be better than my parents' staying married, my experience convinced me that divorce is almost inevitably difficult for the children. Having your daily life split between households is unsettling, even if that's the routine. If I close my eyes, I can still picture the small, rectangular, flowery suitcase that I carried between my mother's house and father's house during many childhood years. The green was a bit olivey;

the reds contained a bit of magenta; the flowers were rendered with a seventies aesthetic. The case had a plastic, rectangular handle and a gold-brass clasp—as might be on a journal—that slid into place. I absolutely hated it. Not the suitcase itself; I hated what it represented. We went back and forth at a dizzying rate. The prevailing wisdom of the time was that young children should not be separated from their mothers for very long, so we had a staccato rhythm that had us at our dad's a night, our mom's for two, our dad's again for sometime, our mom's, our dad's . . . working out to five days with our father out of every fourteen. My sister—nearly three years my junior—and I were in constant motion. Divorce required that we keep track of our schedule and our stuff and each other.

More so, divorce—at least the peripatetic version I experienced—made me feel that I lacked something I truly longed for: a home. Read carefully: a home, one home, you know, of the "there's no place like home" variety. Two houses do not equal a home. Two houses are more houses, less home.

I am not arguing stay-in-it-for-the-kids'-sake. I'm noting, though, that it makes sense to try really hard before letting go of a marriage in process. But let's assume that you do decide to divorce and want to figure out how to do right by your kids. Begin by remembering that your kids did not ask you to marry, have them, or divorce. What I'm really trying to say here holds whether parents stay together or live apart: it's that parents can sabotage their children's happiness by pitting kids in the middle of angry impasses, warring tactics, and dysfunctional communication. That is not fair. While it is extremely hard to parent like a good crew team, pulling oars in unison, winning a race isn't the goal. Unison doesn't have to mean complete agreement to ensure good coparenting. Rather than attempting to win a race, try to get the rowboat across the lake in reasonable fashion.

A key reason that divorce has a negative impact on children is that it very well may place them in the middle of a rift. As each adult endeavors to create his or her new, solid life, the kids travel between those lives or at least are aware of the two new worlds their parents occupy while their "constant" is that chasm, the space between. Even if both parents are thriving, the children are missing pieces of those experiences. They remain in transit. If one or both parents struggle, the children are extremely aware of that, too.

Now that I'm an adult, I have a number of friends with kids who have divorced. It seems so hard for my friends to fathom that for their kids, there's ongoing loss in the form of dislocation. Sometimes, it seems they try not to think too hard about their children's experiences. They think about the children and parent them when they are present, but they minimize how difficult it might be to negotiate two households constantly and to have to miss a parent and to have to reconnect, in a sense, twice as often as either parent does. Trying to imagine what it's like for the child negotiating two households, two spaces, and two sets of expectations seems critical.

What makes a good divorce? Supposing the couple has tried hard to make a marriage work and remain well supported by the couples or family therapist they toiled with, they can continue to garner support from that person through the untangling of their shared lives into two more separate lives with the large overlapping factor of continuing attachment to their child or children.

What I observe: The "best" divorces—for the kids—are the ones in which the parents remain, in some fashion, friends (in the best marriages, couples are friends as well). Really. I have divorced friends who discuss their children and their own dating lives with similar ease, and who continue to share certain chores or time hanging out with their kids. While there are tensions—if the relationship were perfectly easy, they might still be together—they decided to override those tensions for the sake of their children. Some people let the kids stay in one place and they cycle in and out of the family home, for that first year or for a few years, depending on circumstances.

There's no single perfect formula for a positive divorce. The idea, though, is to keep things comfortable enough that decisions aren't battles and that the adults aren't seething. Without gigantic tensions between the parents, they are more easygoing and can present a more unified front about the most important issues and support one another's choices (where they differ) than they could back when less-than-happily-married.

It seems that the best divorces—again, like the best marriages—have room for flexibility. A special out-of-town friend is visiting at the other house? Stay another night. A kid needs something from the other house? We'll get it. If what's needed is the other parent, we'll get the other parent. Flexibility assumes that parents can still talk to one another, and thus that the kids are safe to rely upon their parents as a team when necessary. Flexibility doesn't mean a complete disregard for the comfort—for all involved—of structure. There's a comfortable interplay between the two, ideally.

Fast-forward through holidays and birthday parties, plays, and sports competitions, and you probably reach graduations, weddings, births, and other family milestones. Even if a couple divorces, once they have children, they are either in one another's lives through these events at the very least, or all events—those significant and lesser events—become somewhat more chopped up for the kids (which parent comes to which occasion?).

A divorce that remains open—I think you could call it "warm"—assumes this underlying principle: The adults want the best not only for their children, but for one another. That's the underlying principle for a good marriage, too.

There's a pattern here: So much that is necessary for a good marriage is also essential for a good divorce. This probably means the best divorces do not emerge from the worst marriages.

I'm sure there are physics involved in these things, and that there's a point where the momentum of one's work within a marriage no longer contributes to its forward movement. There must be some place from which a couple can split with enough positive energy left to propel those energies toward a reasonably happy divorce. Long before reaching that point, though, any unhappy couple—or even more specifically, each member of an unhappy couple—should seek support, through friends, through counseling, and through practicing a whole lot of patience.

Parenting is a very stressful undertaking, after all. Work can be stressful.

Growing into adulthood and adult responsibilities is often stressful. With so much to push through in one's life, it's no wonder that two people, each trying to navigate his or her way along, struggle to negotiate these challenges together. In families, there are an awful lot of moving parts.

No doubt time is a factor, too. Now that my husband and I have reached adolescence with one child, we're very clear that the early years of parenthood—sleepless nights, nap strikes, diapers, crumbs, runny noses, minute-to-minute vigilance—are grueling. Those early years are wonderful— they are fun; they are funny—and grueling. For most of us, those years caring for very small children are not the most romantic ones, and they are not the easiest ones on a marriage.

It's hard in a culture that's so oriented to quick fixes and instant gratification to counsel patience. However, it might be worth weathering those periods before calling a marriage quits if for no other reason than starting anew—as in a next phase that includes a blended family, for example—is not so easy a feat, either. While I am in no way suggesting to anyone to throw up arms and forgo having a satisfying relationship, I'm all for realism. Love and family are work. If possible, it makes more sense to work on finding happiness within the marital relationship before seeking the next phase and the next relationship. Put another way: when kids are involved, divorce is a big deal, and the children ensure that even most divorces don't sever two parents' ties to one another. Even divorce, pulled off with compassion, is a substantive emotional commitment.

In all of this, kids are innocent creatures. Parents really do owe their children protection and love and as stable a foundation as possible. The muse I'd listen to in a troubled marriage with kids is not Tolstoy. Nor would I consult a romantic poet extolling the virtues of true love. Instead, I'd cue Mick Jagger: "You can't always get what you want, but if you try sometimes, you just might find, you get what you need." If what you need is a divorce, remember to be sure you include your children's needs in its construction.

Jane Johnson Struck
and Angela Thomas

 **NO**

Solo Act: Single Mom Angela Thomas Reflects on Raising Kids Alone

"**I** don't think any woman ever envisions herself a single mom," Angela Thomas, author of *My Single-Mom Life* (Thomas Nelson), candidly admits. Angela, 45, is a well-known speaker and author who holds a master's degree from Dallas Theological Seminary. The mom of four—Taylor, 17, Grayson, 14, William, 12, and AnnaGrace, 10—Angela's been divorced for more than six years. Here, she gives TCW readers a firsthand look at the challenges—and blessings—of being a single mom.

Question: Before your divorce, did you harbor any misperceptions about single moms?

Answer: Divorce carries such judgment in the church. I'm sure years ago I judged others the way I've occasionally been judged as a divorced mom.

I didn't fully understand the lives of so many women around me. And I definitely didn't realize the loneliness of that life, the difficulty of parenting alone, or the lost feeling of not being able to lean on anyone. When you solo-parent, no one's coming home to take over. No one's there to bounce ideas off, cover your back, or reinforce your decisions. There's no one to hold you through a tough choice and whisper, "I know you're worn out; I'll handle this."

I've learned to avoid making decisions—about spending, dating, or relocating—out of loneliness. I've also learned some good news about loneliness: it won't kill me—even though at times I feel it might.

I love to tell other single moms, "Receive the lessons loneliness wants to teach."

Question: Today's culture rarely blinks an eye at women intentionally choosing to raise a child outside marriage.

Answer: True. But I know for sure being a single mom is not God's design for parenting. God meant for children to be raised by a mom and dad who love each other, love their children, and live in the same house.

Several of my never-married girlfriends have adopted orphans from all over the world. I applaud these women's selflessness. But even they will tell you single parenting is hard and a child's ideally supposed to have two parents.

Question: You've written, "'Difficult' doesn't even come close to describing [single parenting]." What's the biggest challenge for you?

Answer: It's being afraid—even though I belong to God, trust him, and pray without ceasing. Sometimes I think, The kids seem to be overcoming the damage inflicted by this divorce. Their hearts are tender. God has us. We're going to be OK. But when one of them comes home from school distant and sulky, fear whispers to me, Your children will drag around these wounds forever. Then I begin the spiritual battle to fight back fear again.

But from the very beginning, I've believed Jesus's blood covers my children. I choose not to believe even one negative statistic about children raised in a single-parent home. I trust that when children grow up in a home where God is, they can become amazing, productive, whole people.

Question: What's your opinion on single-mom dating?

Answer: If you're working toward healing, addressing your loneliness issues, experiencing spiritual renewal, and finally seeing clearly, having a dinner and a great conversation with a fun date is OK. I try not to spend time with someone out of loneliness or desperation just to be with anyone. I find it easier to make wise choices about a relationship when I sit across the table from a respectable person who shares my values and commitments.

But dating should take place apart from your relationship with your children. Go to dinner when the kids are visiting their dad. Have lunch while they're in school. Men shouldn't parade through your home. That just isn't fair to your kids.

Question: Do married women find you threatening?

Answer: My single mom-ness doesn't threaten my married girlfriends at all. In fact, they're absolutely sure their husband's not interested in running off with a woman with four kids!

The married men on my street have been more than wonderful to coach my boys in sports, take them camping, or help out with home-repair emergencies. I'm sure these husbands are glad to leave my crazy house and get back to their quiet home with their wife.

However, for the sake of appearances, I never talk to a married man unless his wife's with us. I'm not interested in private conversations with married men; that safeguard keeps my interactions appropriate.

Question: How do you fit into the couples-culture of the church—and even society?

Answer: While some single moms love belonging to a single-parent class at church or a single-mom support group, I love hanging out with couples and their families. Most of my social gatherings involve my suburban neighborhood; that support system works great for me. But everybody needs community. I tell other single moms to keep looking for the right mix of people with whom to connect.

Most of the time, I forget I'm a single mom. My four kids and I are a family. The only time I remember I'm a solo parent is when I'm introduced from a platform or interviewed. Then I remember, Oh yeah, that label again.

Question: What message about single parenting would you most like to share with married moms?

Answer: Be sensitive to the Holy Spirit. A friend told me yesterday, "Remember all those years ago when I ran into you at a conference? I knew your light was gone, but I had no idea you were going through a divorce." Then she said, "I wish I'd listened to my heart that day and stayed closer to you."

If you sense the light's gone from your friend's face, let God lead you to love your friend with compassion.

And remember, if, somehow, some way, you become a single mom, God will amaze you with his love, protection, and provision.

Ultimately the question for everyone—married and single moms alike—is, "This day, in these circumstances, how will I bring glory to God?"

EXPLORING THE ISSUE

Does Divorce Have a Negative Impact on Children?

Critical Thinking and Reflection

- What are some arguments made by each side with which you agree or disagree?
- What are the strengths and weaknesses of the two positions argued in this chapter?
- Pick the side with which you most agree. What are some additional arguments you would make to strengthen the case for or against home divorce?
- Think more broadly of the issue of divorce. What sort of support network do families need when parents are in conflict, whether they are going through divorce or not?

Is There Common Ground?

Both authors agree that there are challenges with divorce, but that there are circumstances and ways to make divorce work best for children. How is the role of faith an issue that affects people on all sides of this question? What can we learn about communication and the best interests of the child from Buttenwieser's article? In many ways, this is an issue in which there is agreement of the challenges but a disagreement over the best path for the family.

Additional Resources

Helpguide.org provides advice for helping children through divorce:

http://www.helpguide.org/mental/children_divorce.htm

Kids Health helps young children understand what divorce is:

http://kidshealth.org/kid/feeling/home_family/divorce.html

Coach Christina McGhee helps parents provide an environment so that their children can thrive after divorce:

http://www.divorceandchildren.com/

The highly respected Mayo Clinic provides advice for helping children through divorce:

http://www.mayoclinic.com/health/divorce/HO00055

The Children and Divorce Web site provides a wide array of resources for parents, children, and professionals:

http://www.childrenanddivorce.com/

ISSUE 3

Should Parents Home-school Their Children?

YES: **Chris Jeub,** from "Home School," *Focus on the Family* (2006)

NO: **Carole Moore,** from "Why Home-schooling Isn't Right for Us," Scholastic.com (2006)

Learning Outcomes

As a result of this issue, readers will be able to:

- Identify the major arguments made for and against home schooling.
- Compare and contrast the competing arguments made for and against home schooling in this issue.
- Evaluate the impact that home schooling has on the larger American society in preparing children for their future.

ISSUE SUMMARY

YES: Chris Jeub, writer and president of Training Minds Ministries, is a former public school teacher with 11 children, all of whom he and his wife have home-schooled. Naming several famous home-schooled individuals, such as Winston Churchill, Benjamin Franklin, and Florence Nightingale, he argues that the home is the best environment in which to teach children, for social, academic, family strengthening, and religious reasons. Home-schooling, he maintains, frees parents to impart their own values to their children without concern for how these beliefs might clash with what is presented in the public school system.

NO: Carole Moore, a freelance writer, discusses how she weighed the options of home-schooling versus public schooling and argues that even though home-schooling might offer some benefits to children, in the end, home-schooling provides children a distorted view of the world at large. Children will, she writes, make good

44

decisions and bad decisions as a part of growing up, and whether they are home-schooled or public schooled is not the determining factor in whether they grow up healthy and well adjusted.

Education for children in the United States was not originally required; it was up to parents to decide whether and how to educate their children, including whether to send them to school. In 1850, however, Massachusetts became the first state to pass a law requiring "schooling" for children. Some of this took place in school buildings, and some was done by parents at home—but requiring that children be educated became more and more commonplace as time went on. And as early as the beginning of the twentieth century, there were proponents who believed that school-based education failed children, and that children were better off educated at home. Much changed regarding the views and role of public education over the next 100 years.

President George W. Bush expanded the role of federal education standards by requiring states that wanted federal funds to develop clear standards in reading and mathematics. This legislation, often referred to as No Child Left Behind, fundamentally changed the emphasis on reading and math skills in many schools across America. President Barack Obama championed Race to the Top, building on No Child Left Behind. Race to the Top encouraged states to compete for federal funding by adherence to developing national standards that include, but are not limited to, reading and mathematics, reforming teacher evaluation systems, expanding charter schools, and plans to reform what are regarded as and classified as failing schools. While these laws do not take away the rights of home-schooled children, these laws create a greater role for the federal government in schools, all based on the rationale that there is a compelling federal interest in more centralized standards and academic development of our nation's students.

According to the Home School Association of California, the home schooling that took place between then and the 1970s tended to be a bit more clandestine and to be found in rural areas. The early 1980s saw the emergence of home-schooling publications and groups that were associated specifically with conservative and religious (in particular, Christian) ideologies. Fearing the "godlessness" of public school, members of these groups received ongoing support for teaching their children at home. As we moved into the 1990s, home-schooled children in the United States increased, with a U.S. federal government survey in 1999 estimating that nearly 900,000 children are being home-schooled in this country, a number that can only have increased over the past years.

In your opinion, what are some of the benefits of children being taught by a certified, professional teacher or teachers? What are some of the benefits of teaching children at home, within the context of one's own family values and without the distractions of other people, noise, and social pressures? There are clear arguments on each side, some of which are expressed in the following selections.

Chris Jeub's reasoning is outlined by topic areas, in which he describes his perceptions—having been a schoolteacher himself—of the ways in which home schooling benefits children, as well as parents, more than traditional education in a shared classroom environment. Home schooling, he argues, gives children much more freedom to pursue individual interests, and parents much more leeway to integrate religious messages into their teaching. Carole Moore considered home schooling very carefully and acknowledges some of the potential strengths, some of which center around safety issues for young people. In the end, however, she chose not to home-school her own child and argues that doing so creates a much more sheltered life for young people, which does not reflect the reality of the world at large.

There is limited research available about how effective school-based education is as opposed to home schooling, much of which cannot control for the myriad factors that come into play. For example, most states exempt children who are home-schooled from standardized testing. In schools, factors include teacher experience, school and district leadership, the socioeconomic status of the community in which the school is located, and more. In home schooling, issues include whether a parent can afford financially to stay home and devote the time and energy necessary to home-school effectively, whether the parent(s) can facilitate a social life for their child(ren) that is comparable to their school-based peers, and whether the child(ren) can still access nonacademic activities such as organized sports, theater, and student clubs.

Ask young people who have been home-schooled whether they liked it, and you will receive a range of responses. A Web site, WikiAnswers.com, asked people to comment on what they felt the longer-term effects of home schooling were; here is what several people had to say:

"I was home-schooled for 1st–9th grade. I attended 10th and part of 11th grade. I took my proficiency test and attended community college on and off for 6 years. My younger brother was home-schooled from 1st–8th grade and attended 9th–12th grade. He did not attend college. Almost all the kids I hung out w/were home-schooled also. We were both socially impaired by it; our parents made a point to keep us in sports and try to keep us socializing w/other kids. But it wasn't enough. Most of our friends were also home-schooled too. Some of us turned out OK, some didn't."

"I am 30 years old now, and was home-schooled through junior high and high school. . . . Part of the answer to [the] question is this: Socialization with adults is improved, while socialization with peers is hindered. . . . There are so many social do's and don'ts that are very arbitrary and are pounded home by peer pressure, teasing, cliques, etc."

"I home-schooled through junior high and high school. I agree that there are some social disadvantages to home-schooling, but I think that they can be avoided or changed. I realized when I was 15 that I was awkward around most of my peers and so I worked really hard at changing that. If parents are careful to involve their children in social groups, the kids will be able to learn the necessary skills. I was lucky; there is a big home-schooling community where I live, with many children to interact with. . . . I am now in college and I don't have any qualms about participating in social-groups with other students, whether home-schooled or not. If done right, [I] don't think home-schooling interferes a whole lot with social skills" (from http://www.faqfarm.com/Q/What_are_the_long-term_effects_of_home-schooling).

Clearly, those who have gone through home schooling, like those who have gone through public schooling, do not speak with one voice. How do the views of these home-schooled students change or reinforce your views about home schooling? Keep these diverse views in mind when reading this issue.

YES

Chris Jeub

Home School

Introduction

She innocently asked, "So, where do your children go to school?"

Of all casual questions one teacher could ask another, this one always creates butterflies in my stomach.

"Well, uh, my wife and I tutor them," I say. Then I try to think of something to change the subject. But I never think of anything quickly enough.

"Tutor them?" she might say, squinting her nose and ruffling her brows as if I had held a cockroach up to her face. "You mean, you home-school them?"

These situations inevitably lead to an hour-long apologetic on why we educate our kids at home. This should not surprise me. Home schooling is still unusual and a bit radical. Teachers and others in education—or in any field, for that matter—naturally question new, innovative practices.

But home education is not so rare anymore. Twenty years ago, there were roughly 15,000 home-schooled students in the United States. By 1991, the U.S. Department of Education figured there were 350,000 home-schools in the U.S. and 40,000 in Canada. Today, estimates stretch over 2 million home-schools nationwide.

The world of education has had to adjust to this exploding movement. There are many magazines and newspapers for home schools, numerous home-school curriculum distributors and countless home-school network and contact groups. Why do parents choose to teach their children at home?

Social Reasons

Home-schooling parents believe that children can learn basic life skills—working together, sharing, showing respect for others—without formal classroom experience. The students can develop social graces by being involved in community and church activities.

Pat Farenga, publisher of *Growing Without Schooling*, a catalog of home-school resources, has written: "Group experiences are a big part of education, and home schoolers have plenty of them.

They write to us about how they form or join writing clubs, book discussion groups, and local home-schooling groups. Home schoolers also take part in school sports teams and music groups [in nearby public schools], as well as in the many public and private group activities our communities provide. These young people can and do experience other people and cultures without going to school."

Our children have many church and neighborhood friends. Our community has a home-school contact group where they often get together for field trips and outings that give our kids more than enough socialization. We have gone on camping trips, facilitated soccer tournaments, traveled to speech and debate tournaments, and coordinated educational classes.

But not all socialization is necessarily good for a child. Certain social plagues like drugs, alcohol, premarital sex, violence, and gangs damage a child's growth and development. A home-school environment frees the child from the increasingly persuasive peer pressure prevalent in many schools.

The positive side of socialization—building respect and communication, getting along with and relating to others—is wonderfully fulfilled in a home-school setting. Behavioral psychologist Urie Bronfenbrenner concluded that "meaningful human contact" is best accomplished with few people.

Academic Reasons

While some parents choose to teach at home to promote positive socialization, others make the decision for academic reasons. Any teacher will agree that the smaller the class size, the more learning takes place. The one-on-one tutoring atmosphere is the healthiest, most productive and most progressive atmosphere for a student's academic success.

Take a look at some famous home-schooled students: Andrew Carnegie, Charlie Chaplin, Agatha Christie, Winston Churchill, Charles Dickens, Thomas Edison, Benjamin Franklin, Florence Nightingale, Woodrow Wilson, and the Wright brothers.

People ask how parents—especially parents with little or no post-secondary education—can teach children every discipline available to public school students. Although I have my degree in English, am I qualified to teach math or science to my kids? My wife has a business administration degree; is she able to teach the language arts? With sufficient information and dedication to the task, we certainly are.

Even if parents do not have an abundance of academic training themselves, they can find solutions to fill the gaps. For example, many home schools will team up with other home schools to exchange skills. I traded skills with another home-school family by going to their house once a week to teach English to three of their sons. In return, their mom taught algebra to my two oldest daughters.

Most communities today have enrichment classes students can sign up for, much like college students sign up for electives. Here in Colorado Springs, the High Plains Christian Home Educators support group has hired a full-time administrator who coordinates 60 classes for over 200 students. Cooperatives such as this are becoming more popular as home schooling grows.

But education is more than individual academic courses—more than teaching what the teacher knows or training students in a particular skill. It is actually passing on a worldview. Separating the disciplines—as if English had nothing to do with math, and science were unrelated to civics—promotes a fragmented vision of true education.

A wise man once said, "A good teacher teaches himself out of a job." When I taught English in the public schools, I was not merely repeating what I learned in college; I was teaching students to love and passionately engage in the language arts. And when I taught, I integrated all disciplines—history science, social studies, even math—into my lessons. Treating any learning discipline as separate from others misrepresents real life. Real life is interdisciplinary, and home-school instruction lends itself to a cross-disciplinary approach.

Students have the freedom to pursue their interests and strengths. They also receive the attention needed to improve skills in their more difficult learning areas. Pat Farenga explains the benefits of solitary reflection: "Children, like adults, need time to be alone to think, to muse, to read freely, to daydream, to be creative, to form a self independent of the barrage of mass culture." Granting such a time presents a struggle in traditional schools, but home schools allow such freedom.

Family Reasons

Home-school parents see their role as the single most important responsibility they carry. The family helps to build strong minds and healthy personalities.

Along with strengthening the family and setting firm foundations for kids, home-school parents discover some personal pluses. Wendy and I are now much closer to our kids, more in touch with their needs and feelings. Alicia and Alissa attended public school through first- and third-grade, respectively, until I completed college and Wendy returned home from full-time work (to unpaid full-time work).

While Alicia's grades were excellent, she needed to be home for security's sake. Alissa, on the other hand, loved the social contact at school but struggled in basic writing and reading skills. Wendy and I noticed positive changes immediately in Alicia's esteem and Alissa's academics. They both became more confident. I can only accredit this improvement to the loving and affirming atmosphere of the family.

Religious Reasons

It is no secret that public schools have not taken religion seriously. Fear of church and state laws keep some schools from even mentioning the influence of religion in American life. Instead of recognizing religion as part of our culture, civil liberties organizations have fought hard in the courts to make religion illegal in the classroom.

This has been too bad. With the exclusion of religion, many parents have felt compelled to go elsewhere—even to their own homes—to teach their children basic moral and religious truths to provide a well-rounded and liberal education.

Teaching our kids at home frees us to handle religious questions and spiritual training without worrying about public school issues. While some districts restrict the discussion of religious influence in history, literature, and science, home schools can incorporate the impact of spiritual beliefs into all curricula.

Mutual Respect

Home schooling is being recognized by professional educators and by society as a reasonable educational option for families. Some public schools and private schools have formed alliances with home education groups and have adopted programs that suit the home education lifestyle.

Home schooling is not so much a rebellion against public schools as it is a choice made on social, academic, family, and religious grounds. As educators and home schoolers get to know one another, we will see that we share many of the same goals for our children.

Why Home-schooling Isn't Right for Us

I became interested in home-schooling a few years ago when a friend told me how much she loved it. A former cop turned writer, I approached the editor at the newspaper where I worked and convinced him to let me write a series on the topic. I interviewed dozens of home-schooling parents and students. All told, including the work on the series plus my own follow-up research, I spent over a year studying the possibility and debating whether learning at home would be best for my kids—a daughter, then age 10, and a son, age 8.

I learned that many families home-schooled because they didn't like the secular curriculum. Others complained that classes were dumbed down, which caused boredom and restlessness in bright students. A lot chose to remove their kids from what they perceived as an unhealthy social atmosphere. All were convinced they'd done the right thing.

They explained the differences in the types of home-schooling to me: Some followed rigorous religious-based curricula, while others used the same materials as their public schools. A few, called unschoolers, followed nothing but their hearts and let the kids themselves pick what they wanted to study. Many bartered with other parents on subjects requiring special expertise, such as trading French instruction for piano lessons.

The kids' education seemed balanced and academically sound, but most appealing was the bond they shared with their parents. My own daughter, anxious to grow up, nibbled at her ties to me, with her younger brother fast on her heels. I wondered if home-schooling could bring us closer.

Still, as I spoke with home-schooling families from one coast to the other, certain troubling questions bubbled to the surface—many of them familiar to me from my days in law enforcement.

Our community is nowhere near a major city. Still, my children went to elementary school with a girl whose father committed suicide in her presence, kids with both parents in prison, and youngsters who couldn't read, yet knew all the words to filthy rap songs. As a police officer, I often dealt with adolescent drug dealers, pregnant teens, and runaways—kids whose lives were out of control. Certainly the largest majority of them were enrolled in public schools, but not all. Some of the most troubled kids I dealt with came from homes where they'd been very sheltered.

I remember one teenager in particular. After years of alternately being home-schooled and attending a very strict, small, church-based school, she moved to a public school—where she spiraled out of control. She drank. She took drugs. And she had sex. Her parents were appalled; that was not how they'd raised their daughter.

Some would blame the influence of the public school system. They'd say she made friends with bad kids. And they'd be right. But that wasn't the only reason she got into so much trouble. In my opinion, her problem went much deeper: she didn't know how to handle the sudden combination of freedom and exposure to a side of life she'd never personally confronted. Her parents had talked about these things. She'd heard about them in church. But talk alone isn't a substitute for reality and the forbidden often looms sweet and tantalizing by virtue of its mystery.

Academics form only part of the equation when it comes to teaching life skills. Kids need to know how to write a persuasive essay but they also should learn about real life and, in the process, develop the skills they need to cope with it.

My daughter, who now attends a public high school, has made good choices in both her academic and social lives so far. We've talked about sex, but nothing I've ever said to her has provided as strong a deterrent to casual, early sex as the girl in her class with the ever-expanding belly. Nothing makes my daughter more aware of the effects of drugs than seeing burnt-out kids. And nothing brings home the consequences of drinking and driving more than the empty seat of a boy who did just that.

They're tough lessons, but ones she will never forget. Seeing the aftermath of negative behavior with her own eyes impresses her much more than simple words or even our own good examples.

Do I like that my children are exposed to life's underbelly? Of course not. I'd much prefer to bring them up in an atmosphere of innocence and trust. But we can't raise our children in carefully controlled environments and expect them to instinctively know how to handle evil. Pretending that it doesn't exist won't make it go away.

Home-schooling would have built a wall around my kids and kept them safe—for a little while. Ultimately, they would have had to go out into the real world. Public school has exposed them to bad influences as well as good ones. I believe they're stronger for having had to make tough choices. And going through it together has strengthened our relationship, making it easier for me to start letting go of their hands.

EXPLORING THE ISSUE

Should Parents Home-school Their Children?

Critical Thinking and Reflection

- What are some arguments made by each side with which you agree or disagree?
- What are the strengths and weaknesses of the two positions made in this chapter?
- Pick the side with which you most agree. What are some additional arguments you would make to strengthen the case for or against home schooling?
- Think more broadly of the issue of home schooling. What sort of support network do families need when they home-school their children, and what can public schools do to create a more welcoming school environment for all students?

Is There Common Ground?

One of the challenges—as well as one of the wonderful qualities—of public schools is that they are a place in American society that bring diverse individuals and families together. Our courts have interpreted the First Amendment to keep schools from establishing religion, which means that teachers cannot place one religion over another or even put religion above nonreligion.

However, students have lots of rights to express their own religion freely at school, so long as that expression does not adversely interfere with the school's educational mission. What are some ways we can ensure a greater understanding of students' rights to express their religion freely in school? How can we ensure that parents better understand the different criteria for a school establishing a religion versus students' freely exercising their religion? Additionally, how can home-schooled students get involved with a school's extracurricular activities?

Additional Resources

R. Barfield, *Real-Life Homeschooling: The Stories of 21 Families Who Teach Their Children at Home* (New York: Simon & Schuster Adult Publishing Group, 2002).

S. Bielick, K. Chandler, and S. P. Broughman, *Homeschooling in the United States: 1999* (2001). Accessible online at http://nces.ed.gov/programs/quarterly/Vol_3/3_3/q3-2.asp.

R. H. Davis, "Homeschooling a Personal Choice, not a Movement." *Teachers College Record* (May 16, 2005). Accessible online at www.tcrecord.org/Content .asp?ContentID=11876.

P. T. Hill, "Home Schooling and the Future of Public Education." *Peabody Journal of Education* (vol. 75, no. 1&2, 2000: 20–31).

J. Kaufield, *Homeschooling for Dummies* (Hoboken, NJ: John Wiley & Sons, 2001).

C. Lubienski, "Whither the Common Good? A Critique of Home Schooling," *Peabody Journal of Education* (vol. 75, no. 1&2, 2000: 207–32).

———, "A Critical View of Home Education," *Evaluation and Research in Education* (vol. 17, no. 2/3, 2003: 167–78).

R. G. Medlin, "Home Schooling and the Question of Socialization," *Peabody Journal of Education* (vol. 75, no. 1&2, 2000: 107–23).

ISSUE 4

Do Mothers Who Work Outside the Home Have a Negative Impact on Their Children?

YES: Jeanne Brooks-Gunn, Wen-Jui Han, and Jane Waldfogel, from "Maternal Employment and Child Cognitive Outcomes in the First Three Years of Life: The NICHD Study of Early Child Care," *Child Development* (July/August 2002)

NO: Thomas M. Vander Ven et al., from "Home Alone: The Impact of Maternal Employment on Delinquency," *Social Problems* (May 2001)

Learning Outcomes

As a result of this issue, readers will be able to:

- Identify the major arguments made for and against mothers working outside the home.
- Compare and contrast the competing arguments made for and against mothers working outside the home in this issue.
- Evaluate the impact of mothers working outside the home on the larger American society in preparing children for their future.

ISSUE SUMMARY

YES: Child developmentalists Jeanne Brooks-Gunn, Wen-Jui Han, and Jane Waldfogel assert that their findings show many types of negative effects from maternal employment on the later cognitive and educational outcomes of children.

NO: Professor of sociology and anthropology Thomas M. Vander Ven and his colleagues argue that their studies show that a working mother will have relatively little or no negative influence on the social, emotional, and behavioral functioning of her children.

Over a decade ago, former First Lady Hillary Rodham Clinton made what became an often-quoted statement from an African proverb: "It takes a village to raise a child." While some embraced this saying as it captured the larger, societal responsibility for the well-being of children, others criticized Mrs. Clinton as a denial of the responsibilities that parents have to raise their own children properly.

Although there are those who would agree with this sentiment, the role of the mother and, in particular, the child's biological mother—has received and continues to receive intense scrutiny. Even with so many members of a family or a "village," a belief exists toward the effects a mother has on her child's development—good, bad, or indifferent.

Since the 1950s, this scrutiny has focused on working women—those who work professional jobs outside the home in addition to parenting a child or children. As some know, during World War II, thousands of women in the United States felt it was their patriotic duty to fill in for their husbands and other men who were fighting overseas in the war by working in factories and doing other jobs that traditionally had been held by men. This kept many industries alive in the 1940s. However, when U.S. soldiers returned stateside, the women were expected to give up their jobs and return home, resulting in what historians call a "baby boom." The United States had lost a lot of young lives as a result of World War II. At the end of the war, many Americans, men and women, wanted to have children. That didn't mean that women wanted to give up working permanently, but that is precisely what they were expected to do.

In the 1960s and 1970s, the women's rights movement gave women much more support for working outside the home—although this meant that many women who did *not* want to work outside the home, who wanted to be stay-at-home mothers, were criticized for making this choice. Some people are invested in keeping women at home, for a range of reasons—not the least of which, they say, is that it is vitally important for a woman to be with her child during the child's early years.

Over the past decades, the number of women who have entered or returned to the workforce has risen from 31 percent to 59 percent. It is currently estimated that 70 percent of mothers with children who are their dependents are working today. Furthermore, what some are calling the Great Recession (the challenging economic times during the Bush–Obama years), many job sectors are seeing men losing their jobs in higher proportions than women.

Researchers have been curious about and explored what effects working mothers who place their children in some kind of care— whether in an organized day care or with a nanny—have on children's early development. The results vary, and there are strong opinions on both sides of the argument— those who maintain that not having a mother at home with a child, particularly an infant, is harmful, and those who insist it is not. The "harms" cited range from impaired cognitive development (e.g., challenges in thought and learning processes) to delinquency (e.g., either illegal or antisocial behavior).

There are many claims that a woman who works outside the home will not bond as effectively with her child, claims that those who disagree would say are simply a conservative viewpoint and unsubstantiated by research. They believe that the push to have women return home rather than remain in the workplace is an ongoing backlash against the feminism that paved the way for it to be acceptable for a woman to be a mother as well as a full-time professional.

What do you think? Is it enough for mothers to be home with their children during off-work hours? What about the other people in their lives— like their partners or spouses or other family members? Is it important for a child to bond with any significant adult, or must that adult be the biological mother?

In the YES selection, Jeanne Brooks-Gunn, Wen-Jui Han, and Jane Waldfogel argue that the data show that there are significant long-term negative effects on cognitive development for children whose mothers work outside the home during the child's earlier years. Conversely, in the NO selection, Thomas M. Vander Ven and his colleagues maintain that a child who is born to a mother who works outside the home is not more likely to exhibit delinquent behavior—unless, at the very basic level, supervision of the child is an issue.

For working class and middle class families, it can be difficult to make ends meet without having two incomes. For single-parent homes, it is even more necessary for a parent to work if the family wants to avoid living in poverty. Working mothers can result in additional benefits for their children, such as living in a better school district, having more support in terms of enrichment activities and athletics.

In many family situations where there are two parents, both parents are working not because they think it is an important aspect of their identity or self-esteem, but because they need to in order to survive. Getting by with one income is workable for an investment banker on Wall Street, but it would be far more challenging for a sanitation worker and his partner, a city bus driver. For many parents, therefore, working is a necessity that is not up for discussion, not a luxury, a hobby, or part of a political viewpoint. In fact, some working parents would rather not work outside the home but find that they cannot afford the alternative.

There are no easy answers, and there are certainly arguments for and against parents working outside the home if they even have the capacity to entertain that argument. Regardless of how one feels about this issue, however, it is important to avoid judging a parent's decision about whether to work or stay home; guaranteed, whatever decision was made was very likely a difficult one to make.

YES ← Jeanne Brooks-Gunn, Wen-Jui Han, and Jane Waldfogel

Maternal Employment and Child Cognitive Outcomes in the First Three Years of Life

The past few decades have seen an unprecedented increase in early maternal employment. The share of mothers who return to work before their child's first birthday doubled from 1976 to 1998, rising from 31% to 59% (Bachu & O'Connell, 1998). Women are now nearly as likely to be working when they have an infant as they are when they have an older preschooler (U.S. Department of Labor, Bureau of Labor Statistics, 2000). Yet, questions remain as to what the impact of this rapid shift toward early maternal employment might be. With increased attention being paid on the part of parents and policy makers to the importance of early experiences for children, establishing what links might exist between early maternal employment and child cognitive outcomes is more important than ever.

The potential impacts of early maternal employment and early child care on child development have been extensively studied (for reviews, see Belsky, 2001; Bornstein, Gist, Hahn, Haynes, & Voigt, 2001; Lamb, 1998; Shonkoff & Phillips, 2000; Weinraub & Jaeger, 1990). Most relevant to the present study are the results from (1) studies using the National Longitudinal Survey of Youth–Child Supplement (NLSY-CS) to examine the effects of early maternal employment on child outcomes, and (2) studies using the National Institute of Child Health and Human Development Study of Early Child Care (NICHD-SECC) to examine the effects of early child care on child development.

A large literature has studied the effects of early maternal employment on children's cognitive outcomes using data on children born to respondents of the NLSY-CS (for a helpful overview of this dataset, see Chase-Lansdale, Mott, Brooks-Gunn, & Phillips, 1991). Because these NLSY-CS studies are reviewed elsewhere (see, e.g., Han, Waldfogel, & Brooks-Gunn, 2001), only a brief overview is provided here. The studies that have examined the effects of first-year maternal employment separately from the effects of employment later in the preschool years have tended to find negative effects of first-year maternal employment on children's later cognitive outcomes (see, e.g., Baydar & Brooks-Gunn, 1991; Belsky & Eggebeen, 1991; Blau & Grossberg, 1992; Han et al., 2001; Hill, Waldfogel, Brooks-Gunn, & Han, 2001; Ruhm, 2000;

Waldfogel, Han, & Brooks-Gunn, 2002; but see also Harvey, 1999). An important limitation of these studies is that none have been able to control for the quality of the child-care settings in which the children of the working mothers are placed. Although the NLSY-CS contains retrospective data on the type of child care in which children are placed, it does not contain any assessment of the quality of that care. A further limitation is that none of the NLSY-CS studies have been able to control for the quality of the mothers' interactions with their children. The NLSY-CS contains no direct assessment of the sensitivity of the mother's care for the child. The NLSY-CS does contain data on one measure of the quality of the home environment, the Home Observation of the Measurement of the Environment (HOME) Scale, but it did not start administering the HOME until 1986, so for many children in the sample (children born in 1983 or earlier) this measure was not administered until they were age 3 or older and therefore no data on the earlier home environment are available.

Thus, when studies using the NLSY-CS have found that early maternal employment has negative effects on children's later cognitive outcomes, the extent to which these effects might be due to the poor quality of child care experienced by these children and/or the poor quality of their home environments has not been clear. Establishing the mechanism by which early maternal employment is linked to poorer cognitive outcomes, and the role played by child care or home environments, is critical to understanding the source of the links and also potential policy remedies.

For this reason, the present study turned to newly available data from the NICHD-SECC. This dataset is extremely well suited to address the limitations of the prior NLSY-CS studies and the questions they could not answer, because it contains data on child-care quality and the quality of children's home environment, as well as detailed data on maternal employment and child outcomes (for an excellent overview of this dataset, see NICHD Early Child Care Research Network, in press). It also contains a rich set of data on child and mother characteristics, including a measure of maternal depression, which is not available in the NLSY-CS. The NICHD-SECC dataset has not been used to study the effects of early maternal employment. It was designed as a study of the effects of early child care on child development and has been used extensively to study that topic (for results on the effects of early child care on children's development at age 54 months, see, e.g., NICHD Early Child Care Research Network, in press). . . .

Methods

Data for the present study were obtained from the NICHD-SECC, a unique longitudinal dataset that has followed 1,364 children from 10 sites around the nation since the time of their birth in 1991. (For a detailed description of the dataset, including how the sample was selected and interviewed, see NICHD Early Child Care Research Network, 2000, in press.) It is important to note that some groups were excluded from the sample (e.g., mothers under 18, families who anticipated moving, infants who were multiple births or had health problems or disabilities, mothers who did not speak English, mothers with medical problems or substance-abuse problems, or families living in a dangerous neighborhood). A total of 1,525 families were deemed eligible for inclusion in the study and agreed to be interviewed; of these, 1,364 completed an interview and became participants in the study.

The NICHD-SECC conducted home visits to the children in the sample at 1, 6, 15, 24, and 36 months, supplemented by phone interviews every 3 months to track maternal employment and child-care use. The study also conducted visits to the children's child-care settings at 6, 15, 24, and 36 months (if children were in care more than 10 hr per week). In addition, the children were assessed at home and in the laboratory at ages 15, 24, and 36 months (later visits and assessments were also conducted, but those data have not yet been released for public use). . . .

Discussion

The present study took advantage of a newly available dataset, the NICHD-SECC, to examine the effects of early maternal employment on children's cognitive outcomes at ages 15, 24, and 36 months, controlling for child care (quality and type) and home environment (assessed with the HOME Scale and a rating of maternal sensitivity). The study analyzed three related sets of questions: (1) Is maternal employment in the first year of life associated with negative child cognitive outcomes in the first 3 years of life and, if so, are these effects more pronounced when mothers work full-time? (2) Are there subgroups for whom these effects are more likely to be found? and (3) To what extent are these effects mediated by quality of child care and home environment in the first 3 years of life? These analyses took as their point of departure the literature on the timing of early maternal employment, which has relied mainly on analyses of the NLSY-CS. Because this literature (with important input from developmentalists, economists, and sociologists) has been increasingly concerned with issues of selection bias and model specification, the present study included a large array of covariates that were not available in the NLSY-CS, such as measures of child care and the early home environment. It also drew extensively on the literature on the effects of early child care, in particular the recent work by the NICHD Early Child Care Research Network on the timing and intensity of early child care. The work of the NICHD Early Child Care Research Network was followed closely in terms of how the rich child-care and child-assessment data available in the NICHD-SECC dataset were utilized and also in how the factors that might mediate the effects of early maternal employment on later child outcomes were conceptualized. However, unlike the NICHD Early Child Care Research Network, the focus in the present research was on early maternal employment rather than early child care, reflecting our interest in extending and updating the prior work from the NLSY-CS as well as contributing to the literature regarding women and employment. Thus, we believe the results of the present study complement those of the NICHD Early Child Care Research Network, because it tackled essentially different questions than those addressed in that group's work.

To review the main findings, with regard to the first research question, this study found that children whose mothers worked at all by the ninth month of their life had lower scores on the Bracken [School Readiness Scale] at 36 months than did children whose mothers did not work by that time. The effects of any maternal employment by 1, 3, 6, or 12 months were also negative, although only the effect of maternal employment by 9 months was statistically significant (the effect of employment by 6 months was marginally significant at $p < .10$). This pattern of results suggests that there may be something particularly problematic about having a mother who went to work between 6 and 9 months and/or something unusual about the children whose mothers began employment at this time (which about 5% of the sample did), and the few prior studies that had examined timing effects of maternal employment within the first year (Baydar & Brooks-Gunn, 1991; Han et al., 2001) provided some support for this idea. However, it is also important to note that these results provided some evidence of negative effects of earlier employment as well. Moreover, once the intensity of employment was taken into account, larger negative effects were found, which were statistically significant for employment beginning by 6 months as well as 9 months. Specifically, the negative effect of having a mother who began employment by the ninth month was most pronounced for children whose mothers worked longer hours (30 hr or more per week) in the first year; the same was true for children whose mothers began employment by the sixth month.

The significant negative effects found on the Bracken at 36 months for any employment by the ninth month, and for employment of 30 hr or more per week by the sixth month or ninth month, were consistent with previous findings from the NLSY indicating that early maternal employment had significant negative effects on children's PPVT-R [Peabody Picture Vocabulary Test-Revised] at 36 months (see, e.g., Han et al., 2001; Waldfogel et al., 2002). The fact that these effects were strongest for European American non-Hispanic children was also consistent with prior findings from the NLSY-CS. No effects were found for early maternal employment on children's Bayley MDI [Mental Development Index] scores at 15 or 24 months. The fact that there were negative effects of early maternal employment on the Bracken at 36 months but not on the Bayley MDI in the first 2 years of life is most likely due to the different cognitive competencies tapped in the first 2 years compared with the later preschool years. The cognitive competencies tapped at 15 and 24 months may be less likely to be influenced by environmental events than those tapped later on. Studies that looked at the effects of poverty, for example, found few effects on cognition in the first 18 months of life using the Bayley MDI, but found effects when language and reasoning were assessed in the third year of life (see, e.g., Klebanov et al., 1998). In addition, competencies tapped in the first 2 years of life may not be as predictive of later functioning (McCall, 1983; McCall, Hogarty, & Hurlbut, 1972).

With regard to the second research question, the present results showed that some subgroups of children were more likely to be affected than were others. The effects of early and full-time maternal employment were larger for children whose mothers were rated as insensitive at 6 months (compared with those whose mothers were rated as sensitive), for boys (compared with girls), and for children with married parents (compared with single mothers). The finding on sensitivity was consistent with prior results from the NICHD-SECC (i.e., investigators found that children whose mothers were rated as not sensitive and were in early child care more than 10 hr per week were more vulnerable to attachment problems than were other children in care more than 10 hr per week; NICHD Early Child Care Research Network, 1997). The findings on differences by gender and by parents' marital status were consistent with prior results from the NLSY-CS (see Desai et al., 1989, on gender; Han et al., 2001, on marital status). With regard to the more negative impacts for boys, some analysts have observed that boys are more vulnerable to early stressors in general (see, e.g., Rutter, 1979; Zaslow & Hayes, 1986) and that boys may be more affected by nonmaternal child care as well (for an excellent discussion on this topic, see Bornstein et al., 2001). With regard to the more negative impacts for children of married parents, one possible explanation is that the extra income generated by the mothers' employment may be more valuable, on average, to families headed by unmarried mothers than it is to married-couple families. If so, to the extent that positive income effects offset otherwise negative effects of early maternal employment, this would explain why the observed effects of early maternal employment seemed to be more negative in married-couple families. These differences by subgroup are intriguing and warrant further research, which might shed more light on the mechanisms that underlie the effects of early maternal employment on child cognitive outcomes. In this regard, it would also be useful to conduct research on individual differences in children's vulnerability to early and full-time maternal employment.

With regard to the third research question, it was found that both child care (quality and type) and home environment (as measured by both maternal sensitivity and the HOME Scale) mattered for children's Bracken scores at 36 months. Also found was some evidence that early and full-time maternal employment was negatively associated with the quality of subsequent child care and home environments. Children whose mothers worked more than 30 hr per week by 9 months were in lower quality child-care settings at 36 months than children whose mothers worked fewer hours per week in the first year. Moreover, children whose mothers worked more than 30 hr per week by 9 months had mothers who were rated as providing less sensitive care at 36 months than children whose mothers did not work in the first year (this result is consistent with the finding of the NICHD Early Child Care Research Network, 1999, that children who spent more hours in early child care had mothers who provided less sensitive care at 36 months), although their home environments (as assessed by the HOME Scale) were not significantly different (this latter result may indicate that early and full-time maternal employment may have offsetting effects, reducing some resources due to the limitations on mothers' time available for activities with their children but increasing other resources due to the increased income available to the family through the mothers' employment). However, even after controlling for child care and home environment, a negative association was still found between full-time employment begun in the first 9 months of children's lives and the children's Bracken scores at 36 months.

Because the NICHD-SECC is an observational (rather than experimental) study, it is important to be cautious in interpreting these results. It is possible that mothers' entry into full-time work in the first 9 months did adversely affect their children's cognitive performance at age 3. If this is correct, then one could conclude that encouraging mothers who would otherwise be employed full-time to stay home or work part-time during the first year would produce children with higher Bracken School Readiness scores. However, the NICHD-SECC did not experimentally assign mothers to employment or non-employment, so it is not known from these estimates whether full-time maternal employment by 9 months was causing the lower Bracken School Readiness scores. It is possible that there were pre-existing differences between mothers who did and did not work full-time in the first 9 months of their children's lives that were not observed in the data and that mattered for children's cognitive outcomes. These differences may have had to do with characteristics of the mothers, or with the reasons that they were working. Although selection bias in the present study was controlled for to the extent possible by including a large set of covariates (several of which were not available in prior work with the NLSY-CS), clearly, further work on this topic is needed.

The results of the present study do have some implications for policy. One clear implication is the need to improve the quality of child care that children experience in the first 3 years of life. The results confirm that quality of care matters and also document that, all else equal, children whose mothers work full-time in the first year of life go on to experience poorer quality care in their first 3 years. This lower quality of care in part explains why cognitive outcomes are worse at 36 months for children whose mothers worked full-time rather than part-time in the first year of life. This suggests that improving the quality of child care used by the children of full-time working mothers might help to mitigate the observed negative effects of mothers' early and full-time employment on children's cognitive development. It is important to keep in mind that the present study examined a specific group of children who were infants and toddlers in the early 1990s, and was, therefore, situated in the context of the quality of child care available in the United States during those years. If the quality of that care was, on average, lower than the quality of care that the children's mothers would have offered had they not been working, then that "mismatch" could help to explain the negative relation between early and full-time maternal employment and cognitive development at age 36 months reported in this article. (It was not possible to control for this directly because we did not observe the care that the mother would have provided had she not been working; we only observed the care that she did provide, which may have been affected by the fact that she was employed.) Studies in other countries in which the quality of care is higher have reported different results (see, e.g., Andersson, 1989, 1992, who found that Swedish children who entered child care earlier in the first year of life had better cognitive outcomes than those who entered care later).

A second implication has to do with family leave policy. The United States currently has family leave provisions that guarantee less than 3 months of leave for new mothers as compared with an average of 10 months in the advanced industrialized nations who are members of the Organization for Economic and Community Development (OECD); the United States also differs from peer industrialized nations by not providing paid leave and by having a national law that covers less than half the private sector workforce (Kamerman, 2000; Waldfogel, 2001a). If any maternal employment by the ninth month (and maternal employment of 30 hr or more per week by the sixth or ninth month) has adverse effects on children's cognitive development, this is relevant to consideration of proposals to extend U.S. leave provisions to the 10-month OECD average, provide paid leave, and provide coverage for a larger portion of the U.S. workforce (see, e.g., Kamerman, 2000; Waldfogel, 2001a).

A third implication has to do with family-friendly policies that make it easier for mothers (and fathers) to combine work and family responsibilities. In addition to child care and family leave, such policies include flexible hours, part-time or job-sharing arrangements, and other workplace policies that might reduce the stress or fatigue experienced by working parents with young children. Although, as noted above, the United States lags behind other countries in its provision of family leave, it has at least made some progress in this area with the passage of the Family and Medical Leave Act (FMLA) in 1993. The same is not true of other family-friendly benefits for families with young children. The share of employers who provide such benefits is quite low and has not increased in recent years (Waldfogel, 2001b).

Taken together, the results of the present study illustrate the extent to which the effects of early maternal employment on children's cognitive outcomes depend crucially on both the quality of care that children receive at home and the quality of care that children receive in child care. Good-quality care at home, and good-quality child care, can go a long way toward buffering the negative links between early maternal employment and later child outcomes. Nevertheless, it is concerning that even after controlling for home-environment quality and child-care quality, full-time maternal employment by the ninth month was found to be associated with lower Bracken scores at 36 months. Until there is better understanding with regard to what causes this association and how to buffer it, it would be prudent for policy makers to go slow on measures (such as the recent Temporary Assistance to Needy Families reforms) that would require mothers to enter the labor force (full-time) early in the first year of life and to consider measures (such as proposed FMLA extensions) that would allow more mothers to choose to delay their return to the labor force and/or to work part-time until later in the first year of life. More generally, we concur with the conclusions of the recent National Academy of Sciences expert panel on the science of early development (Shonkoff & Phillips, 2000), that call for policies to improve the quality of child care, extend family leave provisions, and expand other family-friendly policies, to give parents more and better choices about how to balance their work and family responsibilities in the first year of their children's lives.

Thomas M. Vander Ven et al.  **NO**

Home Alone: The Impact of Maternal Employment on Delinquency

In recent decades, American family life has been transformed dramatically. Family scholars debate the causes and consequences of these major changes, routinely clashing over whether family forms are changing for the better (Stacey 1993) or whether our most important social institution is experiencing a moral and functional freefall (Gill 1993; Poponoe 1993).

One of the most profound changes is the unprecedented number of women who have entered the paid workforce since the 1950s. Census data show that female labor force participation rose from approximately 28 percent in 1940 to close to 60 percent in 1992 (U.S. Bureau of Census 1993). This wave of women entering the labor force was accompanied by a large increase in maternal employment. While only 16 percent of all children had working mothers in 1950, close to 70 percent of all mothers with dependent children work today (Coontz 1977). Recent estimates show that over half of those with children less than one year old are employed outside the home and over 60 percent of those with children younger than six are employed (Gerson 1996).

While the mass entrance of women and mothers into the labor market might be regarded as a sign of social progress, many Americans are worried about the trend and have been for some time (Greenberger, Goldberg, Crawford, and Granger 1988). And in what may be seen as part of the "backlash" to feminist political victories (Faludi 1991), politicians, social critics, and parenting "experts" have frequently pointed to the working mother as the cause of many of our social problems.

While supporting empirical evidence is scarce, the political Right charges that feminist philosophies damage the American family by encouraging women to choose work and self-fulfillment over family obligations (Cohen and Katzenstein 1988). Additionally, noted psychologists argue that the neglected child of the working mother may suffer from an attachment disorder, which is widely believed to be a major causal factor in the production of extreme child behavior problems. One pediatrician and TV personality warns that mothers should stay home to raise their infants or risk the disruption of the critical mother-child bonding period: "if he doesn't have that through infancy, it's

From *Social Problems*, vol. 48. no. 2, May 2001, pp. 236–57 (refs. and notes omitted). Copyright © 2001 by University of California Press. Reprinted by permission via Rightslink.

hard to put it in later . . . and these kids that never get it . . . will become difficult in school, they'll never succeed in school, they'll make everybody angry, they'll become delinquents later and eventually they'll become terrorists" (see Eyer 1996:6).

Although there is no shortage of claims that maternal employment causes negative child outcomes, there is little evidence that this is the case. Recent research shows that the children of working mothers are no less attached than other children (Chira 1998) and that they experience no deficits in social, emotional, or behavioral functioning (Harvey 1999; Hoffman 1989; Parcel and Menaghan 1994). While no work and family issue attracts more scholarly attention than the potential effects of maternal employment on children's development (Barling 1990), few researchers have investigated the possible link between working mothers and delinquency.

In this context, we analyze the impact of maternal employment—of kids being left "home alone"—on delinquency using models that include different characteristics of maternal employment (e.g., hours, workplace controls), variations in maternal non-employment (e.g., welfare reliance), and child care arrangements. Our analysis is influenced by the research program of Parcel and Menaghan (1994, 1994a), who investigated the impact of various dimensions of parental work on a range of social, cognitive, and behavioral outcomes. Similarly, we test models that consider the number of hours usually employed, working conditions, and the timing of work. This more comprehensive measurement of maternal work improves upon past research on maternal employment and delinquency, where mother's work was simply divided into "working mother" and "non-working mother" categories (e.g., Glueck and Glueck 1950; Hirschi 1969; Sampson and Laub 1993).

Furthermore, in an attempt to isolate the independent effects of maternal work, we simultaneously consider the impact of maternal resources (i.e., maternal cognitive skills, maternal education, family income), child care arrangements, and marital status. By controlling for maternal resources, we are better able to isolate the independent effects of maternal employment. . . .

Although there is a tremendous body of literature on the effects of maternal employment on child outcomes, studies on the link between maternal work and delinquency are relatively scarce. Early researchers tended to find a small positive effect of maternal employment on delinquency, which they usually assumed was the consequence of low maternal supervision (Glueck and Glueck 1950; Hirschi 1969; Nye 1963; Roy 1963; see also Sampson and Laub 1993). Most contemporary researchers found little or no connection between maternal work status and delinquency (Broidy 1995; Hillman and Sawilowsky 1991; Riege 1972; Wadsworth 1979). Other studies suggest that delinquency is less common among the children of regularly employed mothers (Farnworth 1984; West 1982; Zhao, Cao, and Cao 1997). In some cases, maternal work actually served as insulation against delinquent risks because working mothers effectively raised the family income, thus improving the living conditions of their children. Maternal employment, then, should be considered as an economic dimension of family life and may be most beneficial for children when the alternative is poverty or welfare dependency (Baca-Zinn 1989).

When examined closely, the extant literature on maternal employment and delinquency suggests that working conditions are an important factor that must be included in analytical models. Glueck and Glueck (1950), for example, found that delinquency was highest among the children of occasionally employed mothers. This finding is provocative because occasional or sporadic work may be indicative of secondary labor market employment. Employment in the secondary labor market is often erratic and coercive due to the vulnerability of the low-skilled, uneducated workers at this level (Edwards 1979). Such employment may be criminogenic if coercive workplace experiences negatively shape parenting techniques (Colvin and Pauly 1983).

In a related vein, Roy (1963) found that maternal work was related to delinquency in urban settings, but not in rural areas. This effect, also, may reflect important differences between working conditions in urban vs. rural communities. It may be that maternal work in urban centers and among minority populations is, on average, more likely to be coercive, secondary labor market work (see Haurin 1992). In light of these findings, better measures of maternal employment—including measures for workplace controls and regularity of employment (part-time vs. full-time) are needed. . . .

Methodology

Sample

In the 1960s, the United States Department of Labor hired the Center for Human Resource Research at the Ohio State University to gather longitudinal data on the labor market experiences of four representative target groups among the U.S. population (Fahey 1995). A fifth cohort of men and women between the ages of 14 and 22 was identified in 1979. Known as the National Longitudinal Survey of Youth (NLSY), this project involved a multistaged stratified random sampling that produced 12,686 subjects, 11,404 of whom were interviewed annually about their occupational, educational, familial, and childbearing experiences (see Chase-Landsdale, Mott, Brooks-Gunn, and Phillips 1991, Parcel and Menaghan 1994).

By 1994, 10,042 children of sample mothers were identified to report on their home environment, family relations, and school experiences in addition to taking a number of inventories designed to measure cognitive and socioemotional development. To investigate the relationship between maternal work and delinquency, we conduct our analysis on a sample of 707 adolescents who were between the ages of 12 and 14 in 1994. These children are the offspring of female respondents originally interviewed in 1979. Each of these respondents completed the Child Self-Administered Supplement (CSAS) in 1992 and in 1994. This self-report booklet collects information on a wide range of variables including child-parent interaction, peer relationships, and involvement in various delinquent activities. . . .

Dependent Variable: Delinquency

The 1994 CSAS includes nine highly correlated items that assess involvement in deviant and delinquent acts. Five of the items measure relatively minor to moderate acts of youth deviance: breaking parents' curfew, dishonesty (i.e., lying to a parent), school problems (i.e., parent came to school because of child behavior), truancy, and staying out all night. The other four items involve more serious acts of lawbreaking: alcohol abuse, vandalism (i.e., damaged school property on purpose), store theft, and violence (i.e., hurt some one badly enough to need bandages or a doctor). These nine items are summed to create our scale measuring youth deviance and delinquency (alpha = .78). . . .

Independent Variables

Maternal employment status. A continuous measure of hours usually worked is used in this analysis. In past studies (e.g., Parcel and Menaghan 1994, 1994a), investigators assigned missing values to work-hour variables for non-employed mothers, who were then excluded from the analysis. Thus, these studies focused on the effects of paid maternal employment among a sub-group of working mothers only. Other studies include non-employed mothers but as a dummy category that is used in equations with other dummy variables capturing increasing levels of time commitment to paid employment (e.g., part-time, full-time, overtime) (Baydar and Brooks-Gunn 1991; Muller 1995; Parcel, Nickoll, and Dufur 1996). Measuring maternal work hours via a series of dummy variables is arguably a good strategy for organizing information and for detecting non-linear effects (see Harvey 1999). As Harvey points out, however, this method is problematic because the dummy categories are formed from continuous variables so there are infinite ways one could create categories and arbitrary boundaries between categories are often created. Moreover, using continuous variables does not prevent the detection of nonlinear effects (Harvey 1999). Based on this rationale, we use a continuous measure of hours worked in our primary analysis. . . .

Occupational class. We measure occupational class in two ways. First, following Parcel and Menaghan (1994), we construct a 19-item-based occupational complexity scale by matching occupational titles reported by NLSY respondents to job descriptions reported in the Dictionary of Occupational Titles. . . .

Our primary measure of workplace conditions is developed based on the work of Mark Colvin (Colvin 2000; Colvin and Pauly 1983). Drawing from Kohn (1977) and Edwards (1979), Colvin links the workplace controls experienced by parents to the patterns and styles of control parents exert upon children. Unskilled, non-unionized employees (Fraction I workers) are subjected to "simple control" in the workplace, which is coercive and alienating. . . .

Skilled laborers and craftspersons (Fraction II workers), who often belong to labor unions, experience greater job security, and are controlled via "technical control"—the machine-paced atmosphere of manufacturing and industrial workplaces where workers are motivated to produce by wage increases and job security. . . .

Fraction III workers are those skilled workers, technicians, salaried professionals, and supervisory staff who experience greater self-direction, job complexity, and job security in the workplace. . . .

Family income.   Total family income is included in all models. By employing a family income measure, we are able to assess the impact of the mother's employment experiences while controlling for the total standard of living of each family included in the analysis. Controlling for family income helps to isolate the independent effects of occupational variables in the analysis.

Child care.   Following Parcel and Menaghan (1994), we measure child care with a series of dummy variables. Dummy variables representing professional daycare settings, child care provided by a relative (including fathers), and child care provided by a non-relative are included. . . .

Discussion

Are the children of working mothers more likely to be delinquent than other children? According to past studies and to the results of our analysis, the answer is a qualified "No." The present study demonstrates that regardless of how this issue is examined, having a working mother has only a small and indirect effect on delinquency. This general pattern holds whether we considered maternal employment in a child's preschool years or maternal work in adolescence. Furthermore, with the lone exception of maternal supervision, maternal employment has little influence on several known pathways to delinquency.

Like Parcel and Menaghan (1994, 1994a) and more recent findings by Harvey (1999), our research suggests that the widespread concern over the fates of working women and their children is largely unsupported. Rather than being a social problem whose untoward effects can be demonstrated empirically, the maternal employment–delinquency connection is better understood as a socially constructed problem. As a perceived social problem, the dark side of maternal employment has a long history in America. Fueled by scientific data on the link between early family processes and delinquency and by cherished popular beliefs in the sanctity of the "first relationship" (the coupling of mother and child-for decades) politicians and social commentators have pointed to modern trends in female labor participation to explain social problems such as crime. But if the unprecedented entrance of mothers into the paid workforce is related to delinquency, it must be because working mothers fail their children by depriving them of the support and discipline they need. The current study adds to the growing literature that casts doubt on these assumptions.

Our findings suggest other notable conclusions. First, it is maternal and family resources, rather than the characteristics of maternal work, that most influence some well-known pathways to delinquency in our study. Maternal AFQT [Armed Forces Qualifications Test] score, a measure of intellectual resources, affects both parental support and mother-child bonds in early childhood and in adolescence: mothers who draw from greater cognitive resources are more supportive in parenting and raise more securely attached children.

Although the AFQT measures an individual's intellectual capacity, it reflects the subject's developed abilities rather than a biologically assigned aptitude (Menaghan and Parcel 1991). The AFQT score varies with family of origin, geographic region, and years of schooling, which implies that, like maternal education, an AFQT score reflects relative social advantage or disadvantage (Maume, Cancio, and Evans 1996; Menaghan and Parcel 1991). Our findings should be interpreted as further evidence that social disadvantage is reproduced partly through its effect on parent-child relations. Consistent with this theme, our analysis found that an important family resource, family income, exerts a positive influence on warm and responsive parenting in adolescence, while welfare reliance has the opposite effect. This relationship is consistent with past research that identified economic hardship as a strain on family functioning (McLoyd 1990; Siegal 1984).

The most powerful predictors of delinquency in our analysis are maternal supervision, delinquent peer association, and school attachment. Adolescents who are supervised more closely, those who have fewer delinquent peers, and those who are more attached to school show less involvement in delinquency. This result supports a large body of research that identifies these factors as important to the production of antisocial behavioral patterns. We reiterate, here, our discovery that maternal employment had relatively little negative impact on these important pathways to delinquency.

In one instance, however, workplace controls had a small indirect effect on delinquency. Specifically, bureaucratic work controls were negatively related to maternal supervision and, thus, had a slightly positive effect on delinquency. One interpretation of this result is that professional mothers may invest more time in their careers than the average mother does, which may diminish their ability to monitor children. On the other hand, the negative effect of bureaucratic controls on supervision may not reflect a difference in time spent with children so much as a difference in parenting style. The freedom and autonomy experienced by the professional parent may translate into a parenting style characterized by less overt supervision and greater attempts to equip children with internal normative controls.

Conversely, we found that maternal work hours were indirectly related to lower involvement in delinquency, through their positive effect on supervision. Again, although the effect is small, maternal work hours is actually related to greater supervision in our sample. This may be due to the stabilizing influence of steady employment on family life. As Wilson (1996:73) has argued, a job "constitutes a framework for daily behavior and patterns of interaction because it imposes disciplines and regularities" upon a parent.

Furthermore, while no maternal employment variable is related to delinquent peer association, neighborhood disorder is. This finding is consistent with social disorganization theory (Shaw and Mckay 1942): the breakdown of informal neighborhood controls leaves children at a greater risk for being socialized in intimate delinquent peer groups. It is instructive that our analysis points to community breakdown, as it operates through delinquent peer influence, as a cause of delinquency rather than family breakdown related to the absence of a working mother.

Finally, if improving family life is a goal of crime control policy, it would make good sense to aim at addressing the structural factors that limit maternal and family resources and that contribute to community disorder. Our study suggests that policy debates should avoid ideological attacks on working mothers, which portray them as leaving their children "home alone," and concentrate instead on the economic and educational inequalities that weaken families and neighborhoods.

Note

1. Contrary to past work by Parcel and Menaghan (e.g., 1994), we did not find that mothers' working conditions had a substantial impact on parenting or home environment. In their research, higher-quality work was related to higher-quality home environments. Whether we measured mothers' working conditions with the occupational complexity scale favored by Parcel and Menaghan or our series of dummy variables representing the three fractions of the working class, we found no such effect. Our contradictory findings may be explained, in part, by the measurement of our pathway variables. As discussed earlier, many of our delinquency pathway variables are one-item measures that lack the sensitivity of the multi-item family and home variables used by Parcel and Menaghan.

EXPLORING THE ISSUE

Do Mothers Who Work Outside the Home Have a Negative Impact on Their Children?

Critical Thinking and Reflection

- What are some arguments made by each side with which you agree or disagree?
- What are the strengths and weaknesses of the two positions made in this chapter?
- Pick the side with which you most agree. What are some additional arguments you would make to strengthen the case for or against mothers working outside the home?
- Think more broadly of mothers working outside the home. What are some of the ways in which children benefit from having a greater presence of their mother versus familial independence?

Is There Common Ground?

What everyone cares about is what is in the best interest of the child or children. Additionally, there is probably more room for common ground than ever before. More and more mothers and fathers are working from home. While they are busy at work, their break time can be used for parent–child interactions. An increasing number of companies are finding it advantageous to allow for such arrangements. While this will not work for a wide range of professions, what is the impact on children of the changing workplace? Beyond the changing workplace, what are some of the different ways in which parents and other caregivers impact children?

In the end, does it help to know the effects that mothers working outside of the home have on the development of their children if there is nothing a mother can do about it? What about the effects of fathers? It is interesting how biased so many cultures are toward mothers and against fathers. Although there is research looking at the effects of a mother's working on her child's development, what about the effects of a father working? What about families in which there are two mothers? Families in which there is no mother, but another adult caregiver?

Additional Resources

Family Education provides advice and support for working mothers:

http://life.familyeducation.com/mothers/working-parents/34415.html

Pew Research on Working Mothers:

http://pewresearch.org/pubs/536/working-women

The Christian Woman provides advice for Christian mothers:

http://www.thechristianwoman.com/christian-women-topics/
should-christian-mother-work.html

La Leche League provides advice for working mothers who breastfeed:

http://www.llli.org/llleaderweb/lv/lvdecjan06p123.html

Eileen Bailey tells working moms not to feel guilty:

http://eileen-bailey.suite101.com/working-moms-need-not-feel-guilty-a42841

Internet References . . .

Sexuality Information and Education Council of the United States

The Sexuality Information and Education Council of the United States is a national organization advocating for comprehensive sexuality education, sexual health programs and services, and sexual rights.

http://www.siecus.org

For Health Freedom

For Health Freedom is a nonpartisan, nonprofit research center, or "think tank," based in Washington, DC. It does not endorse any health care treatment, product, provider, or organization; rather, it aims to present the ethical and economic case for strengthening personal health freedom.

http://www.forhealthfreedom.org

Intersex Society of North America

The Intersex Society of North America is devoted to systemic change to end shame, secrecy, and unwanted genital surgeries for people born with an anatomy that someone decided is not standard for male or female.

http://www.isna.org/

The American Society for Human Genetics

The American Society of Human Genetics (ASHG), founded in 1948, is the primary professional membership organization for human geneticists in the Americas, including researchers, academicians, clinicians, laboratory practice professionals, genetic counselors, nurses, and others involved in or with special interest in human genetics.

http://www.ashg.org

National Right to Life Committee

The National Right to Life Committee (NRLC) was founded in 1973 in direct response to the U.S. Supreme Court's decision in the *Roe v. Wade* case, which guaranteed women the right to access abortion in the first trimester of their pregnancy, with some exceptions.

http://www.nrlc.org

Planned Parenthood Federation of America

Planned Parenthood Federation of America is the nation's oldest and largest reproductive health organization, believing in "the fundamental right of each individual, throughout the world, to manage his or her fertility, regardless of the individual's income, marital status, race, ethnicity, sexual orientation, age, national origin, or residence."

http://www.plannedparenthood.org

Parental Control and Children's Rights

*M*ost people can recall at one time or another being a child, and wanting to do something their parent didn't want them to do. When they asked their parent, "Why not?" the answer that came back was, "Because I said so." Parents have an enormous amount of social control over children, from a very young age. This power extends, however, beyond decisions about who a child can play with, how long she or he can stay up at night, or whether she or he can watch television for 10 more minutes. These decisions extend into areas that can affect a child for the rest of her or his life, including health and education. How much say should parents have in these types of decisions? How much say should a young child have? A teenager?

This section examines four particularly challenging parental decisions:

- Should Illegal Immigrant Families Be Able to Send Their Children to Public Schools?

- Should Parents Be Able to Select the Biological Sex of Their Children?

- Should Grandparents Have Visitation Rights for Their Grandchildren?

- Should Courts Be Able to Discriminate Against Immigrant Fathers?

- Do Parents Have the Right to Deny Their Children Lifesaving Medical Care Due to Their Religious Convictions?

ISSUE 5

Should Illegal Immigrant Families Be Able to Send Their Children to Public Schools?

YES: **William Brennan**, from Majority Opinion, *Plyler v. Doe* (1982)

NO: **Warren Burger**, from Dissenting Opinion, *Plyler v. Doe* (1982)

Learning Outcomes
As a result of this issue, readers will be able to: • Identify legal criteria such as the due process clause, the equal protection clause, and fundamental rights.   • Compare and contrast whether the U.S. Constitution protects undocumented immigrant children who reside in the United States.   • Evaluate the impact of this Supreme Court decision on illegal U.S. border crossings.

ISSUE SUMMARY

YES: William Brennan is regarded as one of the greatest intellectual leaders of the twentieth-century Supreme Court. He was regarded for writing extraordinarily forward-thinking opinions, especially regarding civil rights and civil liberties. This case proves no exception, as he captures an issue that seems even more pertinent today than when the Supreme Court addressed it. Brennan believes that children who are in the country and undocumented have a constitutional right to a public education.

NO: Warren Burger was the Chief Justice of the Supreme Court during a time in which it was slowly moving in a more conservative direction. He was an instrumental voice in many cases before the Supreme Court that had a more conservative outcome. Burger believes that undocumented immigrant children have no constitutional right to an education.

$\mathbf{A}$lthough the percentage of the U.S. population that is foreign born has not increased significantly, there is a significant change in the country of origin from decades past. According to the Census Bureau, during 1960, 75 percent of those who were foreign born were from Europe. By 2009, over 80 percent of those who are foreign born are from Latin American and Asian countries (53.1 percent from Latin America, 27.7 percent from Asia, 12.7 percent from Europe, 3.9 percent from Africa, and 2.7 percent from other regions).

When looking at the data from specific countries, Mexico was the largest, accounting for almost 30 percent of foreign-born population, totaling approximately 11.5 million. The second-largest country of birth was China, representing just over 5 percent of the foreign-born population.

In 1960, the foreign born settled in traditional gateway states: New York, California, Texas, Florida, and Illinois. Today, foreign-born residents are increasingly likely to settle in states and communities that may not have a history of having large populations of foreign-born residents. Despite this, half of all foreign-born residents today live in California, New York, Texas, and Florida. According to public opinion polling, Gallup regularly asks a random sample of Americans the following question, "In your view, should immigration be kept at its present level, increased, or decreased?" In 2011, 43 percent of respondents, a plurality, argued that it should be decreased, 35 percent felt it should remain at its present level, and 18 percent of respondents felt it should be increased. How do these numbers compare and contrast with the general public's views at other periods in American history? According to their polling, there were periods of time in which larger numbers of Americans wanted to see decreased immigration, such as after 9/11 (58 percent) and during the mid-1990s (65 percent), when California voters supported reporting undocumented immigrant students to the Immigration and Naturalization Service. The poll's 18 percent support for increased immigration is tied for the highest percentage that response has ever received: in 1965, the first year that Gallop asked that question. Most Americans view immigration as a good thing for the country (57 percent) versus a bad thing (37 percent). The face of immigration has changed in the United States over recent decades. While in the previous decades it was largely European, more recently it is largely Hispanic and African. It is also found in more varied places than the traditional states associated with immigration. While in the mid-1990s the backlash to immigration was seen in California, today the backlash often occurs from untraditional places, sometimes rural and fairly distant from the U.S.-Mexican border.

Views about immigration are not necessarily the same as views about illegal immigration. For example, the state of Arizona passed a highly restrictive law targeting undocumented immigrants, and the United States filed suit, saying that the law is unconstitutional. However, 50 percent of Americans oppose the U.S. lawsuit while only 33 percent support it. When divided by political ideology, support for the lawsuit varies significantly: 56 percent of Democrats, 27 percent of Independents, and 11 percent of Republicans support the lawsuit. The concern that many states have is over undocumented immigration. In some cases, undocumented immigrants can comprise a sizable number of students. In challenging economic times when many districts are laying off teachers, a number of U.S.-born citizens voicing dismay and even anger at the public resources that are directed toward undocumented immigrants. There are school districts across the United States that were accustomed to having a small population of students who speak English as a second language. Today, many districts are seeing a steady increase in the number of speakers of English as a second language. Sometimes a backlash ensues, and visitors are looking for ways to adjust their instruction to correspond with this need. A case like this raises critical questions about the role of education and the role of the Constitution regarding education:

- What is the purpose and function of education in the United States today?
- What is the cost of sending undocumented immigrants to public schools?
- What is the value of sending undocumented immigrants to public schools?
- What is the cost of keeping undocumented immigrants out of public schools?
- What is the value of keeping undocumented immigrants out of public schools?

Immigration has played a critical role throughout American history, as has education. Public education has historically allowed many generations to improve their economic situation compared to that of their parents. Many children who are here illegally, and may have been here since they were infants, want the same opportunities as everyone else. At the same time, there are limited resources directed to public education. Adding more students, and in many cases adding more specialized teachers, creates additional expenses that the public education system would otherwise not need to assume. Also, allowing undocumented immigrants access to public schooling arguably proves to be a compelling incentive to come to the country illegally. The U.S. Constitution provides a wide array of protections. This case raises important questions not just about public education, but also constitutional rights:

- Do those rights and protections in the U.S. Constitution apply to everyone within the U.S. borders?
- Do the rights and protections in the U.S. Constitution apply only to U.S. citizens?
- Do constitutional protections vary depending on whether or not something is a fundamental right?

The U.S. Constitution applies certain rights regardless of popular opinion. In fact, the entire point of having rights enumerated in the Constitution is to keep certain rights from being at the whim of the majority. When the Constitution was written, there was not the sort of formal process for immigration that exists today.

Another perspective to view this from is one of safety and security. For example, proponents of the rights of undocumented immigrants will often say that it is dangerous to leave children on the streets all day. Having them behaving productively in schools will keep them engaged in ways that are beneficial to the larger society. Opponents of the rights of undocumented immigrants argue that such a system encourages dangerous and violent people to come to the United States, and that they use our laws to take advantage of U.S. citizens. Last, analyze the role of race and how that affects views about immigration:

- What role do you feel that race plays in views about immigration today?
- How are the changing demographics of American society influencing views about immigration and public education?
- How would you compare and contrast social problems and immigration (e.g., violence caused by immigrants) between generations past and today?
- How would you compare and contrast ingenuity and immigration between generations past and today?

Race has often played a significant role in American society, and definitions of whiteness and racial minorities have been reconstructed throughout American history. Immigration today, both documented and undocumented, is having a clear impact on American demographics and American culture. The relationship between race and immigration is a topic that merits close examination. This chapter contains excerpts from a Supreme Court opinion about whether undocumented immigrants have a right to attend public schools. This court case is not a recent one, yet the topic remains a priority and a major concern for a large number of Americans. What do we learn from the fact that such an issue remains divisive within our society for decades? When examining the articles in this chapter, apply them to the Legal Framework overview in the Introduction. Do your beliefs in this case fit more under Originalism or Living Document? Consider the larger implications of these decisions.

YES

Majority Opinion, *Plyler v. Doe*

J ustice Brennan delivered the opinion of the Court.

The question presented by these cases is whether, consistent with the Equal Protection Clause of the Fourteenth Amendment, Texas may deny to undocumented school-age children the free public education that it provides to children who are citizens of the United States or legally admitted aliens. . . .

I

In May, 1975, the Texas Legislature revised its education laws to withhold from local school districts any state funds for the education of children who were not "legally admitted" into the United States. The 1975 revision also authorized local school districts to deny enrollment in their public schools to children not "legally admitted" to the country. These cases involve constitutional challenges to those provisions.

This is a class action, filed in the United States District Court for the Eastern District of Texas in September, 1977, on behalf of certain school-age children of Mexican origin residing in Smith County, Tex., who could not establish that they had been legally admitted into the United States. The action complained of the exclusion of plaintiff children from the public schools of the Tyler Independent School District. . . . The State of Texas intervened as a party-defendant. After certifying a class consisting of all undocumented school-age children of Mexican origin residing within the School District, the District Court preliminarily enjoined defendants from denying a free education to members of the plaintiff class. In December, 1977, the court conducted an extensive hearing on plaintiffs' motion for permanent injunctive relief. . . .

II

The Fourteenth Amendment provides that

[n]o State shall . . . deprive any person of life, liberty, or property, without due process of law; nor deny to *any person within its jurisdiction* the equal protection of the laws.

(emphasis added.) Appellants argue at the outset that undocumented aliens, because of their immigration status, are not "persons within the jurisdiction" of the State of Texas, and that they therefore have no right to the equal protection of Texas law. We reject this argument. Whatever his status

Supreme Court of the United States, 1982.

under the immigration laws, an alien is surely a "person" in any ordinary sense of that term. Aliens, even aliens whose presence in this country is unlawful, have long been recognized as "persons" guaranteed due process of law by the Fifth and Fourteenth Amendments. Indeed, we have clearly held that the Fifth Amendment protects aliens whose presence in this country is unlawful from invidious discrimination by the Federal Government. . . .

The Fourteenth Amendment to the Constitution is not confined to the protection of citizens. It says:

Nor shall any state deprive any person of life, liberty, or property without due process of law; nor deny to any person within its jurisdiction the equal protection of the laws.

These provisions are universal in their application, to all persons within the territorial jurisdiction, without regard to any differences of race, of color, or of nationality, and the protection of the laws is a pledge of the protection of equal laws.

In concluding that "all persons within the territory of the United States," including aliens unlawfully present, may invoke the Fifth and Sixth Amendments to challenge actions of the Federal Government, we reasoned from the understanding that the Fourteenth Amendment was designed to afford its protection to all within the boundaries of a State. Our cases applying the Equal Protection Clause reflect the same territorial theme:

Manifestly, the obligation of the State to give the protection of equal laws can be performed only where its laws operate, that is, within its own jurisdiction. It is there that the equality of legal right must be maintained. That obligation is imposed by the Constitution upon the States severally as governmental entities, each responsible for its own laws establishing the rights and duties of persons within its borders. . . .

Is it not essential to the unity of the people that the citizens of each State shall be entitled to all the privileges and immunities of citizens in the several States? Is it not essential to the unity of the Government and the unity of the people that all persons, *whether citizens or strangers, within this land,* shall have equal protection in every State in this Union in the rights of life and liberty and property?

Senator Howard, also a member of the Joint Committee of Fifteen, and the floor manager of the Amendment in the Senate, was no less explicit about the broad objectives of the Amendment, and the intention to make its provisions applicable to all who "may happen to be" within the jurisdiction of a State:

The last two clauses of the first section of the amendment disable a State from depriving not merely a citizen of the United States, but *any person, whoever he may be,* of life, liberty, or property without due process of law, or from denying to him the equal protection of the laws of the State. This abolishes all class legislation in the States and does away with the injustice of subjecting one caste of persons to a code not applicable to another. . . . It will, if adopted by the States, forever disable every one of them from passing laws trenching upon those fundamental rights and privileges which pertain to citizens of the United States, *and to all persons who may happen to be within their jurisdiction.* . . .

Our conclusion that the illegal aliens who are plaintiffs in these cases may claim the benefit of the Fourteenth Amendment's guarantee of equal protection only begins the inquiry. The more difficult question is whether the Equal Protection Clause has been violated by the refusal of the State of Texas to reimburse local school boards for the education of children who cannot demonstrate that their presence within the United States is lawful, or by the imposition by those school boards of the burden of tuition on those children. It is to this question that we now turn. . . .

III

A

Sheer incapability or lax enforcement of the laws barring entry into this country, coupled with the failure to establish an effective bar to the employment of undocumented aliens, has resulted in the creation of a substantial "shadow population" of illegal migrants—numbering in the millions—within our borders. This situation raises the specter of a permanent caste of undocumented resident aliens, encouraged by some to remain here as a source of cheap labor, but nevertheless denied the benefits that our society makes available to citizens and lawful residents. The existence of such an underclass presents most difficult problems for a Nation that prides itself on adherence to principles of equality under law.

The children who are plaintiffs in these cases are special members of this underclass. Persuasive arguments support the view that a State may withhold its beneficence from those whose very presence within the United States is the product of their own unlawful conduct. These arguments do not apply with the same force to classifications imposing disabilities on the minor children of such illegal entrants. At the least, those who elect to enter our territory by stealth and in violation of our law should be prepared to bear the consequences, including, but not limited to, deportation. But the children of those illegal entrants are not comparably situated. Their "parents have the ability to conform their conduct to societal norms," and presumably the ability to remove themselves from the State's jurisdiction; but the children who are plaintiffs in these cases "can affect neither their parents' conduct nor their own status." Even if the State found it expedient to control the conduct of adults by acting against their children, legislation directing the onus of a parent's misconduct against his children does not comport with fundamental conceptions of justice.

[V]isiting . . . condemnation on the head of an infant is illogical and unjust. Moreover, imposing disabilities on the . . . child is contrary to the basic concept of our system that legal burdens should bear some relationship to individual responsibility or wrongdoing. Obviously, no child is responsible for his birth, and penalizing the . . . child is an ineffectual—as well as unjust—way of deterring the parent.

Of course, undocumented status is not irrelevant to any proper legislative goal. Nor is undocumented status an absolutely immutable characteristic, since it is the product of conscious, indeed unlawful, action. But [the Texas law] is directed against children, and imposes its discriminatory burden on the basis of a legal characteristic over which children can have little control. It is thus difficult to conceive of a rational justification for penalizing these children for their presence within the United States. Yet that appears to be precisely the effect of [the Texas law].

Public education is not a "right" granted to individuals by the Constitution. But neither is it merely some governmental "benefit" indistinguishable from other forms of social welfare legislation. Both the importance of education in maintaining our basic institutions and the lasting impact of its deprivation on the life of the child mark the distinction. The "American people have always regarded education and [the] acquisition of knowledge as matters of supreme importance." But neither is it merely some governmental "benefit" indistinguishable from other forms of social welfare legislation. Both the importance of education in maintaining our basic institutions and the lasting impact of its deprivation on the life of the child mark the distinction. The "American people have always regarded education and [the] acquisition of knowledge as matters of supreme importance." We have recognized "the public schools as a most vital civic institution for the preservation of a democratic system of government." We have recognized "the public schools as a most vital civic institution for the preservation of a democratic system of government," and as the primary vehicle for transmitting "the values on which our society rests" (BRENNAN, J., concurring), and as the primary vehicle for transmitting "the values on which our society rests."

[A]s . . . pointed out early in our history, . . . some degree of education is necessary to prepare citizens to participate effectively and intelligently in our open political system if we are to preserve freedom and independence.

And these historic perceptions of the public schools as inculcating fundamental values necessary to the maintenance of a democratic political system have been confirmed by the observations of social scientists.

In addition, education provides the basic tools by which individuals might lead economically productive lives to the benefit of us all. In sum, education has a fundamental role in maintaining the fabric of our society. We cannot ignore the significant social costs borne by our Nation when select groups are denied the means to absorb the values and skills upon which our social order rests.

In addition to the pivotal role of education in sustaining our political and cultural heritage, denial of education to some isolated group of children poses an affront to one of the goals of the Equal Protection Clause: the abolition of governmental barriers presenting unreasonable obstacles to advancement on the basis of individual merit. Paradoxically, by depriving the children of any disfavored group of an education, we foreclose the means by which that group might raise the level of esteem in which it is held by the majority. But more directly, "education prepares individuals to be self-reliant and self-sufficient participants in society." Illiteracy is an enduring disability. The inability to read and write will handicap the individual deprived of a basic education each and every day of his life. The inestimable toll of that deprivation on the social, economic, intellectual, and psychological wellbeing of the individual, and the obstacle it poses to individual achievement, make it most difficult to reconcile the cost or the principle of a status based denial of basic education with the framework of equality embodied in the Equal Protection Clause. What we said 28 years ago in 221. Illiteracy is an enduring disability. The inability to read and write will handicap the individual deprived of a basic education each and every day of his life. The inestimable toll of that deprivation on the social, economic, intellectual, and psychological wellbeing of the individual, and the obstacle it poses to individual achievement, make it most difficult to reconcile the cost or the principle of a status-based denial of basic education with the framework of equality embodied in the Equal Protection Clause. What we said 28 years ago in *Brown v. Board of Education* (1954) still holds true:

Today, education is perhaps the most important function of state and local governments. Compulsory school attendance laws and the great expenditures for education both demonstrate our recognition of the importance of education to our democratic society. It is required in the performance of our most basic public responsibilities, even service in the armed forces. It is the very foundation of good citizenship. Today it is a principal instrument in awakening the child to cultural values, in preparing him for later professional training, and in helping him to adjust normally to his environment. In these days, it is doubtful that any child may reasonably be expected to succeed in life if he is denied the opportunity of an education. Such an opportunity, where the state has undertaken to provide it, is a right which must be made available to all on equal terms.

B

These well-settled principles allow us to determine the proper level of deference to be afforded [the Texas law]. Undocumented aliens cannot be treated as a suspect class, because their presence in this country in violation of federal law is not a "constitutional irrelevancy." Nor is education a fundamental right; a State need not justify by compelling necessity every variation in the manner in which education is provided to its population. But more is involved in these cases than the abstract question whether [the Texas law] discriminates against a suspect class, or whether education is a fundamental right. [The Texas law] imposes a lifetime hardship on a discrete class of children not accountable for their disabling status. The stigma of illiteracy will mark them for the rest of their lives. By denying these children a basic education, we deny them the ability to live within the structure of our civic institutions, and foreclose any realistic possibility that they will contribute in even the smallest way to the progress of our Nation. In determining the rationality of [the Texas law], we may appropriately take into account its costs to the Nation and to the innocent children who are its victims. In light of these countervailing costs, the discrimination contained in [the Texas law] can hardly be considered rational unless it furthers some substantial goal of the State. . . .

IV

As we recognized in *De Canas v. Bica* (1976), the States do have some authority to act with respect to illegal aliens, at least where such action mirrors federal objectives and furthers a legitimate state goal. In *De Canas,* the State's program reflected Congress' intention to bar from employment all aliens except those possessing a grant of permission to work in this country. *Id.* at 361. In contrast, there is no indication that the disability imposed by [the Texas law] corresponds to any identifiable congressional policy. The State does not claim that the conservation of state educational resources was ever a congressional concern in restricting immigration. More importantly, the classification reflected in [the Texas law] does not operate harmoniously within the federal program.

To be sure, like all persons who have entered the United States unlawfully, these children are subject to deportation. But there is no assurance that a child subject to deportation will ever be deported. An illegal entrant might be granted federal permission to continue to reside in this country, or even to become a citizen. In light of the discretionary federal power to grant relief from deportation, a State cannot realistically determine that any particular undocumented child will in fact be deported until after deportation proceedings have been completed. It would, of course, be most difficult for the State to justify a denial of education to a child enjoying an inchoate federal permission to remain. . . .

V

First, appellants appear to suggest that the State may seek to protect itself from an influx of illegal immigrants. While a State might have an interest in mitigating the potentially harsh economic effects of sudden shifts in population, [the Texas law] hardly offers an effective method of dealing with an urgent demographic or economic problem. There is no evidence in the record suggesting that illegal entrants impose any significant burden on the State's economy. To the contrary, the available evidence suggests that illegal aliens underutilize public services, while contributing their labor to the local economy and tax money to the state. The dominant incentive for illegal entry into the State of Texas is the availability of employment; few if any illegal immigrants come to this country, or presumably to the State of Texas, in order to avail themselves of a free education. Thus, even making the doubtful assumption that the net impact of illegal aliens on the economy of the State is negative, we think it clear that "[c]harging tuition to undocumented children constitutes a ludicrously ineffectual attempt to stem the tide of illegal immigration," at least when compared with the alternative of prohibiting the employment of illegal aliens.

Second, while it is apparent that a State may "not . . . reduce expenditures for education by barring [some arbitrarily chosen class of] children from its schools," appellants suggest that undocumented children are appropriately singled out for exclusion because of the special burdens they impose on the State's ability to provide high-quality public education. But the record in no way supports the claim that exclusion of undocumented children is likely to improve the overall quality of education in the State. . . .

Finally, appellants suggest that undocumented children are appropriately singled out because their unlawful presence within the United States renders them less likely than other children to remain within the boundaries of the State, and to put their education to productive social or political use within the State. Even assuming that such an interest is legitimate, it is an interest that is most difficult to quantify. The State has no assurance that any child, citizen or not, will employ the education provided by the State within the confines of the State's borders. In any event, the record is clear that many of the undocumented children disabled by this classification will remain in this country indefinitely, and that some will become lawful residents or citizens of the United States. It is difficult to understand precisely what the State hopes to achieve by promoting the creation and perpetuation of a subclass of illiterates within our boundaries, surely adding to the problems and costs of unemployment, welfare, and crime. It is thus clear that whatever savings might be achieved by denying these children an education, they are wholly insubstantial in light of the costs involved to these children, the State, and the Nation.

VI

If the State is to deny a discrete group of innocent children the free public education that it offers to other children residing within its borders, that denial must be justified by a showing that it furthers some substantial state interest. No such showing was made here. Accordingly, the judgment of the Court of Appeals in each of these cases is

Affirmed.
* Together with No. 80-1934, Texas et al. v. Certain Named and Unnamed Undocumented Alien Children et al., also on appeal from the same court.

Warren Burger  **NO**

Dissenting Opinion, *Plyler v. Doe*

Chief Justice Burger, with whom Justice White, Justice Rehnquist, and Justice O'Connor join, dissenting.

Were it our business to set the Nation's social policy, I would agree without hesitation that it is senseless for an enlightened society to deprive any children—including illegal aliens—of an elementary education. I fully agree that it would be folly—and wrong—to tolerate creation of a segment of society made up of illiterate persons, many having a limited or no command of our language. However, the Constitution does not constitute us as "Platonic Guardians," nor does it vest in this Court the authority to strike down laws because they do not meet our standards of desirable social policy, "wisdom," or "common sense." We trespass on the assigned function of the political branches under our structure of limited and separated powers when we assume policymaking role as the Court does today.

The Court makes no attempt to disguise that it is acting to make up for Congress' lack of "effective leadership" in dealing with the serious national problems caused by the influx of uncountable millions of illegal aliens across our borders. The failure of enforcement of the immigration laws over more than a decade and the inherent difficulty and expense of sealing our vast borders have combined to create a grave socioeconomic dilemma. It is a dilemma that has not yet even been fully assessed, let alone addressed. However, it is not the function of the Judiciary to provide "effective leadership" simply because the political branches of government fail to do so.

The Court's holding today manifests the justly criticized judicial tendency to attempt speedy and wholesale formulation of "remedies" for the failures—or simply the laggard pace—of the political processes of our system of government. The Court employs, and, in my view, abuses, the Fourteenth Amendment in an effort to become an omnipotent and omniscient problem solver. That the motives for doing so are noble and compassionate does not alter the fact that the Court distorts our constitutional function to make amends for the defaults of others.

I

In a sense, the Court's opinion rests on such a unique confluence of theories and rationales that it will likely stand for little beyond the results in these particular cases. Yet the extent to which the Court departs from principled

Supreme Court of the United States, 1982.

constitutional adjudication is nonetheless disturbing. I have no quarrel with the conclusion that the Equal Protection Clause of the Fourteenth Amendment *applies* to aliens who, after their illegal entry into this country, are indeed physically "within the jurisdiction" of a state. However, as the Court concedes, this "only begins the inquiry." The Equal Protection Clause does not mandate identical treatment of different categories of persons.

The dispositive issue in these cases, simply put, is whether, for purposes of allocating its finite resources, a state has a legitimate reason to differentiate between persons who are lawfully within the state and those who are unlawfully there. The distinction the State of Texas has drawn—based not only upon its own legitimate interests but on classifications established by the Federal Government in its immigration laws and policies—is not unconstitutional.

A

The Court acknowledges that, except in those cases when state classifications disadvantage a "suspect class" or impinge upon a "fundamental right," the Equal Protection Clause permits a state "substantial latitude" in distinguishing between different groups of persons. Moreover, the Court expressly—and correctly—rejects any suggestion that illegal aliens are a suspect class or that education is a fundamental right. Yet by patching together bits and pieces of what might be termed quasi-suspect-class and quasi-fundamental-rights analysis, the Court spins out a theory custom-tailored to the facts of these cases.

In the end, we are told little more than that the level of scrutiny employed to strike down the Texas law applies only when illegal alien children are deprived of a public education. If ever a court was guilty of an unabashedly result-oriented approach, this case is a prime example.

(1)

The Court first suggests that these illegal alien children, although not a suspect class, are entitled to special solicitude under the Equal Protection Clause because they lack "control" over or "responsibility" for their unlawful entry into this country. Similarly, the Court appears to take the position that [the Texas law] is presumptively "irrational" because it has the effect of imposing "penalties" on "innocent" children. However, the Equal Protection Clause does not preclude legislators from classifying among persons on the basis of factors and characteristics over which individuals may be said to lack "control." Indeed, in some circumstances, persons generally, and children in particular, may have little control over or responsibility for such things as their ill health, need for public assistance, or place of residence. Yet a state legislature is not barred from considering, for example, relevant differences between the mentally healthy and the mentally ill, or between the residents of different counties simply because these may be factors unrelated to individual choice or to any "wrongdoing." The Equal Protection Clause protects against arbitrary and irrational classifications, and against invidious discrimination stemming from prejudice and hostility; it is not an all-encompassing "equalizer" designed to eradicate every distinction for which persons are not "responsible."

The Court does not presume to suggest that appellees' purported lack of culpability for their illegal status prevents them from being deported or otherwise "penalized" under federal law. Yet would deportation be any less a "penalty" than denial of privileges provided to legal residents? Illegality of presence in the United States does not—and need not—depend on some amorphous concept of "guilt" or "innocence" concerning an alien's entry. Similarly, a state's use of federal immigration status as a basis for legislative classification is not necessarily rendered suspect for its failure to take such factors into account.

The Court's analogy to cases involving discrimination against illegitimate children is grossly misleading. The State has not thrust any disabilities upon appellees due to their "status of birth." Rather, appellees' status is predicated upon the circumstances of their concededly illegal presence in this country, and is a direct result of Congress' obviously valid exercise of its "broad constitutional powers" in the field of immigration and naturalization. This Court has recognized that, in allocating governmental benefits to a given class of aliens, one "may take into account the character of the relationship between the alien and this country." When that "relationship" is a federally prohibited one, there can, of course, be no presumption that a state has a constitutional duty to include illegal aliens among the recipients of its governmental benefits.

(2)

The second strand of the Court's analysis rests on the premise that, although public education is not a constitutionally guaranteed right, "neither is it merely some governmental 'benefit' indistinguishable from other forms of social welfare legislation." Whatever meaning or relevance this opaque observation might have in some other context it simply has no bearing on the issues at hand. Indeed, it is never made clear what the Court's opinion means on this score.

The importance of education is beyond dispute. Yet we have held repeatedly that the importance of a governmental service does not elevate it to the status of a "fundamental right" for purposes of equal protection analysis. In *San Antonio Independent School Dist.*, JUSTICE POWELL, speaking for the Court, expressly rejected the proposition that state laws dealing with public education are subject to special scrutiny under the Equal Protection Clause. Moreover, the Court points to no meaningful way to distinguish between education and other governmental benefits in this context. Is the Court suggesting that education is more "fundamental" than food, shelter, or medical care?

The Equal Protection Clause guarantees similar treatment of similarly situated persons, but it does not mandate a constitutional hierarchy of governmental services. JUSTICE POWELL, speaking for the Court in *San Antonio Independent School Dist.* put it well in stating that, to the extent this Court raises or lowers the degree of "judicial scrutiny" in equal protection cases according to a transient Court majority's view of the societal importance of the interest affected, we "assum[e] a legislative role, and one for which the Court lacks both authority and competence." Yet that is precisely what the Court does today.

The central question in these cases, as in every equal protection case not involving truly fundamental rights "explicitly or implicitly guaranteed by the Constitution," *San Antonio Independent School Dist.* is whether there is some legitimate basis for a legislative distinction between different classes of persons. The fact that the distinction is drawn in legislation affecting access to public education—as opposed to legislation allocating other important governmental benefits, such as public assistance, health care, or housing—cannot make a difference in the level of scrutiny applied.

B

Once it is conceded—as the Court does—that illegal aliens are not a suspect class, and that education is not a fundamental right, our inquiry should focus on and be limited to whether the legislative classification at issue bears a rational relationship to a legitimate state purpose.

The State contends primarily that [the Texas law] serves to prevent undue depletion of its limited revenues available for education, and to preserve the fiscal integrity of the State's school-financing system against an ever-increasing flood of illegal aliens—aliens over whose entry or continued presence it has no control. Of course such fiscal concerns alone could not justify discrimination against a suspect class or an arbitrary and irrational denial of benefits to a particular group of persons. Yet I assume no Member of this Court would argue that prudent conservation of finite state revenues is, *per se*, an illegitimate goal. Indeed, the numerous classifications this Court has sustained in social welfare legislation were invariably related to the limited amount of revenues available to spend on any given program or set of programs. The significant question here is whether the requirement of tuition from illegal aliens who attend the public schools—as well as from residents of other states, for example—is a rational and reasonable means of furthering the State's legitimate fiscal ends.

Without laboring what will undoubtedly seem obvious to many, it simply is not "irrational" for a state to conclude that it does not have the same responsibility to provide benefits for persons whose very presence in the state and this country is illegal as it does to provide for persons lawfully present. By definition, illegal aliens have no right whatever to be here, and the state may reasonably, and constitutionally, elect not to provide them with governmental services at the expense of those who are lawfully in the state. In *De Canas v. Bica* (1976), we held that a State may protect its fiscal interests and lawfully resident labor force from the deleterious effects on its economy resulting from the employment of illegal aliens.

And, only recently, this Court made clear that a State has a legitimate interest in protecting and preserving the quality of its schools and "the right of its own *bona fide residents* to attend such institutions on a preferential tuition basis." The Court has failed to offer even a plausible explanation why illegality of residence in this country is not a factor that may legitimately bear upon the bona fides of state residence and entitlement to the benefits of lawful residence.

It is significant that the Federal Government has seen fit to exclude illegal aliens from numerous social welfare programs, such as the food stamp program, the old-age assistance, aid to families with dependent children, aid to the blind, aid to the permanently and totally disabled, and supplemental security income programs, the Medicare hospital insurance benefits program, and the Medicaid hospital insurance benefits for the aged and disabled program. Although these exclusions do not conclusively demonstrate the constitutionality of the State's use of the same classification for comparable purposes, at the very least they tend to support the rationality of excluding illegal alien residents of a state from such programs so as to preserve the state's finite revenues for the benefit of lawful residents.

The Court maintains—as if this were the issue—that "barring undocumented children from local schools would not necessarily improve the quality of education provided in those schools." However, the legitimacy of barring illegal aliens from programs such as Medicare or Medicaid does not depend on a showing that the barrier would "improve the quality" of medical care given to persons lawfully entitled to participate in such programs. Modern education, like medical care, is enormously expensive, and there can be no doubt that very large added costs will fall on the State or its local school districts as a result of the inclusion of illegal aliens in the tuition-free public schools. The State may, in its discretion, use any savings resulting from its tuition requirement to "improve the quality of education" in the public school system, or to enhance the funds available for other social programs, or to reduce the tax burden placed on its residents; each of these ends is 'legitimate.'" The State need not show, as the Court implies, that the incremental cost of educating illegal aliens will send it into bankruptcy, or have a "'grave impact on the quality of education;'" that is not dispositive under a "rational basis" scrutiny. In the absence of a constitutional imperative to provide for the education of illegal aliens, the State may "rationally" choose to take advantage of whatever savings will accrue from limiting access to the tuition-free public schools to its own lawful residents, excluding even citizens of neighboring States.

Denying a free education to illegal alien children is not a choice I would make were I a legislator. Apart from compassionate considerations, the long-range costs of excluding any children from the public schools may well outweigh the costs of educating them. But that is not the issue; the fact that there are sound policy arguments against the Texas Legislature's choice does not render that choice an unconstitutional one.

II

The Constitution does not provide a cure for every social ill, nor does it vest judges with a mandate to try to remedy every social problem. Moreover, when this Court rushes in to remedy what it perceives to be the failings of the political processes, it deprives those processes of an opportunity to function. When the political institutions are not forced to exercise constitutionally allocated powers and responsibilities, those powers, like muscles not used, tend to atrophy. Today's cases, I regret to say, present yet another example of unwarranted judicial action which, in the long run, tends to contribute to the weakening of our political processes.

Congress, "vested by the Constitution with the responsibility of protecting our borders and legislating with respect to aliens" bears primary responsibility for addressing the problems occasioned by the millions of illegal aliens flooding across our southern border. Similarly, it is for Congress, and not this Court, to assess the "social costs borne by our Nation when select groups are denied the means to absorb the values and skills upon which our social order rests." While the "specter of a permanent caste" of illegal Mexican residents of the United States is indeed a disturbing one, it is but one segment of a larger problem, which is for the political branches to solve. I find it difficult to believe that Congress would long tolerate such a self-destructive result—that it would fail to deport these illegal alien families or to provide for the education of their children. Yet instead of allowing the political processes to run their course—albeit with some delay—the Court seeks to do Congress' job for it, compensating for congressional inaction. It is not unreasonable to think that this encourages the political branches to pass their problems to the Judiciary.

The solution to this seemingly intractable problem is to defer to the political processes, unpalatable as that may be to some.

1. It does not follow, however, that a state should bear the costs of educating children whose illegal presence in this country results from the default of the political branches of the Federal Government. A state has no power to prevent unlawful immigration, and no power to deport illegal aliens; those powers are reserved exclusively to Congress and the Executive. If the Federal Government, properly chargeable with deporting illegal aliens, fails to do so, it should bear the burdens of their presence here. Surely if illegal alien children can be identified for purposes of this litigation, their parents can be identified for purposes of prompt deportation.

2. The Department of Justice recently estimated the number of illegal aliens within the United States at between 3 and 6 million.

3. The Court implies, for example, that the Fourteenth Amendment would not require a state to provide welfare benefits to illegal aliens.

4. Both the opinion of the Court and JUSTICE POWELL's concurrence imply that appellees are being "penalized" because their parents are illegal entrants. However, Texas has classified appellees on the basis of their own illegal status, not that of their parents. Children born in this country to illegal alien parents, including some of appellees' siblings, are not excluded from the Texas schools. Nor does Texas discriminate against appellees because of their Mexican origin or citizenship. Texas provides a free public education to countless thousands of Mexican immigrants who are lawfully in this country.

5. Appellees "lack control" over their illegal residence in this country in the same sense as lawfully resident children lack control over the school district in which their parents reside. Yet in *San Antonio Independent School Dist. v. Rodriguez* we declined to review under "heightened scrutiny" a claim that a State discriminated against residents of less wealthy school districts in its provision of educational benefits. There was no suggestion in that case that a child's "lack of responsibility" for his residence in a particular school district had any relevance to the proper standard of review of his claims. The

result was that children lawfully here but residing in different counties received different treatment.

6. Indeed, even children of illegal alien parents born in the United States can be said to be "penalized" when their parents are deported.

7. It is true that the Constitution imposes lesser constraints on the Federal Government than on the states with regard to discrimination against lawfully admitted aliens. This is because "Congress and the President have broad power over immigration and naturalization which the States do not possess," Hampton, supra, at 95, and because state discrimination against legally resident aliens conflicts with and alters the conditions lawfully imposed by Congress upon admission, naturalization, and residence of aliens in the United States or the several states. However, the same cannot be said when Congress has decreed that certain aliens should not be admitted to the United States at all.

8. In support of this conclusion, the Court's opinion strings together quotations drawn from cases addressing such diverse matters as the right of individuals under the Due Process Clause to learn a foreign language; the First Amendment prohibition against state-mandated religious exercises in the public schools; the First Amendment prohibition against state-mandated religious exercises in the public schools; and state impingements upon the free exercise of religion; and state impingements upon the free exercise of religion. However, not every isolated utterance of this Court retains force when wrested from the context in which it was made. . . .

10. The Texas law might also be justified as a means of deterring unlawful immigration. While regulation of immigration is an exclusively federal function, a state may take steps, consistent with federal immigration policy, to protect its economy and ability to provide governmental services from the "deleterious effects" of a massive influx of illegal immigrants. The Court maintains that denying illegal aliens a free public education is an "ineffectual" means of deterring unlawful immigration, at least when compared to a prohibition against the employment of illegal aliens. Perhaps that is correct, but it is not dispositive; the Equal Protection Clause does not mandate that a state choose either the most effective and all-encompassing means of addressing a problem or none at all. Texas might rationally conclude that more significant "demographic or economic problem[s]" are engendered by the illegal entry into the State of entire families of aliens for indefinite periods than by the periodic sojourns of single adults who intend to leave the State after short-term or seasonal employment. It blinks reality to maintain that the availability of governmental services such as education plays no role in an alien family's decision to enter, or remain in, this country; certainly, the availability of a free bilingual public education might well influence an alien to bring his children, rather than travel alone for better job opportunities.

11. The Court suggests that the State's classification is improper because "[a]n illegal entrant might be granted federal permission to continue to reside in this country, or even to become a citizen." However, once an illegal alien is given federal permission to remain, he is no longer

subject to exclusion from the tuition-free public schools under [the Texas law]. The Court acknowledges that the Tyler Independent School District provides a free public education to any alien who has obtained, or is in the process of obtaining, documentation from the United States Immigration and Naturalization Service. Thus, Texas has not taken it upon itself to determine which aliens are or are not entitled to United States residence. JUSTICE BLACKMUN's assertion that the Texas [law] will be applied to aliens "who may well be entitled to . . . remain in the United States," is wholly without foundation.

12. The Court's opinion is disingenuous when it suggests that the State has merely picked a "disfavored group" and arbitrarily defined its members as nonresidents. Appellees' "disfavored status" stems from the very fact that federal law explicitly prohibits them from being in this country. Moreover, the analogies to Virginians or legally admitted Mexican citizens entering Texas are spurious. A Virginian's right to migrate to Texas, without penalty, is protected by the Constitution; and a lawfully admitted alien's right to enter the State is likewise protected by federal law.

13. The District Court so concluded primarily because the State would decrease its funding to local school districts in proportion to the exclusion of illegal alien children. 458 F.Supp. at 577.

14. I assume no Member of the Court would challenge Texas' right to charge tuition to students residing across the border in Louisiana who seek to attend the nearest school in Texas.

15. Professor Bickel noted that judicial review can have a "tendency over time seriously to weaken the democratic process." He reiterated James Bradley Thayer's observation that

> "the exercise of [the power of judicial review], even when unavoidable, is always attended with a serious evil, namely, that the correction of legislative mistakes comes from the outside, and the people thus lose the political experience, and the moral education and stimulus that comes from fighting the question out in the ordinary way, and correcting their own errors. The tendency of a common and easy resort to this great function, now lamentably too common, is to dwarf the political capacity of the people, and to deaden its sense of moral responsibility."

EXPLORING THE ISSUE

Should Illegal Immigrant Families Be Able to Send Their Children to Public Schools?

Critical Thinking and Reflection

- What are some arguments made by each side with which you agree or disagree?
- What are the strengths and weaknesses of the two positions made in this chapter?
- This issue focuses on what is constitutional. In some cases, a person's morals may be in contradiction to the law. How do constitutional rights in this case relate to what you feel is morally right or morally wrong?
- Think more broadly about the role of immigration, both documented and undocumented, in the United States today. Considering the ruling in this case, what remedies would be best for the creation of an immigration system that is in the best interest of the United States?

Is There Common Ground?

There are clear and distinct differences in this case regarding what should occur related to undocumented immigrant rights and public schooling. However, there is little disagreement that there are a substantial number of undocumented immigrants in the United States today. Some estimates say that the number of undocumented immigrants meets or exceeds 11 million. Many of these undocumented immigrants are children in public schools. The result is that some children are not U.S. citizens but will spend their entire childhood in this country, therefore feeling little different about their place in the United States than that of those who are citizens. Most would agree that immigration has historically had a positive impact on American society. Whether one agrees with the current system that is in place, everyone has a vested interest in fostering a system of immigration that is in the best interest of America's future. How should this affect acceptance, financial aid, and state tuition rates for colleges and universities? What are the implications on this ruling for future citizenship of undocumented immigrants?

Additional Resources

The American Civil Liberties Union on immigrant rights:

http://www.aclu.org/immigrants-rights

Taking action on immigration reform through Change.org:

http://immigration.change.org/

The National Network for Immigration and Refugee Rights:

http://www.nnirr.org/

End Illegal Immigration works to stop undocumented immigration:

http://www.endillegalimmigration.com/

Conservative USA calls to stop illegal immigration immediately:

http://www.conservativeusa.org/immigration.htm

ISSUE 6

Should Parents Be Able to Select the Biological Sex of Their Children?

YES: John A. Robertson, from "Preconception Gender Selection," *The American Journal of Bioethics* (vol. 1, no. 1, Winter 2001)

NO: Norman Daniels et al., from "It Isn't Just the Sex . . . ," *The American Journal of Bioethics* (vol. 1, no. 1, Winter 2001)

Learning Outcomes

As a result of this issue, readers will be able to:

- Identify the major arguments made for and against parents choosing the biological sex of their children.
- Compare and contrast the competing arguments made for and against parents selecting the biological sex of their children in this issue.
- Evaluate the implications of choosing the biological sex of children and the ways in which it affects them in childhood, adolescence, and adulthood.

ISSUE SUMMARY

YES: Professor John A. Robertson of the University of Texas at Austin's School of Law argues that preconception Gender selection of infants in utero for medical purposes should be allowed, and that insufficient data exist to demonstrate that any clear harm exists in allowing parents to do so.

NO: Norman Daniels and contributors argue that one aspect of allowing such a procedure as preconception gender selection, introduces socioeconomic status inequality since the procedure would likely not be covered by health insurance.

Biological sex is determined by the male sperm cell, hundreds of millions of which are present in semen after ejaculation. Among the chromosomes a sperm cell will contain is a sex chromosome, typically either an "X" chromosome or a "Y" chromosome. A woman's egg carries an "X" sex chromosome. When a sperm and egg meet, they create the chromosomal blueprint for the sex of the offspring of any resulting pregnancy. If a man's sperm carries an "X" chromosome, the resulting "XX" baby will typically be a girl. If it carries a "Y" chromosome, the baby will typically be a boy. A man can also contain no sex chromosome, resulting in an "XO" baby; an extra "Y" chromosome, resulting in an "XYY" baby; and other chromosomal differences that result in a range of biological sex variations, usually referred to as "intersex" conditions. Many people recognize intersex individuals by the previous name, *hermaphrodites.*

Many people believe that parents cannot currently select the biological sex of their children, yet preconception sex selection (PSS) has existed since the 1970s. Technology has been developed to determine whether a sperm carries either an X or a Y chromosome and implant it accordingly, although doing so is not always reliable, is an invasive medical procedure, and can be quite costly. It has been understood, therefore, that cases involving PSS have typically been done to avoid some kind of genetic disease that can be linked to either an X or a Y chromosome. Like with any medical procedure, however, there are those who may be able to access it for other reasons, and those who may not.

Why else would some people choose to select the sex of their children? For some families, having a first-born child who is either a boy or a girl is important to them. Others who know they plan to only have one child may have a strong preference for that child to be a boy or a girl. Still others may have a child of one sex and wish to ensure gender variance within their family. Regardless of the reason, one concern that medical practitioners have is about parents who carry an erroneous preconceived notion that having a girl or boy will yield a particular type of child. What happens, for example, when a father who wants a son so that he can teach him sports, only to end up with a son who hates sports? When a mother who looks forward to taking her daughter shopping and for manicures ends up with a daughter who is an outstanding athlete and not interested in shopping and manicures? Adults, they say, connect sex (biology) to gender (how we express our biological sex), when the manners in which a child expresses her or his femaleness or maleness can be quite broad.

In the following selections, John Robertson outlines the arguments both for and against PSS, concluding that there is no ethical reason against it. He disagrees that a potential exists for the practice of PSS for gender variance in the family alone could potentially be sexist, and argues that, so long as parents keep the well-being of their child(ren) in mind, they should be able to have the family composition they wish. Norman Daniels, Carson Strong, Mary B. Mahowald, and Mark V. Sauer each address one aspect of Robertson's arguments to demonstrate why preconception gender selection should not be allowed unless there is a medically necessary reason to do so.

The idea of being able to select a child's biological sex is as fascinating as it is controversial. It is also nothing new. Throughout the late nineteenth and early twentieth centuries, people discussed and debated genetic engineering of children in order to eliminate so-called "undesirable" traits. Initially referring to disease, eugenicists (those who study or espouse the improvement of the human race through controlled selective breeding—www.dictionary.com) were eventually regarded as racism, sexism, and other biases. What one person thinks would improve the human race others would see as tantamount to annihilation or extinction. Hitler's campaign to create a superior human race during World War II is a clear example of the impact of taking eugenics to its extreme.

For some, the argument for PGS is about rights—people have the fundamental right to control their reproductive potential in all ways, including whether and when to have a child, and what sex their child will be. Others oppose PGS because if sex selection takes place for any other reason other than medical necessity, society is opening a Pandora's box of ethical issues that would be impossible to close.

Take, for example, any other traits that human beings possess. What if there were a test to determine eye color of a child, and prospective parents decided that they wanted their child's eyes to match theirs? Should they be able to genetically alter their child to reflect that? What about another physical characteristic, like height?

What about something that is not physical, yet still inborn—our sexual orientation, or the gender(s) of the people to whom we are attracted physically or romantically? There is a fascinating fictional movie called *The Twilight of the Golds,* in which a woman finds that she is pregnant and takes a genetic test that determines within a certain percentage of certainty that the child that she will have will be gay. The movie centers around whether she will choose to carry the pregnancy to term or end it through having an abortion. Clearly, the different ways people might wish to affect their children can be endless, and endlessly controversial.

In 2001, the ethics committee of the American Society for Reproductive Medicine (ASRM) released a position statement in which they discussed primordial germ cell (PGC) selection for medical and non-medical reasons. The ASRM stresses that medical professionals must inform that the only current method of PGC selection available (separating X-bearing and Y-bearing sperm cells) is still an experimental procedure. If it were to become safer and eventually approved for PGC selection so that parents could select the gender of their children, the ASRM believes that PGC selection should only be offered:

- In clinic settings
- To couples who are seeking gender variety in their families
- If the couples are made fully aware of the risks of failure
- To couples who state that they would fully accept a child of a different sex should the PCG process fail

- To couples after counseling that their expectations of what it may be like to have a child of a particular gender may not match the eventual reality
- To couples who are given the opportunity to participate in a research study so that medical professionals can continue to track such issues as safety as effectively as possible

As the medical world continues to advance in leaps and bounds, this debate is far from over—in fact, we probably cannot even imagine how far it will reach in the years to come.

YES

John A. Robertson

Preconception Gender Selection

Advances in genetics and reproductive technology present prospective parents with an increasing number of choices about the genetic makeup of their children. Those choices now involve the use of carrier and prenatal screening techniques to avoid the birth of children with serious genetic disease, but techniques to choose nonmedical characteristics will eventually be available. One nonmedical characteristic that may soon be within reach is the selection of offspring gender by preconception gender selection (PGS).

Gender selection through prenatal diagnosis and abortion has existed since the 1970s. More recently, preimplantation sexing of embryos for transfer has been developed (Tarin and Handyside 1993; The Ethics Committee of the American Society of Reproductive Medicine 1999). Yet prenatal or preimplantation methods of gender selection are unattractive because they require abortion or a costly intrusive cycle of in vitro fertilization (IVF) and embryo discard. Attempts to separate X- and Y-bearing sperm for preconception gender selection by sperm swim-up or swim-through techniques have not shown consistent X- and Y-sperm cell separation or success in producing offspring of the desired gender.

The use of flow cytometry to separate X- and Y-bearing sperm may turn out to be a much more reliable method of enriching sperm populations for insemination. Laser beams passed across a flowing array of specially dyed sperm can separate most of the 2.8% heavier X- from Y-bearing sperm, thus producing an X-enriched sperm sample for insemination. Flow cytometry has been used successfully in over 400 sex selections in rabbit, swine, ovine, and bovine species, including successive generations in swine and rabbit (Fugger et al. 1998). A human pregnancy was reported in 1995 (Levinson, Keyvanfar, and Wu 1995).

The United States Department of Agriculture (USDA), which holds a patent on the flow cytometry separation process, has licensed the Genetics and IVF Institute in Fairfax, Virginia, to study the safety and efficacy of the technique for medical and "family balancing" reasons in an institutional review board-approved clinical trial. In 1998 researchers at the Institute reported a 92.9% success rate for selection of females in 27 patients, with most fertilizations occurring after intrauterine insemination (Fugger et al. 1998). A lower success rate (72%) was reported for male selection.

From *The American Journal of Bioethics*, vol. 1, no. 1, Winter 2001, pp. 2–9. Copyright © 2001 by Routledge/Taylor & Francis Group. Reprinted by permission via Rightslink. www.informaworld.com.

At this early stage of development, much more research is needed to establish the high degree of safety and efficacy of flow cytometry methods of PGS that would justify widespread use. With only one published study of outcomes to date, it is too soon to say whether the 92% success rate in determining female gender will hold for other patients, much less that male selection will reach that level of efficacy. Animal safety data have shown no adverse effect of the dye or laser used in the technique on offspring, but that is no substitute for more extensive human studies (Vidal et al. 1999). In addition, if flow cytometry instruments are to be used for sperm separation purposes, they may be classified as medical devices that require U.S. Food and Drug Administration (FDA) approval. Finally, the holder of the process patent—the USDA—will have to agree to license the process for human uses.

If further research establishes that flow cytometry is a safe and effective technique for both male and female PGS, and regulatory and licensing barriers are overcome, then a couple wishing to choose the gender of their child would need only provide a sperm sample and undergo one or more cycles of intrauterine insemination with separated sperm. A clinic or physician that offers assisted reproductive technologies (ART) and invests in the flow cytometry equipment could run the separation and prepare the X- or Y-enriched sperm for insemination, or it could have the sperm processed by a clinic or firm that has made that investment. Flow cytometry separation would not be as cheap and easy as determining gender by taking a pill before intercourse, but it would be within reach of most couples who have gender preferences in offspring.

Demand for Preconception Gender Selection

Unknown at present is the number of people who have offspring gender preferences robust enough to incur the costs and inconvenience of PGS. Although polls have often shown a preference for firstborn males, they have not shown that a large number of couples would be willing to forego coital conception in order to select the gender of their children. If PGS proves to be safe and effective, however, it may be sought by two groups of persons with gender preferences.

One group would seek PGS in order to have a child of a gender different from that of a previous child or children. A preference for gender variety in offspring would be strongest in families that have already had several children of one gender. They may want an additional child only if they can be sure that it will be of the gender opposite to their existing children. Couples who wish to have only two children might use PGS for the second child to ensure that they have one child of each gender. If social preferences for two-child families remain strong, some families may use PGS to choose the gender of the second child.

A second group of PGS users would be those persons who have strong preferences for the gender of the first child. The most likely candidates here are persons with strong religious or cultural beliefs about the role or importance of children with a particular gender. Some Asian cultures have belief systems that strongly prefer that the firstborn child be a male. In some cases, the preference reflects religious beliefs or traditions that require a firstborn son to perform funeral rituals to assure his parents' entrance into heaven (for a discussion of son preferences in India and China, see Macklin 1999, 148–151). In others, it simply reflects a deeply embedded social preference for males over females. The first-child preference will be all the stronger if a one-child-per-family policy is in effect, as occurred for a while in China (Greenlagh and Li 1995, 627). While the demand for PGS for firstborn children is likely to be strongest in those countries, there has been a sizable migration of those groups to the United States, Canada, and Europe. Until they are more fully assimilated, immigrant groups in Western countries may retain the same gender preferences that they would have held in their homelands.

Other persons with strong gender preferences for firstborn children would be those who prize the different rearing or relational experiences they think they would have with children of a particular gender. They may place special value on having their firstborn be male or female because of personal experiences or beliefs. Numerous scenarios are likely here, from the father who very much wants a son because of a desire to provide his child with what he lacked growing up, to the woman who wants a girl because of the special closeness that she thinks she will have with a daughter (Belkin 1999).

The Ethical Dilemma of Preconception Gender Selection

The prospect of preconception gender selection appears to pose the conflict—long present in other bioethical issues—between individual desires and the larger common good. Acceding to individual desires about the makeup of children seems to be required by individual autonomy. Yet doing so leads to the risk that children will be treated as vehicles of parental satisfaction rather than as ends in themselves, and could accelerate the trend toward negative and even positive selection of offspring characteristics. The dilemma of reconciling procreative liberty with the welfare of offspring and families will only intensify as genetic technology is further integrated with assisted reproduction and couples seek greater control over the genes of offspring.

Arguments for Preconception Gender Selection

The strongest argument for preconception gender selection is that it serves the needs of couples who have strong preferences about the gender of their offspring and would not reproduce unless they could realize those preferences. Because of the importance of reproduction in an individual's life, the freedom to make reproductive decisions has long been recognized as a fundamental moral and legal right that should not be denied to a person unless exercise of that right would cause significant harm to others (Robertson 1994, 2–12). A corollary of this right, which is now reflected in carrier and prenatal screening practices to prevent the birth of children with genetic disease, is that prospective parents have the right to obtain preconception or prenatal information about the genetic characteristics of offspring, so that they may decide in a particular case whether or not to reproduce (Robertson 1996, 124–135).

Although offspring gender is not a genetic disease, a couple's willingness to reproduce might well depend on the gender of expected offspring. Some couples with one or more children of a particular gender might refuse to reproduce if they cannot use PGS to provide gender variety in their offspring or to have additional children of the same gender (E. F. Fugger, personal communication to author). In other cases, they might have such strong rearing preferences for their firstborn child that they might choose not to reproduce at all if they cannot choose that child's gender. Few persons contemplating reproduction may fall into either group; but for persons who strongly hold those preferences, the ability to choose gender may determine whether they reproduce.

In cases where the gender of offspring is essential to a couple's decision to reproduce, the freedom to choose offspring gender would arguably be part of their procreative liberty (Robertson 1996, 434). Since respect for a right is not dependent on the number of persons asserting the right, they should be free to use a technique essential to their reproductive decision unless the technique would cause the serious harm to others that overcomes the strong presumption that exists against government interference in reproductive choice. Until there is a substantial basis for thinking that a particular use of PGS would cause such harms, couples should be free to use the technique in constituting their families. The right they claim is a right against government restriction or prohibition of PGS. It is not a claim that society or insurers are obligated to fund PGS or that particular physicians must provide it.

Arguments Against Preconception Gender Selection

There are several arguments against preconception gender selection. Although such methods do not harm embryos and fetuses or intrude on a woman's body as *prenatal* gender selection does, they do raise other important issues. One concern is the potential of such techniques to increase or reinforce sexism, either by allowing more males to be produced as first or later children, or by paying greater attention to gender itself. A second concern is the welfare of children born as a result of PGS whose parents may expect them to act in certain gender specific ways when the technique succeeds, but who may be disappointed if the technique fails. A third concern is societal. Widely practiced, PGS could lead to sex-ratio imbalances, as have occurred in some parts of India and China due to female infanticide, gender-driven abortions, and a one-child-per-family policy (Sen 1990). Finally, the spread of PGS would be another incremental step in the growing technologization of reproduction and genetic control of offspring. While each step alone may appear to be justified, together they could constitute a threat to the values of care and concern that have traditionally informed norms of parenting and the rearing of children.

Evaluation of Ethical and Social Issues

Concerns about sex-ratio imbalances, welfare of offspring, and technologizing reproduction may be less central to debates over PGS than whether such practices would be sexist or contribute to sexism. If the number of persons choosing PGS is small, or the technique is used solely for offspring gender variety, sex-ratio imbalances should not be a problem. If use patterns did produce drastic changes in sex ratios, self-correcting or regulatory mechanisms might come into play. For example, an over-abundance of males would mean fewer females to marry, which would make being male less desirable and provide incentives to increase the number of female births. Alternatively, laws or policies that required providers of PGS to select for males and females in equal numbers would prevent such imbalances. A serious threat of a sex-ratio imbalance would surely constitute the compelling harm necessary to justify limits on reproductive choice.

It may also be difficult to show that children born after PGS were harmed by use of the technique. Parents who use PGS may indeed have specific gender role expectations of their children, but so will parents who have a child of a preferred gender through coitus. Children born with the desired gender after PGS will presumably be wanted and loved by the parents who sought this technique. Parents who choose PGS should be informed of the risk that the technique will not succeed, and counseled about what steps they will take if a child of the undesired gender is born. If they commit themselves in advance to the well-being of the child, whatever its gender, the risk to children should be slight. However, it is possible that some couples will abort if the fetus is of the undesired gender. PGS might thus inadvertently increase the number of gender-selection abortions.

Finally, technological assistance in reproduction is now so prevalent and entrenched that a ban on PGS would probably have little effect on the use of genetic and reproductive technologies in other situations. With some form of prenatal screening of fetuses occurring in over 80% of United States pregnancies, genetic selection by negative exclusion is already well-installed in contemporary reproductive practice. Although there are valid concerns about whether positive forms of selection, including nonmedical genetic alteration of offspring genes, should also occur, drawing the line at all uses of PGS will not stop the larger social and technological forces that lead parents to use genetic knowledge to have healthy, wanted offspring. If a particular technique can be justified on its own terms, it should not be barred because of speculation of a slippery slope toward genetic engineering of offspring traits (for an analysis of the slippery-slope problem with genetic selection, see Robertson 1994, 162–165).

Is Gender Selection Inherently Sexist?

A central ethical concern with PGS is the effect of such practices on women, who in most societies have been subject to disadvantage and discrimination because of their gender. Some ethicists have argued that any attention to gender, male or female, is per se sexist, and should be discouraged, regardless of whether one can show actual harmful consequences for women (see Grubb and Walsh 1994; and Wertz and Fletcher 1989). Others have argued that there are real differences between male and female children that affect parental rearing experiences and thus legitimate nonsexist reasons for some couples to prefer to rear a girl rather than a boy or vice versa, either as a single child or after they have had a child of the opposite gender.

To assess whether PGS is sexist, we must first be clear about what we mean by sexism. *The Compact OED* (1991, 1727) defines sexism as "the assumption that one sex is superior to the other and the resultant discrimination practised against members of the supposed inferior sex, especially by men against women." By this definition, sexism is wrong because it denies the essential moral, legal, and political equality between men and women. Under this definition, if a practice is not motivated by judgments or evaluations that one gender is superior to the other, or does not lead to discrimination against one gender, it is not sexist.

Professor Mary Mahowald, an American bioethicist writing from an egalitarian feminist perspective, makes the same point with a consequentialist twist:

> Selection of either males or females is justifiable on medical grounds and *morally defensible in other situations* [emphasis added] so long as the intention and the consequences of the practice are not sexist. Sexist intentions are those based on the notion that one sex is inferior to the other; sexist consequences are those that disadvantage or advantage one sex vis-à-vis the other. (2000, 121)

In my view, the *OED* definition, modified by Mahowald's attention to consequences, is a persuasive account of the concept of sexism. If that account is correct, then not all attention to the biologic, social, cultural, or psychological differences between the sexes would necessarily be sexist or disadvantage females. That is, one could recognize that males and females have different experiences and identities because of their gender, and have a preference for rearing a child of one gender over another, without disadvantaging the dispreferred gender or denying it the equal rights, opportunities, or value as a person that constitutes sexism.

If this conjecture is correct, it would follow that some uses of PGS would clearly be sexist, while others would clearly not be. It would be sexist to use PGS to produce males because of a parental belief that males are superior to females. It would be nonsexist to use PGS to produce a girl because of a parental recognition that the experience of having and rearing a girl will be different than having a boy. In the latter case, PGS would not rest on a notion of the greater superiority of one gender over another, nor, if it occurred in countries that legally recognize the equal rights of women, would it likely contribute to sexism or further disadvantage women. As Christine Overall, a British feminist bioethicist, has put it, "sexual similarity or sexual complementarity are morally acceptable reasons for wanting a child of a certain sex" (1987, 27; quoted in Mahowald 2000, 117).

Psychological research seems to support this position. It has long been established that there are differences between boys and girls in a variety of domains, such as (but not limited to) aggression, activity, toy preference, psychopathology and spatial ability (Maccoby and Jacklin 1974; Gilligan 1980; Kimura and Hampson 1994; Feingold 1994; Collaer and Hines 1995; and Halpern 1997). Whether these differences are primarily inborn or learned, they are facts that might rationally lead people to prefer rearing a child of one gender rather than another, particularly if one has already had one or more children of a particular gender. Indeed, Supreme Court Justice Ruth Bader Ginsburg, a noted activist for women's rights before her appointment to the Supreme Court, in her opinion striking down a male-only admissions policy at the Virginia Military Institute (*United States v. Virginia*, 116 S. Ct. 2264 [1996]), noted that:

> Physical differences between men and women . . . are enduring: "[T]he two sexes are not fungible; a community made up exclusively of one [sex] is different from a community composed of both." . . . "Inherent differences" between men and women, we have come to appreciate, remain cause for celebration.

Some persons will strongly disagree with this account of sexism and argue that any attention to gender difference is inherently sexist because perceptions of gender difference are themselves rooted in sexist stereotypes. They would argue that any offspring gender preference is necessarily sexist because it values gender difference and thus reinforces sexism by accepting the gendered stereotypes that have systematically harmed women (Grubb and Walsh 1994; and Wertz and Fletcher 1989, 21). According to them, a couple with three boys who use PGS to have a girl are likely to be acting on the basis of deeply engrained stereotypes that harm women. Similarly, a couple's wish to have only a girl might contribute to unjustified gender discrimination against both men and women, even if the couple especially valued females and would insist that their daughter receive every benefit and opportunity accorded males.

Resolution of this controversy depends ultimately on one's view of what constitutes sexism and what actions are likely to harm women. Although any recognition of gender difference must be treated cautiously, I submit that recognizing and preferring one type of childrearing experience over the other can occur without disadvantaging women generally or denying them equal rights and respect. On this view, sexism arises not from the recognition or acceptance of difference, but from unjustified reactions to it. Given the biological and psychological differences between male and female children, parents with a child of one gender might without being sexist prefer that their next child be of the opposite gender. Similarly, some parents might also prefer that their firstborn or only child be of a particular gender because they desire a specific rearing and companionship experience.

If it is correct that using PGS for offspring diversity is sexist, then those who deny that biological gender differences exist, or who assume that any recognition of them always reinforces sexism or disadvantages women, will not have carried the burden of showing that a couple's use of PGS for offspring gender variety or other nonintentionally sexist uses is so harmful to women that it justifies restricting procreative choice. Until a clearer ethical argument emerges, or there is stronger empirical evidence that most choices to select the gender of offspring would be harmful, policies to prohibit or condemn as unethical all uses of nonmedically indicated PGS would not be justified.

The matter is further complicated by the need to respect a woman's autonomy in determining whether a practice is sexist. If a woman is freely choosing to engage in gender selection, even gender-selection abortion, she is exercising procreative autonomy. One might argue in response that the woman choosing PGS or abortion for gender selection is not freely choosing if her actions are influenced by strong cultural mores that prefer males over females. Others, however, would argue that the straighter path to equal rights is to respect female reproductive autonomy whenever it is exercised, even if particular exercises of autonomy are strongly influenced by the sexist norms of her community (Mahowald 2000, 188).

Public Policy and Preconception Gender Selection

Because of the newness of PGS and uncertainties about its effects, the best societal approach would, of course, be to proceed slowly, first requiring extensive studies of safety and efficacy, and then at first only permitting PGS for increasing the gender variety of offspring in particular families. Only after the demographic and other effects of PGS for gender variety have been found acceptable should PGS be available for firstborn children.

However, given the close connection between parental gender preferences for offspring and reproductive choice, public policies that bar all nonmedical uses of PGS or that restrict it to choosing gender variety in offspring alone could be found unconstitutional or illegal. If there are physical, social, and cultural differences between girls and boys that affect the rearing or relational experiences of parents, individuals and couples would have the right to implement those preferences as part of their fundamental procreative liberty. The risk that exercising rights of procreative liberty would hurt offspring or women—or contribute to sexism generally—is too speculative and uncertain to justify infringement of those rights.

The claim of a right to choose offspring gender is clearest in the case of PGS for gender variety. If flow cytometry or other methods of PGS are found to be safe and effective, there would be no compelling reason to ban or restrict their nonmedical use by persons seeking gender variety in the children they rear. Couples with one child or several children of a particular gender might, without being sexist or disadvantaging a particular gender, prefer to have an additional child of the opposite gender. ART clinics should be free to proceed with PGS for offspring variety in cases where couples are aware of the risk of failure and have undergone counseling that indicates that they will accept and love children of the dispreferred gender if PGS fails. Clinics providing PGS should also ask couples to participate in research to track and assess the effects of PGS on children and families.

The use of PGS to determine the gender of firstborn children is a more complicated question. The choice to have one's first or only child be female has the least risk of being sexist, because it is privileging or giving first place to females, who have traditionally been disfavored. The use of PGS to select firstborn males is more problematic because of the greater risk that this choice reflects sexist notions that males are more highly valued. It is also more likely to entrench male dominance. The danger of sexism is probably highest in those ethnic communities that place a high premium on male offspring, but it could exist independently of those settings.

Yet restricting PGS to offspring gender variety and firstborn females may be difficult to justify. Given that individuals could prefer to have a boy rather than a girl because of the relational and rearing experiences he will provide, just as they might prefer a girl for those reasons, it might be difficult to show that all preferences for firstborn males are sexist. Nor could one easily distinguish firstborn male preferences when the couple demanding them is of a particular ethnic origin. Although the risk that firstborn male preferences would be sexist is greatest if the PGS occurred in a country in which those beliefs prevailed, the chance that PGS would contribute to societal sexism lessens greatly if the child is reared in a country that legally protects the equal status of women and men.

If prohibitions on some or all nonmedical uses of PGS could not be justified and might even be unconstitutional, regulation would have to take different forms. One form would be to deny public or private insurance funding of PGS procedures, which would mean that only those willing to pay out-of-pocket would utilize them. Another form would be for the physicians who control access to PGS techniques to take steps to assure that it is used wisely. If they comply with laws banning discrimination, physician organizations or ART clinics could set guidelines concerning access to PGS. They might, for example, limit its use to offspring gender variety or firstborn female preferences only. As a condition of providing services, they might also require that any couple or individual seeking PGS receive counseling about the risks of failure and commit to rear a child even if its gender is other than that sought through PGS. Although such guidelines would not have the force of statutory law, they could affect the eligibility of ART clinics to list their ART success rates in national registries and could help define the standard of care in malpractice cases.

Conclusion

The successful development of flow cytometry separation of X- and Y-bearing sperm would make safe, effective, and relatively inexpensive means of non-medical preconception gender selection available for selecting female, if not also male, offspring. The nonmedical use of PGS raises important ethical, legal, and social issues, including the charge that any or most uses of PGS would be sexist and should therefore be banned or discouraged. Assessment of this charge, however, shows that the use of PGS to achieve offspring gender variety and (in some cases) even firstborn gender preference, may not be inherently sexist or disadvantaging of women. Although it would be desirable to have extensive experience using PGS to increase the variety of offspring gender before extending it to firstborn gender preferences, it may not be legally possible to restrict the technique in this way. However, practitioners offering PGS should restrict their PGS practice to offspring gender variety until further debate and analysis of the issues has occurred. In any event, physicians offering PGS should screen and counsel prospective users to assure that persons using PGS are committed to the well-being of their children, whatever their gender.

A policy solution that gives practitioners and patients primary control without direct legal or social oversight, although not ideal, may be the best way to deal with new reprogenetic techniques. Society should not prohibit or substantially burden reproductive decisions without stronger evidence of harm than PGS now appears to present. Ultimately, the use of PGS and other reprogenetic procedures will depend on whether they satisfy ethical norms of care and concern for children while meeting the needs of prospective parents.

Norman Daniels et al.

 **NO**

It Isn't Just the Sex . . .

John Robertson argues that preconception sex selection (PSS) should remain a moral and legal prerogative of parental family planning, provided certain other conditions are met, including caveats about harms to others. If sound, his argument also applies to parental prerogatives to select offspring having any one of a family of traits that have properties and effects similar to sex (or sex selection). Bringing out this more general formulation will help us evaluate his argument.

Suppose, as Robertson does with regard to flow cytometry, that a specific sex-selection technology exists and has the following properties:

A. It is safe;
B. It imposes no harm on any fetus (because it is preconception);
C. It has quantifiably high reliability;
D. There is parental demand for using the technique (even though other techniques are much cheaper and more enjoyable); and
E. Some parents would not reproduce if they could not use it.

Now suppose that we also have techniques for preconception selection of traits other than sex, such as height, greater immune capacities, calmer temperament, or better memory, and that these techniques also have properties A–E. Property E may now seem more problematic than when it was applied only to sex selection. Robertson imagines a family that has several children of one gender and would rather not reproduce again unless it could raise a child of a different gender. Similarly, we can imagine parents refusing to reproduce further unless they can have a much taller or much calmer child—one different from the ones they already have.

Exactly what role does property E play in Robertson's argument? Property E does clearly show the strength of the parental preference, but strength of preference seems irrelevant to establishing that we have a right to gender or other trait selection. For Robertson, the point of property E seems to be this: if the parents would not reproduce at all unless they could have a child with a particular gender or other trait, then state prohibitions on gender or other trait selection technologies interfere with their basic moral and legal liberty to make reproductive choices, unless, of course, there are harms to others that the prohibition is aimed at preventing. In contrast, if parents prefer to select for a particular trait but would choose to reproduce even if they could not—that is, if property E is missing—then the state has not interfered with their liberty to make reproductive choices if it prohibits use of trait selection technologies.

Robertson's appeal to property E seems misguided. Consider Table 1:

Table 1

Agents	First Choice	Second Choice	Third Choice
Ben and Lily	gender selection	take chances	no offspring
Max and Sophie	gender selection	no offspring	(take chances?)

Property E is present for Max and Sophie but not Ben and Lily. If gender selection is denied either couple, they get their second choice. The prohibition on sex selection affects both couple's reproductive choices in the same way. Perhaps it seems worse for Max and Sophie because they are then "driven" to have no children, whereas Ben and Lily still reproduce, but the result in both cases is determined by each couple's choice in the absence of their first choice. Property E thus seems to do no work in the argument, and I believe it should be dropped.

Perhaps what motivates Robertson's appeal to E is a narrow (perhaps legally constrained) interpretation of reproductive liberty: it is a negative right against government interference with the choice to reproduce or not. Given this narrow interpretation, we might still be able to derive a right against interference with some cases of gender selection if property E did the work that I have argued it fails to do. Since property E fails to do what this alternative requires, we have two options. We can adopt and justify a broader interpretation of reproductive liberties, one that provides a right against interference with reproductive choices about trait selection, provided there are no harms to others. Alternatively, we can retain the narrow interpretation of reproductive liberty but argue for an additional, broader (negative) right of parents to pursue what they think is best for their children (and their families) through the selection, shaping, and development of the traits of their offspring. This broader right will include means other than reproductive choices (Buchanan et al. 2000, 187–191).

Much of Robertson's paper focuses on the reasons for thinking that gender selection either poses no harm to others or poses harms that can be countered in ways that infringe less on liberty than would prohibitions on gender selection. The disjunction of conditions (F–H) that Robertson's argument appeals to as constraints on gender selection constrains selection for other traits as well.

F. Neither individual cases of selection, nor the aggregate effect of many such selections, imposes (nonspeculative) harms on others;
G. Where there is a potential harm to others, it will correct itself in a reasonable time period (as in some cases of gender ratio imbalance); or
H. Any potential harm to others can be eliminated through regulation that does not directly infringe on basic reproductive liberties.

Robertson should have emphasized more the way in which the estimate of harms, and thus the justification of a liberty to select a trait, is sensitive to empirical facts about a society. He correctly argues that the case of family gender balancing does not by itself reinforce sexist beliefs or practices. When societies have a strong gender bias, permitting preconception sex selection beyond family balancing would reinforce existing biases and might lead to sex ratio imbalances. Under these conditions, permitting sex selection would require rigorous regulation of the grounds for selection. Robertson fails to emphasize the ways in which such regulations would appear to many as intrusions into basic parental liberties and how politically difficult it might be to sustain them.

One kind of harm Robertson does not mention, perhaps because it is not raised by gender selection, is the competitive or positional disadvantage that might result from allowing trait selection for certain traits, but financing them only through out-of-pocket payments. Advantages in wealth will then lead to the further transmission of advantage through access to trait selection. Fairness issues must be addressed in this case (for a discussion of these issues, see Buchanan et al. 2000, chs. 5–6).

Reference

Buchanan, A., D. Brock, N. Daniels, and D. Wikler. 2000. *From chance to choice: Genetics and justice.* New York: Cambridge University Press.

⋖◉⋗

Can't You Control Your Children?

In his paper "Preconception Gender Selection" (PGS), John Robertson (2001) discusses two issues: What limitations, if any, should the government impose on use of PGS? And what restrictions, if any, would be justifiable for physicians to impose on prospective parents who request PGS? For both issues, the focus is on PGS for parental preference, as opposed to prevention of sex-linked diseases The issue requires the use of our constitutional law framework. According to that framework, procreative liberty is a *fundamental* right, which entails that government restrictions must be justified by compelling state interests. Meeting the test of being "compelling" requires especially strong reasons for infringing procreative liberty; according to Robertson, meeting the test typically requires showing that substantial harm to others would occur. The second issue does not require the constitutional framework. Here the question is whether some individuals—either individual physicians or groups of physicians—are justified in refusing to carry out patients' requests for PGS. In arguing that it is ethically justifiable for physicians to refuse such requests, it is not necessary to show that there are compelling reasons for the refusal. It is only necessary to show that the arguments for refusing are better than the arguments for carrying out the requests.

Unfortunately, this basic difference between constitutional and professional ethical argumentation is not clearly acknowledged in Robertson's article.

Throughout the paper, he appeals to the more demanding constitutional framework, even where the less demanding framework for professional ethical justifiability is all that is required. For example, he argues that PGS for offspring diversity is ethically permissible, despite the objection of some ethicists that it is sexist. He concludes his argument by stating:

> If this view is correct, then those who deny that biological gender differences exist, or who assume that any recognition of them always reinforces sexism or disadvantages women, will not have carried the burden of showing that a couple's use of PGS for offspring gender variety or other nonintentionally sexist uses is so harmful to women that it justifies restricting procreative choice. Until a stronger basis for finding harm to others from PGS exists, policies to prohibit or substantially restrict its use would not be justified.

Here Robertson appeals to the test of substantial harm. Later he advocates physician guidelines that permit PGS for gender diversity, but the only arguments for such guidelines that can be found in the paper appeal, like this one, to the test of substantial harm. This blurring of constitutional and professional ethics argumentation creates a problem in trying to justify physician guidelines. Robertson seems to approve of guidelines that permit PGS for gender diversity because objections to such guidelines do not meet the demanding "compelling reasons" test. But objections to physician guidelines simply do not have to meet this high standard.

This problem is significant because there are important arguments bearing on the issue of physician guidelines that Robertson does not address. In particular, in discussing concerns about the genetic control of offspring, he does not present those concerns in a particularly forceful form. As a result, his paper does not engage those issues very well. There are at least two concerns that should be discussed, and although they overlap, I believe it is useful to distinguish between them. First, there are concerns about the genetic enhancement of offspring. Second, there are concerns about parental genetic control of offspring characteristics irrespective of whether the purpose of the control is properly labeled "enhancement" (as in the case of control for offspring diversity, eye and hair color, or various other possibilities).

Let me begin with the first set of concerns, which is relevant to the issue of physician response to requests for PGS for firstborn male offspring. I want to emphasize that sex selection is not itself a form of enhancement. To claim otherwise is to imply that one gender is superior to the other. However, it is obvious that in our male-dominated society, being male confers advantages upon a person. Parents who seek genetically to enhance the ability of offspring to succeed in life could easily reason that being male would enhance that ability. When physicians allow PGS for firstborn male offspring, they are at least in some circumstances allowing parents who think this way to pursue their vision of genetic enhancement. Those who would want additional forms of genetic enhancement in the future could point to this as a precedent; we would *already* be a distance down the proverbial slippery slope. Let me mention two arguments that have been given to explain why we should be wary of the genetic enhancement of offspring. First, such technologies likely would not be available to all, but would be skewed among different socio-economic and ethnic groups. The economically advantaged would be better able to afford the costs of the technology. Because enhancement can improve the offspring's opportunities, unequal access to it would exacerbate current social and economic inequities (for a similar argument in the context of germ-line genetic modification, see Zimmerman 1991). Second, allowing parents to choose enhancements might erode our opposition to state-sponsored programs that promote (or carry out) enhancements of offspring. There is wide concern that abuses might occur, as has happened in all previous eugenics programs, or that efforts would be made to redesign human nature, resulting in more harm than benefit (Wertz and Fletcher 1989; Anderson 1989).

It should be acknowledged that enhancement could have positive consequences, as well. In some cases, it might promote the happiness of parents and children and the quality of family life. Also, it has been pointed out that we do not have sufficient information to assess the risks and benefits of positive eugenics, and that we should not assume that it is automatically wrong (Munson and Davis 1992). Admittedly, it is difficult to predict the long-term consequences of enhancement. However, the arguments against enhancement of offspring raise concerns significant enough to suggest that we should not proceed with enhancement without a better understanding of where it might take us (Strong 1997, 143–144). These considerations, in addition to the argument from sexism, provide important reasons why, for now at least, physicians should not carry out requests for PGS for firstborn male offspring.

The concern about parental control of offspring characteristics applies to all uses of PGS, including its use for offspring diversity and for firstborn female offspring based on a parental desire for the rearing and companionship experiences that would be involved. There is a legitimate worry that genetic control of offspring characteristics, if it becomes common and is applied to many characteristics, would alter parent-child relationships and that children would become more like "products" (Botkin 1990; Strong 1997, 143–144). When offspring characteristics are under parental control (whether they are properly labeled "enhancement" or not), parents might be less willing to accept the shortcomings of their children. Such designing might undermine a child's ability to have self-esteem. Less parental tolerance of children's imperfections might result in less compassion for the handicapped. Also, there would be a greater tendency to blame parents for their children's imperfections. The question, "Can't you control your children?" might take on a darker meaning. Children themselves might blame their parents, and this could harm family relationships. These sorts of considerations suggest that we should be more wary about proceeding with PGS than Robertson would have us be. It is not necessary to have compelling reasons for physician refusal to carry out requests for PGS based on parental gender preferences. It is only necessary to have good reasons. Concerns about what we might be doing to our future seem to justify a cautionary approach. They support the view that, for now at least, physicians should not carry out any requests for PGS for parental preference.

References

Anderson, W. F. 1989. Human gene therapy: Why draw a line? *Journal of Medicine and Philosophy* 14:681–693.

Botkin, J. R. 1990. Prenatal screening: Professional standards and the limits of parental choice. *Obstetrics and Gynecology* 75:875–880.

Munson, R., and L. H. Davis. 1992. Germ-line gene therapy and the medical imperative. *Kennedy Institute of Ethics Journal* 2:137–158.

Robertson, J. A. 2001. Preconception gender selection. *American Journal of Bioethics,* 1(1) 2–9.

Strong, C. 1997. *Ethics in reproductive and perinatal medicine: A new framework.* New Haven: Yale University Press.

Wertz D. C, and J. Fletcher 1989. Fatal knowledge? Prenatal diagnosis and sex selection. *Hastings Center Report* 19:21–27.

Zimmerman, B. K. 1991. Human germ-line therapy: The case for its development and use. *Journal of Medicine and Philosophy* 16:593–612.

⋅◈⋅

Reverse Sexism? Not to Worry

I concur with John Robertson that preconception sex selection (PSS) would be morally objectionable if it were sexist, and that it is not necessarily sexist (any more than post conception sex selection is necessarily sexist).[1] I disagree, however, that PSS is morally permissible on grounds of procreative liberty or the right to reproduce. Further, I believe that PSS is more likely than not to be sexist in its intent or in its consequences. Robertson appears to think otherwise.

According to Robertson, procreative liberty is the "freedom to reproduce or not to reproduce in the genetic sense." It also includes the freedom to gestate "whether or not there is a genetic connection to the resulting child" (Robertson 1996, 22–23). He deploys this definition in support of PSS by arguing that a couple who wish to have a biologically related child only if the child is of one sex rather than the other are deprived of their "fundamental right" to reproduce if PSS is not available to them. This argument erroneously assumes that the right to reproduce implies the right to reproduce a child of a specific kind. As Rebecca Dresser observes, "helping people to have children is different from helping them to have a particular kind of child" (Dresser 2001). It would be as wrong to say a couple have a fundamental right to reproduce a child who is a clone of one of them or to reproduce a child who has the same disabilities that they have. Although Robertson may affirm procreative liberty in these situations also, neither right is implied by the right to reproduce.

In *Children of Choice,* Robertson (1996, 22) acknowledges that the right to reproduce is separable from the right to raise a child, but he does not fully examine the implications of that separability for sex selection. This leaves me wondering how he might respond to scenarios not addressed in his article. Would he defend the right to reproduce a child of the desired sex solely on grounds of that right even if the reproducing person had no intention of raising the child? Would a sperm "donor," for example, be entitled to flow cytometry so as to ensure, or to maximize the chance, that any embryo developed from his gametes is male?[2] Would a potential egg "donor" be entitled to require that embryos formed from her gametes be transferred to the recipient only if they are determined to be female? Or would a woman who desires to gestate the genetic offspring of another be entitled to exclude some embryos from that offer on grounds of their sex? In none of these cases is the rationale for sex selection necessarily sexist. But as Robertson defines it, the right to reproduce entails the right to sex selection in all of these cases, as well as those where the right to reproduce is exercised by those who intend to raise the child.

Neither does the right not to reproduce imply the right to terminate a pregnancy at any point during gestation for any reason. *Roe v. Wade* (410 U.S. 113 [1973]) allows the states to proscribe abortion after viability only if the pregnant woman's health is not threatened by continuation of the pregnancy. The rationale for this caveat is not simply procreative freedom but the woman's right to avoid harm to herself. Even those who, like me, do not agree with Robertson's claim that the right to reproduce includes the right to PSS, may support PSS on this basis. We may argue, for example, that the anticipation of social stigmatization or ostracization may provide moral justification for PSS by individuals in particular cultural milieux. However, this is not equivalent to justification of permissive policies for PSS.

In addition to his affirmation of procreative liberty, Robertson apparently supports permissive policies for PSS because such policies are unlikely to be sexist in their intent or consequences. In contrast, I think that sexist intent and sexist consequences are more likely than not to be associated with the social and legal permissibility of PSS. Neither Robertson nor I have empirical data to buttress our positions, in part because intent is difficult if not impossible to verify in most cases. The mere fact that individuals prefer to have a boy or girl as a first, only, or additional child does not count as evidence of sexism. But sexist consequences are evident in situations where sex selection is practiced, despite its illegality, because the preponderance of boys in such situations shows that in general, male children are more valued than female children.

Even if male children are more valued for morally defensible reasons such as economic security or to avoid discriminatory or oppressive practices towards son-less women and their daughters, this constitutes complicity in sexism. Individuals themselves may not have sexist reasons for PSS, but their practice inevitably supports the view that one sex is inferior to the other. On an individual level, sexism may also be practiced by those who choose to have female children—if the intent or consequences of their choices are based on the notion that men are inferior to women. If and when a preponderance of female children in the general population shows them to be more valued than male children, we may then need to worry that the permissibility of PSS has led to "reverse sexism." Present circumstances lend little weight to that worry.

References

Dresser, R. 2001. Cosmetic reproductive services and professional integrity. *American Journal of Bioethics*, 1(1):11–12.

Mahowald, M. B. 2000. *Genes, women, equality.* New York: Oxford University Press.

Robertson, J. A. 1996. *Children of choice: Freedom and the new reproductive technologies.* Princeton: Princeton University Press.

Notes

1. My own views on sex selection, whether it is practiced prior to conception, prenatally or postnatally, are developed in Mahowald (2000, 115–121).

2. I put the term "donor" in quotation marks to call attention to the fact that the literal meaning of the term, i.e., one who gives a gift, is typically inapplicable in this context. In most cases, those who provide gametes to others are vendors rather than donors. Whether gamete providers are in fact donors or vendors, however, their right to reproduce does not imply a right to select the sex of their genetic offspring.

◦◦◦

Preconception Sex Selection: A Commentary

Gender selection of offspring created through assisted reproductive technology (ART) has been hotly debated since the inception of the method of in vitro fertilization (IVF). Given the broad range of innovation enjoyed throughout the development of IVF, it should not be surprising that couples would ask whether or not predetermination of gender is possible. Thus, early on, attempts at controlling outcomes began through the development of techniques that would preferentially select the desired sex of the embryo. What has never been universally agreed upon, however, is what, if any, situation should warrant attempts to manipulate the gender of the offspring.

The issue of sex selection through prenatal determination is one of the more difficult subjects facing clinicians. Ultimately physicians must decide whether or not to offer services; such decisions are based largely on the soundness of the medical and ethical practice. Today, couples choosing to select the gender of their children have essentially three options:

1. to terminate a pregnancy already established after the sex has been determined by chorionic villus sampling or amniocentesis;
2. to undergo preimplantation genetic diagnosis (PGD) by embryonic biopsy prior to embryo transfer; or
3. to alter the population of inseminated sperm so as to increase the likelihood of achieving a pregnancy of the desired sex.

Karyotyping a fetus or embryo is inherently invasive, expensive, and potentially dangerous to the mother and/or the pregnancy. However, it is the only way to guarantee that the sex of the embryo is the one desired by the mother.

Manipulating the insemination is appealing since the intervention occurs prior to conception, and avoids most issues involving abortion. From this perspective, sperm separation techniques would appear to have a decisive advantage over traditional methods. Unfortunately, to this date all techniques involving sperm separation are flawed since none guarantee success. As John Robertson points out, at best between 8% and 18% of pregnancies will result in the "wrong sex," even using flow cytometry to separate sperm of X and Y genotype. It is this fact of life that troubles most of us responsible for "assisting" in the creation of these lives. What happens to the pregnancies of the wrong sex? I would guess that many would choose to abort. As noted, "paying greater attention to gender" than to the importance of the life itself in many ways perverts the original intent of helping the infertile to conceive. Knowing that we live in a sexist world, there can be no doubt that many (mostly female) embryos would be terminated in the name of "procreative liberty."

All agree that the right of the individual to reproduce is fundamental. What isn't always clear is whether or not the pursuit of reproductive interventions requires regulation. Society and individuals speaking on behalf of the unborn have an equal right to object to gender selection when performed without clear medical justification. Physicians and patients with genetic diseases generally agree that the avoidance of X-linked illness is a valued reason for gender selection, whether through invasive or noninvasive means. However, "family balancing" is a politically correct euphemism that does little to diminish the valid concerns related to societal sexism.

The flow cytometry method has been neither clinically tested nor approved by the U.S. Food and Drug Administration. Yet, it has been discussed in the international press and news media and profiled as a treatment option in the medical literature. Naturally, patients are inquiring as to its efficacy even though the procedure remains largely unavailable. Typically, the debate over whether or not it should be used is obscured by debate over the clinical success of the method.

Unfortunately, throughout the history of reproductive medicine, sensational press has often dictated medical practice. Many techniques in ART were introduced in this manner (e.g., intracytoplasmic sperm injection, cryopreservation, assisted hatching, and blastocyst culturing). Even IVF itself was equally unorthodox in its development and presentation. With respect to preconception sex selection, I agree with Robertson's assessment as to the need to "proceed slowly." In order for individuals to give informed consent, more needs to be known of the long-term effects, both medical and psychosocial, of flow cytometry. More importantly, I believe ethics committees at each institution should discuss how best to implement policy related to gender selection, and physicians should abide by these recommendations.

The Ethics Committee at Columbia University believes gender selection should not be performed except in instances in which a clear medical indication exists (e.g., a known genetic X-linked carrier status). Undoubtedly, many will disagree with that opinion. However, public debate is good for the field, and each physician should take a clear stand prior to introducing yet another untested procedure.

EXPLORING THE ISSUE

Should Parents Be Able to Select the Biological Sex of Their Children?

Critical Thinking and Reflection

- What are some arguments made by each side with which you agree or disagree?
- What are the strengths and weaknesses of the two positions made in this chapter?
- Pick the side with which you most agree. What are some additional arguments you would make to strengthen the case for or against parents choosing the biological sex of their children?
- Think more broadly of the issue of parents choosing the biological sex of their children.
- Specifically, think about it from the children's perspective as they grow older. What are the challenges of growing up without being clearly male or female? What are the challenges of the wrong sex being chosen for a person?

Is There Common Ground?

When talking about sex and gender, is it most important to fit in? Or is it most important to be yourself? Many people act as if we have a gender continuum, a world of only boys and girls. However, nature actually gives us a gender continuum in which most people, but not all, fit into different places on the continuum.

Beyond that, science provides different capabilities every day. Regardless of our decision on this particular issue, what are some of the things that we can do to reduce the stigma for those who are intersex? What kind of education needs to occur to reduce the automatic assumption of a binary gender system (that everyone is born either male or female)?

Additional Resources

M. Darnovsky, "Revisiting Sex Selection: The Growing Popularity of New Sex Selection Methods Revives An Old Debate," *GeneWatch* (vol. 17, no. 1, January/February 2004). Accessible online at http://www.gene-watch.org/genewatch/articles/17-1darnovsky.html.

——— "Sex Selection Moves to Consumer Culture—Ads For 'Family Balancing' in *The New York Times*," *Genetic Crossroads: The Newsletter of the Center for*

Genetics and Society (vol. 33, August 20, 2003). Accessible online at http://www.genetics-and-society.org/newsletter/archive/33.html#II.

D. King, "Eugenic Tendencies in Modern Genetic," in B. Tokar, ed., *Redesigning Life?* (New York: Zed Books, 2001).

R. Mallik, "A Less Valued Life: Population Policy and Sex Selection in India," The Center for Gender and Health Equity, 2002. Accessible online at www.genderhealth.org/pubs/MallikSexSelectionIndiaOct2002.pdf.

R. McDougall, "Acting Parentally: An Argument Against Sex Selection," *Journal of Medical Ethics* (vol. 31, no. 10, 2005).

P. Moore and L. Moore, *Baby Girl or Baby Boy: Choose the Sex of Your Child* (Tallahassee, FL: Washington Publishers, 2004).

J. Savulescu and E. Dahl, "Sex Selection and Preimplantation Diagnosis: A Response to the Ethics Committee of the American Society of Reproductive Medicine," *Human Reproduction* (vol. 15, no. 9, September 2000).

R. Shettles and D. M. Rorvik, *How to Choose the Sex of Your Baby* (New York: Broadway Books, 2006).

I. Simoncelli, "Preimplantation Genetic Diagnosis and Selection: From Disease Prevention to Customized Conception," *Different Takes: The Newsletter on Population and Development Program at Hampshire College* (no. 24, Spring 2003). Accessible online at http://www.genetics-and-soci-ety.org/resources/cgs/200303_difftakes_simoncelli.pdf.

ISSUE 7

Should Grandparents Have Visitation Rights for Their Grandchildren?

YES: Jennifer Russell, from "Grandparents Play an Essential Role in the Lives of Their Grandchildren," written for *Taking Sides: Family and Personal Relationships* (2011)

NO: Sandra Day O'Connor, from Plurality Opinion, *Troxel v. Granville* (2000)

Learning Outcomes

As a result of this issue, readers will be able to:

- Identify the agreed-upon rights and responsibilities associated with both parents and grandparents.
- Compare and contrast the arguments made for parents' rights versus those made for grandparents' rights.
- Evaluate the impact of the Supreme Court on states and how they might enact different laws and policies.

ISSUE SUMMARY

YES: Jennifer Russell is an attorney at SeniorLAW Center. She provides legal services to grandparents and other seniors raising relative children. Russell contends that grandparent custody and visitation statutes should be upheld, and argues that grandparents often play an essential role in their grandchildren's lives, especially during times of family turmoil.

NO: Sandra Day O'Connor was the first woman appointed to the United States Supreme Court. For much of her time on the court, she was the justice most likely to wind up in the majority opinion. O'Connor argues that the rights of parents trumps grandparents. As a result, grandparents would not have the right to see their grandchildren.

$\mathbf{G}$randparents play an essential and unique role in today's diverse family structures, but there is significant debate over whether that role deserves special recognition and protection under the law when those protections interfere with the rights of parents to choose what is best for their children. There can be no denying that many children live in homes where grandparents have assumed a variety of critical roles, greatly influencing a child's emotional, physical and mental development, and well-being. The 2000 United States Census revealed that 5.8 million grandparents lived with their minor grandchildren, 2.4 million of whom had the primary responsibility for these grandchildren. These numbers are growing. In 2008, the U.S. Census reported that 6.4 million grandparents had minor grandchildren living with them. Recognizing the reality of a significant grandparent role in American families and the benefits children derive from relationships with their grandparents, all 50 states have enacted statutes over the past half-century granting grandparents the ability to seek visitation or partial custody of their grandchildren. This issue will look at arguments for both sides, using a case from the U.S. Supreme Court to argue that it is a parent's right to determine what is the best for his or her child, while a case from the Pennsylvania Supreme Court is used to argue that grandparent rights must be protected.

Grandparent visitation rights and partial custody statutes are rooted in recognition of the vital role grandparents play in a child's development. Although the relationship between a parent and a child is primary, legislatures have determined that grandparents' rights must be protected under the law, especially in situations where the link between the grandparent and the parent has been interfered with through the parent's illness, divorce, or even death. The traditional image of the happy grandparent holding the bouncing grandchild while the parent looks lovingly on the scene is an image that often conflicts with the reality of modern life, which finds many stresses on the family affecting these multigenerational relationships. Yet it is precisely in these highly stressed situations that the admittedly vital role of the grandparent needs to be weighed against the primary rights of the parent to decide what is best for the child. All states must ensure compliance with the spirit of *parens patriae*, the public policy doctrine that allows states to intervene in a family's affairs to the extent necessary to protect a child in need. But absent a showing that the child will be harmed significantly by a parent's choice to limit or end contact with a grandparent, a parent's decision should not be interfered with by government action. It is crucial to defend a parent's rights, especially in times of family flux and turmoil. Whatever benefit a grandparent may provide a grandchild, no one is better situated to determine what is in the best interests of a child than the parent.

Included in this issue is language from *Troxel v. Granville*, 530 U.S. 57 (2000), hereinafter "*Troxel*." In *Troxel*, a plurality of the U.S. Supreme Court ruled against a grandparent's visitation rights and affirmed the trial court's decision to invalidate a Washington State third-party visitation statute on constitutional grounds. The Washington statute was found to be overly broad because it allowed any third party to petition for custody at any time. The statute also failed to allow fit parents the presumption that they were acting in their child's best interests when, for example, they chose to eliminate contact with the child by a third party. The main question in *Troxel* was whether the Washington statute, which allows any person to petition for a court-ordered right to see a child over a custodial parent's objection if such visitation is found to be in the child's best interest, unconstitutionally interfere with the fundamental right of parents to rear their children? The Court concluded, in a 6–3 decision delivered by Justice Sandra Day O'Connor, that the Washington statute violated the right of parents, under the due process clause of the Constitution's Fourteenth Amendment, to make decisions concerning the care, custody, and control of their children. Justice O'Connor wrote for the Court that "[t]he liberty interest at issue in this case—the interest of parents in the care, custody, and control of their children—is perhaps the oldest of the fundamental liberty interests recognized by this Court." Because the Court rested its decision on the sweeping breadth of *the Washington law* and the application of that broad, unlimited power in this case, it did not consider the primary constitutional question of this case—whether the Due Process Clause requires all non-parental visitation statutes to include a showing of harm or potential harm to the child as a condition precedent to granting visitation. Clearly, though, this case highlights that the constitutionality of any standard for awarding visitation turns on the specific manner in which that standard is applied and that the constitutional protections in this area are best "elaborated with care." The following language outlines the arguments that can be made to support a parent's right to choose for his or her child what relationship that child will have with his or her grandparent.

YES

Jennifer Russell

Grandparents Play an Essential Role in the Lives of Their Grandchildren

Grandparents play an essential and unique role in today's diverse family structures, one which deserves special recognition and protection. Many children live in homes where grandparents have assumed a variety of critical roles, greatly influencing a child's emotional, physical, and mental development and well-being. The 2000 U.S. Census revealed that 5.8 million grandparents lived with their minor grandchildren, 2.4 million of whom had the primary responsibility for these grandchildren. These numbers are growing. In 2008, the U.S. Census reported that 6.4 million grandparents had minor grandchildren living with them. Recognizing the reality of a significant grandparent role in American families and the benefits children derive from relationships with their grandparents, all fifty states have enacted statutes over the past half century granting grandparents the ability to seek visitation or partial custody of their grandchildren.

All states must ensure compliance with the spirit of *parens patriae*, the public policy doctrine that allows states to intervene in a family's affairs to the extent necessary to protect a child in need. It is crucial to defend grandparent visitation and custody rights under this doctrine because grandparents often provide a vital source of stabilization for children during times of family flux and turmoil and play an essential role in a child's development and well-being. For example, after the loss of a parent, arbitrary termination of a child's supportive and nurturing relationship with a grandparent by the surviving parent can be very detrimental to the child. States have an interest in seeing that children in disrupted families are not arbitrarily deprived of the benefit of these relationships. This article will discuss *Hiller v. Fausey*, 588 Pa. 342 (2006), hereinafter *"Hiller,"* the Pennsylvania Supreme Court case that upheld a grandparent visitation and partial custody statute in Pennsylvania. The purpose of this article is to advocate for the continued rights of grandparents to seek visitation and partial custody, especially during times of crisis in a child's life.

The Pennsylvania statute at issue in *Hiller*, 23 Pa.C.S. §5311, hereinafter called "the Pennsylvania law," allowed a grandparent or great-grandparent to seek visitation or partial custody of an unmarried grandchild (or great-grandchild) upon the death of the parent who was related to the petitioner.

However, before an award of visitation or partial custody, the court must find that it will be in the child's best interests, and that it will not interfere with the relationship between the child and surviving parent. The statute also required courts to consider the amount of previous contact between the grandparent or great-grandparent petitioner and child.

In *Hiller,* a maternal grandmother was arbitrarily denied visitation with the child in question, her grandson, by the child's father after the death of the child's mother. The grandmother shared a close relationship with her grandson before his mother's death, and the denial of contact by the father eventually caused her to seek partial custody of the child over the father's objections. This case highlights the conflict between parents' rights to rear their children and the government's interest in protecting children from harm. Parents have a constitutionally protected right to make decisions concerning the care, custody, and control of their children. States, however, have a compelling interest in protecting the health and emotional welfare of children. The *Hiller* case advanced to the Pennsylvania Supreme Court, where the court sided with the grandmother and affirmed the award of partial custody to the child's grandmother. The court held that the compelling interest of the state and best interests of the child outweighed the father's decision to cut off the grandmother's nurturing relationship with her grandson.

The paramount concern in all custody disputes is the "best interests of the child."[1] The goal is to "foster those relationships which will be meaningful for the child, while protecting the child from situations which would have a harmful effect."[2] A best interest analysis requires courts to consider all factors relevant to the physical, intellectual, emotional, and spiritual well-being of a child.[3] In *Hiller,* the child and his grandmother shared a close relationship, seeing each other on an almost daily basis during the last two years of his mother's life as she was battling cancer. After his mother's death, the grandmother made repeated attempts to maintain contact with her grandson but was denied any contact by her grandson's father. At trial, the grandmother was able to rebut the presumption afforded to the father that his decision to deny contact was in the child's best interests. She was able to prove instead that partial custody was in her grandson's best interests, and also that it would not interfere with the parent–child relationship, as required by the statute. The trial court awarded her partial custody for one weekend per month and one week per summer.

The child's father appealed the trial court's decision to the Pennsylvania Superior Court, the mid-level Pennsylvania court that reviews such decisions, asserting that application of the Pennsylvania statute violated his due process rights under the Fourteenth Amendment of the U.S. Constitution. The Due Process Clause of the Fourteenth Amendment protects the fundamental right of parents to make decisions concerning the care, custody, and control of their children.[4] When a party raises an infringement of a fundamental right under the Fourteenth Amendment, the court typically applies a "strict scrutiny analysis." This analysis asks if the infringement of the individual's right by the state law or action is necessary to promote a compelling state interest, and also whether it is narrowly tailored to further that compelling state interest.

The Pennsylvania Superior Court began its analysis by comparing the Pennsylvania statute, which allowed the grandmother to seek partial custody, with a Washington State statute that the U.S. Supreme Court found unconstitutional in *Troxel v. Granville*, 530 U.S. 57 (2000), hereinafter "*Troxel.*" In *Troxel*, the U.S. Supreme Court affirmed the Washington Supreme Court's decision to invalidate a Washington non-parental visitation statute on constitutional grounds. The Washington statute at issue allowed *any third party* to seek visitation of a child *at any time* and permitted the court to authorize visitation if it served the child's best interests. The Court found the statute to be overly broad because it allowed any third party to seek visitation of a child at any time. The statute also failed to allow fit parents the presumption that they were acting in their child's best interests when, for example, they chose to eliminate contact with the child by a third party. Finding the statute had violated a parent's constitutional right to make decisions concerning the care, custody, and control of their child, the Court affirmed the lower court's decision to invalidate the statute.

The Pennsylvania Superior Court in *Hiller* found the Pennsylvania statute was distinguishable from the Washington statute that the U.S. Supreme Court found unconstitutional. It found the Pennsylvania statute did not violate the father's rights under the Fourteenth Amendment, and it upheld the trial court's application of the Pennsylvania statute and the award of partial custody to the *Hiller* grandmother. It concluded that although the trial court presumed that the father, as a fit parent, was acting in his child's best interests, the grandmother overcame this presumption by demonstrating that granting her partial custody was in the child's best interests, due in part to the loving and supportive relationship she provided to her grandson as he worked through his grief. The grandmother also demonstrated that partial custody would not interfere with the parent-child relationship.

Unsatisfied with the Superior Court's decision, the father then appealed to the Pennsylvania Supreme Court, arguing that a grandparent should be required to show compelling circumstances, such as harm to the child resulting from denial of visitation, before a court can interfere with a parent's constitutional right to make decisions concerning the care, custody, and control of the child. The Pennsylvania Supreme Court granted review to determine whether the trial court's application of the Pennsylvania law violated the father's rights under the Fourteenth Amendment.

The Pennsylvania Supreme Court first discussed *Troxel* and found all of the U.S. Supreme Court justices, with the exception of one, "recognized the existence of a constitutionally protected right of parents to make decisions concerning the care, custody, and control of their children, which includes determining which third parties may visit with their children and to what extent."[5] A majority of the U.S. Supreme Court also agreed that "fit parents are entitled to a presumption that they act in the best interests of their children."[6]

In light of the U.S. Supreme Court's findings in *Troxel*, the father in *Hiller* requested the Pennsylvania Supreme Court find the lower courts erred in concluding that application of the Pennsylvania statute was constitutional in his case. He maintained that the lower courts did not afford his decision to deny contact with the child's grandmother the special weight it deserved. He asserted that grandparents should be required to show "compelling circumstances such as unfitness of the parent or significant harm to the child resulting from denial of visitation or partial custody" before courts can interfere with parental decisions regarding the child.[7] The grandmother rejected the father's assertion that the Constitution requires she first demonstrate parental unfitness or harm to the child before allowing her partial custody. In *Troxel*, the U.S. Supreme Court did not determine whether this was required.

The grandmother distinguished the Washington statute at issue in *Troxel* from the Pennsylvania statute at issue in *Hiller*. She argued the Pennsylvania statute was a perfect balance between protecting parents' fundamental rights and the state's interest in protecting the best interests and welfare of a child who had lost a parent and is at risk of losing the relationship with a grandparent. She believed the trial court properly applied the Pennsylvania statute and weighed all factors necessary to render a decision that both promoted the child's best interests and protected the parent's due process rights. The trial court made detailed findings with regard to the child's best interests, found partial custody would not interfere with the parent–child relationship, and found the father would not provide contact for the grandmother with the child absent a court order.

The Pennsylvania Supreme Court analyzed the constitutionality of the Pennsylvania law and found little merit in the father's attempt to diminish the importance in the clear differences between the Pennsylvania statute and the Washington statute invalidated by the U.S. Supreme Court. The court acknowledged that the right to make decisions regarding the care, custody, and control of one's child is one of the oldest fundamental rights protected by the Due Process Clause of the Fourteenth Amendment. The Pennsylvania Supreme Court then applied a strict scrutiny analysis of this infringement on the father's fundamental right, first analyzing whether the infringement was supported by a compelling state interest and then whether the infringement was narrowly tailored to effectuate that interest.

The court acknowledged and confirmed that the state has a longstanding interest in protecting the health and emotional welfare of children. The court also confirmed that the state can apply the *parens patriae* doctrine to intervene in a family's private affairs to the extent necessary to protect a child's health and welfare. This is allowed over the objections of a parent, thus infringing on that parent's fundamental right regarding the child. Recognizing that the state's compelling interest in protecting children's welfare can be the basis for infringing on a parent's fundamental right, the court then asked whether the infringement premised upon this interest was narrowly tailored to effectuate the interest. The court found the infringement was narrowly tailored because the Pennsylvania statute at issue was limited to a grandparent (or great-grandparent) whose deceased child (or grandchild) was the parent of the child for whom custody was sought. This was in stark contrast with the overly broad Washington statute invalidated by the U.S. Supreme Court in *Troxel* that allowed *any third party* to petition for visitation of a child *at any time.*

The Pennsylvania Supreme Court also found the statute properly protected parents' fundamental rights in that Pennsylvania courts are not only required to ensure that visitation or partial custody will serve the best interests of the child, but also that it *will not interfere* with the parent–child relationship. Additionally, courts must consider the amount of previous contact between the child and petitioner, allowing for an assessment of their prior relationship. Moreover, Pennsylvania precedent requires courts to provide a presumption in favor of a fit parent's decision, which is exactly what the U.S. Supreme Court faulted the trial court in *Troxel* for failing to do. Pennsylvania precedent already gives special weight and deference to the parent–child relationship, properly tipping controversies with third parties in the parent's favor.

The U.S. Supreme Court in *Troxel* did not decide whether the Due Process Clause requires all non-parental visitation statutes to include a showing of harm or potential harm as a condition precedent to granting visitation or partial custody to a third party. In declining to make this determination, the Court left the decision to individual states. The Pennsylvania Supreme Court in *Hiller* disagreed with the father's argument that the Pennsylvania statute should require a showing of harm, concluding this requirement would vitiate the purpose of the statute as well as Pennsylvania's policy of assuring "continuing contact of the child or children with the grandparent when the parent is deceased, divorced, or separated."[8] While the parent–child relationship must be given special weight and deference, and should not typically be disturbed unless there is a showing of harm, the court found that it can be disturbed without a showing of harm if circumstances "clearly indicate the appropriateness of awarding custody to a non-parent."[9]

The Pennsylvania Supreme Court held the stringent requirements of the Pennsylvania law, combined with the presumption in Pennsylvania legal precedent that fit parents act in their children's best interests, sufficiently protects parents' fundamental rights. The court found that a grandparent or great-grandparent did not have to demonstrate parental unfitness or a showing of harm when seeking visitation or partial custody. The Pennsylvania statute thus survived its constitutional challenge. The statute's application in *Hiller* was upheld because it was properly applied by the lower courts, and the child was able to continue his beneficial and nurturing relationship with his maternal grandmother following the tragic death of his mother.

In *Troxel,* the U.S. Supreme Court reaffirms its view that the Due Process Clause of the Fourteenth Amendment protects parents' interest in the care, custody, and control of their children. However, the Court also made clear that non-parental visitation statutes are constitutional, provided they are carefully tailored, contain procedures and/or provisions that are respectful of the parent–child relationship, further a compelling state interest, and protect the best interests of the child. All the justices in *Troxel,* except one, agreed on a state's interest in establishing non-parental visitation and partial custody laws, clearly recognizing the changing reality of the American family and the crucial role that grandparents and other third parties play in children's lives.

In *Hiller,* the Pennsylvania Supreme Court recognized that the Pennsylvania law met all requirements set forth by the U.S. Supreme Court for a constitutional non-parental visitation statute. The statute is narrowly drawn to limit the class of third persons to parents or grandparents of the deceased parent, requires any award of visitation or partial custody to be in the child's best interests and mandates it not interfere with the parent–child relationship. The statute also requires courts to consider the amount of prior contact between the petitioner and child. For a court to override a parent's decision to deny contact, a grandparent petitioner must provide evidence that their request is truly in the child's best interests.

By enacting this law, the Pennsylvania legislature acknowledged that children who have experienced the death of a parent may need protection against unilateral terminations of the child's relationships with kin of the deceased parent. Without this statute, a child would have no recourse against this additional loss, thus compounding his tragedy. The Pennsylvania law carefully balances the rights of parents against the state's compelling interest. It protects the welfare of children who have experienced the death of a parent while promoting a beneficial relationship between grandparents and grandchildren, crucial in our increasingly intergenerational and interconnected society.

As *Hiller* highlights, grandparents can play an essential role in the protection of a child's development and welfare in today's families. Pennsylvania has recognized that this role deserves special recognition and protection and allows grandparents to petition for custody and/or supervised physical custody (visitation) in a variety of circumstances. So many children are raised in single-parent, intergenerational, and kinship care homes, where relatives such as grandparents have primary responsibility for the children, that the conventional nuclear family is no longer America's norm. Children that are raised in environments with a great deal of family flux can suffer detrimental effects on their development and well-being. The stabilizing relationship and various forms of support and security that many grandparents provide are critical to ensuring a grandchild's mental, physical, and emotional development.

This source of stability and support from a grandparent with whom the child has a close relationship is even more crucial when that child has suffered the tragic loss of a parent. Loss of a parent can lead to depression and other emotional disturbances; severing another deep family attachment can exacerbate a child's pain and cause additional harm to the child. It is not in a child's best interests to arbitrarily be denied contact with that nurturing grandparent after the loss of a parent, particularly when the child has had a longstanding relationship with the grandparent. The fundamental right of parents to the custody of their children, which includes the ability to deny third-party relationships, must be balanced with and restricted by the state's interest, which includes the emotional development and well-being of a grieving child.

Hiller focused on the Pennsylvania statute allowing grandparents and great-grandparents to seek partial custody or visitation upon the death of a parent. Pennsylvania grandparents can also seek custody or visitation in other circumstances. Although much of the substance of custody law remains the same since *Hiller* was decided in 2006, changes were made to Pennsylvania's custody laws in January 2011. Grandparents and great-grandparents continue to have the right to petition for partial physical and supervised physical custody (previously, "visitation") when the parent of the child who is related to the petitioner is deceased, when the parents are separated for at least six months or have commenced divorce proceedings, or when the child has resided with the grandparent or great-grandparent for one year and is then subsequently removed from the home by the parents.[10] The Pennsylvania law at issue in *Hiller* now falls under the revised custody laws.[11]

Grandparents in Pennsylvania can petition for *any* form of physical or legal custody if 1) their relationship with the child began with the consent of a parent or under court order, 2) they have assumed or are willing to assume responsibility for the child, and 3) the child has been determined to be a dependent child under state law, or is substantially at risk due to parental abuse, neglect, drug or alcohol abuse or incapacity, or was living with that grandparent for one year and is then removed from the home by the parents.[12] The variety of circumstances under which a grandparent can seek "visitation" or custody of their grandchild in Pennsylvania is a strong testament to, and acknowledgment by the legislature of, the role that grandparents play in the development and well-being of children, especially in families suffering from disruption, loss, and broken relationships.

Many grandparents are *in loco parentis* to their grandchildren, meaning they have assumed all of the parental rights and duties of, and obligations for, the child, and are acting as the child's parent, but are doing so without a court order in place. This is problematic because caregivers cannot obtain necessary medical or mental health care for a child without the necessary legal decision-making authority. Under Pennsylvania's current custody law, individuals who are *in loco parentis* now have a statutorily-conferred right to petition for any form of physical or legal custody of that child, providing many grandparent caregivers with the relief they need.[13]

A child's best interest is the guiding force by which custody determinations are made. However, custody law continues to evolve and develop in light of our changing society. While parents have constitutionally protected parental rights, grandparents are increasingly afforded greater authority, rights and liberties in light of their crucial role and the support they provide to children and families across the United States.

In *Hiller,* the Pennsylvania Supreme Court found the grandmother had a nurturing and loving relationship with her grandson that was highly beneficial for the child. Recognizing that this relationship was in the "best interests of the child," the court affirmed the grandmother's legal right to continue her involvement in her grandson's life. This landmark decision highlights the vital role grandparents play in the lives of many children, especially in times of crisis. As states continue to seek ways to protect the health and welfare of children, the evolution of grandparent visitation and partial custody statutes reflects the recognition of the vital role grandparents play in maintaining the well-being of children and families alike.

Notes

1. *Douglas v. Wright,* 801 A.2d 586, 591 (2002)
2. *Id.*
3. *Id.*
4. *Troxel v. Granville,* 530 U.S. 57, 66 (2000)
5. *Hiller v. Fausey,* 904 A.2d 875, 883 (2006)
6. *Id.*
7. *Id.* at 884.
8. 23 Pa.C.S. §5301
9. *Id.* at 889–90.
10. 23 Pa.C.S. §5325
11. 23 Pa.C.S. §5325(1)
12. 23 Pa.C.S. §5324(3)
13. 23 Pa.C.S. §5324(2)

Sandra Day O'Connor

 **NO**

Plurality Opinion

J ustice O'Connor announced the judgment of the Court and delivered an opinion, in which the Chief Justice, Justice Ginsburg, and Justice Breyer join.

Section 26.10.160(3) of the Revised Code of Washington *(editor's note—hereinafter called "the Washington law")* permits "[a]ny person" to petition a superior court for visitation rights "at any time," and authorizes that court to grant such visitation rights whenever "visitation may serve the best interest of the child." Petitioners Jenifer and Gary Troxel petitioned a Washington Superior Court for the right to visit their grandchildren, Isabelle and Natalie Troxel. Respondent Tommie Granville, the mother of Isabelle and Natalie, opposed the petition. The case ultimately reached the Washington Supreme Court, which held *the Washington law* unconstitutionally interferes with the fundamental right of parents to rear their children.

The demographic changes of the past century make it difficult to speak of an average American family. The composition of families varies greatly from household to household. While many children may have two married parents and grandparents who visit regularly, many other children are raised in single-parent households. Understandably, in these single-parent households, persons outside the nuclear family are called upon with increasing frequency to assist in the everyday tasks of child rearing. In many cases, grandparents play an important role.

The nationwide enactment of nonparental visitation statutes is assuredly due, in some part, to the States' recognition of these changing realities of the American family. Because grandparents and other relatives undertake duties of a parental nature in many households, States have sought to ensure the welfare of the children therein by protecting the relationships those children form with such third parties. The States' nonparental visitation statutes are further supported by a recognition, which varies from State to State, that children should have the opportunity to benefit from relationships with statutorily specified persons—for example, their grandparents. The extension of statutory rights in this area to persons other than a child's parents, however, comes with an obvious cost. For example, the State's recognition of an independent third-party interest in a child can place a substantial burden on the traditional parent–child relationship.

The Washington law permits "any person" to petition a superior court for visitation rights "at any time," and authorizes that court to grant such visitation rights whenever "visitation may serve the best interest of the child."

Supreme Court of the United States, 2000.

Petitioners Jenifer and Gary Troxel petitioned a Washington Superior Court for the right to visit their grandchildren, Isabelle and Natalie Troxel. Respondent Tommie Granville, the mother of Isabelle and Natalie, opposed the petition. The case ultimately reached the Washington Supreme Court, which held that *the Washington law* unconstitutionally interferes with the fundamental right of parents to rear their children.

Tommie Granville and Brad Troxel shared a relationship that ended in June 1991. The two never married, but they had two daughters, Isabelle and Natalie. Jenifer and Gary Troxel are Brad's parents, and thus the paternal grandparents of Isabelle and Natalie. After Tommie and Brad separated in 1991, Brad lived with his parents and regularly brought his daughters to his parents' home for weekend visitation. Brad committed suicide in May 1993. Although the Troxels at first continued to see Isabelle and Natalie on a regular basis after their son's death, Tommie Granville informed the Troxels in October 1993 that she wished to limit their visitation with her daughters to one short visit per month.

In December 1993, the Troxels commenced the present action by filing, in the Washington Superior Court for Skagit County, a petition to obtain visitation rights with Isabelle and Natalie. *The Washington law (under which they brought this action)* provides: "Any person may petition the court for visitation rights at any time including, but not limited to, custody proceedings. The court may order visitation rights for any person when visitation may serve the best interest of the child whether or not there has been any change of circumstances." At trial, the Troxels requested two weekends of overnight visitation per month and two weeks of visitation each summer. Granville did not oppose visitation altogether, but instead asked the court to order one day of visitation per month with no overnight stay. In 1995, the Superior Court issued an oral ruling and entered a visitation decree ordering visitation one weekend per month, one week during the summer, and four hours on both of the petitioning grandparents' birthdays.

Granville appealed, during which time she married Kelly Wynn. Before addressing the merits of Granville's appeal, the Washington Court of Appeals remanded the case to the Superior Court for entry of written findings of fact and conclusions of law. On remand, the Superior Court found that visitation was in Isabelle and Natalie's best interests:

> "The Petitioners [the Troxels] are part of a large, central, loving family, all located in this area, and the Petitioners can provide opportunities for the children."
> ". . . The court took into consideration all factors regarding the best interest of the children and considered all the testimony before it. The children would be benefitted from spending quality time with the Petitioners, provided that that time is balanced with time with the childrens' [sic] nuclear family. The court finds that the childrens' [sic] best interests are served by spending time with their mother and stepfather's other six children."
> Approximately nine months after the Superior Court entered its order on remand, Granville's husband formally adopted Isabelle and Natalie.

The Washington Court of Appeals reversed the lower court's visitation order and dismissed the Troxels' petition for visitation, holding that nonparents lack standing to seek visitation unless a custody action is pending. In the Court of Appeals' view, that limitation on nonparental visitation actions was "consistent with the constitutional restrictions on state interference with parents' fundamental liberty interest in the care, custody, and management of their children." The Washington Supreme Court granted the Troxels' petition for review and, after consolidating their case with two other visitation cases, affirmed. The court disagreed with the Court of Appeals' decision on the statutory issue and found that *the Washington law* gave the Troxels standing to seek visitation, irrespective of whether a custody action was pending. The Washington Supreme Court nevertheless agreed with the Court of Appeals' ultimate conclusion that the Troxels could not obtain visitation of Isabelle and Natalie pursuant to *the Washington law*. The court rested its decision on the Federal Constitution, holding that *the Washington law* unconstitutionally infringes on the fundamental right of parents to rear their children. In the court's view, there were at least two problems with the nonparental visitation statute. First, according to the Washington Supreme Court, the Constitution permits a State to interfere with the right of parents to rear their children only to prevent harm or potential harm to a child. *The Washington law* fails that standard because it requires no threshold showing of harm. Second, by allowing "'any person' to petition for forced visitation of a child at 'any time' with the only requirement being that the visitation serve the best interest of the child," the Washington visitation statute sweeps too broadly. "It is not within the province of the state to make significant decisions concerning the custody of children merely because it could make a 'better' decision." The Washington Supreme Court held that "parents have a right to limit visitation of their children with third persons," and that between parents and judges, "the parents should be the ones to choose whether to expose their children to certain people or ideas."

The demographic changes of the past century make it difficult to speak of an average American family. The composition of families varies greatly from household to household. While many children may have two married parents and grandparents who visit regularly, many other children are raised in single-parent households. The nationwide enactment of nonparental visitation statutes is assuredly due, in some part, to the States' recognition of these changing realities of the American family. Because grandparents and other relatives undertake duties of a parental nature in many households, States have sought to ensure the welfare of the children therein by protecting the relationships those children form with such third parties. The States' nonparental visitation statutes are further supported by a recognition, which varies from State to State, that children should have the opportunity to benefit from relationships with statutorily specified persons—for example, their grandparents. The extension of statutory rights in this area to persons other than a child's parents, however, comes with an obvious cost. For example, the State's recognition of an independent third-party interest in a child can place a substantial burden on the traditional parent–child relationship.

The Fourteenth Amendment provides that no State shall "deprive any person of life, liberty, or property, without due process of law." We have long recognized that the Amendment's Due Process Clause, like its Fifth Amendment counterpart, "guarantees more than fair process." The Clause also includes a substantive component that "provides heightened protection against government interference with certain fundamental rights and liberty interests."

The liberty interest at issue in this case—the interest of parents in the care, custody, and control of their children—is perhaps the oldest of the fundamental liberty interests recognized by this Court. More than 75 years ago, in *Meyer v. Nebraska,* 262 U.S. 390 (1923), we held that the "liberty" protected by the Due Process Clause includes the right of parents to "establish a home and bring up children" and "to control the education of their own." Two years later, in *Pierce v. Society of Sisters,* 268 U.S. 510 (1925), we again held that the "liberty of parents and guardians" includes the right "to direct the upbringing and education of children under their control." We explained in *Pierce* that "the child is not the mere creature of the State; those who nurture him and direct his destiny have the right, coupled with the high duty, to recognize and prepare him for additional obligations."

In subsequent cases also, we have recognized the fundamental right of parents to make decisions concerning the care, custody, and control of their children. See, e.g., *Stanley v. Illinois,* 405 U.S. 645 (1972) ("It is plain that the interest of a parent in the companionship, care, custody, and management of his or her children 'comes to this Court with a momentum for respect lacking when appeal is made to liberties which derive merely from shifting economic arrangements'"); *Wisconsin v. Yoder,* 406 U.S. 205(1972) ("The history and culture of Western civilization reflect a strong tradition of parental concern for the nurture and upbringing of their children. This primary role of the parents in the upbringing of their children is now established beyond debate as an enduring American tradition".) In light of this extensive precedent, it cannot now be doubted that the Due Process Clause of the Fourteenth Amendment protects the fundamental right of parents to make decisions concerning the care, custody, and control of their children.

The Washington law, as applied to Granville and her family in this case, unconstitutionally infringes on that fundamental parental right. The Washington nonparental visitation statute is breathtakingly broad. According to the statute's text, "*any person* may petition the court for visitation rights *at any time,*" and the court may grant such visitation rights whenever "visitation may serve *the best interest of the child.*" That language effectively permits any third party seeking visitation to subject any decision by a parent concerning visitation of the parent's children to state-court review. Once the visitation petition has been filed in court and the matter is placed before a judge, a parent's decision that visitation would not be in the child's best interest is accorded no deference. *The Washington law* contains no requirement that a court accord the parent's decision any presumption of validity or any weight whatsoever. Instead, the Washington statute places the best-interest determination solely in the hands of the judge. Should the judge disagree with the parent's estimation of the child's best interests, the judge's view necessarily prevails. Thus, in practical effect, in the State of Washington, a court can disregard and overturn *any* decision by a fit custodial parent concerning visitation whenever a third party affected by the decision files a visitation petition, based solely on the judge's determination of the child's best interests.

Turning to the facts of this case, the record reveals that the Superior Court's order was based on precisely the type of mere disagreement we have just described and nothing more. The Superior Court's order was not founded on any special factors that might justify the State's interference with Granville's fundamental right to make decisions concerning the rearing of her two daughters. To be sure, this case involves a visitation petition filed by grandparents soon after the death of their son—the father of Isabelle and Natalie—but the combination of several factors here compels our conclusion that *the Washington law,* as applied, exceeded the bounds of the Due Process Clause.

First, the Troxels did not allege, and no court has found, that Granville was an unfit parent. That aspect of the case is important, for there is a presumption that fit parents act in the best interests of their children. As this Court explained in *Parham*:

> "Our constitutional system long ago rejected any notion that a child is the mere creature of the State and, on the contrary, asserted that parents generally have the right, coupled with the high duty, to recognize and prepare [their children] for additional obligations. . . . The law's concept of the family rests on a presumption that parents possess what a child lacks in maturity, experience, and capacity for judgment required for making life's difficult decisions. More important, historically it has recognized that natural bonds of affection lead parents to act in the best interests of their children."

Accordingly, so long as a parent adequately cares for his or her children (i.e., is fit), there will normally be no reason for the State to inject itself into the private realm of the family to further question the ability of that parent to make the best decisions concerning the rearing of that parent's children.

The problem here is not that the Washington Superior Court intervened, but that when it did so, it gave no special weight at all to Granville's determination of her daughters' best interests. More importantly, it appears that the Superior Court applied exactly the opposite presumption. In reciting its oral ruling after the conclusion of closing arguments, the Superior Court judge explained:

> "The burden is to show that it is in the best interest of the children to have some visitation and some quality time with their grandparents. I think in most situations a commonsensical approach [is that] it is normally in the best interest of the children to spend quality time with the grandparent, unless the grandparent, *[sic]* there are some issues or problems involved wherein the grandparents, their lifestyles are going to impact adversely upon the children. That certainly isn't the case here from what I can tell."

The judge's comments suggest that he presumed the grandparents' request should be granted unless the children would be "impacted adversely." In effect, the judge placed on Granville, the fit custodial parent, the burden of *disproving* that visitation would be in the best interest of her daughters. The judge reiterated moments later: "I think [visitation with the Troxels] would be in the best interest of the children and I haven't been shown it is not in [the] best interest of the children."

The decisional framework employed by the Superior Court directly contravened the traditional presumption that a fit parent will act in the best interest of his or her child. In that respect, the court's presumption failed to provide any protection for Granville's fundamental constitutional right to make decisions concerning the rearing of her own daughters. In an ideal world, parents might always seek to cultivate the bonds between grandparents and their grandchildren. Needless to say, however, our world is far from perfect, and in it, the decision whether such an intergenerational relationship would be beneficial in any specific case is for the parent to make in the first instance. And, if a fit parent's decision of the kind at issue here becomes subject to judicial review, the court must accord at least some special weight to the parent's own determination. . . .

Considered together with the Superior Court's reasons for awarding visitation to the Troxels, the combination of these factors demonstrates that the visitation order in this case was an unconstitutional infringement on Granville's fundamental right to make decisions concerning the care, custody, and control of her two daughters. . . .

EXPLORING THE ISSUE

Should Grandparents Have Visitation Rights for Their Grandchildren?

Critical Thinking and Reflection

- What are some arguments made by each side with which you agree or disagree?
- What are the strengths and weaknesses of the two positions made in this chapter?
- Compare and contrast the competing arguments made for parents' rights versus grandparents' rights. Which legal arguments are stronger? How does this fit with your views of what is morally right and morally wrong?
- Think more broadly about the role of child visitation and custody rights. While this chapter focuses on the rights of parents versus the rights of grandparents, this chapter also raises an important question: what is in the best interest of children?

Is There Common Ground?

Many believe that parents should play the primary role in raising their children, while also acknowledging the critical role of extended family, particularly grandparents, in child rearing. How do we determine the right balance when there are disputes within families? Almost everyone would agree that they want to do what is best for the children, yet so often that can get lost in the competing needs and rights of parents and grandparents. While this chapter focuses on different court cases, most would agree that regardless of the verdict, everyone is harmed if we get to the point that we drag a family through court. What are some ways to find peace through this conflict without subjecting the family, and particularly the children, to a drawn-out court battle?

Additional Resources

The following Web sites are resources for grandparents' rights:

http://www.grandparents.com/gp/content/expert-advice/legal/article/
dograndparentshavetherightstheyshould.html

http://www.grandparentsrights.org/

http://www.caringgrandparents.com/

http://family-law.freeadvice.com/family-law/child_custody/grandparents_
visitation_rights.htm

ISSUE 8

Should Courts Be Able to Discriminate Against Immigrant Fathers?

YES: Neal Kumar Katyal et al., from "On Writ of Certiorari: Brief for the United States," *Ruben Flores-Villar v. United States of America*, 2010.

NO: Steven F. Hubachek et al., from "On Writ of Certiorari: Brief for Petitioner," *Ruben Flores-Villar v. United States of America*, 2010.

Learning Outcomes

As a result of this issue, readers should be able to:

- Identify basic arguments made for and against holding fathers to a different standard than mothers involving the citizenship of their children.
- Compare and contrast the competing arguments regarding the role of gender equality when examining the citizenship of immigrants' children.
- Evaluate the implications of this policy on immigrants and U.S. society.

ISSUE SUMMARY

YES: Neal Kumar Katyal served as Acting Solicitor General in the Obama administration at the time of this case. Katyal argues that Congress created legislation with a different standard of citizenship for biological fathers versus biological mothers and that this different standard served a rational interest and should be upheld.

NO: Steven Hubachek is the Counsel of Record for the Federal Defenders of San Diego, Inc. Hubachek argues that this law discriminates against men because it makes it more difficult for immigrant fathers to pass on their citizenship to their children than for immigrant mothers.

Generally speaking, the law prohibits discrimination on the basis of a person's biological sex. Despite this fact, there are longstanding beliefs that women are more nurturing than men. Some people take an essentialist perspective and say that this is how women have always been for innate reasons. Others take a social constructionist perspective and argue that women are seen as more nurturing due to how females are raised and the social constructions of gender roles. Divorce courts traditionally have difficulty in determining child custody, and some argue that mothers are placed at an unfair advantage. In fact, many fathers' rights groups will strenuously argue that courts discriminate against fathers on a decision-by-decision basis. They argue that the anti-father bias in society and reflected in our courts is damaging not only to fathers but also to children. Of course, this view is not shared by all. Others argue that courts are looking for what is in the best interest of the children rather than what is in the best interest of the father.

The U.S. Constitution provides certain protections from being discriminated against due to a person's sex. As a result, many laws, including our court system in most divorce cases, are expected to approach the topic of divorce from a gender-neutral standpoint. The question of this issue, however, is what happens when contemporary views of sex and gender are interjected with views about immigration and naturalization. Does determining citizenship merit a different standard for immigrant citizens versus natural-born citizens? According to the U.S. government, the answer to that question is yes.

There are some cases in which treating people differently based on their biological sex is required by law. Specifically, courts are instructed to treat immigrant fathers differently from how they would treat immigrant mothers, with fathers held to a higher standard in order for their children to have U.S. citizenship when they are born outside the United States. For this reason, it is important to examine this issue not just from a perspective of biological sex, but also immigration. According to the U.S. Census Bureau, during 2009 there were 38.5 million people living in the United States, which represents 12.5 percent of the population. Most of these foreign-born residents are here on legal visas or are naturalized citizens. Of the 38.5 million foreign-born population, it is estimated that approximately 12 million are neither naturalized citizens nor here on a valid visa, often referred to as undocumented immigrants or illegal immigrants. Immigration was at its height between the late 1800s and early 1900s, when foreign-born residents accounted for 13–15 percent of the entire U.S. population. The average American tends to believe in and expect equal treatment under the law for men and women alike. In the case of immigration and citizenship, many are surprised to learn that this is not the case. Indeed, citizenship is far more complex than many realize. The most simple rule of citizenship is the one with which people are most familiar: all persons born in the United States are citizens of the United States. What happens if your parent is a naturalized U.S. citizen, but you are born outside the United States and you are born out of wedlock? This is where the law particularly becomes more complicated and varied. If you are born out of wedlock to a mother who is a naturalized U.S. citizen, there is one criterion to meet: she must have resided in the United States for one year prior to the birth of the child. Today, if you are born out of wedlock to a father who is a naturalized U.S. citizen, the following must be proven:

- He lived in the United States for at least ten years prior to the birth of the child.
- Five of the ten years must have occurred after turning 14 years old.

Many fathers' rights groups and others complain that courts are systematically discriminatory toward men by assuming that women play a primary role in child rearing. They argue that this occurs for fathers who are U.S.-born citizens. Although this is an area of debate in our society, here we have a statutory law that holds children of undocumented immigrants to a different standard depending on whether it is a father or a mother who is a U.S. citizen. When discussing immigration, are you surprised to see why there might be different criteria for fathers and mothers? What are some reasons that you think people might support different treatment based on gender? What are some reasons that you think people might oppose different treatment based on gender? This is a way in which U.S. law unequivocally creates a different standard for males than for females. Although the U.S. Constitution does not contain an Equal Rights Amendment that would prohibit discrimination based on biological sex, it does contain an Equal Protection Clause in the Fourteenth Amendment, which states that the government cannot "deny to any person within its jurisdiction equal protection under the law." This amendment was passed after the Civil War, so there is some debate about how it should be interpreted. Most would agree that it should provide equal protection if one is discriminated against due to race, as that was the intent when it was passed. If they are discriminated against due to their biological sex, however, there is less agreement. Generally speaking, the courts extend protection if discrimination is based on biological sex, but it is a lower level of protection than would be extended based on race. This issue contains excerpts from a court case on this matter. Here we see the U.S. government making its case for immigration policy, as well as those supportive of immigrant rights making the case for those adversely affected by this law. This raises questions regarding why there should be a different standard in the cases of immigrant parents. Is there a compelling state interest to hold different standards based on the biological sex of the parent? Or does this have more to do with immigration and border control?

YES

Neal Kumar Katyal et al.

On Writ of Certiorari: Brief for the United States

In order for a United States citizen who has a child abroad with a non–United States citizen to transmit his or her citizenship to the foreign-born child, the U.S. citizen parent must have been physically present in the United States for a particular period of time prior to the child's birth. The question presented is: Whether Congress's decision to impose a shorter physical-presence requirement on unwed citizen mothers of foreign-born children than on other parents of foreignborn children through [the law] (1970) violates the Fifth Amendment's guarantee of equal protection.

Article I of the United States Constitution assigns to Congress the "Power To establish an uniform Rule of Naturalization throughout the United States." [The] U.S. Const. Art. I. Pursuant to that authority, Congress has elected to confer United States citizenship by statute on certain persons born outside the United States through various provisions in the Immigration and Nationality Act (INA). At the time of petitioner's birth in 1974, a child born outside the United States to married parents, only one of whom was a U.S. citizen, could acquire citizenship through his or her U.S. citizen parent if, before the child's birth, the citizen parent had been physically present in the United States for a total of ten years, at least five of which were after the parent had turned fourteen years of age. The same physical-presence requirement applied if the child was born out of wedlock and the father was a U.S. citizen (and if the paternity was established through legitimation while the child was under age 21). If, however, the child was born out of wedlock outside the United States and only his mother was a U.S. citizen, [the law] transmits U.S. citizenship to the child if the mother was a citizen of the United States at the time of the child's birth and had been physically present in the United States before the child's birth for a continuous period of at least one year.

In 1974, petitioner was born in Tijuana, Mexico, to unmarried parents. His mother is a citizen and national of Mexico, and his father, who was 16 years old at the time of petitioner's birth, is a U.S. citizen who resided in the United States for much of his life. Although petitioner's father was a U.S. citizen from birth, petitioner's father did not obtain formal documentation of that fact until May 24, 1999 (almost 25 years after petitioner was born), when he was issued a certificate of citizenship upon his own application. Petitioner's father was confirmed as a citizen from birth based on the fact that his mother— petitioner's paternal grandmother—was a U.S. citizen by birth in the United States, and

Supreme Court of the United States, 2010.

met the requirements of [the law] to transmit citizenship to her out-of-wedlock child (petitioner's father) at the time of his birth. It is not clear that petitioner's father was aware of his U.S. citizenship prior to adulthood.

When petitioner was two months old, his father and paternal grandmother brought him to the United States to receive medical treatment. After petitioner was released from the hospital, he lived with his father and grandmother in the San Diego area, where he grew up. Although petitioner's father is not listed on his birth certificate, in 1985 the father acknowledged petitioner as his son by filing an acknowledgment of paternity with the Civil Registry in Mexico.

On March 17, 1997, petitioner was convicted of importation of marijuana, in violation of [US law], and was sentenced to 24 months of imprisonment. After serving his sentence, petitioner was ordered removed from the United States, and he was removed on October 16, 1998. Petitioner repeatedly returned to the United States following removal, resulting in additional removal proceedings in 1999 (when he was twice deported) and again in 2002. In June 2003, following another illegal reentry, petitioner was convicted of two counts of illegal entry into the United States in violation of [the law], and was again removed in October 2003. Petitioner again reentered the United States illegally and was once again removed in March 2005, after which he yet again unlawfully returned to the United States.

On February 24, 2006, petitioner was arrested and charged with being a deported alien found in the United States after deportation, in violation of [U.S. law]. Petitioner has since served his sentence and been released under supervision and then deported. The completion of petitioner's sentence and his deportation do not, however, render the present proceeding moot. After his indictment, petitioner filed an application for a certificate of citizenship with the Department of Homeland Security (DHS). DHS denied petitioner's application (and his administrative appeal) because it was physically impossible for petitioner's father, who was 16 years old when petitioner was born, to have been present in the United States for five years after his fourteenth birthday, but prior to petitioner's birth, in order for him to transmit U.S. citizenship to petitioner.

The government filed a motion in limine in petitioner's illegal-reentry prosecution to exclude evidence of petitioner's purported citizenship because petitioner did not qualify for citizenship under the [law]. The district court granted the motion after concluding that no reasonable juror could find that petitioner's father satisfied the transmission-of-citizenship requirements of the [law]. The district court also rejected petitioner's equal protection challenge to application of the physical-presence requirements to his father. Following a bench trial on stipulated facts, petitioner was convicted of violating [US law] by illegally entering the United States without permission after having been removed. He was sentenced to 42 months of imprisonment.

On appeal, petitioner reasserted his contention that the versions of Sections 1401(a)(7) and 1409 applicable at the time of his birth violated the equal protection component of the Fifth Amendment's Due Process Clause because they required a U.S. citizen father of a child born abroad out of wedlock to have been physically present in the United States for a total of at least five years following his fourteenth birthday in order to transmit his citizenship to his child, while a U.S. citizen mother in such a situation need only have been physically present in the United States for a continuous period of one year. The court of appeals rejected petitioner's contention and affirmed his conviction. The court concluded that the answer to petitioner's equal protection argument "follows from the Supreme Court's opinion in *Nguyen v. INS*." In *Nguyen*, this Court held that [the law] does not discriminate on the basis of gender in violation of equal protection principles by requiring a citizen father—but not a citizen mother—to take steps to establish his connection (through legitimation, adjudication, or acknowledgment) to a child born out of wedlock outside the United States before he can transmit U.S. citizenship to the child.

Assuming that intermediate scrutiny applies to petitioner's equal protection challenge, the court of appeals determined that, "[a]lthough the means at issue are different in this case—an additional residence requirement for the unwed citizen father—the government's interests are no less important, and the particular means no less substantially related to those objectives, than in *Nguyen*." The court reasoned that applying different physical-presence requirements to unwed citizen mothers and fathers was substantially related to the important government interests in minimizing the risk of statelessness of foreign-born children and in "assuring a link between an unwed citizen father, and this country, to" the child. The court relied on its analysis in *Runnett v. Shultz*, (9th Cir. 1990), in which it observed that "illegitimate children are more likely to be 'stateless' at birth" because "if the U.S. citizen mother is not a dual national, and the illegitimate child is born in a country that does not recognize citizenship by *jus soli* (citizenship determined by place of birth), the child can acquire no citizenship other than his mother's at birth." The court found that concern about statelessness justified a shorter physical-presence requirement for mothers of out-of-wedlock children to "insure that the child will have a nationality at birth." The Court acknowledged that the "fit" between the means and the objectives was "not perfect," but found it "sufficiently persuasive in light of the virtually plenary power that Congress has to legislate in the area of immigration and citizenship."

Summary of Argument

Pursuant to its authority under Article I of the Constitution, Congress has enacted comprehensive rules governing immigration and naturalization. One subset of those rules governs the acquisition of citizenship by children born abroad to U.S. citizen parents. When a U.S. citizen has a child abroad with a non-citizen, Congress requires that the U.S. citizen parent have satisfied a physical-presence requirement prior to the child's birth before the parent may transmit his or her citizenship to the child as of birth. That requirement applies to married fathers and married mothers—and it applies to unmarried fathers such as petitioner's. In an effort to reduce the number of children who may be born stateless, Congress has applied a shorter physical-presence requirement to unmarried U.S. citizen mothers who give birth abroad. Such physical-presence requirements on the U.S. citizen parents of children born abroad ensure that foreign-born children will have sufficient connections to the United States to merit citizenship, and this Court has long upheld Congress's decision to require such a connection.

Petitioner asserts an equal protection challenge to this statutory framework on behalf of his father. But petitioner's father has never asserted such a claim on his own behalf, and petitioner cannot demonstrate any hindrance to his father's having done so. Petitioner therefore lacks third-party standing to assert his father's equal protection claim.

Congress's choice of rules governing naturalization is entitled to deference by this Court and is subject to review under rational basis standards. But even if heightened review is applied to the equal protection challenge asserted here on behalf of petitioner's father, the statutory provisions are constitutional. There is no serious dispute that reducing the number of children born stateless is an important government objective. Congress chose to pursue that objective by applying a shorter physical-presence requirement to unwed U.S. citizen mothers of foreign-born children than to other U.S. citizen parents. That statutory scheme is constitutionally permissible because it is substantially related to the government's important interest.

As Congress knew, most countries apply *jus sanguinis* citizenship laws, pursuant to which a child's citizenship is determined at birth through his blood relationship to a parent rather than with reference to his place of birth. In most of those countries—as indeed in most *jus soli* countries such as the United States—the only parental relationship that is legally recognized or formalized at birth for a child born out of wedlock is usually that of his mother. Thus, at birth, the child's only means of taking citizenship is through his mother. Although such a child's father may subsequently take actions to establish a legally recognized parental relationship, there is no guarantee that he will ever do so. Because impediments to an unwed mother's ability to transmit her citizenship to a child at birth create a substantially higher risk that a child will be born stateless, Congress eased the requirements for acquisition of U.S. citizenship by the children of those mothers.

The fact that Congress did not eliminate the possibility that any foreign-born child of a U.S. citizen parent would be stateless, either at birth or at some point later in his life, does not render its chosen framework unconstitutional. No foreign-born person has a free-standing constitutional right to U.S. citizenship, and no U.S. citizen has a free-standing right to transmit his or her citizenship to a foreign-born child. Congress balances competing interests in enacting laws governing naturalization. The carefully measured rules Congress enacted serve the important governmental interest in ensuring that children born abroad have sufficient ties to this country to merit citizenship and the interest in reducing statelessness—and consequently do not violate equal protection.

Even if this Court were to determine that the differing physical-presence requirements in [the law] violated equal protection, petitioner is not entitled to the relief he seeks, namely a reversal of his criminal conviction based on a determination that he has been a citizen from birth. The fact that Congress chose to apply the more stringent physical-presence requirements in [the law] to a substantial majority of U.S. citizen parents of foreign-born children, the need to preserve necessary flexibility for Congress, as well as adherence to this Court's longstanding treatment of naturalization requirements lead to the conclusion that the proper way to cure any equal protection violation would be to apply the longer physical-presence requirements in [the law], on a prospective basis, to unwed citizen mothers. Petitioner's suggestions that the Court either extend the shorter physical-presence requirement in [the law] to unmarried fathers (but not to married parents of either gender) or retain the unequal treatment but reduce the length of the physical-presence requirement applicable to unmarried men make little sense and could foreclose future revision by Congress. Equalizing the treatment of all citizen parents of foreign-born children as suggested here would eliminate any equal protection problem and most faithfully preserve Congress's policy choices.

Argument

Petitioner Lacks Standing to Assert the Equal Protection Rights of his Father

Petitioner has not suffered any differential treatment by virtue of his own gender. Petitioner's equal protection complaint instead is that his father is treated less favorably than a U.S. citizen mother with respect to the ability to transmit U.S. citizenship to a child born abroad out of wedlock. That claim is properly raised by petitioner's father, who is the subject of the allegedly unconstitutional differential treatment.

This Court has held that a party ordinarily "cannot rest his claim to relief on the legal rights or interests of third parties." In such a case, a litigant may not assert the constitutional rights of an absent third party unless the litigant has a "close relation" to the party whose rights are asserted, and there is "some hindrance to the third party's ability to protect his or her own interests." Those restrictions "arise from the understanding that the third-party right holder may not, in fact, wish to assert the claim in question, as well as from the belief that 'third parties themselves usually will be the best proponents of their rights.'"

Although we may assume that petitioner has a close relationship with his father, petitioner cannot satisfy this Court's limits on *jus tertii* standing because, as the court of appeals found, "the record discloses no obstacle that would prevent [petitioner's father] from asserting his own constitutional rights." It is true that petitioner's father is not entitled to intervene in petitioner's criminal case in order to assert his equal protection challenge; but the inquiry is not whether a third party may assert his own rights in this particular case, but whether he may effectively assert them at all. Petitioner has not demonstrated any "daunting" or "considerable practical" barriers— or indeed, any barriers at all—to his father's protection of his own rights if he chose to do so.

Shortly after petitioner's birth in 1974, his father brought him to the United States to receive medical care. After his release from the hospital, petitioner lived with his father and paternal grandmother near San Diego. J.A.

Although petitioner's father formally acknowledged his paternity in 1985 in Mexico, he took no steps to have petitioner declared a U.S. citizen. Petitioner's father did not, for example, apply for a certificate of citizenship on behalf of petitioner when petitioner was a minor. If that application was turned down, petitioner's father could have brought an action on petitioner's behalf challenging that denial under [the law], and raising the claim that his inability to transmit citizenship to petitioner violated his Fifth Amendment rights. Nor did petitioner's father ever apply to have petitioner naturalized when petitioner was a child (father initially filed suit with foreign-born child seeking such a declaration).

Petitioner offers no justification for his father's failure to assert his equal protection claim by bringing his own action. It is true that petitioner's father did not himself obtain a certificate of citizenship until 1999, when petitioner was already 24 years old. But petitioner's father was automatically a citizen at birth by virtue of his mother's citizenship, and his ignorance of that fact does not constitute the type of hindrance to assertion of his own rights that would confer on petitioner third-party standing to raise those rights.

Moreover, once petitioner became an adult, petitioner's father could have joined an equal protection claim a later suit by petitioner himself under [the law], following a denial of an application by petitioner for such a certificate (father asserted claim under the Fifth Amendment by participating in child's petition for judicial review of removal order). Petitioner is correct that a majority of the Court in *Miller* found that the petitioner in that case had third-party standing to assert her citizen father's equal protection rights. But that finding in *Miller* was based on the existence of an actual hindrance to the citizen father's demonstrated efforts to pursue his equal protection claim. In *Miller*, the petitioner and her father had together sought a declaration that the father's inability to transmit citizenship to his foreign born daughter violated the Fifth Amendment. At the government's urging, the district court had dismissed the petitioner's father from the suit and the father had failed to appeal that ruling. The Court concluded that, under those circumstances, the right-holder (the petitioner's father) faced a sufficient barrier to the actual assertion of his rights to confer third-party standing on his daughter.

That holding does not apply to petitioner in this case, however, because two crucial elements are missing: (1) unlike petitioner's father, the father in *Miller* had in fact taken steps to attempt to assert his equal protection rights; and (2) the father in *Miller* was prevented through dismissal from the suit from pursuing vindication of his rights, while no obstacle prevented petitioner's father from pursuing those rights in the proper manner. "Here, although we have an injured party before us, the party actually discriminated against is both best suited to challenging the statute and available to undertake that task." Petitioner has failed to demonstrate that his father is unable "to advance his own rights," because of a "genuine obstacle" that rises to the level of a hindrance.

 **NO**

On Writ of Certiorari: Brief for Petitioner

Petitioner, Ruben Flores-Villar, was born out of wedlock on October 7, 1974, in Tijuana, Mexico. His father, Ruben Trinidad Floresvillar, was then a 16-year-old U.S. citizen. Although he would have testified at trial that he resided in the United States for at least ten years before [his son's] birth, he was too young to have five years' presence after turning 14 as required for transmission of citizenship.

When two months old, [the] father and paternal grandmother brought him into the United States for medical treatment. Thereafter, the hospital sent, on Petitioner's father's behalf, a letter to border authorities requesting a permit for Petitioner to enter the United States. Petitioner's mother authorized his release from the hospital to his paternal grandmother for adoption planning. Although Petitioner was not adopted, his mother took no part in his upbringing.

Petitioner grew up in San Diego county with his father, attending local schools. Petitioner's father formally recognized him by filing a paternity acknowledgment in the Tijuana civil registry in 1985, when Petitioner was 11, and claimed Petitioner as his son on his United States income taxes.

In 2006, Petitioner was indicted for being a deported alien found in the United States, in violation of [U.S. law]. On September 22, 2006, Petitioner filed an application seeking a Certificate of Citizenship. Petitioner's father and paternal grandmother submitted supporting declarations. *Id.* 84-90. On December 14, 2006, his application was denied:

> The fact of your legitimation is not in question. . . . Since your father was only sixteen at the time of your birth, it is physically impossible for him to have [the] required physical presence necessary (five years after age fourteen) in order for you to acquire United States citizenship through him.

Petitioner nonetheless sought to defend by contending that he is a citizen. The government moved to preclude the defense. Petitioner responded that the statutory scheme in place at his birth violated the Fifth Amendment's equal protection guarantee. Petitioner sought a jury instruction applying the shorter physical presence requirement to his father. His father would have testified in

Supreme Court of the United States, 2010.

Petitioner's defense, but the district court precluded the testimony. The district court found Petitioner guilty and sentenced him to 42 months' custody.

Since 1940, citizen fathers, but not citizen mothers, have been required to meet a lengthy residency requirement before transmitting citizenship to their foreign-born, non-marital children. The 1952 Act, effective at Petitioner's birth, perpetuated the discrimination, maintaining a physical presence requirement under which men below age 19 could not transmit citizenship. Age never prevented transmission of citizenship to a woman's non-marital child.

Because this statutory scheme discriminates against fathers of non-marital children based on gender, it denies equal protection. Intermediate scrutiny is warranted because of our Nation's history of sex discrimination in laws governing transmission of citizenship, and the significance of citizens' interest in transmitting citizenship to their children. The "plenary power" doctrine, which the Court has applied in the context of the entry of aliens into the United States, does not warrant some lesser standard of scrutiny, because acquisition of citizenship at birth is fundamentally different from the immigration or naturalization of an alien. Further, even if the plenary power doctrine applies, the classification of a congressional power as "plenary" does not exempt congressional action in that area from constitutional scrutiny.

Regardless, the discriminatory scheme at issue survives neither intermediate scrutiny nor rational basis review. While the government has consistently contended that Congress adopted the discriminatory, sex-based residence requirements to avoid statelessness of non-marital children of U.S. citizen mothers, it has not met its burden to demonstrate that avoiding statelessness was the actual purpose of the discriminatory residency requirements. Moreover, the risk of statelessness applies to the non-marital children of U.S. citizen mothers *and* fathers. The discriminatory scheme actually creates new risks of statelessness for non-marital children of U.S. fathers. Thus, the "statelessness" rationale cannot justify the discrimination under any standard.

Nguyen v. INS (2001) is not to the contrary. *Nguyen* approved distinctions that were biologically based: by delivering a child, a woman necessarily had strong evidence of parentage and at least an opportunity to form a relationship with the child. By requiring the father to take a formal act prior to the child's 18th birthday, the statutory scheme provided the evidence and opportunity that biology had guaranteed the mother. The residence requirements posed by the instant scheme have no biological basis: there is no reason to believe that mothers are more adept at forming ties to the United States than are fathers or that fathers' non-marital children experience statelessness in any different way.

The denial of equal protection effected by gender discrimination can and should be fully remedied by extension of the benefit offered by [the law]—the limited residence requirement—to both men and women. Extension of benefits is a traditional remedy for equal protection violations and is supported by the INA's severability provision.

Alternatively, severance of the application of former section 1401(g)'s requirement of 5 years' residence in the United States after age 14, which disables some younger men, but not younger women, from transmitting citizenship to their non-marital children, could partially remedy the discrimination against Petitioner's father such that Petitioner could at least offer evidence of his father's 10-year U.S. residence at trial. Even if the equal protection violation cannot be remedied by a grant of citizenship, the government nonetheless should be estopped from invoking that unconstitutional scheme to support a criminal conviction.

Finally, Petitioner meets the requirements of third-party standing to litigate the gender discrimination against his father in defending against this government-initiated prosecution.

The Statutory Scheme for Acquisition of Citizenship by Non-Marital, Foreign-Born Children Discriminates Based on Gender

Since 1940, citizen fathers, but not citizen mothers, have been required to meet a lengthy residency requirement before transmitting citizenship to their foreign-born, non-marital children. The 1940 Act required an unwed citizen father to demonstrate ten years' physical presence in the United States prior to the child's birth, five of which had to be after the age of sixteen. Fathers under age 21 could not transmit citizenship. Prior residence of any length was sufficient for women. The 1952 Act, in effect at Petitioner's birth, perpetuated the discrimination, maintaining the ten years' physical presence requirement, before the nonmarital child's birth, five of which had to be after age 14. Men under 19 were disabled from transmitting citizenship. For women, the law required only one year's residence prior to the non-marital child's birth. A woman's age never prevented transmission of citizenship to her non-marital child.

Petitioner was born out of wedlock, in Mexico, to a U.S. citizen father and an alien mother. Although his father legitimated and raised him in the United States from infancy, the district court precluded Petitioner's citizenship defense because his father's age at Petitioner's birth, 16, made it impossible to transmit citizenship. Because the statutory scheme discriminates against fathers of non-marital children by imposing a differential residence requirement based on gender, it denies equal protection.

The 1940 Act Allowed Women Freely to Transmit Citizenship to Non-Marital Children, but Created New Barriers to Transmission of Citizenship to Legitimated Children by Men

Explicitly addressing non-marital children for the first time, Congress adopted [the law], which provided that men could transmit citizenship after satisfying an age-calibrated, 10-year residence requirement and upon legitimation of the child during the child's minority. As to women, [the law] provided that, absent legitimation, her non-marital child would be a U.S. citizen if she "had the nationality of the United States at the time of the child's birth, and had previously resided in the United States or one of the outlying possessions."

The framework established in the 1940 Act remains in place today, albeit with a less onerous residence requirement.

Commentary published before passage of the 1940 Act suggested the non-marital, foreign-born children of both men *and* women were at risk of statelessness. If Congress had sought to alleviate concerns that the non-marital children of female U.S. citizens would be stateless, it accomplished that by providing for U.S. nationality for the non-marital children of women subject to a modest pre-birth residence requirement, of any length, in the United States. Current law reduces the residence requirement applicable to men to 5 years and imposes a one-year requirement on women. The requirement of pre-birth residence vindicates a well-established Congressional goal of ensuring that citizenship not pass through generations of expatriate citizens living outside the United States for their entire lives.

But the 1940 Act's discriminatory residence requirements lead to very different results as to the children of U.S. citizen fathers, exposing many children of U.S. fathers to risks of statelessness and discouraging such fathers from legitimating their offspring. Congress would have been aware of a significant risk of statelessness on the part of the foreign-born, non-marital children of U.S. citizen fathers, as the Attorney General had suggested that such children were not citizens even when legitimated. "If, in these cases, the country of birth adhered strictly to the principle of *jus sanguinis* in determining nationality, these children had no effective citizenship, unless it was acquired through the mother."

In stark contrast to its solicitousness as to the children of U.S. citizen mothers, Congress's response to this grave risk was to limit severely the ability of fathers to transmit citizenship to non-marital children, requiring lengthy residence (10 years) in the United States for legitimated children and making no provision for non-legitimated children. The incongruity of this approach is illustrated by the study cited to Congress in support of the proposed legislation.

> [T]he Department of State has for a long time followed the rule that an illegitimate child follows the nationality of the mother, in the absence of legitimation according to law by the father. It is significant to observe that the same *lacuna* exists in the statutory law of about half the states studied.

"The majority rule with respect to legal recognition or legitimation is that the child takes the father's nationality."). Thus, as of 1940, many states attributed the mother's nationality to the non-marital child *unless* the father legitimated the child. The legitimated, non-marital children of U.S. fathers therefore faced the prospect of being denied the nationalities of their mothers by virtue of legitimation, leaving them dependent upon their U.S. citizen fathers to provide nationality.

The State Department's witness at the hearings on the proposed code identified a number of countries in which legitimation deprived a child of her mother's nationality. In Iraq, citizenship could not be acquired through the mother, although a child born in Iraq whose father was ordinarily resident in

Iraq at the time of the child's birth could opt for Iraqi citizenship upon attaining his majority (provided the child had not already acquired the nationality of a foreign country). In the Netherlands, a child could only acquire citizenship through the mother if "the child [was] born outside of wedlock [and] acknowledged only by the mother, provided that the mother, at the time of the birth, had the status of a Dutch national . . ." In other countries, such as Japan and Monaco, a child born out of wedlock would only obtain the mother's nationality if the mother acknowledged the child before the father (or in Japan, if the father was unknown or had no nationality). In Jordan, the risk of statelessness would exist regardless of legitimation because citizenship is derived only through the father.

The Congressional scheme, however, would often make it impossible for those fathers to fulfill that need.

By requiring 10 years of residence, Congress created a serious risk that non-marital, legitimated children of U.S. citizen fathers would be rendered stateless unless the father met a stringent residence requirement that no mother of a non-marital child was obliged to satisfy. Moreover, Congress made it impossible, not merely difficult, for a non-marital, legitimated child born to a U.S. citizen father under age 21 to claim U.S. citizenship as of birth because at least 5 of the 10 years' residence in the United States must take place after age 16.

Indeed, a U.S. citizen father who could not meet the residence requirements would be forced to consider carefully whether legitimation was in his child's interest, inasmuch as formal legitimation—even marriage to the child's mother—might result in statelessness, because a claim to the mother's nationality could be extinguished while at the same time no claim to U.S. citizenship would be possible. Children who were not legitimated, of course, would be able to claim the mother's nationality in approximately half the states that Sandifer surveyed. Thus, Congress both visited statelessness upon many legitimated children of U.S. citizen fathers and perversely gave U.S. citizens who fathered non-marital children strong incentives not to legitimate their children.

The government conceded that rules denying citizenship to many legitimated, non-marital children of U.S. citizen fathers create a grave risk of statelessness, acknowledging that, under the 1940 scheme, "[t]here would be a parallel problem of statelessness in the case of children who lost their mother's foreign citizenship due to legitimation by their United States citizen father." Indeed, the government conceded that the risk of statelessness persists today, acknowledging in 2000 that "it remains the case that children born out of wedlock generally are recognized to have the citizenship of the mother *unless and until* legitimated or formally acknowledged by the father." Thus, even today, U.S. citizen fathers who responsibly fulfill their obligations to their non-marital children run the risk of rendering those children stateless if the father cannot meet a residence requirement that is not imposed upon mothers of non-marital children.

Even if statelessness concerns prompted differential residence requirements, concerns that the children of U.S. mothers might be stateless in no way justifies disabling a class of U.S. fathers—those under 21 under the 1940

Act and those under 19 under the 1952 Act—from transmitting citizenship to their legitimated children. No class of U.S. citizen mothers is so disabled from ensuring that her non-marital child has a nationality.

Thus, Congress in 1940 was faced with challenges to practices under which both the non-marital, foreign-born children of women and legitimated children of men had claims to U.S. citizenship. Congress codified the practice as to women bearing non-marital children, but adopted a discriminatory scheme that offered narrow protection to fathers. It exposed citizen-fathers' non-marital children to risks of statelessness if the fathers were younger, or could not meet a 10-year residence requirement, or had not legitimated their children. The 1940 Act therefore tolerated substantial risks of statelessness as to non-marital children of men.

EXPLORING THE ISSUE

Should Courts Be Able to Discriminate Against Immigrant Fathers?

Critical Thinking and Reflection

- What are some arguments made by each side with which you agree or disagree?
- What are the strengths and weaknesses of the two positions made in this issue?
- This issue focuses on what is legal. In some cases, a person's morals may be in contradiction to the law. How do legal rights in this case relate to what you feel is morally right or morally wrong?
- Think more broadly about the role of immigration, both legal and illegal, in the United States today. Considering the ruling in this case, what remedies would be best for the creation of a policy for citizenship for immigrants' children that is in the best interest of the United States?

Is There Common Ground?

The vast majority of people would agree that children of U.S. citizens should themselves be citizens. Conversely, the vast majority would agree that the United States has a right and an obligation to create a system of immigration that is best for the nation's long-term goals. The challenges arise in determining how to balance these competing values and interests. In order to meet this challenge, the following questions must be addressed: What are the rights of naturalized immigrant fathers? What are the rights of naturalized immigrant mothers? What is necessary to ensure the best interest of the United States?

Additional Resources

The American Civil Liberties Union on immigrant rights:

http://www.aclu.org/immigrants-rights

Taking action on immigration reform through Change.org:

http://immigration.change.org/

National Network for Immigration and Refugee Rights:

http://www.nnirr.org/

End Illegal Immigration works to stop undocumented immigration:

http://www.endillegalimmigration.com/

Conservative USA calls to stop illegal immigration immediately:

http://www.conservativeusa.org/immigration.htm

ISSUE 9

Do Parents Have the Right to Deny Their Children Lifesaving Medical Care Due to Their Religious Convictions?

YES: Calvin P. Johnson Law Firm, from "Closing Statement for Parents: In Re the Matter of the Welfare of the Child of Colleen and Anthony Hauser," Minnesota, District Court, Fifth Judicial District (2009)

NO: John R. Rodenberg, from "Opinion of the Court: In the Matter of the Welfare of the Child of Colleen and Anthony Hauser,"Minnesota, District Court, Fifth Judicial District (2009)

Learning Outcomes

As a result of this issue, readers will be able to:

- Identify the major arguments made for and against parents denying their child lifesaving medical treatment.
- Compare and contrast the competing arguments made for and against parents denying their child lifesaving medical treatment in this chapter.
- Evaluate the implications of parents denying their child lifesaving medical treatment on children's health as well as religious liberty.

ISSUE SUMMARY

YES: Calvin P. Johnson, Esq., is the attorney for the parents, Colleen and Anthony Hauser. Johnson argues that the government forcing medical care for the Hauser child violates his religious liberty and is abusive to this child.

NO: Judge John R. Rodenberg is the District Court judge in this case. Rodenberg argues that all parties are acting out of convictions for the best interest of the child. He also argues that the state has a compelling interest to act against Hauser's religious views for medical care since the child is only thirteen years old.

The use of chemotherapy as a cancer treatment dates back to the early twentieth century. It was designed as the use of chemicals to treat disease. In 1935, the National Cancer Institute was set up and provided an organized system for screening drugs that treated cancer. However, the level of toxicity of the drugs proved to be a challenge for wider use of this treatment.

During World War II, it was noted that when troops were exposed to sulfur mustards due to an accidental spill, more purposeful research occurred to better understand the impact of these chemicals on things like cancer.

While initially highly controversial, attempts to treat cancer with chemotherapy would enjoy wide levels of support over the coming decades. Within the past couple of decades, it has become a highly regarded method for treating cancer.

Christian Scientists have received a considerable amount of attention for refusing medical care for themselves and their children, sometimes for even life-threatening illnesses such as cancer. Generally speaking, many Christian scientists are expected to heal themselves through prayer of minor sicknesses such as the cold and flu as well as life-threatening conditions such as cancer. However, if a child dies as a result of his or her parents denying their child lifesaving medical care, then the parents are sometimes charged and prosecuted.

Although Christian Scientists receive perhaps the highest profile for this belief, they are by no means the only religion that subscribes to such a belief. The Nemenhah and Indigenous Traditional Organization, also known as the Oklevueha Native American church of Nemenhah, was established by self-determination in 2002. They describe themselves as a "restoration of the Pre-Colonial and Pre-Conquest Nomadic Indigenous People which inhabited parts of Central America, North America, the Pacific Islands, Japan, Korea, China, and Tibet anciently." Their Web site states that they focus on "the Healing of the Body Physical, the Body Familial, the Body Societal and the Whole Earth." The Nemenhah are committed to natural healing.

The Nemenhah Constitution states the following:

- We believe in miracles, such as cures, healings, prophecies, visions . . . and that it is the right of all people to heal and be healed without restriction from any earthly government, for natural medicine and natural modalities of healing are gifts of the Creator.
- The Sacred Sahaptan Healing Way is that body of knowledge which is compiled into a uniform curriculum for the systematic training and education of the Medicine Men and Medicine Women of the Band. It is the criteria by which Band Adoption is entered into and the basis and foundation of this spiritual and physical ceremonies.
- Article Fifteen: The right of community members to choose their method and kind of medicine shall not be denied or abridged in any

way and the councils shall not enact any counsel that shall place one profession or modality of medicine over any other, except when such professions or modalities tend to render a person unable to earn a living, or when they threaten to do so.

Clearly, this religion possesses the basic tenet that they have their own rights to determine the best course for healing when sick. That course includes a denial of intervention for modern Western remedies.

The First Amendment to the U.S. Constitution says, "Congress shall make no law respecting an establishment of religion, or prohibiting the free exercise thereof." The First Amendment provides us with this right, known as the Free Exercise Clause, as one that is so important that it is often referred to as a fundamental right.

What sort of limitations do we place on fundamental rights? Should we allow human sacrifice? Use of drugs? Wearing a weapon such as a knife, which also has strong religious significance in some cultures, in schools? Opting out of a class at school because a child feels that it violates his or her religious convictions?

In short, we are attempting to determine when there is a compelling state interest to intervene. In the case of the Hausers, which is explored in this chapter, the question is how do we protect a child with cancer. The Hausers argued in court that they should be free to intervene as they wish with their son's cancer. Their son had Hodgkin's lymphoma. His story would generate national headlines.

Doctors argued that with proper medical treatment, Daniel had a 90% chance of survival. Without the treatment, he would have only a 5% chance of survival. The Hausers, who belong to the Nemenhah faith, believe that their son is a medicine man and can best determine his path in healing his body and spirit.

The judge ruled that Daniel had to get chemotherapy. As a result, Daniel's mother took him and fled.

Jeffrey Toobin, CNN senior legal analyst, says that the state must intervene: "Virtually all the time the court says that what this mother is doing, while we sympathize with her pain, this is child abuse. He is a minor. He is not qualified to make the decision for himself. This is what it means to be a minor: other people make your decisions for you. This is the same thing as if he got hit by a car, blocking the ambulance. If need be, they have to take the kid away, strap him down, and apply chemotherapy. . . . It's life or death."

After Daniel and his mother fled, Daniel was eventually returned after almost one week on the run. The parents consented to have their son undergo his chemotherapy treatment.

The doctors treating Daniel received mail from all over the country, ranging from those who believe in natural medicine to anti-abortion activists to conspiracy theorists. One opponent of the medical intervention created a Web site of a needle being injected into a monkey and said that doctors were "dripping poison into yet another child."

Daniel did not have a positive reaction to the chemotherapy, explained a family spokesman: "Danny has had a horrible day, he's felt terrible all day long. He's not happy. The doctor changed the number of chemotherapy drugs in the protocol submitted to the court. Danny is not tolerating the drugs well and has been vomiting all day. He is understandably angry and depressed about being forced to go through the ravages of chemotherapy again."

Daniel Hauser's lymphoma went into remission after his radiation treatment. Although his doctors credit the radiation, the Hausers credit Daniel's good diet.

In this issue, you have excerpts from the primary sources from the court case, representing both sides. You can determine the reasoning of the Hausers, as well as the court, in informing your decision.

YES

Closing Statement for Parents: In Re the Matter of the Welfare of the Child of Colleen and Anthony Hauser

Respondents, Colleen and Anthony Hauser, submit this legal memorandum in support of their closing arguments in this matter.

Thank you to all, with your words of encouragement. And thank you to those on the other side, for genuinely believing in their position.

Most importantly, I thank Danny Hauser, a true Medicine man. This thirteen-year-old young man has turned this community upside down and inside out. A world is listening.

I respectfully submit that he is one of the more powerful medicine men around.

Danny is a Medicine man by virtue of his ranking as a male in the family. That is contained in the Nemenhah Constitution that you could not understand. It is written in clear language.

This Court has always held, from day one, to the steadfast principle of protecting our children. We do not harm our children. We do not torture our children.

Yet the path advocated by the State is one of torture and criminal action.

There is a reason why 91% of the oncologists on staff at McGill Cancer Centre in Montreal do not take chemotherapy or allow their family members to take it for cancer treatment. It's too toxic, and not effective. This is exactly as the standard of medical care advocated and pronounced by Dr. Shealy.

This matter has been pummeled to death with the percentage of a 90% cure rate. And yet we come to find that a cure rate can be defined as "tumor shrinkage" but not the elimination of cancer, at all. In fact, given the statistics as provided to this Court, and demonstrated by a reputable, peer-reviewed, journal (*Clinical Oncology*, 2004; 16:549–560.), the real rate of survival hovers around 35–40%.

Apparently, if a study predicts a 6% success rate, and they achieve 12%, the cancer industry reports that as a 50% increase in their success rates. It is

United States District Court, Minnesota, Fifth Judicial District, 2009.

unconscionable that the absolute numbers were not given to the Hausers in this particular matter. It is unconscionable that the cancer industry would perpetrate a number that does not stand up to actual fact. And it is unconscionable that we had to enter into an emotional issue when the true issue is the care of a thirteen-year-old young man, and the ability of that young man and his parents to realistically assess their best survival rates from reputable, peer-reviewed medical journals, before making their decision.

To condense the posture of this case, it looks like this:

A doctor went to a state official and said we have a 90% chance that this young man is going to die if he does not use my product.

By legal definition, if you use the product, it constitutes felony assault, and may very well constitute torture, when you force the use of the product against the will of the victim.

It will seriously damage the largest component of this young man's body: his immune system.

It may kill him.

Without question, it will cause serious disfigurement, including the fact that there will probably be no progeny of this thirteen-year-old young man.

It will cost $92,900 just for the first round of chemotherapeutic agents and initial testing, and we will apply it five to six more times.

We cannot tell you the manner in which we can do this against the will of the child.

When we promise a 90% cure rate, that really only amounts to 40.3%, as measured by the best statistics available from our very own peer-reviewed medical journals.

We will not rebut a very prominent surgeon's opinion that chemotherapy constitutes torture.

We will make this application five or six more times, over the course of six months.

If the young man is still alive after that time, we will apply radiation to him.

We will do this against his religious beliefs, and we will try to convince the Court that his religion is not his.

Further, we will make sure that you cannot consider any other modes or options for health treatment, because they are not approved by a "standard of care" that does nothing to address this soul's individual consciousness.

If I brought a client in front of this Court and asked for permission to do this, you would look at me and ask that I be locked up, not just my client. If we would make a proposal to exercise torture on any of the detainees at Guantanamo, in the same measure as advocated by the doctors in this case, our country's reputation would be in a shambles. It is too easy to fall prey to that 90% number. This is a real case, involving real issues, and involving freedom of consciousness.

The Hausers . . . have integrated a process of pH-balanced therapy that is and has been accepted in much of the world. This water machine that Danny told the Court (Kangen water) is found in practically every major hospital in Japan.

We have long known the history of the pH balance. After World War II, the only survivors of Hiroshima and Nagasaki were the Japanese monks who focused on a diet of miso soup and short-grained brown rice, a pH-balanced diet. They lived. The others died horrible deaths.

It is entirely fitting that Japan would be a leader in this "standard of care." It would be a shame to preclude a modality of healing for a thirteen-year-old because we determined it is more fitting to torture and to assault the juvenile, with poisons he does not want.

The point is simple: the Hausers have elected forms of alternative health-care that they believe to be more effective and more beneficial than those recommended by the cancer industry.

This trial is the act of two loving parents who will go to any length to save their child from assault and torture.

This Court has a long and strong history of protecting children. Now is the time to do so, according to the dictates of Danny and his family's con-sciousness and spiritual being. The fact remains, that there are an abundance of scientifically proven, medical therapies available for Danny. If this Court wants to intervene, consistent with their conscious and religious beliefs, It must follow the reasonable path of healing as articulated by our evidence.

The Guardian Ad Litem takes no consideration of the spiritual path cho-sen by the parties. Nor does she give any power of the parents to help with the spiritual education of their son.

What is without question is the verification of Danny's status as a mem-ber of the Nemenhah band. This has not been refuted.

What is without question is that we, even the Guardian Ad Litem, must allow Danny's conscience to worship God as he sees fit. His conscience shall not be infringed. She cannot infringe upon it now. Nor shall she control or interfere with his right of conscience. Nor can the State. The State is attempt-ing to do so, by their act.

We qualify our "liberty of conscience" in that we cannot exercise acts of licentiousness or justify practices inconsistent with the peace or safety of the State. We do not assault our children. We do not torture the juveniles of this state. We are a bright and shining beacon for freedom and justice for the rest of the world.

We come to understand that healing is more than just a physical act of the administration of drugs or chemicals. It begins at the deep level of Soul, and continues through the mind, emotional and physicals bodies.

The confidence of healing is of paramount concern. Danny holds this confidence, and is self-sufficient in his understanding of healing. He is self-actualized, and not in that group of 99.2% of those people who will die in the next fifteen years, from their beliefs.

What has happened is, by his very acts and deeds, Danny has become a torch bearer of an important message: the people of this state have the right to chose their own reasonable medical modality. We have the ability to go beyond those standards established by the courts, and the medical "religion," and to go beyond the "standard of care" advocated and compelled upon all doctors in this state.

We heard the testimony of Dr. Bostrom, who indicated that Danny could be part of a study.

It is entirely reasonable for parents to reject experimentation upon their son, especially when his life is on the line.

It is ironic that the parents have to fight for their right not to have radiation on Danny, and yet, by the flip of a coin, if Danny is selected in one of the factions of the study group, he won't get radiation.

Finally, before you get to the heart of my legal argument, I would ask the court to consider the definition of a medicine man. Again, like all these computer people, I go to Wikipedia for a first review.

Medicine man, Role in Native Society:

"The primary function of these 'medicine elders' is to secure the health of the spiritual world, including the Great Spirit, for the benefit of the entire community. Sometimes the help sought may be for the sake of healing disease, sometimes it may be for the sake of healing the psyche, sometimes the goal is to promote harmony between human groups or between humans and nature."

I realize that Ms. Oliver doesn't know what a Medicine man looks like. In seeing and understanding the changes brought about by this thirteen-year-old young man, we are coming to understand what a Medicine man does.

We are moving into a new arena of consciousness. We are rejecting a modality of treatment that is assaultive and torturous. We are relying upon our bodies to do what the good Lord intended: to heal.

Legal Argument as Applied from the Facts

The Guardian Ad Litem's Testimony Constitutes an Impermissible Imposition of a Religious Test

Religious freedoms are constitutionally protected by both the United States Bill of Rights, as well as by our Minnesota Constitution. Specifically, these documents state:

U.S. Bill of Rights: Amendment I

Congress shall make no law respecting an establishment of religion, or prohibiting the free exercise thereof; or abridging the freedom of speech, or of the press; or the right of the people peaceably to assemble, and to petition the Government for a redress of grievances.

Minnesota State Constitution: Article I, Bill of Rights

Sec. 16. Freedom of conscience; no preference to be given to any religious establishment or mode of worship. The enumeration of rights in this constitution shall not deny or impair others retained by and inherent in the people. The right of every man to worship God according to the dictates of his own conscience shall never be infringed; nor shall any man be compelled to attend, erect or support any place of worship, or to maintain any religious or ecclesiastical ministry, against his consent; nor shall any control of or interference with the rights of conscience be permitted, or any preference be given by law to any religious establishment or mode of worship; but the liberty of conscience hereby secured shall not be so construed as to excuse acts of licentiousness or justify practices inconsistent with the peace or safety of the state, nor shall any money be drawn from the treasury for the benefit of any religious societies or religious or theological seminaries.

Sec. 17. Religious tests and property qualifications prohibited. No religious test or amount of property shall be required as a qualification for any office of public trust in the state. No religious test or amount of property shall be required as a qualification of any voter at any election in this state; nor shall any person be rendered incompetent to give evidence in any court of law or equity in consequence of his opinion upon the subject of religion.

"Religious liberty is a precious right," *State v. Hershberger* (Minn. 1990). The people of this state have always cherished religious liberty, and the high importance of protecting this right is demonstrated by its treatment in our constitution, where it appears even before any reference to the formation of a government. *State by Cooper v. French* (Minn. 1990). The Minnesota Supreme Court has consistently held that article I, section 16 of the Minnesota Constitution affords greater protection against governmental action affecting religious liberties than the First Amendment of the federal constitution. "Whereas the first amendment establishes a limit on government action at the point of *prohibiting* the exercise of religion, section 16 precludes even an *infringement* on or an *interference* with religious freedom," *Hershberger*. Thus, government action that is permissible under the federal constitution because it does not prohibit religious practices but merely infringes on or interferes with religious practices may nonetheless violate the Minnesota Constitution.

Minnesota courts employ a heightened "compelling state interest balancing test" when determining whether a challenged law infringes on or interferes with religious practices. The test has four prongs: (1) whether the objector's beliefs are sincerely held; (2) whether the state regulation burdens the exercise of religious beliefs; (3) whether the state interest in the regulation is overriding or compelling; and (4) whether the state regulation uses the least restrictive means.

As the Court will recall, the Guardian Ad Litem had stipulated to the genuineness of both the parents' and Daniel's religious beliefs. However, during trial, the Guardian Ad Litem broke her word when said she was now challenging the agreed-upon Pre-Trial Stipulation. Mr. and Mrs. Hauser have been prejudiced, because they were not adequately informed that this would be an issue for trial. In fact, they were told the opposite.

As argued in Respondents' previous Memorandum, parents have a significant interest in establishing a spiritual path for their child. The State may not come in and qualify that path. To do so violates State and Federal Constitutional Protections.

The qualification by the Guardian Ad Litem is limited in this situation. While she indicated that she read the Constitution of the Nemenhah Spiritual

Path, she testified that she did not understand it. She further testified that she did not see any of the principals embodied in the way of life of the Hausers. She could not tell the Court why Danny is a medicine man.

On the contrary, the Hausers have demonstrated an ability to walk their path in all aspects of their lives. They will do no harm. They eat food from the land, not polluted by pesticides and herbicides. They use oils, herbs, and other remedies to promote and maintain healthy bodies. They act as a harmonious family together.

In the present case, Danny's Guardian Ad Litem has attempted to qualify his membership and beliefs in the Nemenhah spiritual path. Her doing so constitutes an impermissible religious test, in violation of both the Federal and Minnesota Constitutions. There is no evidence contradicting Danny's beliefs in the Nemenhah faith or its spiritual path, or that these beliefs are anything but sincere. Certainly, the interference that is being advocated in this case, that of forcing Danny to undergo chemotherapy when such treatment is in direct violation of these religious beliefs burdens Danny's exercise of his religious beliefs. The state has failed to demonstrate a compelling interest in this matter that would justify imposition of the propounded medical treatment in violation of Danny's religious beliefs.

Opinion of the Court: In the Matter of the Welfare of the Child of Colleen and Anthony Hauser

The Court is today determining that the Petition alleging Daniel Hauser to be a child in need of protection or services has been proven by clear and convincing evidence. The Court is also concluding that the State of Minnesota, through Brown County Family Services ("BCFS"), has demonstrated a compelling state interest in the life and welfare of Daniel sufficient to override the fundamental constitutional rights of both the parents and Daniel to the free exercise of religion and the due process right of the parents to direct the religious and other upbringing of their child.

This much is certain and the Court so finds: All of the actions of the parties which bring this matter before the Court have been done in good faith. The parents, Daniel, the treating doctors, the child welfare agency, the Brown County Attorney and the Guardian ad Litem have at all times acted in good faith herein.

. . .

Daniel Hauser is currently 13 years of age. He has been diagnosed as suffering from nodular sclerosing Hodgkin's disease, stage IIB. The Hauser family's local family practice doctor, Dr. Joyce, correctly identified on January 21, 2009 that "lymphoma certainly seems likely" when Daniel presented with a persistent cough, fatigue, swollen lymph nodes and other symptoms. Dr. Joyce made a referral to oncology specialists at Children's Hospitals. The diagnosis was made there and it was determined that the cancer was readily treatable by therapies including chemotherapy.

Daniel's mother consented to the administration of the recommended chemotherapy beginning on February 5, 2009. The gravity and imminence of Daniel's situation limited the available options. Mrs. Hauser effectively consented to the initiation of chemotherapy after being adequately informed of her rights as Daniel's parent.

Daniel's lymphoma responded well to the initial round of chemotherapy.

Unfortunately Daniel also had adverse side effects to the administration of chemotherapy. While this was not unusual, both Daniel and his parents

United States District Court, Minnesota, Fifth Judicial District, 2009.

were justifiably quite concerned. The parents, acting in absolute parental good faith, chose to seek out a second opinion and consulted with Mayo Clinic. Mayo Clinic doctors concurred with the earlier medical advice. The parents, again in complete good faith, sought a third medical opinion, this time from the University of Minnesota Hospitals. Again, the recommendation was that the additional course of chemotherapy should be undertaken.

The doctors at these facilities, which are among the finest available in this part of the country, agree that Daniel has a very good chance of a complete recovery with additional chemotherapy and possibly radiation. Estimates of complete 5-year remission with this course range from 80% to 95%. These doctors are also in agreement that Daniel has very little chance of surviving 5 years without the prescribed course of treatment. If the mediastinal tumor were to increase in size and become resistant to chemotherapy, as all of these doctors opine that it will without the prescribed treatment, the long-term prospects for Daniel decrease significantly, even if the chemotherapy is resumed in the future.

The family has also consulted with Dr. Kotulski, an osteopathic physician practicing in Mankato, Minnesota. Dr. Kotulski agrees with the recommended chemotherapy. The Hauser family's local doctor, Dr. Joyce, also agrees with the recommendations of the oncologists.

In short, five (5) different medical doctors, three (3) of whom specialize in pediatric oncology, have all agreed upon the necessary medical care for Daniel.

There were several experts testifying at trial who believe in alternatives to chemotherapy for treatment of some cancers in some instances. However, there was absolutely no evidence presented at trial from any health care practitioner who has examined Daniel and who recommends any course of treatment different than that prescribed by the oncologists and medical doctors. The evidence is uncontroverted that Hodgkin's lymphoma, stage IIB, is best treated by chemotherapy and possible later radiation.

The family has a genuine and strong belief in the benefits of holistic medicine and, specifically, in Nemenhah. Nemenhah is based upon Native American healing practices. Daniel is deemed to be a "medicine man" by Nemenhah and does not wish to receive any additional chemotherapy.

Daniel Hauser is an extremely polite and pleasant young man. While he is 13 years of age, Daniel is unable to read. He does not know what the term "elder" means, although he claims to be one. He knows he is a medicine man under Nemenhah teachings, but is unable to identify how he became a medicine man or what teachings he has had to master to become one. He believes in the principle of "do no harm" and attributes his belief to Nemenhah teachings. He lacks the ability to give informed consent to medical procedures.

The doctors who have filed reports with Brown County concerning Daniel and who testified in this case have acted in conformity with their duties under well-established Minnesota statutory law. Brown County has properly brought this matter before the Court for determination and has filed a Petition with the Court as it is authorized to do by [law]. The parents and Daniel have properly asserted their positions in the matter in a very orderly and respectful fashion, with the capable assistance of counsel. The Guardian ad Litem, whose role it is to advocate for the best interests of a child claimed to be in need of protection or services, has carefully considered the matter and has expressed her opinions as to the child's best interests consistent with her obligation to the Court.

There are sharp differences in the positions of the parties.

The Hauser family members have a constitutional right to freedom of belief. The parents also have a right to parent their child that is based in the Due Process Clause of the United States Constitution. These constitutional freedoms can be overcome only upon a showing of a compelling state interest.

Correspondingly, there can scarcely be imagined a governmental interest more compelling than protecting the life of a child.

Minnesota has a long-standing statutory requirement that parents must provide "necessary medical care" for a child and providing that "complementary and alternative health care" is not sufficient. Multiple Minnesota statutes so provide. The legislature has also mandated by statute that both medical providers and "complementary and alternative practitioners" must report to child welfare authorities any situation in which a child is not being provided with "necessary medical care."

As applied to this case, Minnesota's statutory provisions have an effect upon the religious practices of the Hauser family. The mother asserts that a core tenet of Nemenhah is "first do no harm." The mother asserts that God intends that the body should be healed the natural way and that chemotherapy and radiation are poisons. Daniel also professes to the primacy of the "do no harm" tenet.

Under the relevant authorities and as applied to the facts in this case, Brown County has demonstrated a compelling state interest in seeing to it that Daniel's prospects for life are maximized by his being found in need to protection or services. The parents are free to provide Daniel with complementary or alternative therapies, but under Minnesota law, as applied here consistent with both federal and state constitutions, the parents must provide "necessary medical care" to Daniel.

As set forth below, the Court is intending to leave Daniel in the custody of his parents and to allow the parents the maximum legally-permissible range of choices for treatment of Daniel. Daniel loves his parents and they love him. He should remain with them as long as he receives treatment complying with the minimum standards of parental care provided by Minnesota law.

The issue in this case is not whether the State of Minnesota should have enacted the law as it did. The Court is obligated to apply the law as it is written unless to do so would violate a constitutional right. Settled state and federal case law establish that the State of Minnesota may constitutionally intervene in the present matter.

Surely many will think that the law should be different. With issues as sensitive as these, there are bound to be strong feelings both ways about what the law should be. To the extent that the parties involved in this case and members of the public in general believe that [the Minnesota law] or any other statute should be revisited, those arguments are properly made to the Minnesota Legislature. The Court is resolving this matter solely with reference to the relevant legal authorities, and not based upon the Court's personal opinion with regard to what Minnesota substantive law should be. The only personal observation the Court makes is this: If the Minnesota Legislature ever reconsiders the relevant statutes, I am confident that I join all of the others involved in this matter in hoping, and indeed in praying, that Daniel Hauser lives to testify at that hearing.

. . .

Conclusions of Law

- Daniel Hauser is a child in need of protection or services within the meaning of [Minnesota law].
- The parents and Daniel have made their arguments with respect to the free exercise clause of the First Amendment to the United States Constitution. "Congress shall make no law respecting an establishment of religion, or prohibiting the free exercise thereof; or abridging the freedom of speech, or of the press; or the right of the people peaceably to assemble, and to petition the Government for a redress of grievances." The Minnesota Constitution also contains a provision relating to religious liberty. "The right of every man to worship God according to the dictates of his own conscience shall never be infringed . . . nor shall any control of or interference with the rights of conscience be permitted. . . ." This provision of the Minnesota Constitution affords greater protection for religious liberties against governmental action than the first amendment of the federal constitution. The Court is analyzing the free exercise claim under both provisions. In that that state constitution affords greater protection to the free exercise of religion and imposes a higher standard in order to justify any state action the impinges upon the free exercise of religion and conscience, it follows that if Brown County is able to satisfy the requirements of the Minnesota Constitution in this matter, then it will also have satisfied the requirements of the federal constitution.
  . . .
- The State of Minnesota has legislatively determined that ensuring that children receive necessary medical care is very important state interest. This state interest is also reflected in the requirement imposed upon both medical doctors and practitioners of complimentary or alternative therapies to report to child welfare agencies any failure to provide "necessary medical care."
- The law does not condone the injury of children, nor will it accommodate danger for children. The welfare of children is a matter of paramount concern. The power of the courts to protect children is now exercised by the state as an attribute of its sovereignty. The state as *parens patriae* has authority to assume parental authority over a child who because of misfortune or helplessness is unable to properly care for himself.
- *Wisconsin v. Yoder* (1972) involved Amish parents who refused to send their children to school past the 8th grade. The Amish claimed that the compulsory attendance statute encroached on their rights and the rights of their children to the free exercise of the religious

beliefs they and their forbears had adhered to for almost three centuries. The U.S. Supreme Court wrote that: "In evaluating those claims we must be careful to determine whether the Amish religious faith and their mode of life are, as they claim, inseparable and interdependent. A way of life, however virtuous and admirable, may not be interposed as a barrier to reasonable state regulation of education if it is based on purely secular considerations; to have the protection of the Religion Clauses, the claims must be rooted in religious belief." Wisconsin argued that its interest in its system of compulsory education was compelling, such that even the established religious practices of the Amish needed to give way. Wisconsin argued that its system of compulsory education prepared children to participate in our political system so as to preserve freedom and independence and also that education prepares individuals to be self-reliant and self-sufficient participants in society. The U.S. Supreme Court accepted those propositions but determined that the State had not made a sufficient showing to justify the severe interference with religious freedom entailed by compulsory education, in light of evidence that the Amish were a successful, though nonconventional, society in America. Wisconsin also asserted a *parens patriae* interest in the well-being and educational opportunities of Amish children. The Supreme Court wrote that: "if the State is empowered, as *parens patriae* to 'save' a child from himself or his Amish parents by requiring an additional two years of compulsory formal high school education, the State will in large measure influence, if not determine, the religious future of the child. When the interests of parenthood are combined with a free exercise claim of the nature revealed by this record, more than merely a 'reasonable relation to some purpose within the competency of the State' is required to sustain the validity of the State's requirement under the First Amendment. To be sure, the power of the parent, even when linked to a free exercise claim, may be subject to limitation . . . if it appears that parental decisions will jeopardize the health or safety of the children, or have a potential for significant social burdens." (bolding added). The Supreme Court determined that "the record strongly indicated that accommodating the religious objections of the Amish by forgoing one, or at most two, additional years of compulsory education will not impair the physical or mental health of the child. . . ."

- Minnesota courts have enunciated and applied a balancing test, balancing the state's interest in cases such as this against the actor's free-exercise interest in religious-based conduct. Where it is undisputed that the religious belief is sincerely held and that the religious belief would be burdened by the proposed regulation, the balancing test requires proof of a compelling state interest. Minnesota has a compelling interest in protecting the welfare of children. A parent may exercise genuinely held religious beliefs; but the resulting conduct, though motivated by religious belief, must yield when—judged by accepted medical practice—it jeopardizes the life of a child. Religious practices must bend to the state's interest in protecting the welfare of a child whenever the child might die without the intervention of conventional medicine. This is settled Minnesota law.

- In Hofbauer v. Saratoga County Department of Social Services (N.Y. App. 1979), a case similar to this matter, a county filed a petition to have an eight-year-old child, who was suffering from Hodgkin's Disease, adjudged to be a child neglected by his parents. The parents were not following the treating physician's recommendations for radiation and chemotherapy, but instead entrusted the child to the care of a duly licensed physician advocating nutritional or metabolic therapies, including laetrile injections. The New York appellate court held that the decision as to whether the parents were providing adequate medical care must be "whether the parents, once having sought accredited medical assistance and having been made aware of the seriousness of their child's affliction and the possibility of cure if a certain mode of treatment is undertaken, have provided for their child a treatment which is recommended by their physician and which has not been totally rejected by all responsible medical authority."
- The present situation is *unlike* that in the Hoffbauer case. There, a medical authority was monitoring the treatment. If there were to be a medically approved way to treat Daniel's Hodgkin's lymphoma different than what the five different medical/osteopathic doctors have thus far opined, then the parents here would be free to pursue such an option under the statute. Where there is unanimity of medical opinion and where the matter is an important one of life and death, the State has a compelling State interest sufficient to overcome the parents' Free Exercise and Due Process rights.
- The Court's resolution of the issue presented is limited to the specific factual situation present. What is not before the Court in this matter is the issue of whether there would ever be the case of an older or particularly mature minor who expresses a position opposed to medical treatment and who might therefore have a constitutional right to direct his or her own treatment contrary to what is "medically necessary." This matter, as more fully described above, involves a 13-year-old child who has only a rudimentary understanding at best of the risks and benefits of chemotherapy. He genuinely opposes the imposition of chemotherapy. However, he does not believe he is ill currently. The fact is that he is very ill currently. He has Hodgkin's lymphoma which is apparently not in remission from the available evidence. In this case, the state has a compelling state interest sufficient to override the minor's genuine opposition.

    . . .

EXPLORING THE ISSUE

Do Parents Have the Right to Deny Their Children Lifesaving Medical Care Due to Their Religious Convictions?

Critical Thinking and Reflection

- What are some arguments made by each side with which you agree or disagree?
- What are the strengths and weaknesses of the two positions made in this chapter?
- Pick the side with which you most agree. What are some additional arguments you would make to strengthen the case for or against parents denying their children lifesaving medical treatment?
- Think more broadly of the issue of religious liberty and the medical care of children.
- How do you balance a fundamental right with science and an adolescent's life?

Is There Common Ground?

Even the judge in this case acknowledged that everyone involved was looking out for the best interest of Daniel Hauser. The right to express our religion is a fundamental right that enjoys wide protection in our society. At the same time, protecting the health and welfare of children is critical in any caring society. How much power should be ceded to medical professionals? Although the state did not support the position of Daniel's parents, what might have caused a different outcome? What if Daniel's illness were not fatal? In what circumstances, if any, would you let parents' decision-making rights supersede the states decision based on the testimony of medical professionals?

Additional Resources

Nemenah and Traditional Indigenous Organization:

http://www.nemenhah.org/

Christian Science:

http://christianscience.com/

Washington Post article about prayer and healing:

http://www.washingtonpost.com/wp-dyn/content/article/2006/03/23/
AR2006032302177.html

Healing Scripture:

http://healingscripture.com/

Religious tolerance and medical care:

http://www.religioustolerance.org/medical1.htm

Internet References . . .

Child Rights Information Network

The Child Rights Information Network (CRIN) is a global network that disseminates information about the Convention on the Rights of the Child and child rights among non-governmental organizations, U.N. agencies, intergovernmental organizations, educational institutions, and other child rights experts.

http://www.crin.org/

Eagle Forum's Mission

Eagle Forum's Mission enables conservative and pro-family men and women to participate in the process of self-government and public policy making.

http://www.eagleforum.org/

UNICEF

UNICEF is mandated by the U.N. General Assembly to advocate for the protection of children's rights, to help meet their basic needs, and to expand their opportunities to reach their full potential.

http://www.unicef.org/

Nontraditional Families and Relationships

*T*he American family today is decidedly different than during the Leave-it-to-Beaver era. Children grow up in a wide array of families: two married parents, single parents, grandparents raising children, lesbian and gay parents, and many other family structures. As the composition of a family changes, it is critical to take a closer look at the twenty-first-century family. What does a changing family mean for modern-day America?

This section examines five critical questions:

- Should Same-Sex Couples Be Able to Legally Marry?
- Should Private Sexual Acts Between Gay Couples Be Illegal?
- Are Traditional Families Better for Children?
- Should Lesbian and Gay Individuals Be Able to Adopt Children?
- Are Teenagers Too Young to Become Parents?

ISSUE 10

Should Same-Sex Couples Be Able to Legally Marry?

YES: Human Rights Campaign, from "Answers to Questions About Marriage Equality," *HRC's FamilyNet Project* (2004)

NO: Peter Sprigg, from "Questions and Answers: What's Wrong with Letting Same-Sex Couples 'Marry'?" *Family Research Council* (2004)

Learning Outcomes

As a result of this issue, readers will be able to:

- Identify the major arguments made for and against same-sex marriage.
- Compare and contrast the competing arguments made for and against same-sex marriage in this issue.
- Evaluate the implications of same-sex marriage on individual relationships, as well as on the larger fabric of American society.

ISSUE SUMMARY

YES: The Human Rights Campaign (HRC), America's largest lesbian and gay organization, outlines the disparities American lesbian and gay couples experience when they are not allowed to marry legally, as well as the logistical considerations involved in granting same-sex couples the right to marry.

NO: Peter Sprigg, director of the Center for Marriage and Family Studies at the Family Research Council, outlines why nonheterosexual relationships do not carry with them the same validity as heterosexual relationships, and therefore gays and lesbians should not be allowed to marry legally.

The past few years have seen the topic of same-sex marriage rush into the forefront of the news and other media. As of January 2012, six states (Connecticut, Iowa, Massachusetts, New Hampshire, New York, Vermont) and Washington, D.C. allow same-sex marriage, although that is being challenged by those who want to amend the United States Constitution to ban same-sex marriage. Same-sex couples in other states are challenging current laws by suing for the right to marry legally and are now able to marry in a handful of states and Washington, D.C. In most cases, marriage rights to same-sex couples are being extended through the state courts. However, in some states, such as New York, rights are extended through the legislative process. California has seen an array of reactions: the state Supreme Court ruling on behalf of same-sex marriage, the state's voters taking away that right, and the 9th Circuit federal courts extending that right (that right had a stay pending appeal at the time of publication).

At the same time, many states voted to amend their constitutions to define marriage as being exclusively between a man and a woman, a list of states that includes but is not limited to Idaho, Colorado, South Dakota, Virginia, Tennessee, South Carolina, Wisconsin, and Alabama.

As of the writing of this issue, Connecticut, Iowa, Massachusetts, New Hampshire, New York, Vermont, and Washington, D.C., are the only jurisdictions to have a marriage license or refer to their union as a marriage, with benefits that are the same as they would be for a heterosexual marriage. These unions, however, are not recognized in most other states. This is due in part to the Defense of Marriage Act, which was signed into law in 1996 by then-president Bill Clinton. This Act says that no state is required to recognize a same-sex union and defines marriage as being between a man and a woman only. Therefore, same-sex unions that are legal in one state do not have to be recognized as legal in another. Over 30 states have passed legislation saying they would not recognize a same-sex union that took place in another state. Furthermore, even if your state allows for same-sex marriage, there are no federal rights that apply to heterosexual married couples. For example, Social Security benefits are not extended.

Those who oppose same-sex marriage believe that marriage is, and always has been, between a man and a woman. They believe that a key part of marriage for many heterosexual couples is reproduction or another type of parenting arrangement, such as adoption. In those cases, they believe that any child should have two parents, one male and one female. Many do not oppose granting domestic partner benefits to same-sex partners, or even, in some cases, civil unions. They do, however, believe that if lesbian and gay couples were allowed to marry and to receive the legal and social benefits thereof, it would serve only to further erode the institution of marriage as it is currently defined in the United States.

Supporters of same-sex marriage believe that if lesbian and gay couples wish to make a lifetime commitment, they should be afforded the same rights, privileges, and vocabulary as heterosexual couples. Although some would be as happy with the term "civil union," accompanied by equal rights, others believe that making marriage available to all is the only way to go. Some lesbian and gay couples who are in committed, loving relationships resent that they have fewer rights than a heterosexual couple who experience alcohol or drug abuse or domestic violence.

An argument that is raised in this debate is that granting same-sex couples the right to marry would open the door for adult pedophiles to petition to marry the children with whom they engage in their sexual relationships. Most lesbian and gay individuals and their supporters find this offensive, as well as an invalid comparison. What do you think?

In the YES and NO selections, both the HRC and Peter Sprigg raise the most common questions pertaining to same-sex marriage. The HRC enumerates the rights that are not currently available to same-sex couples in long-term committed relationships and maintains that granting equal rights to these couples is good not only for them, but also for society as a whole. One of the concerns Peter Sprigg raises pertains to the expectation that a purpose of heterosexual marriage is to raise children, and that a same-sex couple is a harmful setting in which to do that.

Part of this discussion is that marriage is a civil right, not an inherent or moral one. Those supporting marriage rights for lesbian and gay couples cite the struggles of the civil rights movement of the 1960s in their current quest for equality for all couples. Among the points they make is that up until 1967, it was still illegal in some states for people of different races to marry. Many opponents find the idea of comparing same-sex marriage to the civil rights struggles of the 1960s and earlier is offensive, that it is like comparing apples and oranges. Many of these individuals believe that sexual orientation is chosen, rather than an inherent part of who one is—unlike race, which is predetermined. Most experts, however, agree that what "causes" a person to be heterosexual, bisexual, or homosexual is determined before we are born.

Regardless, is marriage a civil right? A fundamental right? A legal right? An inherent right?

We are now seeing the result of years of same-sex marriage being legal. States that allow for same-sex marriage often find that it causes little controversy once implemented. Perhaps that is why public opinion polling has changed so dramatically in just a couple of years. While a few years ago an overwhelming majority of voters were against same-sex marriage, today there is at least a plurality and often a majority of voters who support same-sex marriage.

Of course, public opinion polls often hold little sway for those who hold strong feelings one way or the other. Supporters of same-sex marriage worked to extend marriage rights while the majority of the country was opposed to extending such rights. Today, the opposite appears to be true, but opponents of same-sex marriage are working just as hard to limit further expansion of marriage rights, or even to turn back the clock on the marriage rights for same-sex couples gained thus far.

YES

Answers to Questions About Marriage Equality

Why Same-Sex Couples Want to Marry

Many same-sex couples want the right to legally marry because they are in love—either they just met the love of their lives, or more likely, they have spent the last 10, 20, or 50 years with that person—and they want to honor their relationship in the greatest way our society has to offer, by making a public commitment to stand together in good times and bad, through all the joys and challenges family life brings.

Many [same-sex] parents want the right to marry because they know it offers children a vital safety net and guarantees protections that unmarried parents cannot provide.

And still other people—both gay and straight—are fighting for the right of same-sex couples to marry because they recognize that it is simply not fair to deny some families the protections all other families are eligible to enjoy.

Currently in the United States, same-sex couples in long-term, committed relationships pay higher taxes and are denied basic protections and rights granted to married heterosexual couples. Among them:

- **Hospital visitation.** Married couples have the automatic right to visit each other in the hospital and make medical decisions. Same-sex couples can be denied the right to visit a sick or injured loved one in the hospital.
- **Social Security benefits.** Married people receive Social Security payments upon the death of a spouse. Despite paying payroll taxes, gay and lesbian partners receive no Social Security survivor benefits—resulting in an average annual income loss of $5,528 upon the death of a partner.
- **Immigration.** Americans in binational relationships are not permitted to petition for their same-sex partners to immigrate. As a result, they are often forced to separate or move to another country.
- **Health insurance.** Many public and private employers provide medical coverage to the spouses of their employees, but most employers do not provide coverage to the life partners of gay and lesbian employees. Gay employees who do receive health coverage for their partners must pay federal income taxes on the value of the insurance.

From Human Rights Campaign Foundation's FamilyNet Project (www.hrc.org). Copyright © 2004 by Human Rights Campaign. Reprinted by permission.

- **Estate taxes.** A married person automatically inherits all the property of his or her deceased spouse without paying estate taxes. A gay or lesbian taxpayer is forced to pay estate taxes on property inherited from a deceased partner.
- **Retirement savings.** While a married person can roll a deceased spouse's 401(k) funds into an IRA without paying taxes, a gay or lesbian American who inherits a 401(k) can end up paying up to 70 percent of it in taxes and penalties.
- **Family leave.** Married workers are legally entitled to unpaid leave from their jobs to care for an ill spouse. Gay and lesbian workers are not entitled to family leave to care for their partners.
- **Nursing homes.** Married couples have a legal right to live together in nursing homes. Because they are not legal spouses, elderly gay or lesbian couples do not have the right to spend their last days living together in nursing homes.
- **Home protection.** Laws protect married seniors from being forced to sell their homes to pay high nursing home bills; gay and lesbian seniors have no such protection.
- **Pensions.** After the death of a worker, most pension plans pay survivor benefits only to a legal spouse of the participant. Gay and lesbian partners are excluded from such pension benefits.

Why Civil Unions Aren't Enough

Comparing marriage to civil unions is a bit like comparing diamonds to rhinestones. One is, quite simply, the real deal; the other is not. Consider:

- Couples eligible to marry may have their marriage performed in any state and have it recognized in every other state in the nation and every country in the world.
- Couples who are joined in a civil union in Vermont (the only state that offers civil unions) have no guarantee that its protections will even travel with them to neighboring New York or New Hampshire— let alone California or any other state.

Moreover, even couples who have a civil union and remain in Vermont receive only second-class protections in comparison to their married friends and neighbors. While they receive state-level protections, they do not receive any of the *more than 1,100 federal benefits and protections of marriage.*

In short, civil unions are not separate but equal—they are separate *and* unequal. And our society has tried separate before. It just doesn't work. . . .

Answers to Questions People Are Asking

I Believe God Meant Marriage for Men and Women.
How Can I Support Marriage for Same-Sex Couples?
Many people who believe in God—and fairness and justice for all—ask this question. They feel a tension between religious beliefs and democratic values that has been experienced in many different ways throughout our nation's history. That

is why the framers of our Constitution established the principle of separation of church and state. That principle applies no less to the marriage issue than it does to any other.

Indeed, the answer to the apparent dilemma between religious beliefs and support for equal protections for all families lies in recognizing that marriage has a significant religious meaning for many people, but that it is also a legal contract. And it is strictly the legal—not the religious—dimension of marriage that is being debated now.

Granting marriage rights to same-sex couples would *not* require Christianity, Judaism, Islam, or any other religion to perform these marriages. It would not require religious institutions to permit these ceremonies to be held on their grounds. It would not even require that religious communities discuss the issue. People of faith would remain free to make their own judgments about what makes a marriage in the eyes of God—just as they are today.

Consider, for example, the difference in how the Catholic Church and the U.S. government view couples who have divorced and remarried. Because church tenets do not sanction divorce, the second marriage is not valid in the church's view. The government, however, recognizes the marriage by extending to the remarried couple the same rights and protections as those granted to every other married couple in America. In this situation—as would be the case in marriage for same-sex couples—the church remains free to establish its own teachings on the religious dimension of marriage while the government upholds equality under law.

It should also be noted that there are a growing number of religious communities that have decided to bless same-sex unions. Among them are Reform Judaism, the Unitarian Universalist Association, and the Metropolitan Community Church. The Presbyterian Church (USA) also allows ceremonies to be performed, although they are not considered the same as marriage. The Episcopal Church and United Church of Christ allow individual churches to set their own policies on same-sex unions.

"This Is Different from Interracial Marriage.
Sexual Orientation Is a Choice."
. . . Decades of research all point to the fact that sexual orientation is not a choice, and that a person's sexual orientation cannot be changed. Who one is drawn to is a fundamental aspect of who we are.

In this way, the struggle for marriage equality for same-sex couples is just as basic as the fight for interracial marriage was. It recognizes that Americans should not be coerced into false and unhappy marriages but should be free to marry the person they love—thereby building marriage on a true and stable foundation.

"Won't This Create a Free-for-All and Make the
Whole Idea of Marriage Meaningless?"
Many people share this concern because opponents of gay and lesbian people have used this argument as a scare tactic. But it is not true. Granting same-sex couples the right to marry would in no way change the number of people who

could enter into a marriage (or eliminate restrictions on the age or familial relationships of those who may marry). Marriage would continue to recognize the highest possible commitment that can be made between two adults, plain and simple. . . .

"I Strongly Believe Children Need a Mother and a Father."

Many of us grew up believing that everyone needs a mother and father, regardless of whether we ourselves happened to have two parents, or two *good* parents.

But as families have grown more diverse in recent decades and as the researchers have studied how these different family relationships affect children, it has become clear that the *quality* of a family's relationship is more important than the particular *structure* of families that exist today. In other words, the qualities that help children grow into good and responsible adults—learning how to learn, to have compassion for others, to contribute to society and be respectful of others and their differences—do not depend on the sexual orientation of their parents, but on their parents' ability to provide a loving, stable, and happy home, something no class of Americans has an exclusive hold on.

That is why research studies have consistently shown that children raised by gay and lesbian parents do just as well on all conventional measure of child development, such as academic achievement, psychological well-being, and social abilities, as children raised by heterosexual parents.

That is also why the nation's leading child welfare organizations, including the American Academy of Pediatrics, the American Academy of Family Physicians, and others, have issued statements that dismiss assertions that only heterosexual couples can be good parents—and declare that the focus should now be on providing greater protections for the 1 million to 9 million children being raised by gay and lesbian parents in the United States today. . . .

"How Could Marriage for Same-Sex Couples Possibly Be Good for the American Family—or Our Country?"

. . . The prospect of a significant change in our laws and customs has often caused people to worry more about dire consequences that could result than about the potential positive outcomes. In fact, precisely the same anxiety arose when some people fought to overturn the laws prohibiting marriage between people of different races in the 1950s and 1960s. (One Virginia judge even declared that "God intended to separate the races.")

But in reality, opening marriage to couples who are so willing to fight for it could only strengthen the institution for all. It would open the doors to more supporters, not opponents. And it would help keep the age-old institution alive.

As history has repeatedly proven, institutions that fail to take account of the changing needs of the population are those that grow weak; those that recognize and accommodate changing needs grow strong. For example, the U.S. military, like American colleges and universities, grew stronger after permitting African Americans and women to join its ranks.

Similarly, granting same-sex couples the right to marry would strengthen the institution of marriage by allowing it to better meet the needs of the true diversity of family structures in America today. . . .

*"Can't Same-Sex Couples Go to a Lawyer to
Secure All the Rights They Need?"*
Not by a long shot. When a gay or lesbian person gets seriously ill, there is no legal document that can make their partner eligible to take leave from work under the federal Family and Medical Leave Act to provide care—because that law applies only to married couples.

When gay or lesbian people grow old and in need of nursing home care, there is no legal document that can give them the right to Medicaid coverage without potentially causing their partner to be forced from their home—because the federal Medicaid law only permits married spouses to keep their home without becoming ineligible for benefits.

And when a gay or lesbian person dies, there is no legal document that can extend Social Security survivor benefits or the right to inherit a retirement plan without severe tax burdens that stem from being "unmarried" in the eyes of the law.

These are only a few examples of the critical protections that are granted through more than 1,100 federal laws that protect only married couples. In the absence of the right to marry, same-sex couples can only put in place a handful of the most basic arrangements, such as naming each other in a will or a power of attorney. And even these documents remain vulnerable to challenges in court by disgruntled family members.

"Won't This Cost Taxpayers Too Much Money?"
No, it wouldn't necessarily cost much at all. In fact, treating same-sex couples as families under law could even save taxpayers money because marriage would require them to assume legal responsibility for their joint living expenses and reduce their dependence on public assistance programs, such as Medicaid, Temporary Assistance to Needy Families, Supplemental Security Income disability payments, and food stamps.

Put another way, the money it would cost to extend benefits to same-sex couples could be outweighed by the money that would be saved as these families rely more fully on each other instead of state or federal government assistance.

For example, two studies conducted in 2003 by professors at the University of Massachusetts, Amherst, and the University of California, Los Angeles, found that extending domestic partner benefits to same-sex couples in California and New Jersey would save taxpayers millions of dollars a year.

Specifically, the studies projected that the California state budget would save an estimated $8.1 million to $10.6 million each year by enacting the most comprehensive domestic partner law in the nation. In New Jersey, which passed a new domestic partner law in 2004, the savings were projected to be even higher—more than $61 million each year.

(Sources: "Equal Rights, Fiscal Responsibility: The Impact of A.B. 205 on California's Budget," by M. V. Lee Badgett, Ph.D., IGLSS, Department of Economics, University of Massachusetts, and R. Bradley Sears, J.D., Williams Project, UCLA School of Law, University of California, Los Angeles, May 2003, and "Supporting Families, Saving Funds: A Fiscal Analysis of New Jersey's

Domestic Partnership Act," by Badgett and Sears with Suzanne Goldberg, J.D., Rutgers School of Law-Newark, December 2003.)

"Where Can Same-Sex Couples Marry Today?"

In 2001, the Netherlands became the first country to extend marriage rights to same-sex couples. Belgium passed a similar law two years later. The laws in both of these countries, however, have strict citizenship or residency requirements that do not permit American couples to take advantage of the protections provided.

In June 2003, Ontario became the first Canadian province to grant marriage to same-sex couples, and in July 2003, British Columbia followed suit—becoming the first places that American same-sex couples could go to get married.

In November 2003, the Massachusetts Supreme Judicial Court recognized the right of same-sex couples to marry—giving the state six months to begin issuing marriage licenses to same-sex couples. It began issuing licenses May 17, 2004.

In February 2004, the city of San Francisco began issuing marriage licenses to same-sex couples after the mayor declared that the state constitution forbade him to discriminate. The issue is being addressed by California courts, and a number of other cities have either taken or are considering taking steps in the same direction.

Follow the latest developments in California, Oregon, New Jersey, New Mexico, New York and in other communities across the country. . . .

Other nations have also taken steps toward extending equal protections to all couples, though the protections they provide are more limited than marriage. Canada, Denmark, Finland, France, Germany, Iceland, Norway, Portugal, and Sweden all have nationwide laws that grant same-sex partners a range of important rights, protections, and obligations.

For example, in France, registered same-sex (and opposite-sex) couples can be joined in a civil "solidarity pact" that grants them the right to file joint tax returns, extend social security coverage to each other and receive the same health, employment, and welfare benefits as legal spouses. It also commits the couple to assume joint responsibility for household debts.

Other countries, including Switzerland, Scotland, and the Czech Republic, also have considered legislation that would legally recognize same-sex unions.

"What Protections Other than Marriage Are
Available to Same-Sex Couples?"

At the federal level, there are no protections at all available to same-sex couples. In fact, a federal law called the "Defense of Marriage Act" says that the federal government will discriminate against same-sex couples who marry by refusing to recognize their marriages or providing them with the federal protections of marriage. Some members of Congress are trying to go even further by attempting to pass a Federal Marriage Amendment that would write discrimination against same-sex couples into the U.S. Constitution.

10 FACTS

1. Same-sex couples live in 99.3 percent of all counties nationwide.
2. There are an estimated 3.1 million people living together in same-sex relationships in the United States.
3. Fifteen percent of these same-sex couples live in rural settings.
4. One out of three lesbian couples is raising children. One out of five gay male couples is raising children.
5. Between 1 million and 9 million children are being raised by gay, lesbian, and bisexual parents in the United States today.
6. At least one same-sex couple is raising children in 96 percent of all counties nationwide.
7. The highest percentages of same-sex couples raising children live in the South.
8. Nearly one in four same-sex couples includes a partner 55 years old or older, and nearly one in five same-sex couples is composed of two people 55 or older.
9. More than one in 10 same-sex couples include a partner 65 years old or older, and nearly one in 10 same-sex couples is composed of two people 65 or older.
10. The states with the highest numbers of same-sex senior couples are also the most popular for heterosexual senior couples: California, New York, and Florida.

These facts are based on analyses of the 2000 Census conducted by the Urban Institute and the Human Rights Campaign. The estimated number of people in same-sex relationships has been adjusted by 62 percent to compensate for the widely-reported undercount in the Census. . . .

At the state level, only Vermont offers civil unions, which provide important state benefits but no federal protections, such as Social Security survivor benefits. There is also no guarantee that civil unions will be recognized outside Vermont. Thirty-nine states also have "defense of marriage" laws explicitly prohibiting the recognition of marriages between same-sex partners.

Domestic partner laws have been enacted in California, Connecticut, New Jersey, Hawaii, and the District of Columbia. The benefits conferred by these laws vary; some offer access to family health insurance, others confer co-parenting rights. These benefits are limited to residents of the state. A family that moves out of these states immediately loses the protections.

Peter Sprigg  **NO**

Questions and Answers: What's Wrong with Letting Same-Sex Couples "Marry"?

What's Wrong with Letting Same-Sex Couples Legally "Marry"?
There are two key reasons why the legal rights, benefits, and responsibilities of civil marriage should not be extended to same-sex couples.

The first is that homosexual relationships are not marriage. That is, they simply do not fit the minimum necessary condition for a marriage to exist—namely, the union of a man and a woman.

The second is that homosexual relationships are harmful. Not only do they not provide the same benefits to society as heterosexual marriages, but their consequences are far more negative than positive.

Either argument, standing alone, is sufficient to reject the claim that same-sex unions should be granted the legal status of marriage.

Let's Look at the First Argument.
Isn't Marriage Whatever the Law Says It Is?
No. Marriage is not a creation of the law. Marriage is a fundamental human institution that predates the law and the Constitution. At its heart, it is an anthropological and sociological reality, not a legal one. Laws relating to marriage merely recognize and regulate an institution that already exists.

But Isn't Marriage Just a Way of Recognizing People
Who Love Each Other and Want to Spend Their Lives Together?
If love and companionship were sufficient to define marriage, then there would be no reason to deny "marriage" to unions of a child and an adult, or an adult child and his or her aging parent, or to roommates who have no sexual relationship, or to groups rather than couples. Love and companionship are usually considered integral to marriage in our culture, but they are not sufficient to define it as an institution. . . .

Why Should Homosexuals Be Denied the Right to Marry Like Anyone Else?
The fundamental "right to marry" is a right that rests with *individuals,* not with *couples.* Homosexual *individuals* already have exactly the same "right" to

From *Family Research Council,* Issue no. 256, 2004, pp. 173–79. Copyright © 2004 by Family Research Council. Reprinted by permission.

marry as anyone else. Marriage license applications do not inquire as to a person's "sexual orientation." . . .

However, while every individual person is free to get married, *no* person, whether heterosexual or homosexual, has ever had a legal right to marry simply any willing partner. Every person, whether heterosexual or homosexual, is subject to legal restrictions as to whom they may marry. To be specific, every person, regardless of sexual preference, is legally barred from marrying a child, a close blood relative, a person who is already married, or a person of the same sex. There is no discrimination here, nor does such a policy deny anyone the "equal protection of the laws" (as guaranteed by the Constitution), since these restrictions apply equally to every individual.

Some people may wish to do away with one or more of these longstanding restrictions upon one's choice of marital partner. However, the fact that a tiny but vocal minority of Americans desire to have someone of the same sex as a partner does not mean that they have a "right" to do so, any more than the desires of other tiny (but less vocal) minorities of Americans give them a "right" to choose a child, their own brother or sister, or a group of two or more as their marital partners.

Isn't Prohibiting Homosexual "Marriage" Just as Discriminatory as Prohibiting Interracial Marriage, Like Some States Used to Do?

This analogy is not valid at all. Bridging the divide of the sexes by uniting men and women is both a worthy goal and a part of the fundamental purpose of marriage, common to all human civilizations.

Laws against interracial marriage, on the other hand, served only the purpose of preserving a social system of racial segregation. This was both an unworthy goal and one utterly irrelevant to the fundamental nature of marriage.

Allowing a black woman to marry a white man does not change the definition of marriage, which requires one man and one woman. Allowing two men or two women to marry would change that fundamental definition. Banning the "marriage" of same-sex couples is therefore essential to preserve the nature and purpose of marriage itself. . . .

How Would Allowing Same-Sex Couples to Marry Change Society's Concept of Marriage?

As an example, marriage will open wide the door to homosexual adoption, which will simply lead to more children suffering the negative consequences of growing up without both a mother and a father.

Among homosexual men in particular, casual sex, rather than committed relationships, is the rule and not the exception. And even when they do enter into a more committed relationship, it is usually of relatively short duration. For example, a study of homosexual men in the Netherlands (the first country in the world to legalize "marriage" for same-sex couples), published in the journal *AIDS* in 2003, found that the average length of "steady partnerships" was not more than 2 < years (Maria Xiridou et al., in *AIDS* 2003, 17:1029–1038).

In addition, studies have shown that even homosexual men who are in "committed" relationships are not sexually faithful to each other. While infidelity among heterosexuals is much too common, it does not begin to compare to the rates among homosexual men. The 1994 National Health and Social Life Survey, which remains the most comprehensive study of Americans' sexual practices ever undertaken, found that 75 percent of married men and 90 percent of married women had been sexually faithful to their spouse. On the other hand, a major study of homosexual men in "committed" relationships found that only seven out of 156 had been sexually faithful, or 4.5 percent. The Dutch study cited above found that even homosexual men in "steady partnerships" had an average of eight "casual" sex partners per year.

So if same-sex relationships are legally recognized as "marriage," the idea of marriage as a sexually exclusive and faithful relationship will be dealt a serious blow. Adding monogamy and faithfulness to the other pillars of marriage that have already fallen will have overwhelmingly negative consequences for Americans' physical and mental health. . . .

Don't Homosexuals Need Marriage Rights So That They Will Be Able to Visit Their Partners in the Hospital?

The idea that homosexuals are routinely denied the right to visit their partners in the hospital is nonsense. When this issue was raised during debate over the Defense of Marriage Act in 1996, the Family Research Council did an informal survey of nine hospitals in four states and the District of Columbia. None of the administrators surveyed could recall a single case in which a visitor was barred because of their homosexuality, and they were incredulous that this would even be considered an issue.

Except when a doctor limits visitation for medical reasons, final authority over who may visit an adult patient rests with that patient. This is and should be the case regardless of the sexual orientation or marital status of the patient or the visitor.

The only situation in which there would be a possibility that the blood relatives of a patient might attempt to exclude the patient's homosexual partner is if the patient is unable to express his or her wishes due to unconsciousness or mental incapacity. Homosexual partners concerned about this (remote) possibility can effectively preclude it by granting to one another a health care proxy (the legal right to make medical decisions for the patient) and a power of attorney (the right to make all legal decisions for another person). Marriage is not necessary for this. It is inconceivable that a hospital would exclude someone who holds the health care proxy and power of attorney for a patient from visiting that patient, except for medical reasons.

The hypothetical "hospital visitation hardship" is nothing but an emotional smokescreen to distract people from the more serious implications of radically redefining marriage.

Don't Homosexuals Need the Right to Marry Each Other in Order to Ensure That They Will Be Able to Leave Their Estates to Their Partner When They Die?

As with the hospital visitation issue, the concern over inheritance rights is something that simply does not require marriage to resolve it. Nothing in current law prevents homosexual partners from being joint owners of property such as a home or a car, in which case the survivor would automatically become the owner if the partner dies.

An individual may leave the remainder of his estate to whomever he wishes—again, without regard to sexual orientation or marital status—simply by writing a will. As with the hospital visitation issue, blood relatives would only be able to overrule the surviving homosexual partner in the event that the deceased had failed to record his wishes in a common, inexpensive legal document. Changing the definition of a fundamental social institution like marriage is a rather extreme way of addressing this issue. Preparing a will is a much simpler solution.

Don't Homosexuals Need Marriage Rights So That They Can Get Social Security Survivor Benefits When a Partner Dies?

. . . Social Security survivor benefits were designed to recognize the non-monetary contribution made to a family by the homemaking and child-rearing activities of a wife and mother, and to ensure that a woman and her children would not become destitute if the husband and father were to die.

The Supreme Court ruled in the 1970s that such benefits must be gender-neutral. However, they still are largely based on the premise of a division of roles within a couple between a breadwinner who works to raise money and a homemaker who stays home to raise children.

Very few homosexual couples organize their lives along the lines of such a "traditional" division of labor and roles. They are far more likely to consist of two earners, each of whom can be supported in old age by their own personal Social Security pension.

Furthermore, far fewer homosexual couples than heterosexual ones are raising children at all, for the obvious reason that they are incapable of natural reproduction with each other. This, too, reduces the likelihood of a traditional division of labor among them.

Survivor benefits for the legal (biological or adopted) *children* of homosexual parents (as opposed to their partners) are already available under current law, so "marriage" rights for homosexual couples are unnecessary to protect the interests of these children themselves. . . .

Even If "Marriage" Itself Is Uniquely Heterosexual, Doesn't Fairness Require That the Legal and Financial Benefits of Marriage Be Granted to Same-Sex Couples—Perhaps Through "Civil Unions" or "Domestic Partnerships"?

No. The legal and financial benefits of marriage are not an entitlement to be distributed equally to all (if they were, single people would have as much reason to consider them "discriminatory" as same-sex couples). Society grants benefits to marriage because marriage has benefits for society—including, but not limited to, the reproduction of the species in households with the optimal household structure (i.e., the presence of both a mother and a father).

Homosexual relationships, on the other hand, have no comparable benefit for society, and in fact impose substantial costs on society. The fact that AIDS is at least ten times more common among men who have sex with men than among the general population is but one example. . . .

Isn't It Possible That Allowing Homosexuals to "Marry" Each Other
Would Allow Them to Participate in Those Benefits as Well?
Opening the gates of "marriage" to homosexuals is far more likely to change the attitudes and behavior of heterosexuals for the worse than it is to change the lifestyles of homosexuals for the better. . . .

What About the Argument That Homosexual Relations
Are Harmful? What Do You Mean by That?
Homosexual men experience higher rates of many diseases, including:

- Human Papillomavirus (HPV), which causes most cases of cervical cancer in women and anal cancer in men
- Hepatitis A, B, and C
- Gonorrhea
- Syphilis
- "Gay Bowel Syndrome," a set of sexually transmitted gastrointestinal problems such as proctitis, proctocolitis, and enteritis
- HIV/AIDS (One Canadian study found that as a result of HIV alone, "life expectancy for gay and bisexual men is eight to twenty years less than for all men.")

Lesbian women, meanwhile, have a higher prevalence of:

- Bacterial vaginosis
- Hepatitis C
- HIV risk behaviors
- Cancer risk factors such as smoking, alcohol use, poor diet, and being overweight . . .

Do Homosexuals Have More Mental Health Problems as Well?
Yes. Various research studies have found that homosexuals have higher rates of:

- Alcohol abuse
- Drug abuse
- Nicotine dependence
- Depression
- Suicide

Isn't It Possible That These Problems Result from Society's
"Discrimination" Against Homosexuals?
This is the argument usually put forward by pro-homosexual activists. However, there is a simple way to test this hypothesis. If "discrimination" were the cause of homosexuals' mental health problems, then one would expect those problems to be much less common in cities or countries, like San Francisco or the Netherlands, where homosexuality has achieved the highest levels of acceptance.

In fact, the opposite is the case. In places where homosexuality is widely accepted, the physical and mental health problems of homosexuals are greater, not less. This suggests that the real problem lies in the homosexual lifestyle itself, not in society's response to it. In fact, it suggests that increasing the level of social support *for* homosexual behavior (by, for instance, allowing same-sex couples to "marry") would only increase these problems, not reduce them. . . .

Haven't Studies Shown That Children Raised by Homosexual Parents Are No Different from Other Children?

No. This claim is often put forward, even by professional organizations. The truth is that most research on "homosexual parents" thus far has been marred by serious methodological problems. However, even pro-homosexual sociologists Judith Stacey and Timothy Biblarz report that the actual data from key studies show the "no differences" claim to be false.

Surveying the research (primarily regarding lesbians) in an *American Sociological Review* article in 2001, they found that:

- Children of lesbians are less likely to conform to traditional gender norms.
- Children of lesbians are more likely to engage in homosexual behavior.
- Daughters of lesbians are "more sexually adventurous and less chaste."
- Lesbian "co-parent relationships" are more likely to end than heterosexual ones.

A 1996 study by an Australian sociologist compared children raised by heterosexual married couples, heterosexual cohabiting couples, and homosexual cohabiting couples. It found that the children of heterosexual married couples did the best, and children of homosexual couples the worst, in nine of the thirteen academic and social categories measured. . . .

Do the American People Want to See "Marriages" Between Same-Sex Couples Recognized by Law?

No—and in the wake of the June 2003 court decisions to legalize such "marriages" in the Canadian province of Ontario and to legalize homosexual sodomy in the United States, the nation's opposition to such a radical social experiment has actually grown.

Five separate national opinion polls taken between June 24 and July 27, 2003, showed opponents of civil "marriage" for same-sex couples outnumbering supporters by not less than fifteen percentage points in every poll. The wording of poll questions can make a significant difference, and in this case, the poll with the most straightforward language (a Harris/CNN/Time poll asking "Do you think marriages between homosexual men or homosexual women should be recognized as legal by the law?") resulted in the strongest opposition, with 60 percent saying "No" and only 33 percent saying "Yes."

Even where pollsters drop the word "marriage" itself and use one of the euphemisms to describe a counterfeit institution parallel to marriage, we see a decline in public support for the homosexual agenda. The Gallup Poll, for instance, has asked, "Would you favor or oppose a law that would allow homosexual couples to legally form civil unions, giving them some of the legal rights of married couples?"

This question itself is misleading, in that it downplays the legal impact of "civil unions." Vermont, the only U.S. state to adopt "civil unions" (under coercion of a state court), actually gives all "of the legal rights of married couples" available under state law to people in a same-sex "civil union"—not just "some." But despite this distortion, a 49-percent-to-49-percent split on this question in May 2003 had changed to opposition by a margin of 58 percent to 37 percent when the *Washington Post* asked the identical question in August 2003.

Even the percentage of Americans willing to declare that "homosexual relations between consenting adults" (never mind homosexual civil "marriage") "should be legal" dropped from 60 percent to only 48 percent between May and July of 2003. The biggest drop in support, a stunning 23 percentage points (from 58 percent to 35 percent), came among African Americans—despite the rhetoric of pro-homosexual activists who seek to frame the issues of "gay rights" and same-sex unions as a matter of "civil rights." . . .

EXPLORING THE ISSUE

Should Same-Sex Couples Be Able to Legally Marry?

Critical Thinking and Reflection

- What are some arguments made by each side with which you agree or disagree?
- What are the strengths and weaknesses of the two positions made in this chapter?
- Pick the side with which you most agree. What are some additional arguments you would make to strengthen the case for or against same-sex marriage?
- Think more broadly of the issue of same-sex marriage. How will same-sex marriage impact how people perceive lesbian and gay couples as well as the institution of marriage?

Is There Common Ground?

The topic of same-sex marriage can be a highly divisive issue. Pending action by the U.S. Supreme Court, this issue will continue to be decided by the states. Some additional states will probably pass marriage equality in the coming years. Other states have little chance of seeing marriage rights passed at the state level any time soon. In fact, in most states it is still legal to fire someone for their sexual orientation or gender identity/expression.

What do we do in states in which there appears to be limited debate? For example, in states that have same-sex marriage, are there certain exemptions that can and should be put into place for religious organizations? In states in which same-sex marriage becoming legal is not even on the horizon, are there ways in which other rights short of marriage could be extended? While some argue that civil unions offer insufficient protections, is that better than nothing in states in which the establishment of marital rights for same-sex couples seems implausible at best?

Additional Resources

The opinion of the court in *Perry v. Schwarzeneggar*:

https://ecf.cand.uscourts.gov/cand/09cv2292/

National Organization for Marriage:

http://www.nationformarriage.org/site/c.omL2KeN0LzH/b.3836955/k.BEC6/Home.htm

Human Rights Campaign and Marriage:

http://www.hrc.org/issues/marriage

Out & Equal's Business Case for Marriage Equality:

http://outandequal.org/marriageequality

ISSUE 11

Should Private Sexual Acts Between Gay Couples Be Illegal?

YES: Anthony Kennedy, from Majority Opinion, *Lawrence v. Texas*, U.S. Supreme Court (2003)

NO: Antonin Scalia, from Dissenting Opinion, *Lawrence v. Texas*, U.S. Supreme Court (2003)

Learning Outcomes
As a result of this issue, readers will be able to: • Identify the major arguments made for and against anti-sodomy laws.   • Compare and contrast the competing arguments made for and against anti-sodomy laws in this issue.   • Evaluate the implications of whether or not certain types of private, consensual sexual acts are legal or illegal.

ISSUE SUMMARY

YES: Anthony Kennedy, Associate Justice of the Supreme Court of the United States, was appointed to the Court by President Reagan in 1988. In this case, Kennedy is writing for a six-member majority that overturns a previous case, *Bowers v. Hardwick. Bowers* is overturned by Kennedy's opinion, therefore striking down state anti-sodomy laws.

NO: Antonin Scalia, Associate Justice of the Supreme Court of the United States, was appointed to the Court by President Reagan in 1986. Scalia writes that there are no constitutional protections from discrimination based on sexual orientation and that state sodomy laws should be upheld.

Antisodomy laws have been found throughout Western civilization dating back to the Middle Ages, a time during which the belief became common that non-procreative sex was immoral. The legacy of these morals is still evident in American society today. Throughout American history, homosexuality has been regarded as morally wrong and therefore has often been illegal. Many nineteenth- and twentieth-century religious readers and psychologists regarded homosexuality as a mental illness.

In 1948, Dr. Alfred Kinsey published the groundbreaking book *Sexual Behavior in the Human Male,* which was followed with the 1953 publication of another groundbreaking book, *Sexual Behavior in the Human Female.* In both texts, the longest chapters were specifically about homosexuality. Kinsey's work had a significant impact on challenging American sexual morality, and he was particularly concerned about the discrimination faced by those who were lesbian, gay, and bisexual, a population that at the time was largely regarded as sex criminals. His work, though widely read at the time, did not have an immediate widespread impact on public perceptions of those who were lesbian, gay, or bisexual. In fact, Kinsey's books were published at the onset of the Lavender Scare, a period in which it was official U.S. policy to fire lesbian and gay federal employees.

The American Psychological Association removed homosexuality from its list of mental disorders in 1973. Coming out of the closet became increasingly common, and challenges to state anti-sodomy laws were practically inevitable. In 1986, the U.S. Supreme Court ruled in *Bowers v. Hardwick* to uphold state anti-sodomy laws.

In 2003, the Supreme Court heard a similar anti-sodomy case with *Lawrence v. Texas.* Prior to *Bowers* and *Lawrence,* the Supreme Court had three times ruled in favor of a non-procreative right to sex. In the 1965 case of *Griswold v. Connecticut,* the Supreme Court ruled that married couples have the right to have access to contraception. *Eisenstadt v. Baird* (1972) extended this same right to unmarried couples. In 1973, the Supreme Court ruled in *Roe v. Wade* that women have a constitutional right to obtain an abortion. This right has been upheld in subsequent Supreme Court cases. Although each of these cases deals with non-procreative sexual behaviors, they address neither sodomy nor homosexuality.

Lawrence v. Texas began when John Lawrence, who was not getting along with his neighbor, was engaged in consensual sex in his residence with another man, Tyron Garner. Lawrence's neighbor called the police with a false report of a burglary in Lawrence's residence. The police, having legal grounds to enter Lawrence's residence based on the phone call, entered and found Lawrence and Garner having sex. Lawrence and Garner were arrested, and the police charged them with violating Texas's antihomosexual conduct law. For having been caught engaging in consensual sex in a private residence, both men were found guilty, spent a night in prison, and were fined $200.

Lawrence and Garner appealed their conviction, claiming that their constitutional rights had been violated. Explicit in their argument was a challenge to the constitutional reasoning behind *Bowers v. Hardwick,* essentially arguing that *Bowers* had been wrongly decided and should be overturned. In 2003, *Lawrence v. Texas* reached the Supreme Court of the United States.

Review the legal framework section of the Introduction that examines Original Intent and Living Constitution. The opinions in this case are clear examples of these concepts. Try to identify which opinion is written from an Original Intent perspective and which is written from a Living Constitution perspective.

Lawrence and Garner won the case, and anti-sodomy laws were struck down in the remaining states that had them. Lawrence's neighbor was charged with making a false report to the police. *Lawrence v. Texas* is beginning to be regarded as a landmark Supreme Court case. Although this case was a significant victory for those who advocate for lesbian, gay, and bisexual rights, many students are stunned to find that, until recently, sodomy was illegal in many states. It may be interesting to research the history of anti-sodomy laws in your state.

How would you assess how the political climate has changed since 2003, when this decision was issued? In what ways was Justice Scalia correct and in what ways was he incorrect about the changes he said this decision could lead to?

A significant number of cases dealing with sexual orientation have been decided in state courts. In 2003, same-sex marriage was prohibited in all 50 states and the District of Columbia. As this book reaches publication, same-sex marriage is permitted in six states (Connecticut, Iowa, Massachusetts, New Hampshire, New York, and Vermont) and Washington, D.C. California has 18,000 same-sex married couples who wed during a brief period of legal recognition. Other states, such as California and Maryland, have active efforts to make same-sex marriage legal. In addition, there are states, such as New Jersey, California, and Rhode Island, that have active movements working to ensure that same-sex marriage rights are extended to their states.

In addition to states extending equal marital rights, many large corporations are instituting the equivalent in the workplace. According to the Human Rights Campaign's 2009 Corporate Equality Index, 259 companies employing more than 9 million employees prohibit discrimination based on sexual orientation and gender identity, while providing domestic partner benefits to their employees. These companies, when operating in states that deny lesbian and gay couples the right to marry, treat same-sex couples just as they treat married, heterosexual couples.

Some of the states that permit same-sex marriage have done so through state court order, while others have done so through legislative action. The case of *Lawrence v. Texas* did not serve as cited precedent in any of these state court decisions. However, this chapter demonstrates how quickly societal values have changed on this topic in, historically speaking, a relatively short period of time.

Based on what you learned from reading this chapter, what might be some topics for future Supreme Court cases at the federal level that will be related to sexual orientation? For what types of topics might *Lawrence v. Texas* be a particularly pertinent precedent?

YES

Anthony Kennedy

Majority Opinion, *Lawrence v. Texas*

Liberty protects the person from unwarranted government intrusions into a dwelling or other private places. In our tradition, the State is not omnipresent in the home. And there are other spheres of our lives and existence, outside the home, where the State should not be a dominant presence. Freedom extends beyond spatial bounds. Liberty presumes an autonomy of self that includes freedom of thought, belief, expression, and certain intimate conduct. The instant case involves liberty of the person both in its spatial and more transcendent dimensions.

The question before the Court is the validity of a Texas statute making it a crime for two persons of the same sex to engage in certain intimate sexual conduct.

In Houston, Texas, officers of the Harris County Police Department were dispatched to a private residence in response to a reported weapons disturbance. They entered an apartment where one of the petitioners, John Geddes Lawrence, resided. The right of the police to enter does not seem to have been questioned. The officers observed Lawrence and another man, Tyron Garner, engaging in a sexual act. The two petitioners were arrested, held in custody overnight, and charged and convicted before a Justice of the Peace.

The complaints described their crime as "deviate sexual intercourse, namely anal sex, with a member of the same sex (man)." It provides: "A person commits an offense if he engages in deviate sexual intercourse with another individual of the same sex." The statute defines "[d]eviate sexual intercourse" as follows:

"(A) any contact between any part of the genitals of one person and the mouth or anus of another person; or

"(B) the penetration of the genitals or the anus of another person with an object."

We granted certiorari (2002) to consider three questions:

"1. Whether Petitioners' criminal convictions under the Texas 'Homosexual Conduct' law– which criminalizes sexual intimacy by same-sex couples, but not identical behavior by different-sex couples–violate the Fourteenth Amendment guarantee of equal protection of laws?

"2. Whether Petitioners' criminal convictions for adult consensual sexual intimacy in the home violate their vital interests in liberty and privacy protected by the Due Process Clause of the Fourteenth Amendment?

Majority Opinion: *Lawrence v. Texas,* United States Supreme Court 539 U. S 558 (2003).

"3. Whether *Bowers* v. *Hardwick,* (1986), should be overruled?"

The petitioners were adults at the time of the alleged offense. Their conduct was in private and consensual.

We conclude the case should be resolved by determining whether the petitioners were free as adults to engage in the private conduct in the exercise of their liberty under the Due Process Clause of the Fourteenth Amendment to the Constitution. For this inquiry, we deem it necessary to reconsider the Court's holding in *Bowers*.

There are broad statements of the substantive reach of liberty under the Due Process Clause; but the most pertinent beginning point is our decision in *Griswold* v. *Connecticut* (1965).

In *Griswold,* the Court invalidated a state law prohibiting the use of drugs or devices of contraception and counseling or aiding and abetting the use of contraceptives. The Court described the protected interest as a right to privacy and placed emphasis on the marriage relation and the protected space of the marital bedroom.

"It is true that in *Griswold,* the right of privacy in question inhered in the marital relationship. . . . If the right of privacy means anything, it is the right of the *individual*, married or single, to be free from unwarranted governmental intrusion into matters so fundamentally affecting a person as the decision whether to bear or beget a child."

The opinions in *Griswold* and *Eisenstadt* were part of the background for the decision in *Roe* v. *Wade* (1973). As is well known, the case involved a challenge to the Texas law prohibiting abortions, but the laws of other States were affected as well. Although the Court held the woman's rights were not absolute, her right to elect an abortion did have real and substantial protection as an exercise of her liberty under the Due Process Clause. The Court cited cases that protect spatial freedom and cases that go well beyond it. *Roe* recognized the right of a woman to make certain fundamental decisions affecting her destiny and confirmed once more that the protection of liberty under the Due Process Clause has a substantive dimension of fundamental significance in defining the rights of the person.

In *Carey* v. *Population Services Int'l* (1977), the Court confronted a New York law forbidding sale or distribution of contraceptive devices to persons under 16 years of age. Although there was no single opinion for the Court, the law was invalidated. Both *Eisenstadt* and *Carey*, as well as the holding and rationale in *Roe*, confirmed that the reasoning of *Griswold* could not be confined to the protection of rights of married adults. This was the state of the law with respect to some of the most relevant cases when the Court considered *Bowers* v. *Hardwick*.

The facts in *Bowers* had some similarities to the instant case. A police officer, whose right to enter seems not to have been in question, observed Hardwick, in his own bedroom, engaging in intimate sexual conduct with another adult male. The conduct was in violation of a Georgia statute making it a criminal offense to engage in sodomy. One difference between the two cases is that the Georgia statute prohibited the conduct whether or not the participants were of the same sex, while the Texas statute, as we have seen, applies only to participants of the same sex. Hardwick was not prosecuted, but he brought an action in federal court to declare the state statute invalid. He alleged he was a practicing homosexual and that the criminal prohibition violated rights guaranteed to him by the Constitution. The Court, in an opinion by Justice White, sustained the Georgia law.

The Court began its substantive discussion in *Bowers* as follows: "The issue presented is whether the Federal Constitution confers a fundamental right upon homosexuals to engage in sodomy and hence invalidates the laws of the many States that still make such conduct illegal and have done so for a very long time." That statement, we now conclude, discloses the Court's own failure to appreciate the extent of the liberty at stake. To say that the issue in *Bowers* was simply the right to engage in certain sexual conduct demeans the claim the individual put forward, just as it would demean a married couple were it to be said marriage is simply about the right to have sexual intercourse. The laws involved in *Bowers* and here are, to be sure, statutes that purport to do no more than prohibit a particular sexual act. Their penalties and purposes, though, have more far-reaching consequences, touching upon the most private human conduct, sexual behavior, and in the most private of places, the home. The statutes do seek to control a personal relationship that, whether or not entitled to formal recognition in the law, is within the liberty of persons to choose without being punished as criminals.

This, as a general rule, should counsel against attempts by the State, or a court, to define the meaning of the relationship or to set its boundaries absent injury to a person or abuse of an institution the law protects. It suffices for us to acknowledge that adults may choose to enter upon this relationship in the confines of their homes and their own private lives and still retain their dignity as free persons. When sexuality finds overt expression in intimate conduct with another person, the conduct can be but one element in a personal bond that is more enduring. The liberty protected by the Constitution allows homosexual persons the right to make this choice.

Having misapprehended the claim of liberty there presented to it, and thus stating the claim to be whether there is a fundamental right to engage in consensual sodomy, the *Bowers* Court said: "Proscriptions against that conduct have ancient roots." In academic writings, and in many of the scholarly *amicus* briefs filed to assist the Court in this case, there are fundamental criticisms of the historical premises relied upon by the majority and concurring opinions in *Bowers*. We need not enter this debate in the attempt to reach a definitive historical judgment, but the following considerations counsel against adopting the definitive conclusions upon which *Bowers* placed such reliance.

At the outset, it should be noted that there is no longstanding history in this country of laws directed at homosexual conduct as a distinct matter. Beginning in colonial times, there were prohibitions of sodomy derived from the English criminal laws passed in the first instance by the Reformation Parliament of 1533. The English prohibition was understood to include relations between men and women as well as relations between men and men. Nineteenth-century commentators similarly read American sodomy, buggery, and crime-against-nature statutes as criminalizing certain relations between men and women and between men and men. The absence of legal prohibitions focusing on homosexual conduct may be explained in part by noting that, according to some scholars, the concept of the homosexual as a distinct category of person did not emerge until the late 19th century. Thus, early American sodomy laws were not directed at homosexuals as such, but instead sought to prohibit nonprocreative sexual activity more generally. This does not suggest approval of homosexual conduct. It does tend to show that this particular form of conduct was not thought of as a separate category from like conduct between heterosexual persons.

Laws prohibiting sodomy do not seem to have been enforced against consenting adults acting in private. A substantial number of sodomy prosecutions and convictions for which there are surviving records were for predatory acts against those who could not or did not consent, as in the case of a minor or the victim of an assault. As to these, one purpose for the prohibitions was to ensure there would be no lack of coverage if a predator committed a sexual assault that did not constitute rape as defined by the criminal law. Thus, the model sodomy indictments presented in a 19th-century treatise addressed the predatory acts of an adult man against a minor girl or minor boy. Instead of targeting relations between consenting adults in private, 19th-century sodomy prosecutions typically involved relations between men and minor girls or minor boys, relations between adults involving force, relations between adults implicating disparity in status, or relations between men and animals.

To the extent that there were any prosecutions for the acts in question, 19th-century evidence rules imposed a burden that would make a conviction more difficult to obtain, even taking into account the problems always inherent in prosecuting consensual acts committed in private. Under then-prevailing standards, a man could not be convicted of sodomy based upon testimony of a consenting partner, because the partner was considered an accomplice. A partner's testimony, however, was admissible if he or she had not consented to the act or was a minor, and therefore incapable of consent. The rule may explain in part the infrequency of these prosecutions. In all events, that infrequency makes it difficult to say that society approved of a rigorous and systematic punishment of the consensual acts committed in private and by adults. The longstanding criminal prohibition of homosexual sodomy upon which the *Bowers* decision placed such reliance is as consistent with a general condemnation of nonprocreative sex as it is with an established tradition of prosecuting acts because of their homosexual character.

The policy of punishing consenting adults for private acts was not much discussed in the early legal literature. We can infer that one reason for this was the very private nature of the conduct. Despite the absence of prosecutions, there may have been periods in which there was public criticism of homosexuals as such and an insistence that the criminal laws be enforced to discourage their practices. But far from possessing "ancient roots," American laws targeting same-sex couples did not develop until the last third of the 20th century. The reported decisions concerning the prosecution of consensual, homosexual sodomy between adults for the years 1880–1995 are not always clear in the details, but a significant number involved conduct in a public place.

It was not until the 1970s that any State singled out same-sex relations for criminal prosecution, and only nine States have done so. Post-*Bowers,* even some of these States did not adhere to the policy of suppressing homosexual conduct. Over the course of the last decades, States with same-sex prohibitions have moved toward abolishing them.

In summary, the historical grounds relied upon in *Bowers* are more complex than the majority opinion and the concurring opinion by Chief Justice Burger indicate. Their historical premises are not without doubt and, at the very least, are overstated.

It must be acknowledged, of course, that the Court in *Bowers* was making the broader point that for centuries there have been powerful voices to condemn homosexual conduct as immoral. The condemnation has been shaped by religious beliefs, conceptions of right and acceptable behavior, and respect for the traditional family. For many persons, these are not trivial concerns but profound and deep convictions accepted as ethical and moral principles to which they aspire and which thus determine the course of their lives. These considerations do not answer the question before us, however. The issue is whether the majority may use the power of the State to enforce these views on the whole society through operation of the criminal law. "Our obligation is to define the liberty of all, not to mandate our own moral code." *Planned Parenthood of Southeastern Pa.* v. *Casey.*

Chief Justice Burger joined the opinion for the Court in *Bowers* and further explained his views as follows: "Decisions of individuals relating to homosexual conduct have been subject to state intervention throughout the history of Western civilization. Condemnation of those practices is firmly rooted in Judeo-Christian moral and ethical standards." As with Justice White's assumptions about history, scholarship casts some doubt on the sweeping nature of the statement by Chief Justice Burger as it pertains to private homosexual conduct between consenting adults. In all events, we think that our laws and traditions in the past half century are of most relevance here. These references show an emerging awareness that liberty gives substantial protection to adult persons in deciding how to conduct their private lives in matters pertaining to sex.

In 1955 the American Law Institute promulgated the Model Penal Code and made clear that it did not recommend or provide for "criminal penalties for consensual sexual relations conducted in private." It justified its decision on three grounds: (1) The prohibitions undermined respect for the law by penalizing conduct many people engaged in; (2) the statutes regulated private conduct not harmful to others; and (3) the laws were arbitrarily enforced and thus invited the danger of blackmail. Other States soon followed.

In *Bowers,* the Court referred to the fact that before 1961, all 50 States had outlawed sodomy, and that at the time of the Court's decision, 24 States and the District of Columbia had sodomy laws. Justice Powell pointed out that these prohibitions often were being ignored, however. Georgia, for instance, had not sought to enforce its law for decades.

The sweeping references by Chief Justice Burger to the history of Western civilization and to Judeo-Christian moral and ethical standards did not take account of other authorities pointing in an opposite direction. A committee advising the British Parliament recommended in 1957 repeal of laws punishing homosexual conduct. Parliament enacted the substance of those recommendations 10 years later.

Of even more importance, almost five years before *Bowers* was decided the European Court of Human Rights considered a case with parallels to *Bowers* and to today's case. An adult male resident in Northern Ireland alleged he was a practicing homosexual who desired to engage in consensual homosexual conduct. The laws of Northern Ireland forbade him that right. He alleged that he had been questioned, his home had been searched, and he feared criminal prosecution. The court held that the laws proscribing the conduct were invalid under the European Convention on Human Rights. Authoritative in all countries that are members of the Council of Europe (21 nations then, 45 nations now), the decision is at odds with the premise in *Bowers* that the claim put forward was insubstantial in our Western civilization.

In our own constitutional system, the deficiencies in *Bowers* became even more apparent in the years following its announcement. The 25 States with laws prohibiting the relevant conduct referenced in the *Bowers* decision are reduced now to 13, of which 4 enforce their laws only against homosexual conduct. In those States where sodomy is still proscribed, whether for same-sex or heterosexual conduct, there is a pattern of nonenforcement with respect to consenting adults acting in private. The State of Texas admitted in 1994 that as of that date, it had not prosecuted anyone under those circumstances.

Persons in a homosexual relationship may seek autonomy for these purposes, just as heterosexual persons do. The decision in *Bowers* would deny them this right.

The . . . post-*Bowers* case of principal relevance is *Romer* v. *Evans* (1996). There the Court struck down class-based legislation directed at homosexuals as a violation of the Equal Protection Clause. *Romer* invalidated an amendment to Colorado's constitution which named as a solitary class persons who were homosexuals, lesbians, or bisexual either by "orientation, conduct, practices, or relationships," and deprived them of protection under state antidiscrimination laws. We concluded that the provision was "born of animosity toward the class of persons affected" and, further, that it had no rational relation to a legitimate governmental purpose.

As an alternative argument in this case, counsel for the petitioners and some *amici* contend that *Romer* provides the basis for declaring the Texas statute invalid under the Equal Protection Clause. That is a tenable argument, but we conclude the instant case requires us to address whether *Bowers* itself has continuing validity. Were we to hold the statute invalid under the Equal Protection Clause, some might question whether a prohibition would be valid if drawn differently, say, to prohibit the conduct both between same-sex and different-sex participants.

Equality of treatment and the due process right to demand respect for conduct protected by the substantive guarantee of liberty are linked in important respects, and a decision on the latter point advances both interests. If protected conduct is made criminal and the law which does so remains unexamined for its substantive validity, its stigma might remain even if it were not enforceable as drawn for equal protection reasons. When homosexual conduct is made criminal by the law of the State, that declaration in and of itself is an invitation to subject homosexual persons to discrimination both in the public and in the private spheres. The central holding of *Bowers* has been brought in question by this case, and it should be addressed. Its continuance as precedent demeans the lives of homosexual persons.

The stigma this criminal statute imposes, moreover, is not trivial. The offense, to be sure, is but a class C misdemeanor, a minor offense in the Texas legal system. Still, it remains a criminal offense, with all that imports for the dignity of the persons charged. The petitioners will bear on their record the history of their criminal convictions. Just this Term, we rejected various challenges to state laws requiring the registration of sex offenders. We are advised that if Texas convicted an adult for private, consensual homosexual conduct under the statute here in question, the convicted person would come within the registration laws of a least four States were he or she to be subject to their jurisdiction. This underscores the consequential nature of the punishment and the state-sponsored condemnation attendant to the criminal prohibition. Furthermore, the Texas criminal conviction carries with it the other collateral consequences always following a conviction, such as notations on job application forms, to mention but one example.

The foundations of *Bowers* have sustained serious erosion from our recent decisions in *Casey* and *Romer*. When our precedent has been thus weakened, criticism from other sources is of greater significance. In the United States criticism of *Bowers* has been substantial and continuing, disapproving of its reasoning in all respects, not just as to its historical assumptions. The courts of five different States have declined to follow it in interpreting provisions in their own state constitutions parallel to the Due Process Clause of the Fourteenth Amendment.

To the extent *Bowers* relied on values we share with a wider civilization, it should be noted that the reasoning and holding in *Bowers* have been rejected elsewhere. The European Court of Human Rights has followed not *Bowers* but its own decision in *Dudgeon* v. *United Kingdom*. Other nations, too, have taken action consistent with an affirmation of the protected right of homosexual adults to engage in intimate, consensual conduct. The right the petitioners seek in this case has been accepted as an integral part of human freedom in many other countries. There has been no showing that in this country, the governmental interest in circumscribing personal choice is somehow more legitimate or urgent.

The rationale of *Bowers* does not withstand careful analysis. In his dissenting opinion in *Bowers,* Justice Stevens came to these conclusions:

"Our prior cases make two propositions abundantly clear. First, the fact that the governing majority in a State has traditionally viewed a particular practice as immoral is not a sufficient reason for upholding a law prohibiting the practice; neither history nor tradition could save a law prohibiting miscegenation from constitutional attack. Second, individual decisions by married persons, concerning the intimacies of their physical relationship, even when not intended to produce offspring, are a form of "liberty" protected by the Due Process Clause of the Fourteenth Amendment. Moreover, this protection extends to intimate choices by unmarried as well as married persons."

Justice Stevens' analysis, in our view, should have been controlling in *Bowers* and should control here.

Bowers was not correct when it was decided, and it is not correct today. It ought not to remain binding precedent. *Bowers* v. *Hardwick* should be and now is overruled.

The present case does not involve minors. It does not involve persons who might be injured or coerced or who are situated in relationships where consent might not easily be refused. It does not involve public conduct or prostitution. It does not involve whether the government must give formal recognition to any relationship that homosexual persons seek to enter. The case does involve two adults who, with full and mutual consent from each other, engaged in sexual practices common to a homosexual lifestyle. The petitioners are entitled to respect for their private lives. The State cannot demean their existence or control their destiny by making their private sexual conduct a crime. Their right to liberty under the Due Process Clause gives them the full right to engage in their conduct without intervention of the government. "It is a promise of the Constitution that there is a realm of personal liberty which the government may not enter." The Texas statute furthers no legitimate state interest which can justify its intrusion into the personal and private life of the individual.

Had those who drew and ratified the Due Process Clauses of the Fifth Amendment or the Fourteenth Amendment known the components of liberty in its manifold possibilities, they might have been more specific. They did not presume to have this insight. They knew times can blind us to certain truths and later generations can see that laws once thought necessary and proper in fact serve only to oppress. As the Constitution endures, persons in every generation can invoke its principles in their own search for greater freedom.

The judgment of the Court of Appeals for the Texas Fourteenth District is reversed, and the case is remanded for further proceedings not inconsistent with this opinion.

It is so ordered.

Dissenting Opinion, *Lawrence v. Texas*

Most of the rest of today's opinion has no relevance to its actual holding—that the Texas statute "furthers no legitimate state interest which can justify" its application to petitioners under rational-basis review. Though there is discussion of "fundamental proposition[s]," and "fundamental decisions," *ibid.* nowhere does the Court's opinion declare that homosexual sodomy is a "fundamental right" under the Due Process Clause; nor does it subject the Texas law to the standard of review that would be appropriate (strict scrutiny) if homosexual sodomy *were* a "fundamental right." Thus, while overruling the *outcome* of *Bowers*, the Court leaves strangely untouched its central legal conclusion: "[R]espondent would have us announce . . . a fundamental right to engage in homosexual sodomy. This we are quite unwilling to do." Instead, the Court simply describes petitioners' conduct as "an exercise of their liberty"—which it undoubtedly is—and proceeds to apply an unheard-of form of rational-basis review that will have far-reaching implications beyond this case.

(1) A preliminary digressive observation with regard to the first factor: The Court's claim that *"Planned Parenthood* v. *Casey, supra,* "casts some doubt" upon the holding in *Bowers* (or any other case, for that matter) does not withstand analysis. As far as its holding is concerned, *Casey* provided a *less* expansive right to abortion than did *Roe, which was already on the books when Bowers was decided.* I have never heard of a law that attempted to restrict one's "right to define" certain concepts; and if the passage calls into question the government's power to regulate *actions based on* one's self-defined "concept of existence, etc.," it is the passage that ate the rule of law.

(2) *Bowers,* the Court says, has been subject to "substantial and continuing [criticism], disapproving of its reasoning in all respects, not just as to its historical assumptions." Exactly what those nonhistorical criticisms are, and whether the Court even agrees with them, are left unsaid, although the Court does cite two books. Of course, *Roe* too (and by extension *Casey)* had been (and still is) subject to unrelenting criticism, including criticism from the two commentators cited by the Court today.

Dissenting Opinion: *Lawrence v. Texas,* United States Supreme Court 539 U. S 558 (2003).

(3) That leaves, to distinguish the rock-solid, unamendable disposition of *Roe* from the readily overrulable *Bowers,* only the third factor. "[T]here has been," the Court says, "no individual or societal reliance on *Bowers* of the sort that could counsel against overturning its holding. . . ." *Ante,* at 16. It seems to me that the "societal reliance" on the principles confirmed in *Bowers* and discarded today has been overwhelming. Countless judicial decisions and legislative enactments have relied on the ancient proposition that a governing majority's belief that certain sexual behavior is "immoral and unacceptable" constitutes a rational basis for regulation. We ourselves relied extensively on *Bowers* when we concluded, in *Barnes* v. *Glen Theatre, Inc.* (1991), that Indiana's public indecency statute furthered "a substantial government interest in protecting order and morality." State laws against bigamy, same-sex marriage, adult incest, prostitution, masturbation, adultery, fornication, bestiality, and obscenity are likewise sustainable only in light of *Bowers'* validation of laws based on moral choices. Every single one of these laws is called into question by today's decision; the Court makes no effort to cabin the scope of its decision to exclude them from its holding. See *ante,* at 11 (noting "an emerging awareness that liberty gives substantial protection to adult persons in deciding how to conduct their private lives *in matters pertaining to sex*" (emphasis added)). The impossibility of distinguishing homosexuality from other traditional "morals" offenses is precisely why *Bowers* rejected the rational-basis challenge. "The law," it said, "is constantly based on notions of morality, and if all laws representing essentially moral choices are to be invalidated under the Due Process Clause, the courts will be very busy indeed."

Texas Penal Code (2003) undoubtedly imposes constraints on liberty. So do laws prohibiting prostitution, recreational use of heroin, and, for that matter, working more than 60 hours per week in a bakery. But there is no right to "liberty" under the Due Process Clause, though today's opinion repeatedly makes that claim. The Fourteenth Amendment *expressly allows* States to deprive their citizens of "liberty," so long as "due process of law" is provided:

"No state shall . . . deprive any person of life, liberty, or property, *without due process of law.*"

Our opinions applying the doctrine known as "substantive due process" hold that the Due Process Clause prohibits States from infringing *fundamental* liberty interests, unless the infringement is narrowly tailored to serve a compelling state interest. We have held repeatedly, in cases the Court today does not overrule, that *only* fundamental rights qualify for this so-called "heightened scrutiny" protection—that is, rights which are "'deeply rooted in this Nation's history and tradition.'" All other liberty interests may be abridged or abrogated pursuant to a validly enacted state law if that law is rationally related to a legitimate state interest.

Bowers held, first, that criminal prohibitions of homosexual sodomy are not subject to heightened scrutiny because they do not implicate a "fundamental right" under the Due Process Clause. Noting that "[p]roscriptions against that conduct have ancient roots," *id.,* at 192, that "[s]odomy was a criminal offense at common law and was forbidden by the laws of the original 13 States when they ratified the Bill of Rights," and that many States had retained their bans on sodomy, *Bowers* concluded that a right to engage in homosexual sodomy was not "'deeply rooted in this Nation's history and tradition.'"

The Court today does not overrule this holding. Not once does it describe homosexual sodomy as a "fundamental right" or a "fundamental liberty interest," nor does it subject the Texas statute to strict scrutiny. Instead, having failed to establish that the right to homosexual sodomy is "'deeply rooted in this Nation's history and tradition,'" the Court concludes that the application of Texas's statute to petitioners' conduct fails the rational-basis test, and overrules *Bowers'* holding to the contrary, "The Texas statute furthers no legitimate state interest which can justify its intrusion into the personal and private life of the individual."

The Court's description of "the state of the law" at the time of *Bowers* only confirms that *Bowers* was right. The Court points to *Griswold* v. *Connecticut* (1965). But that case *expressly disclaimed* any reliance on the doctrine of "substantive due process," and grounded the so-called "right to privacy" in penumbras of constitutional provisions *other than* the Due Process Clause. *Eisenstadt* v. *Baird* (1972), likewise had nothing to do with "substantive due process"; it invalidated a Massachusetts law prohibiting the distribution of contraceptives to unmarried persons solely on the basis of the Equal Protection Clause. Of course *Eisenstadt* contains well known dictum relating to the "right to privacy," but this referred to the right recognized in *Griswold*—a right penumbral to the *specific* guarantees in the Bill of Rights, and not a "substantive due process" right.

Roe v. *Wade* recognized that the right to abort an unborn child was a "fundamental right" protected by the Due Process Clause. The *Roe* Court, however, made no attempt to establish that this right was "'deeply rooted in this Nation's history and tradition'"; instead, it based its conclusion that "the Fourteenth Amendment's concept of personal liberty . . . is broad enough to encompass a woman's decision whether or not to terminate her pregnancy" on its own normative judgment that anti-abortion laws were undesirable. We have since rejected *Roe's* holding that regulations of abortion must be narrowly tailored to serve a compelling state interest.

After discussing the history of anti-sodomy laws, the Court proclaims that, "it should be noted that there is no longstanding history in this country of laws directed at homosexual conduct as a distinct matter." This observation in no way casts into doubt the "definitive [historical] conclusion" on which *Bowers* relied: that our Nation has a longstanding history of laws prohibiting *sodomy in general*—regardless of whether it was performed by same-sex or opposite-sex couples:

"It is obvious to us that neither of these formulations would extend a fundamental right to homosexuals to engage in acts of consensual sodomy. Proscriptions against that conduct have ancient roots. *Sodomy* was a criminal offense at common law and was forbidden by the laws of the original 13 States when they ratified the Bill of Rights. In 1868, when the Fourteenth Amendment was ratified, all but 5 of the 37 States in the Union had *criminal sodomy laws*. In fact, until 1961, all 50 States outlawed *sodomy*, and today, 24 States and the District of Columbia continue to provide criminal penalties for *sodomy* performed in private and between consenting adults. Against this background, to claim that a right to engage in such conduct is 'deeply rooted in this Nation's history and tradition' or 'implicit in the concept of ordered liberty' is, at best, facetious."

It is (as *Bowers* recognized) entirely irrelevant whether the laws in our long national tradition criminalizing homosexual sodomy were "directed at homosexual conduct as a distinct matter." Whether homosexual sodomy was prohibited by a law targeted at same-sex sexual relations or by a more general law prohibiting both homosexual and heterosexual sodomy, the only relevant point is that it *was* criminalized—which suffices to establish that homosexual sodomy is not a right "deeply rooted in our Nation's history and tradition." The Court today agrees that homosexual sodomy was criminalized and thus does not dispute the facts on which *Bowers actually* relied.

Next the Court makes the claim, again unsupported by any citations, that "[l]aws prohibiting sodomy do not seem to have been enforced against consenting adults acting in private." *Ante,* at 8. The key qualifier here is "acting in private"—since the Court admits that sodomy laws *were* enforced against consenting adults (although the Court contends that prosecutions were "infrequent"). I do not know what "acting in private" means; surely consensual sodomy, like heterosexual intercourse, is rarely performed on stage. If all the Court means by "acting in private" is "on private premises, with the doors closed and windows covered," it is entirely unsurprising that evidence of enforcement would be hard to come by. (Imagine the circumstances that would enable a search warrant to be obtained for a residence on the ground that there was probable cause to believe that consensual sodomy was then and there occurring.) Surely that lack of evidence would not sustain the proposition that consensual sodomy on private premises with the doors closed and windows covered was regarded as a "fundamental right," even though all other consensual sodomy was criminalized. There are 203 prosecutions for consensual, adult homosexual sodomy reported in the West Reporting system and official state reporters from the years 1880–1995. There are also records of 20 sodomy prosecutions and 4 executions during the colonial period. *Bowers'* conclusion that homosexual sodomy is not a fundamental right "deeply rooted in this Nation's history and tradition" is utterly unassailable.

Realizing that fact, the Court instead says: "[W]e think that our laws and traditions in the past half century are of most relevance here. These references show *an emerging awareness* that liberty gives substantial protection to adult persons in deciding how to conduct their private lives *in matters pertaining to sex*" (emphasis added). Apart from the fact that such an "emerging awareness" does not establish a "fundamental right," the statement is factually false. States continue to prosecute all sorts of crimes by adults "in matters pertaining to sex": prostitution, adult incest, adultery, obscenity, and child pornography. Sodomy laws, too, have been enforced "in the past half century," in which there have been 134 reported cases involving prosecutions for consensual, adult, homosexual sodomy. In relying, for evidence of an "emerging recognition," upon the American Law Institute's 1955 recommendation not to criminalize "'consensual sexual relations conducted in private,'" the Court ignores the fact that this recommendation was "a point of resistance in most of the states that considered adopting the Model Penal Code." Gaylaw 159.

In any event, an "emerging awareness" is by definition not "deeply rooted in this Nation's history and tradition[s]," as we have said "fundamental right" status requires. Constitutional entitlements do not spring into existence because some States choose to lessen or eliminate criminal sanctions on certain behavior. Much less do they spring into existence, as the Court seems to believe, because *foreign nations* decriminalize conduct. The *Bowers* majority opinion *never* relied on "values we share with a wider civilization," but rather rejected the claimed right to sodomy on the ground that such a right was not "'deeply rooted in *this Nation's* history and tradition'" (emphasis added). *Bowers'* rational-basis holding is likewise devoid of any reliance on the views of a "wider civilization." The Court's discussion of these foreign views (ignoring, of course, the many countries that have retained criminal prohibitions on sodomy) is therefore meaningless dicta. Dangerous dicta, however, since "this Court . . . should not impose foreign moods, fads, or fashions on Americans."

I turn now to the ground on which the Court squarely rests its holding: the contention that there is no rational basis for the law here under attack. This proposition is so out of accord with our jurisprudence—indeed, with the jurisprudence of *any* society we know—that it requires little discussion.

The Texas statute undeniably seeks to further the belief of its citizens that certain forms of sexual behavior are "immoral and unacceptable," *Bowers*—the same interest furthered by criminal laws against fornication, bigamy, adultery, adult incest, bestiality, and obscenity. *Bowers* held that this *was* a legitimate state interest. The Court today reaches the opposite conclusion. The Texas statute, it says, "furthers *no legitimate state interest* which can justify its intrusion into the personal and private life of the individual" (emphasis addded). The Court embraces instead Justice Stevens' declaration in his *Bowers* dissent, that "the fact that the governing majority in a State has traditionally viewed a particular practice as immoral is not a sufficient reason for upholding a law prohibiting the practice." This effectively decrees the end of all morals legislation. If, as the Court asserts, the promotion of majoritarian sexual morality is not even a *legitimate* state interest, none of the above-mentioned laws can survive rational-basis review.

Finally, I turn to petitioners' equal-protection challenge, which no Member of the Court save Justice O'Connor, *ante*, at 1 (opinion concurring in judgment), embraces: On its face, §21.06(a) applies equally to all persons. Men and women, heterosexuals and homosexuals, are all subject to its prohibition of deviate sexual intercourse with someone of the same sex. To be sure, §21.06 does distinguish between the sexes insofar as concerns the partner with whom the sexual acts are performed: men can violate the law only with other men, and women only with other women. But this cannot itself be a denial of equal protection, since it is precisely the same distinction regarding partner that is drawn in state laws prohibiting marriage with someone of the same sex while permitting marriage with someone of the opposite sex.

The objection is made, however, that the antimiscegenation laws invalidated in *Loving* v. *Virginia* (1967), similarly were applicable to whites and blacks alike, and only distinguished between the races insofar as the *partner* was concerned. In *Loving*, however, we correctly applied heightened scrutiny, rather than the usual rational-basis review, because the Virginia statute was "designed to maintain White Supremacy." A racially discriminatory purpose is always sufficient to subject a law to strict scrutiny, even a facially neutral law that makes no mention of race. No purpose to discriminate against men or women as a class can be gleaned from the Texas law, so rational-basis review applies. That review is readily satisfied here by the same rational basis that satisfied it in *Bowers*—society's belief that certain forms of sexual behavior are "immoral and unacceptable." This is the same justification that supports many other laws regulating sexual behavior that make a distinction based upon the identity of the partner—for example, laws against adultery, fornication, and adult incest and laws refusing to recognize homosexual marriage.

Justice O'Connor argues that the discrimination in this law which must be justified is not its discrimination with regard to the sex of the partner but its discrimination with regard to the sexual proclivity of the principal actor.

"While it is true that the law applies only to conduct, the conduct targeted by this law is conduct that is closely correlated with being homosexual. Under such circumstances, Texas' sodomy law is targeted at more than conduct. It is instead directed toward gay persons as a class."

Of course, the same could be said of any law. A law against public nudity targets "the conduct that is closely correlated with being a nudist," and hence "is targeted at more than conduct"; it is "directed toward nudists as a class." But be that as it may. Even if the Texas law *does* deny equal protection to "homosexuals as a class," that denial *still* does not need to be justified by anything more than a rational basis, which our cases show is satisfied by the enforcement of traditional notions of sexual morality.

Justice O'Connor simply decrees application of "a more searching form of rational basis review" to the Texas statute. The cases she cites do not recognize such a standard, and reach their conclusions only after finding, as required by conventional rational-basis analysis, that no conceivable legitimate state interest supports the classification at issue. Nor does Justice O'Connor explain precisely what her "more searching form" of rational-basis review consists of. It must at least mean, however, that laws exhibiting "'a . . . desire to harm a politically unpopular group'" are invalid *even though* there may be a conceivable rational basis to support them.

This reasoning leaves on pretty shaky grounds state laws limiting marriage to opposite-sex couples. Justice O'Connor seeks to preserve them by the conclusory statement that "preserving the traditional institution of marriage" is a legitimate state interest. But "preserving the traditional institution of marriage" is just a kinder way of describing the State's *moral disapproval* of same-sex couples. Texas's interest in §21.06 could be recast in similarly euphemistic terms: "preserving the traditional sexual mores of our society." In the jurisprudence Justice O'Connor has seemingly created, judges can validate laws by characterizing them as "preserving the traditions of society" (good); or invalidate them by characterizing them as "expressing moral disapproval" (bad).

Today's opinion is the product of a Court, which is the product of a law-profession culture that has largely signed on to the so-called homosexual agenda, by which I mean the agenda promoted by some homosexual activists directed at eliminating the moral opprobrium that has traditionally attached to homosexual conduct. I noted in an earlier opinion the fact that the American Association of Law Schools (to which any reputable law school *must* seek to belong) excludes from membership any school that refuses to ban from its job-interview facilities a law firm (no matter how small) that does not wish to hire as a prospective partner a person who openly engages in homosexual conduct.

One of the most revealing statements in today's opinion is the Court's grim warning that the criminalization of homosexual conduct is "an invitation to subject homosexual persons to discrimination both in the public and in the private spheres." It is clear from this that the Court has taken sides in the culture war, departing from its role of assuring, as neutral observer, that the democratic rules of engagement are observed. Many Americans do not want persons who openly engage in homosexual conduct as partners in their business, as scoutmasters for their children, as teachers in their children's schools, or as boarders in their home. They view this as protecting themselves and their families from a lifestyle that they believe to be immoral and destructive. The Court views it as "discrimination" which it is the function of our judgments to deter. So imbued is the Court with the law profession's anti-anti-homosexual culture, that it is seemingly unaware that the attitudes of that culture are not obviously "mainstream"; that in most States, what the Court calls "discrimination" against those who engage in homosexual acts is perfectly legal; that proposals to ban such "discrimination" under Title VII have repeatedly been rejected by Congress.

Let me be clear that I have nothing against homosexuals, or any other group, promoting their agenda through normal democratic means. Social perceptions of sexual and other morality change over time, and every group has the right to persuade its fellow citizens that its view of such matters is the best. That homosexuals have achieved some success in that enterprise is attested to by the fact that Texas is one of the few remaining States that criminalize private, consensual homosexual acts. But persuading one's fellow citizens is one thing, and imposing one's views in absence of democratic majority will is something else. I would no more *require* a State to criminalize homosexual acts—or, for that matter, display *any* moral disapprobation of them—than I would *forbid* it to do so. What Texas has chosen to do is well within the range of traditional democratic action, and its hand should not be stayed through the invention of a brand-new "constitutional right" by a Court that is impatient of democratic change. It is indeed true that "later generations can see that laws once thought necessary and proper in fact serve only to oppress," and when that happens, later generations can repeal those laws. But it is the premise of our system that those judgments are to be made by the people, and not imposed by a governing caste that knows best.

One of the benefits of leaving regulation of this matter to the people rather than to the courts is that the people, unlike judges, need not carry things to their logical conclusion. The people may feel that their disapprobation of homosexual conduct is strong enough to disallow homosexual marriage, but not strong enough to criminalize private homosexual acts—and may legislate accordingly. The Court today pretends that it possesses a similar freedom of action, so that that we need not fear judicial imposition of homosexual marriage, as has recently occurred in Canada (in a decision that the Canadian Government has chosen not to appeal). At the end of its opinion—after having laid waste the foundations of our rational-basis jurisprudence—the Court says that the present case "does not involve whether the government must give formal recognition to any relationship that homosexual persons seek to enter." Do not believe it. More illuminating than this bald, unreasoned disclaimer is the progression of thought displayed by an earlier passage in the Court's opinion, which notes the constitutional protections afforded to "personal decisions relating to *marriage*, procreation, contraception, family relationships, child rearing, and education," and then declares that "[p]ersons in a homosexual relationship may seek autonomy for these purposes, just as heterosexual persons do" (emphasis added). Today's opinion dismantles the structure of constitutional law that has permitted a distinction to be made between heterosexual and homosexual unions, insofar as formal recognition in marriage is concerned. If moral disapprobation of homosexual conduct is "no legitimate state interest" for purposes of proscribing that conduct, and if, as the Court coos (casting aside all pretense of neutrality), "[w]hen sexuality finds overt expression in intimate conduct with another person, the conduct can be but one element in a personal bond that is more enduring," what justification could there possibly be for denying the benefits of marriage to homosexual couples exercising "[t]he liberty protected by the Constitution," Surely not the encouragement of procreation, since the sterile and the elderly are allowed to marry. This case "does not involve" the issue of homosexual marriage only if one entertains the belief that principle and logic have nothing to do with the decisions of this Court. Many will hope that, as the Court comfortingly assures us, this is so.

The matters appropriate for this Court's resolution are only three: Texas's prohibition of sodomy neither infringes a "fundamental right" (which the Court does not dispute), nor is unsupported by a rational relation to what the Constitution considers a legitimate state interest, nor denies the equal protection of the laws. I dissent.

EXPLORING THE ISSUE

Should Private Sexual Acts Between Gay Couples Be Illegal?

Critical Thinking and Reflection

- What are some arguments made by each side with which you agree or disagree?
- What are the strengths and weaknesses of the two positions made in this chapter?
- Pick the side with which you most agree.
- What are some additional arguments you would make to strengthen the case for or against anti-sodomy laws?
- Think more broadly of the issue of anti-sodomy laws. This law inherently affects same-sex couples. What do the existence of such laws, or the absence of them, demonstrate about larger views about sexual orientation and power in American society?

Is There Common Ground?

While there might be differences in views regarding what laws should say regarding relationships, what about status related to discrimination? Are there those who would support anti-sodomy laws but also agree that no one should be fired due to their sexual orientation or gender identity/expression? Are there those who oppose anti-sodomy laws but want to work to create a greater understanding about diversity and inclusion?

In addition, if we are going to uphold anti-sodomy laws, what does that mean about other rights? If sodomy can be illegal, can contraception become illegal? After all, is it any different for heterosexuals to have non-procreative sex versus those who are gay or lesbian? What are the implications (good and/or bad) of agreeing that there are no inherent rights to private, sexual behavior?

Additional Resources

Human Rights Campaign:

http://www.hrc.org

Lambda Legal:

http://www.lambdalegal.org/

American Family Association:

http://www.afa.net

Focus on the Family:

http://www.focusonthefamily.com/

ISSUE 12

Are Traditional Families Better for Children?

YES: Allan C. Carlson and Paul T. Mero, excerpts from *The Natural Family: A Manifesto* (2005–2006).

NO: Mark Good, "Nontraditional Families and Childhood Progress through School," written for *Taking Sides: Family and Personal Relationships* (2012)

Learning Outcomes

As a result of this issue, readers will be able to:

- Identify the major arguments made for and against the traditional family.
- Compare and contrast the competing arguments made for and against the traditional family in this issue.
- Evaluate the implications of changing family structure on children and the larger American society.

ISSUE SUMMARY

YES: Allan Carlson is president of the Howard Center for Family, Religion & Society and Distinguished Fellow in Family Policy Studies at the Family Research Council in Washington, D.C. Paul Mero is president of the Sutherland Institute and a trustee of the ALS Foundation. Carlson and Mero argue that America needs to return to a traditional family headed by a man and woman.

NO: Mark Good is a professor of counselor education at West Chester University and the president of Opn-Wyd, a diversity and communication company. Good argues that diversity in traditional and nontraditional families is healthy. In fact, he argues that it can be damaging to hold up the traditional family as the ideal familial structure.

Throughout most of American history, the concept of marriage and parenthood has seen a mild fluctuation. Ages for marriage may have changed a bit. Much has remained steady and intact, but over the past decades, we also have seen a fairly profound change in the nature of family.

Greater access to birth control, which was guaranteed to all married couples by the Supreme Court during the late 1960s, gave couples greater power over the timing of and frequency of child rearing. While women still face discrimination in terms of employment and wages, today's woman has more opportunities in the workplace than in generations past. Indeed, there was a time in American history when marriage was virtually the only way that women could secure their economic future. Today, women face different challenges than men, but millions manage to provide to support single mothers and their children. During times of economic distress, the discrepancy in wages can result in increased job security for women. For example, while there certainly is discrimination based on wages, in 2010, more women were employed than men.

Economic opportunities for women are by no means the only issue reconstructing our definition of families. For example, same-sex marriage, something not recognized in any of the 50 states just one decade ago, is legal in six states and Washington, D.C., and is likely to spread to additional states over the coming years. Today, the number of adults who have never married remains much higher than it had been for generations past. This trend is not absent of having children, as there is also a rise in single parents raising children in the United States.

What do these changes mean? These days, are adult generations living in diverse family structures at the expense of and to the detriment of children? Or have we reached a more democratic, egalitarian family structure that comes closer to embracing our nation's true diversity? The answer divides a wide array of Americans.

Each political party has a different view of the value of traditional versus nontraditional families. The 2008 Republican National Platform states the following:

Preserving Traditional Marriage

Because our children's future is best preserved within the traditional understanding of marriage, we call for a constitutional amendment that fully protects marriage as a union of a man and a woman. . . .

Republicans recognize the importance of having in the home a father and a mother who are married. The two-parent family still provides the best environment of stability, discipline, responsibility, and character. Children in homes without fathers are more likely to commit a crime, drop out of school, become violent, become teen parents, use illegal drugs, become mired in poverty, or have emotional or behavioral problems. We support the courageous efforts of single-parent families to provide a stable home for their children. . . .

As the family is our basic unit of society, we oppose initiatives to erode parental rights.

On which side of this debate would one find the Republican Party? If we look back to the Political Ideology continuum at the start of the chapter, where would the aforementioned views fall along the continuum? While supporting the traditional family, there is an acknowledgment of the "courage" of single parents. Why is this, when they cite a two-parent family as the ideal?

What about examining the Republican position through a Lakoffian Nation as Family framework, also cited in the Introduction. Does this represent Strict Father Morality? Nurturant Parent Morality? What does the language itself tell you about the larger worldview of the Republican Party as stated in this section of their platform?

The Democratic National Committee released its own platform that mentions families without using the word *traditional:*

Children and Families
If we are to renew America, we must do a better job of investing in the next generation of Americans. For parents, the first and most sacred responsibility is to support our children: setting an example of excellence, turning off the TV, and helping with the homework. But we must also support parents as they strive to raise their children in a new era. We must make it easier for working parents to spend time with their families when they need to. . . We also must recognize that caring for family members and managing a household is real and valuable work.

Fatherhood
Too many fathers are missing—missing from too many lives and too many homes. Children who grow up without a father are five times more likely to live in poverty and are more likely to commit crime, drop out of school, abuse drugs, and end up in prison. We need more fathers to realize that responsibility does not end at conception. We need them to understand that what makes a man is not the ability to have a child—it's the courage to raise one.

On which side of this debate would one find the Democratic Party? If we look back to the Political Ideology continuum at the start of the chapter, where would the aforementioned views fall along the continuum? While supporting the family, there is a listing of the qualities of good parents rather than a focus on the structure of the family. Why do Democrats avoid citing the structure of the ideal American family?

What about examining the Democratic position through a Lakoffian Nation as Family framework. Does this represent Strict Father Morality? Nurturant Parent Morality? What does the language itself tell you about the larger worldview of the Democratic Party, as stated in this section of their platform?

This issue contains two articles about whether the traditional family is the ideal family structure. *The Natural Family: A Manifesto* contains excerpts in this book intended to help the reader understand the case for the traditional (i.e., natural) family. The counterpoint by Professor Good argues that family diversity is itself a valuable goal in a pluralistic society.

YES

Allan C. Carlson
and Paul T. Mero

The Natural Family: A Manifesto

What is the natural family? The answer comes to the woman and the man who take the risk of turning their love into promises of lifelong devotion.

In doing so, they will discover the story of the family, at once an ideal vision and a universal reality. In our time, they will also sense crisis, for malignant forces tear at the common source of freedom, order, virtue, and children. To set things right, they will need to look for clear principles, open goals, and a firm course of action. They also will need to reject false charges and weak compromise. Still, through these acts they shall come to know true liberty, a rekindled hearth, and a real homecoming, for themselves and for all humankind.

The Story of the Family

A young man and a young woman draw toward each other. They yearn to be as one. When they see the other, broad smiles appear. They sense the possibility of joy. Alone, they feel partial, incomplete. When together, they feel whole. The people among whom they live bless this bond in the celebration of marriage. The man and the woman exchange public vows with each other, and also with their kindred and neighbors, and the two become one flesh.

Over time, their joy and passion will be tested by the twists and surprises of life. They will cry together, sometimes in happiness, sometimes in sorrow. They will face sickness; they may know poverty; they could face dislocation or natural disaster; they might be torn apart by war. In times of despair or loss, they will find strength in each other. Facing death, they will feel the warm spiritual balm that heals the pain of physical separation. The conjugal bond built on fidelity, mutual duty, and respect allows both of them to emerge into their full potential; they become as their Creator intended, a being complete.

This marriage creates a new family, a home, the first and fundamental unit of human society. Here, husband and wife build a small economy. They share the work of provisioning, drawing on each one's interests, strengths, and skills. They craft a home which becomes a special place on earth. In centuries past, the small farm or the artisan's shop was the usual expression of this union between the sexual and the economic. Today, the urban townhouse, apartment, or suburban home are more common. Still, the small home economy remains the vital center of daily existence.

The wife and husband also build their home as a spiritual place. They learn that family and faith are, in fact, two sides of the same coin. The vital home rests on reverence, worship, and prayer.

From this same natural union flows new human life. Children are the first end, or purpose, of marriage. The couple watch with wonder as their first baby grows within the mother. Joy and awe drive away doubt and fear as they find their love transformed into a living child. Parts of their own beings have gone into the child's making, forming a new and unique person. The new father takes on the protection of the new mother in her time of vulnerability and dependence. A happiness follows the trial of childbirth as the new mother nurses her baby and as the father caresses his first born. Receiving a child through adoption sparks similar feelings. From such amazing moments, these parents are the child's first teachers; their home, the child's first, most vital school. They pass to the child the skills of living and introduce the satisfactions of talking, reading, reasoning, and exploring the world.

Inspired by love, the couple opens its union to additional children, filling their home, and filling the earth. These parents will know the delight of watching brothers and sisters grow together. They will watch with a mix of pride and worry as their children take their first steps, attempt their first chores, take on their first responsibilities. Among the children, there will be bruised knees, quarrels over toys, lost sport contests, tears, and laughter. As the children grow, they enter by steps a broader world. In all this, though, their parents stand as guides and guardians, and the home serves as a shelter and the focus of their common life.

Indeed, the natural family opens its home to other kin. The love and care which flow from parents to young children are mirrored in the care and love that adult children give to their aging parents. The truly rich family draws on the strengths of three or more generations. This family cares for its own. Each generation sees itself as a link in an unbroken chain, through which the family extends from and into the centuries.

A Time of Crisis

And yet, the natural family—*part of the created order, imprinted on our natures, the source of bountiful joy, the fountain of new life, the bulwark of ordered liberty*—stands reviled and threatened in the early 21st century. Foes have mounted attacks on all aspects of the natural family, from the bond of marriage to the birth of children to the true democracy of free homes. Ever more families show weaknesses and disorders. We see growing numbers of young adults rejecting the fullness and joy of marriage, choosing instead cheap substitutes or standing alone, where they are easy prey for the total state. Too many children are born outside of wedlock, ending as wards of that same state. Too few children are born inside married-couple homes, portending depopulation.

What has caused this alienation of humankind from its true nature and real home? Two basic assaults on the natural family have occurred, with their roots reaching back several hundred years: in brief, the challenge of industrialism and the assault of new, family-denying ideas.

On the one hand, the triumph of industrialism brought a "great disruption" or a "great transformation" in human affairs. The creation of wealth accelerated under the regime of industry. Yet this real gain rested on tearing productivity away from the hearth, on a disruption of the natural ecology of family life. The primal bond of home and work appeared to dissolve into air. Family-made goods and tasks became commodities, things to be bought and sold. Centralized factories, offices, and warehouses took over the tasks of the family workshop, garden, kitchen, and storeroom. Husbands, wives, and even children were enticed out of homes and organized in factories according to the principle of efficiency. Impersonal machines undermined the natural complementarity of the sexes in productive tasks. Children were left to fend for themselves, with the perception that their families no longer guided their futures; rather, the children now looked to faceless employers.

Politicians also embraced the industrial ideal and its claims to efficiency. New laws denied children a family-centered education and put them in mass state schools. Fertility tumbled, for "it . . . has yet to be [shown] . . . that any society can sustain stable high fertility beyond two generations of mass schooling." The state also invaded the home, seizing the protection of childhood from parents through the reform school movement and later schemes to "prevent child abuse." Family households, formerly function-rich beehives of useful, productive work and mutual support, tended to become merely functionless, overnight places of rest for persons whose active lives and loyalties lay elsewhere.

More critically, new ideas emerged over the same years that rejected the natural family. Some political thinkers held that the individual, standing alone, was the true cell of society; that family bonds—including those between husband and wife and between mother and child—showed merely the power of one selfish person over another. Other theorists argued that the isolated self, the lone actor in "the state of nature," was actually oppressed by institutions such as family and church. In this view, the central state was twisted into a supposed agent of liberation. It alone could free the enslaved individual from "the chains of tradition." From these premises emerged a terrible cloud of ideologies that shared a common target: the natural family. These idea systems included socialism, feminism, communism, sexual hedonism, racial nationalism, and secular liberalism.

By the 1990's, their campaign was global. Cynically, they used the International Year of the Family, 1994, to launch a series of United Nations conferences designed to tear down the natural family in the developing nations, as well. Cairo, Beijing, Istanbul, and Copenhagen were the arenas where they tried to impose this "post-family" order.

In our time, the partisans of a "post-family" world are still the ones on the offensive. For example, our pro-family movement has failed to restore legal protection to marriage by rolling back the "no-fault" revolution. Instead, by 2005, we are in a desperate fight simply to keep the vital institution of marriage from being fitted to homosexuals. And our two movements have failed to slow the war of governments on human fertility, despite the new likelihood of a catastrophic depopulation of the developed *and* developing nations through the global "empty cradle."

A Vision

And so, we advance here a new vision and a fresh statement of principles and goals appropriate for the 21st century and the third millennium.

We see a world restored in line with the intent of its Creator. We envision a culture—found both locally and universally—that upholds the marriage of a woman to a man, and a man to a woman, as the central aspiration for the young. This culture affirms marriage as the best path to health, security, fulfillment, and joy. It casts the home built on marriage as the source of true political sovereignty, the fountain of democracy. It also holds the household framed by marriage to be the primal economic unit, a place marked by rich activity, material abundance, and broad self-reliance. This culture treasures private property in family hands as the rampart of independence and liberty. It celebrates the marital sexual union as the unique source of new human life. We see these homes as open to a full quiver of children, the source of family continuity and social growth. We envision young women growing into wives, homemakers, and mothers; and we see young men growing into husbands, homebuilders, and fathers.

We see true happiness as the product of persons enmeshed in vital bonds with spouses, children, parents, and kin. We look to a landscape of family homes, lawns, and gardens busy with useful tasks and ringing with the laughter of many children. We envision parents as the first educators of their children. We see homes that also embrace extended family members who need special care due to age or infirmity. We view neighborhoods, villages, and townships as the second locus of political sovereignty. We envision a freedom of commerce that respects and serves family integrity. And we look to nation-states that hold the protection of the natural family to be their first responsibility.

Our Principles

To advance this vision, we advocates for the natural family assert clear principles to guide our work in the new century and millennium.

- We affirm that the natural family, not the individual, is the fundamental unit of society.
- We affirm the natural family to be the union of a man and a woman through marriage for the purposes of sharing love and joy, propagating children, providing their moral education, building a vital home economy, offering security in times of trouble, and binding the generations.
- We affirm that the natural family is a fixed aspect of the created order, one ingrained in human nature. Distinct family systems may grow weaker or stronger. However, the natural family cannot change into some new shape; nor can it be re-defined by eager social engineers.
- We affirm that the natural family is the ideal, optimal, true family system. While we acknowledge varied living situations caused by circumstance or dysfunction, all other "family forms" are incomplete or are fabrications of the state.

- We affirm the marital union to be the authentic sexual bond, the only one open to the natural and responsible creation of new life.
- We affirm the sanctity of human life from conception to natural death; each newly conceived person holds rights to live, to grow, to be born, and to share a home with its natural parents bound by marriage.
- We affirm that the natural family is prior to the state and that legitimate governments exist to shelter and encourage the natural family.
- We affirm that the world is abundant in resources. The breakdown of the natural family and moral and political failure, not human "over-population," account for poverty, starvation, and environmental decay.
- We affirm that human depopulation is the true demographic danger facing the earth in this new century. Our societies need more people, not fewer.
- We affirm that women and men are equal in dignity and innate human rights, but different in function. Even if sometimes thwarted by events beyond the individual's control (or sometimes given up for a religious vocation), the calling of each boy is to become husband and father; the calling of each girl is to become wife and mother. Everything that a man does is mediated by his aptness for fatherhood. Everything that a woman does is mediated by her aptness for motherhood. Culture, law, and policy should take these differences into account.
- We affirm that the complementarity of the sexes is a source of strength. Men and women exhibit profound biological and psychological differences. When united in marriage, though, the whole becomes greater than the sum of the parts.
- We affirm that economic determinism is false. Ideas and religious faith can prevail over material forces. Even one as powerful as industrialization can be tamed by the exercise of human will.
- We affirm the "family wage" ideal of "equal pay for equal family responsibility." Compensation for work and taxation should reinforce natural family bonds.
- We affirm the necessary role of private property in land, dwelling, and productive capital as the foundation of familial independence and the guarantor of democracy. In a just and good society, all families will hold real property.
- And we affirm that lasting solutions to human problems rise out of families and small communities. They cannot be imposed by bureaucratic and judicial fiat. Nor can they be coerced by outside force.

Our Platform

From these principles, we draw out a simple, concrete platform for the new century and millennium. To the world, we say:

- We will build a new culture of marriage, where others would define marriage out of existence.
- We will welcome and celebrate more babies and larger families, where others would continue a war on human fertility.

- We will find ways to bring mothers, fathers, and children back home, where others would further divide parents from their children.
- And we will create true home economies, where others would subject families to the full control of big government and vast corporations.

To do these things, we must offer positive encouragements, and we must also correct the policy errors of the past. Specifically:

To Build a New Culture of Marriage . . .

- We will craft schooling that gives positive images of chastity, marriage, fidelity, motherhood, fatherhood, husbandry, and housewifery. We will end the corruption of children through state "sex education" programs.
- We will build legal and constitutional protections around marriage as the union of a man and a woman. We will end the war of the sexual hedonists on marriage.
- We will transform social insurance, welfare, and housing programs to reinforce marriage, especially the marriage of young adults. We will end state incentives to live outside of marriage.
- We will place the weight of the law on the side of spouses seeking to defend their marriages. We will end state preferences for easy divorce by repealing "no-fault" statutes.
- We will recognize marriage as a true and full economic partnership. We will end "marriage penalties" in taxation.
- We will allow private insurers to recognize the health advantages of marriage and family living, according to sound business principles. We will end legal discrimination against the married and child-rich.
- We will empower the legal and cultural guardians of marriage and public morality. We will end the coarsening of our culture.

To Welcome More Babies Within Marriage . . .

- We will praise churches and other groups that provide healthy and fertile models of family life to the young. We will end state programs that indoctrinate children, youth, and adults into the contraceptive mentality.
- We will restore respect for life. We will end the culture of abortion and the mass slaughter of the innocents.
- We will create private and public campaigns to reduce maternal and infant mortality and to improve family health. We will end government campaigns of population control.
- We will build special protections for families, motherhood, and childhood. We will end the terrible assault on these basic human rights.
- We will celebrate husbands and wives who hold open their sexual lives to new children. We will end the manipulation and abuse of new human life in the laboratories.
- We will craft generous tax deductions, exemptions, and credits that are tied to marriage and the number of children. We will end the oppressive taxation of family income, labor, property, and wealth.

- We will create credits against payroll taxes that reward the birth of children and that build true family patrimonies. We will end existing social insurance incentives toward childlessness.
- We will offer tax benefits to businesses that provide "natal gifts" and "child allowances" to their employees. We will end legal incentives that encourage business corporations to ignore families.

To Bring Mothers, and Fathers, Home . . .

- We will ensure that stay-at-home parents enjoy at least the same state benefits offered to day-care users. We will end all discriminations against stay-at-home parents.
- We will encourage new strategies and technologies that would allow home-based employment to blossom and prosper. We will end policies that unfairly favor large, centralized businesses and institutions.
- We will favor small property that reintegrates home and work. We will end taxes, financial incentives, subsidies, and zoning laws that discourage small farms and family-held businesses.

To Create a True Home Economy . . .

- We will allow men and women to live in harmony with their true natures. We will end the aggressive state promotion of androgyny.
- We will encourage employers to pay a "family wage" to heads of households. We will end laws that prohibit employers from recognizing and rewarding family responsibility.
- We will craft laws that protect home schools and other family-centered schools from state interference. We will give real control of state schools to small communities so that their focus might turn toward home and family. And we will create measures (such as educational tax credits) that recognize the exercise of parental responsibility. We will end discriminatory taxes and policies that favor mass state education of the young.
- We will hold up the primacy of parental rights and hold public officials accountable for abuses of their power. We will end abuse of the "child-abuse" laws.
- We will encourage self-sufficiency through broad property ownership, home enterprise, home gardens, and home workshops. We will end the culture of dependency found in the welfare state.
- We will celebrate homes that are centers of useful work. We will end state incentives for home building that assume, and so create, families without functions.

The Usual Charges

We know that certain charges will be leveled against us. Some will say that we want to turn back the clock, to restore a mythical American suburban world of the 1950's. Others will charge that we seek to subvert the rights of women or that we want to impose white, Western, Christian values on a pluralistic world.

Still others will argue that we ignore science or reinforce patriarchal violence. Some will say that we block inevitable social evolution or threaten a sustainable world with too many children.

So, in anticipation, let us be clear:

We Look Forward with Hope, While Learning from the Past

It is true that we look with affection to earlier familial eras such as "1950's America." Indeed, for the first time in one hundred years, five things happened simultaneously in America (and in Australia and parts of Western Europe, as well) during this time: the marriage rate climbed; the divorce rate fell; marital fertility soared; the equality of households increased; and measures of child well-being and adult happiness rose. These were the social achievements of "the greatest generation." We look with delight on this record and aspire to recreate such results.

However, we also know that this specific development was a one-generation wonder. It did not last. Some children of the "baby boom" rebelled. Too often, this rebellion was foolish and destructive. Still, we find weaknesses in the family model of "1950's America." We see that it was largely confined to the white majority. Black families actually showed mounting stress in these years: a retreat from marriage; more out-of-wedlock births. Also, this new suburban model—featuring long commutes for fathers and tract homes without the central places such as parks and nearby shops where mothers and youth might have found healthy community bonds—proved incomplete. Finally, we see the "companionship marriage" ideal of this time, which embraced psychological tasks to the exclusion of material and religious functions, as fragile. We can, and we will, do better.

We Believe Wholeheartedly in Women's Rights

Above all, we believe in rights that recognize women's unique gifts of pregnancy, birthing, and breastfeeding. The goal of androgyny, the effort to eliminate real differences between women and men, does every bit as much violence to human nature and human rights as the old efforts by the communists to create "Soviet Man" and by the nazis to create "Aryan Man." We reject social engineering, attempts to corrupt girls and boys, to confuse women and men about their true identities. At the same time, nothing in our platform would prevent women from seeking and attaining as much education as they want. Nothing in our platform would prevent women from entering jobs and professions to which they aspire. We do object, however, to restrictions on the liberty of employers to recognize family relations and obligations and so reward indirectly those parents staying at home to care for their children. And we object to current attacks on the Universal Declaration of Human Rights, a document which proclaims fundamental rights to family autonomy, to a family wage for fathers, and to the special protection of mothers.

We Believe That the Natural Family Is Universal, an Attribute of All Humankind

We confess to holding Christian values regarding the family: the sanctity of marriage; the desire by the Creator that we be fruitful and multiply; Jesus' miracle at the wedding feast; His admonitions against adultery and divorce. And yet, we find similar views in the other great world faiths. Moreover, we even find recognition of the natural family in the marriage rituals of animists. Because it is imprinted on our natures as human beings, we know that the natural family can be grasped by all persons who open their minds to the evidence of their senses and their hearts to the promptings of their best instincts. Also, in the early 21st century, there is little that is "Western" about our views. The voices of the "post family" idea are actually today's would-be "Westernizers." They are the ones who largely rule in the child-poor, aging, dying lands of "the European West." It is they who seek to poison the rest of the world with a grim, wizened culture of death. Our best friends are actually to be found in the developing world, in the Third World, in the Middle East, Africa, South Asia, South America. Our staunchest allies tend not to be white, but rather people of color. Others seek a sterile, universal darkness. We seek to liberate the whole world—including dying Europa—for light and life, for children.

We Celebrate the Findings of Empirical Science

Science, honestly done and honestly reported, is the friend of the natural family. The record is clear from decades of work in sociology, psychology, anthropology, sociobiology, medicine, and social history: children do best when they are born into and raised by their two natural parents. Under *any* other setting—including one-parent, step-parent, homosexual, cohabitating, or communal households—children predictably do worse. Married, natural-parent homes bring health, learning, and success to the offspring reared therein. Science shows that these same homes give life, wealth, and joy to wives and husbands, as well. Disease, depression, and early death come to those who reject family life. This result should not really cause surprise. Science, after all, is the study of the natural order. And while the Creator forgives, nature never does.

We Seek to Reduce Domestic Violence

All families fall short of perfection and a few families fail. We, too, worry about domestic violence. We know that people can make bad choices, that they can fall prey to selfishness and their darker instincts. We also know that persons can live in places or times where they have few models of solid homes, few examples of good marriages. All the same, we also insist that the natural family is not the source of these human failures. The research here is clear. Women are safest physically when married and living with their husbands. Children are best sheltered from sexual, physical, and emotional abuse when they live with their married natural parents. In short, the natural family is the *answer* to abuse. We also know that all husbands and wives, all mothers and fathers, need to be nurtured toward and encouraged in their proper roles. These are the first tasks of all worthy social institutions.

We Believe That While Distinct Family Systems Change, the Design of the Natural Family Never Does

Regarding the natural family, we deny any such thing as social evolution. The changes we see are either decay away from or renewal toward the one true family model. From our very origin as a unique creature on earth, we humans have been defined by the long-term bonding of a woman and a man, by their free sharing of resources, by a complementary division of labor, and by a focus on the procreation, protection, and rearing of children in stable homes. History is replete with examples of distinct family systems that have grown strong and built great civilizations, only to fall to atomism, vice, and decay. Even in our Western Civilization, we can identify periods of family decline and disorder, followed by successful movements of renewal. It is true that the last forty years have been a time of great confusion and decay. We now sense a new summons to social rebirth.

We Seek a Sustainable Human Future

With sadness, we acknowledge that the new Malthusian impulse has succeeded in its war against children all too well. Fertility is tumbling around the globe. A majority of nations have already fallen into "the aging trap" of depopulation. As matters now stand, the predictable future is one of catastrophic population decline, economic contraction, and human tragedy. Our agenda actually represents the earth's best hope for a sustainable future.

Looking Forward

That large task requires new ways of thinking and acting. Our vision of the hearth looks forward, not to the past, for hope and purpose. We see the vital home reborn through startling new movements such as home schooling. We marvel at fresh inventions that portend novel bonds between home and work. We are inspired by a convergence of religious truth with the evidence of science around the vital role of the natural family. We see the prospect of a great civil alliance of religious orthodoxies, within nations and around the globe; not to compromise on doctrines held dear, but to defend our family systems from the common foe. With wonder, we find a shared happiness with people once distrusted or feared. We enjoy new friendships rooted in family ideals that cross ancient divides. We see the opportunity for an abundant world order built on the natural family.

We issue a special call to the young, those born over the last three to four decades. You are the children of a troubled age, a time of moral and social disorder. You were conceived into a culture of self-indulgence, of abortion, a culture embracing death. More than all generations before, you have known the divorce of parents. You have lived too often in places without fathers. You have been taught to deny your destinies as young women and young men.

You have been forced to read books that mock marriage, motherhood, and fatherhood. Persons who should have protected you—teachers, judges, public officials—often left you as prey to moral and sexual predators. Many of you are in fact the victims of a kind of cultural rape: seduced into early sexual acts, then pushed into sterility.

And yet, you are also the ones with the power to make the world anew. Where some members of *our* generation helped to corrupt the world, you will be the builders. You have seen the darkness. The light now summons you. It is your time to lead, with the natural family as your standard and beacon. Banish the lies told to you. Claim your natural freedom to create true and fruitful marriages. Learn from the social renewal prompted by "the greatest generation" and call on them for special support. You have the chance to shape a world that welcomes and celebrates children. You have the ability to craft a true homecoming. Your generation holds the destiny of humankind in its hands. The hopes of all good and decent people lie with you.

The Call

A new spirit spreads in the world, the essence of the natural family. We call on all people of goodwill, whose hearts are open to the promptings of this spirit, to join in a great campaign. The time is close when the persecution of the natural family, when the war against children, when the assault on human nature shall end.

The enemies of the natural family grow worried. A triumph that, not so many years ago, they thought complete is no longer sure. Their fury grows. So do their attempts, ever more desperate, at coercion. Yet their mistakes also mount in number. They misread human nature. They misread the times.

We all are called to be the actors, the moral soldiers, in this drive to realize the life ordained for us by our Creator. Our foes are dying, of their own choice; we have a world to gain. Natural families of all races, nations, and creeds, let us unite.

> "TO THE WORLD, WE SAY:
> - We will build a new culture of marriage, where others would define marriage out of existence.
> - We will welcome and celebrate more babies and larger families, where others would continue a war on human fertility.
> - We will find ways to bring mothers, fathers, and children back home, where others would further divide parents from their children.
> - And we will create true home economies, where others would subject families to the full control of big government and vast corporations."

Mark Good  **NO**

Nontraditional Families and Childhood Progress through School

What types of outcomes can be expected for children raised by same-sex couples, relative to children in other types of families? The answer is vitally important both for public policy relating to same-sex marriage and adoption (Eskridge 2002; Koppelman 2002), and for theories of how family structure matters. Supporters and opponents of same-sex marriage rights agree that the legal issue of same-sex marriage rights should revolve around the question of childhood outcomes for children raised by same-sex couples (Alvaré 2005; Patterson 2002). In this paper, I examine progress through school, i.e., normal progress versus grade retention, for children of same-sex couples compared to children of other family types, using data from the 2000 U.S. census.

The debate over same-sex unions and their children draws from and informs a more general literature concerning family structure's effect on children. The literature on family structure has generally focused on structural variations within heterosexual parented families, contrasting heterosexual married couples, heterosexual remarried couples, and (presumably heterosexual) single mothers (Cherlin 1992; McLanahan and Sandefur 1994). Even though same-sex couples are a small minority of all couples (1% of all couples in census 2000 were same-sex couples), the inclusion of same-sex couples can provide researchers with more leverage over the key question of how family structure matters in general.

Studies of family structure and children's outcomes nearly universally find at least a modest advantage for children raised by their married biological parents. The question which has bedeviled researchers, and which remains essentially unresolved, is *why* (Cherlin 1999). Some results have indicated that socioeconomic status explains most or all of the advantage of children raised by married couples (Biblarz and Raftery 1999; Gennetian 2005; Ginther and Pollak 2004), while other scholars find that family structure has an enduring effect on children net of all other factors (McLanahan and Sandefur 1994; Zill 1996). Married couples tend to be the most prosperous type of family unit, and this economic prosperity undoubtedly has certain advantages for children (but also see Mayer 1997).

Literature Review

Same-Sex Parenting

The modern reality of same-sex couples raising children long postdates the classical psychological theories of child development (for example, Freud [1905] 1975). Recent research on childhood socialization to gender roles has emphasized peer groups and genetics as much as direct parental influence (Harris 1998; Maccoby 1990). In-depth studies of the psychosocial development of children raised by lesbians or by same-sex couples has found that these children are normal and well adjusted (Chan, Raboy and Patterson 1998b; Flaks et al. 1995; Golombok et al. 2003), though as I discuss below, there are also critics of the small-N literature on same-sex couples and their children.

Same-sex couples become parents in three main ways. First, through one partner's (generally prior) heterosexual relationship; second, through adoption; third, through donor insemination or surrogate parenting (Stacey 2006). Same-sex couples cannot become parents through misuse or failure of birth control, the way heterosexual couples can. Parenthood is more difficult to achieve for same-sex couples than for heterosexual couples, which implies a stronger selection effect for same-sex parents. If gays and lesbians have to work harder to become parents, it could be the case that the gays and lesbians who do become parents are on average more dedicated to the hard work of parenting than their heterosexual peers, and this could be beneficial for their children.

In Judith Stacey's (2006 p. 39) discussion of gay adoption, she describes the gay men of Los Angeles as having to search through the state's ". . . overstocked warehouse of 'hard to place' children, the majority of whom . . . have been removed from families judged negligent, abusive, or incompetent. Most of the state's stockpiled children . . . are children of color, and disproportionately boys with 'special needs.'" If it is the case that same-sex couples who adopt mainly have access to 'special needs' children, the special needs of these children could exert a downward bias on the average outcomes for children of same-sex couples. Fortunately, the census distinguishes between the head of household's "own children," adopted children, stepchildren, and foster children.

Nearly all children of gay and lesbian parents attend schools and live in neighborhoods whose other children come overwhelmingly from families with heterosexual parents. In other words, children of same-sex couples share a common peer and school environment with children of heterosexual couples. To the extent that peer environment is a primary socializing environment for children (Harris 1998; Maccoby 1990; for a survey, see Rutter 2002), whatever differences sexual orientation of parents makes within the home may well be mediated and diffused by the common peer and school environments that children share regardless of the gender or sexual orientation of their parents.

How the Census Complements the Existing Literature

Our research lists 45 empirical studies of outcomes of children of same-sex couples, comprising all of the journal articles listed in Fiona Tasker's (2005) comprehensive survey which examined childhood outcomes, plus several more recent studies listed by Wald (2006), and all four studies listed by Meezan and Rauch (2005) as the highest quality studies in this field, and all the more recent studies which cite the earlier ones. None of the studies cited in our research find statistically significant disadvantages for children raised by gay and lesbian parents compared to other children.

The uniform finding of no significant disadvantage for children raised by gay or lesbian parents has been convincing to some scholars (Ball and Pea 1998; Meezan and Rauch 2005; Stacey and Biblarz 2001; Wald 2006), though others remain unconvinced (Lerner and Nagai 2001; Nock 2001; Wardle 1997). Several points are worth commenting upon. First, as the critics have noted, convenience sampling dominated this literature in the past (Nock 2001). More recent scholarship has answered this criticism by using nationally representative probability samples derived from the National Longitudinal Study of Adolescent Health (Add Health, see Wainright and Patterson 2006, 2008; Wainright et al. 2004), as well as studies constructed from a hybrid of probability sampling and convenience sampling (Golombok et al. 2003; Perry et al. 2004).

A second critique of the literature, that the sample sizes of the studies are too small to allow for statistically powerful tests, continues to be relevant. The mean number of children of gay or lesbian parents in these studies is 39, and the median is 37, and both numbers would be slightly lower if studies without comparison groups were excluded. The nationally representative studies in the series found only 44 children who were raised by lesbian couples in the Add Health survey. Golombok et al (2003) found only 18 lesbian mothers out of 14,000 mothers in the Avon Longitudinal Study of Parents and Children, which is why they supplemented this sample with snowball sampling and their own convenience sample. The universally small sample sizes of the studies in the existing literature has left room for several critiques, including the critique that small sample studies would not have the statistical power to identify the effects of homosexual parents on childhood outcomes, even if such effects did exist (Lerner and Nagai 2001; Nock 2001). A third potential weakness of this literature is the narrowness of family structures under study (Tasker 2005). Of the 45 studies listed, only seven examined the children of gay fathers, and only two of these seven studies had a more traditional family control group built into the study.

Among the convenience sample studies, several of the most important have been based on samples of women who became parents through assisted reproductive technology (ART-Brewaeys et al. 1997; Chan et al. 1998b; Flaks et al. 1995). Because individuals who become parents through assisted means can be identified through the reproductive clinic and are therefore easier to recruit than the general population of same-sex couple parents, the literature on same-sex couple parenting has tended to feature studies of the kind of women who can afford ART: white upper middle class women. Nationally representative data tends to paint a different picture: in the U.S. census, same-sex couple parents tend to be more working class and are much more likely to be racially nonwhite compared to heterosexual married couples.

The debate over same-sex marriage and gay and lesbian adoption rights revolves around many competing sets of assumptions with political, religious, and ideological axes which cannot be resolved or even fully addressed in this paper. To the extent the debate is an empirical debate, that is to the extent that disagreement remains over the meaning of the empirical literature on the development of children of same-sex couples, this paper offers a new perspective.

To supplement the existing small-scale studies, I offer a large sample study of children from the U.S. Census, including 3,502 children of same-sex couples who had been living with both parents for at least five years (2,030 children living with lesbian mothers and 1,472 children living with gay fathers, see our research), and more than 700,000 children in grades 1–8 from other family types. This sample size more than satisfies Nock's (2001) criteria of 800 as the minimum number of gay and lesbian couples required for statistically useful study.

The U.S. census has several major disadvantages: normal progress through school is the only available children's outcome, and even this outcome is measured with less precision than one would hope for. Although the census data have several important limitations for the research questions considered here, the strengths of the census data (large sample, national representativity, and a full array of family structures) address important lacunae in the literature, and as such, this study offers a potentially useful new perspective on how family structure matters to children. Although the census data are far from ideal for the subject under study here, better data are nowhere on the horizon.

Grade Retention

Grade retention (the opposite of normal progress through school) has been increasing in U.S. schools since President Bill Clinton proposed ending social promotion in schools in his State of the Union address in 1998 (Alexander, Entwisle and Dauber 2003:viii; Hauser 2001). Grade retention is an important childhood outcome because retention in the primary grades is a strong indicator of a lack of childhood readiness for school, and we know that effective parenting is a crucial ingredient in school readiness (Brooks-Gunn and Markman 2005). Brooks-Gunn and Markman argue that the lower school readiness of racial minority children is due, in part, to parenting practices which differ from the authoritative parenting style favored in middle class white homes (Baumrind 1966; Lareau 2003).

Guo, Brooks-Gunn, and Harris (1996) studied grade retention among urban black children and found that some indicators of parental stress such as unemployment and welfare use were associated with increased grade retention for children; in other words, they found childhood grade retention to be a useful measure of difficulties the students were experiencing at home. Guo, Brooks-Gunn, and Harris (1996:218) identify three potential sources of grade retention: "weak cognitive ability, behavioral problems, and lack of engagement in school." Of these three causes of childhood grade retention, the second two might be partly associated with the quality of the home environment. Students with learning disabilities or physical disabilities which affect learning are also at risk of grade retention, and this type of grade retention would not be indicative of parenting deficits.

Grade retention is closely associated with more serious problems later in life. Students who are held back at least once are at much higher risk for eventually dropping out of high school (Alexander, Entwisle, and Horsey 1997; Guo et al. 1996; Moller et al. 2006; Roderick 1994; Rumberger 1987; Tillman, Guo, and Harris 2006). Failure to graduate from high school is associated with low earnings, high unemployment, low self-esteem, and high mortality rates (Guo et al. 1996; McLanahan 1985; Tillman et al. 2006). Even when grade retention takes place in the early grades, the "crystallization" of behaviors and academic abilities implies that difficulties a child experiences when he or she is 7 or 8 carry forward (more so for girls than for boys) into adolescence and young adulthood (Kowalesi-Jones and Duncan 1999).

There are several theoretical reasons for supposing that children of same-sex couples might have lower school readiness (and therefore higher rates of grade retention) than own children of heterosexual married couples, net of race, parental income, and parental education. First, the legal privileges of marriage are numerous and have direct consequences for the well being of children (Eskridge 1996; Pawelski et al. 2006). Second, evolutionary theory suggests that parents invest more in their own biological children (Wilson 2002; but see also Hamilton, Cheng, and Powell 2007), and same-sex couples (absent a prior sex change) cannot both be the biological parents of any one child. Third, the large majority of children of same-sex couples from the 2000 census were children from prior heterosexual relationships (only 11% were stepchildren, adopted children, or foster children of the head of household), meaning that most of the children being raised by same-sex couples at the time of the 2000 census had previously lived through divorce or parental breakup, which research has shown to be traumatic for some children (Amato and Cheadle 2005; Chase-Lansdale, Cherlin, and Kiernan 1995; McLanahan and Sandefur 1994; Wallerstein and Kelly 1980; Wallerstein, Lewis, and Blakeslee 2000).

The Benefits of Legal Marriage

Legal marriage confers a host of protections and advantages both to the couples who marry and to their children. Married couples generally share joint legal custody of their coresident children. In a system of employer-based health care insurance, either spouse in a married couple can usually provide health insurance for both spouses and all their children. Marriage is a long-term contract which allows and encourages parents to make long-term investments in their children (Waite and Gallagher 2000). Divorce rights, which are a corollary to marriage rights, provide guarantees for child support and visitation that are intended to minimize the damage of a breakup to a couple's children. Given the many practical, legal, economic, and social advantages of marriage as a childrearing family structure, it should come as no surprise that children of long-term married couples have the best outcomes (McLanahan and Sandefur 1994). The various benefits of marriage extend far beyond income, so one would generally expect children in married couples to have advantages even after SES is accounted for in regressions.

The moral claim for same-sex marriage rests in part on the many practical and psychological benefits of marriage, benefits which conservative family scholars have made the most careful and enthusiastic case for (Waite and

Gallagher 2000; Wilson 2002). The benefits of marriage, combined with the exclusion of gays and lesbians (and their children) from those benefits, together form one cornerstone of the case for same-sex marriage (Eskridge 1996).

Relevant Comparison Sets for Same-Sex Couples

Along with the standard comparison to heterosexual married couples, heterosexual cohabiting couples are a second logical comparison group for same-sex cohabiting couples. Both heterosexual cohabiters and same-sex cohabiters are two-parent families living without the rights and benefits of marriage. Certainly, there are differences: heterosexual cohabiting couples can marry if they want to, whereas in the United States at the time of the 2000 census, same-sex couples could not marry. The comparison between children of same-sex cohabiting couples and children of heterosexual cohabiting couples allows for a more specific test of the effect of same-sex parenthood on children, while holding constant legal rights and the number of parents.

A third relevant comparison for children of same-sex couples are the children living in group quarters, since these are the children presumably available for adoption, and because same-sex couples are more likely than heterosexual couples to participate in the adoption market. Some of the difference between children in group quarters and children living with parents and guardians must be due to selection effects—the most troubled children available for adoption may not be adopted and may do poorly in school as a result of emotional or physical disabilities. On the other hand, if gay and lesbian adoptive parents are choosing from the middle or the bottom of the adoptive pool (Stacey 2006), rather than from the population of the most desirable potential adoptees, then the selection effect will be less important. In either case, the census, as a cross-sectional survey, is poorly suited to the analysis of selection effects. Nonetheless, census 2000 does provide strong controls for individual student disabilities, and any comparison between children living with families and children living in group quarters will be made after individual disabilities have been controlled for.

First-Order Predictors of Childhood Grade Retention

Because denominator school populations cover four years (grades 1–4, grades 5–8), but the students who can be identified as over age for their grade come only from the last grade of each four-year span (grades 4 and 8)5, the implied grade retention rate is four times higher than the observed grade retention rate. Our research shows both the observed grade retention rate and the implied grade retention rate, for primary school students using weighted data from the 2000 census.

Our research suggests that childhood grade retention is correlated with family type. Children of heterosexual married couples had the lowest implied rate of grade retention, 6.8%. Children of lesbian mothers and gay fathers had grade retention rates of 9.5% and 9.7%, respectively. Children of heterosexual cohabiting parents had a grade retention rate of 11.7%, while children of single parents had grade retention rates between 11.1% and 12.6%.

The differences in childhood grade retention between all types of non-group-quarters households were dwarfed by the high grade retention rates of children living in group quarters. According to our research, children living in group homes, many of them awaiting adoption or foster parents, had an implied grade retention rate of 34.4%. Children who were incarcerated had a grade retention rate of 78.0%. Later in the paper, I show that the enormous difference in grade retention between children raised in families and children living in group quarters remains even after individual level student disabilities are accounted for.

One way to gauge the advantage of living with families is to note that adopted children (10.6% grade retention) who spent the five years prior to the census living with their adoptive parents, and foster children (20.6% grade retention) with five years of residential stability performed considerably better than children who spent the same 5 years living at a single-group-quarters address (34.4% grade retention for non-inmates). The performance hierarchy which favors own children, and then (in declining order of school performance) adopted children, then foster children, then children in group quarters confirms the long standing research finding that children do best when living with parents who make a long term commitment to the children's development (Bartholet 1999). Selection bias (wherein the children with the most severe disabilities or children who have suffered the worst abuse are the least likely to be adopted) must also play a role, which unfortunately cannot be quantified with these data.

The rest of our research shows implied grade retention along several other dimensions. Asian children had the lowest rates of grade retention, while black children had the highest. Girls were less likely to be held back in the primary grades than boys were. Suburban schools had lower rates of grade retention than city schools, which in turn were lower than rural schools. Household socioeconomic status (SES) was a crucial predictor of childhood school performance. In households with income less than $25,000, 12.6% of the primary school students were left back, compared to only 5.3% for children in households with incomes over $100,000. Householder's education had an even stronger effect on children's progress through school: parents who had less than a high school degree had primary school children who were retained 14.3% of the time, whereas householders with college degrees had children who were retained only 4.4% of the time.

Our research shows that the strongest factor in making normal progress through elementary school is living with a family rather than living in group quarters. For children living in a family, whether the family is headed by a heterosexual married couple or by some less traditional parenting arrangement, the second most important factor in childhood progress through school appears to be parental educational attainment.

Socioeconomic Status by Family Type

Our research shows that gays and lesbians had a higher-than-average educational attainment of 13.6 years (i.e., 1.6 years of college) compared to 13.4 years for heterosexual married heads of household. Across family types, gay couples had the highest median household income at $61,000 per household. It should also be noted that men have higher earnings than women, and gay male couples are the only household type that relied on the earnings of two men. The second Nontraditional Families and Childhood Grade Retention P. 17 four family types are all single-parent (i.e., single-income) families, so their household incomes were roughly half as high as the household incomes of the first four family types.

Despite the fact that the cost of becoming parents may be higher for gays and lesbians than for heterosexual couples, our research shows that gay and lesbian couples who did have children had substantially lower income and educational attainment than gay and lesbian couples in general. While gay and lesbian cohabiters had relatively high household incomes, gay and lesbian parents had lower SES than heterosexual married parents ($50 thousand per household for gay parents compared to $58 thousand for heterosexual married parents). Excluding marital status recodes, the income and educational level of gay and lesbian parents was even lower. Among gay and lesbian couples, those with lower incomes are more likely to be raising children. Not only were heterosexual married parents economically advantaged, the heterosexual married couples were also racially advantaged. Only 22.9% of children of heterosexual married couple were black or Hispanic, whereas 41.6% of children of gay men were black or Hispanic, and this percentage rose to 53.7% when dual marital status recodes were excluded. The children of lesbians were similarly likely (37.1%) to be black or Hispanic. Never-married mothers were the most likely parenting family type to have black or Hispanic children. The racial breakdown of parents was similar to the racial breakdown of children described in our research. Among heterosexual married heads of household, 22.2% were black or Hispanic, while 40.4% of gay fathers were black or Hispanic, and 36.1% of lesbian mothers were black or Hispanic (not shown in our research).

Among all family types, children of lesbian mothers were the most likely (more than 12%) to be adopted children, stepchildren, or foster children. Because economic disadvantage, minority racial status, and experience with the adoption or foster care system are all challenges for children, a careful analysis of the school performance of children of gay and lesbian parents must take these disadvantages into account.

Comparisons with Children of Unmarried Heterosexual Couples

Our research revisits the regressions from our research (with the same models, covariates, and summary statistics), comparing children raised by same-sex couples to children raised by heterosexual cohabiting couples. Our research shows that children raised by same-sex couples are more likely to make normal progress through school compared to children raised by heterosexual cohabiting couples, but the difference is statistically significant only in Model 1, before parental SES has been accounted for. If children living with dual marital status recoded couples are excluded, the signs are reversed (meaning children raised by heterosexual cohabiting couples do better), but none of the coefficients are statistically significant. These results suggest that (for the outcome of normal progress through school) children raised by same-sex cohabiting couple parents are no different, and perhaps slightly advantaged, compared to children being raised by heterosexual cohabiting couples. The similarity in school performance between children of same-sex couples and children of heterosexual cohabiting couples fails to support the gender essentialist theories of parenting, which argue that child development depends on having parental role models from both gender groups (Alvaré 2005; Popenoe 1996; Wardle 1997).

Comparisons with Children in Group Quarters

Our research represents a different variation on the type of analysis from. In our research, the sample of children includes children in group quarters, and these children are the comparison category for the analysis. Because neither household income nor parental education can be associated with children in group quarters, these variables are dropped from the analysis. The sample of children in our research includes own children, adopted children, stepchildren, group quarters children, and foster children. Since the children in group-quarters have no head of household to have a relationship with, it seemed appropriate to use the broadest definition of "children" for children who were living with families. Furthermore, the adopted and foster children probably include some children who formerly lived in group quarters.

Our research confirms the robustness of a previous finding from our research, that children who live with parents regardless of family type are much more likely to make normal progress through school than children living in group quarters. Even after student disabilities (more common among group-quarters children than among children living with families) are taken into account, the difference remained between children raised by families and children living in group quarters. Children living at least five years with same-sex couples and children living at least five years with unmarried heterosexual cohabiting couples had odds of making good progress through school that were twice as high as non-inmate children who had spent the previous five years in group-quarters. Using coefficients from Model 2 of our research, which controls for children's race and disabilities, children raised by same-sex couples had odds of making good progress through school that were 2.43 times higher than children living in group quarters (e.886 = 2.43). Children raised by heterosexual cohabiting couples were similarly advantaged compared to children in group quarters (e.810 = 2.25, coefficients from Model 2). The advantage of children raised by same-sex couples over children living in group quarters remains positive and statistically significant across all four models even after marital status recoded couples are excluded.

Discussion

Children raised by same-sex couples are one of the most difficult populations in the United States to study systematically because of their small numbers and their geographic dispersion. The census data are far from ideal, and better data would, of course, be welcome. However, until such time as better nationally representative data are available, the U.S. census is the only nationally representative dataset with a large enough sample of children raised by same-sex couples to allow for statistically powerful comparisons with children of other family types.

To the extent that normal progress through primary school is a useful and valid measure of child development, the results confirm that children of same-sex couples appear to have no inherent developmental disadvantage. Heterosexual married couples are the most economically prosperous, the most likely to be white, and the most legally advantaged type of parents; their children have the lowest rates of grade retention. Parental SES accounts for more than half of the relatively small gap in grade retention between children of heterosexual married couples and children of same-sex couples. When one controls for parental SES and characteristics of the students, children of same-sex couples cannot be distinguished with statistical certainty from children of heterosexual married couples.

Children of all non–group quarters family types, including households headed by same-sex couples, are dramatically more likely to make normal progress through school than students living in group quarters. Any policy that would deny gay and lesbian parents the right to adopt or foster children would force some children to remain in group quarters. A longer stay in group quarters would seem to be contrary to the best interest of the children. In recent years, scholars have arrived at a consensus that moving children out of group homes and into adoptive families should be the goal of public policy. Families, even suboptimal families, are better equipped than the state to raise children (Bartholet 1999; Goldstein, Freud, and Solnit 1979).

Historical restrictions against interracial adoption in the United States represent one relevant historical precedent for the current debate over the adoption rights of same-sex couples. Randall Kennedy (2003) argues that even though restrictions against interracial adoption have been proposed as a way of protecting children, such restrictions have victimized children by taking them away from loving homes or by forcing children to remain in group quarters for too long. Policies which limit the kinds of families that can adopt or foster children ignore the enormous advantages of personal attention that families have (even single parents and other nontraditional family types) over the state in raising children well.

The prior literature has found no evidence that children raised by same-sex couples suffer any important disadvantages (Chan et al. 1998b; Patterson 1995; Stacey and Biblarz 2001; Wald 2006). Yet this same literature has been heavily criticized on the methodological grounds that universally small sample sizes prevent the studies from having the statistical power to identify differences that might actually exist (Alvaré 2005; Lerner and Nagai 2001; Nock 2001). The analysis in this paper, using large-sample, nationally representative data for the first time, shows that children raised by same-sex couples have no fundamental deficits in making normal progress through school. The core finding here offers a measure of validation for the prior, and much debated, small-sample studies.

EXPLORING THE ISSUE

Are Traditional Families Better for Children?

Critical Thinking and Reflection

- What are some arguments made by each side with which you agree or disagree?
- What are the strengths and weaknesses of the two positions made in this issue?
- Pick the side with which you most agree. What are some additional arguments you would make to strengthen the case for or against the traditional family?
- Think more broadly about the issue of the traditional family. Are there some changes in family structure that you support but others you oppose? Why or why not?

Is There Common Ground?

While we can debate the value of the traditional versus the nontraditional family, changing family structure is difficult to alter significantly. However, there are other qualities that need to be provided to ensure that children are afforded as many opportunities as possible. Let's identify those opportunities and advantages. What are some of the ways in which both traditional and nontraditional families can provide such opportunities?

Family structure will not remain static. Perhaps nontraditional families will be on the increase. Perhaps they will be on the decrease. What sort of projections would you make about changing family structure in the future? How should a pluralistic democracy approach such changes in family structure?

Additional Resources

Human Rights Campaign:

http://www.hrc.org

Lambda Legal:

http://www.lambdalegal.org/

American Family Association:

http://www.afa.net

Focus on the Family:

http://www.focusonthefamily.com/

ISSUE 13

Should Lesbian and Gay Individuals Be Able to Adopt Children?

YES: Joan Biskupic, from "Same-Sex Couples Redefining Family Law in USA," (February 17, 2003) *USA Today*

NO: Timothy J. Dailey, from "State of the States: Update on Homosexual Adoption in the U.S.," *Family Research Council* (no. 243, 2004).

Learning Outcomes

As a result of this issue, readers will be able to:

- Identify the major arguments made for and against lesbian and gay couples adopting children.
- Compare and contrast the competing arguments made for and against lesbian and gay couples adopting children in this issue.
- Evaluate the implications of lesbian and gay couples adopting children on families and the larger impact on American society.

ISSUE SUMMARY

YES: Joan Biskupic, legal affairs correspondent for *USA Today,* discusses the personal challenges for same-gender couples attempting to adopt in states that are not friendly to them and provides an update of legal issues and options available to lesbian and gay couples; these indicate a changing tide of acceptance toward couples of the same gender, as well as lesbian and gay individuals, adopting children.

NO: Timothy J. Dailey, senior research fellow at the Center for Marriage and Family Studies, provides an overview of state laws pertaining to adoption by lesbian or gay parents. He points to studies showing that children do much better in family settings that include both a mother and a father, and that the sexual behaviors same-sex parents engage in make them, by definition, inappropriate role models for children.

Currently, there are thousands of children awaiting adoption. In many cases, there are strict requirements as to who can and cannot adopt. In one country, for example, a heterosexual couple must be married for at least four years—and if they already have one child, they can only adopt a child of a different gender. Most countries do not allow same-sex couples or openly lesbian or gay individuals to adopt children.

In the United States, same-sex couples can adopt in a number of ways. Some will adopt as single parents, even though they are in a long-term, committed relationship with another person, because the state or agency does not permit same-sex couples to adopt together. Others will do what is called "second-parent" adoption—where one partner is the biological parent of the child and the other can become the other legal parent by going through the court system. In other cases, the biological parent must terminate her or his own rights so that there can be a "joint adoption." Both parents jointly adopt the child and become equal, legal parents. This applies to unmarried different-sex couples, too.

There is a range of feelings about who should or should not parent children. Some individuals feel that children should be raised by a man and a woman who are married, not by a gay or lesbian individual or couple. Starting with the premise that homosexuality is wrong, they feel that such a relationship is an inappropriate context in which to raise children. For some of these opponents of lesbian and gay parenting, homosexuality is defined by behaviors. Because they fear that sexual orientation and behaviors can be learned, they also fear that a child raised by a lesbian or gay couple will be more likely to come out as lesbian or gay herself or himself.

Other people do not believe that a person's sexual orientation determines her or his ability to parent. Whether a person is raised by one parent, two men, two women, or a man and a woman is less important than any individual's or couple's ability to love, support, and care for a child. They oppose the concept that a heterosexual couple in which there is abuse or where there are inappropriate sexual boundaries would be considered preferable to a lesbian or gay couple in a long-term, committed relationship who care for each other and their children. They point to the fact that most lesbian, gay, and bisexual adults were raised by heterosexual parents. Therefore, they believe, being raised by a lesbian or gay couple will not create lesbian, gay, or bisexual children, any more than being raised by a heterosexual, married couple would guarantee heterosexuality.

Some state laws support same-sex couples' right to adopt children, and some do not. In eight states (New Jersey, California, Connecticut, Massachusetts, New York, Illinois, Pennsylvania, and Vermont) as well as Washington, D.C., for example, joint or second-parent adoption is currently available. In Utah, married heterosexual couples are given priority for foster or adoptive children, and in Mississippi, there is a law that outright bans a same-sex couple from being able to adopt children.

As you read this issue, think about what you think the characteristics of a good parent are. Can these characteristics be found only in heterosexual relationships, or can they be fulfilled by a same-sex relationship? Does the gender of a same-sex relationship affect your feelings on the subject? For example, do you find two women raising a child more or less threatening than two men?

In the following selections, Joan Biskupic discusses the assertive steps that lesbian, gay, and bisexual individuals have made to gain footage in the legal arena when it comes to adoption rights. She provides an overview of individual state statutes pertaining to adoption by same-gender couples, citing an increased focus on creating "functional" parents—regardless of the gender(s) of the parents involved. Timothy J. Dailey asserts that gay men are sexually promiscuous and are therefore poor role models and parents for children. Lesbians, he believes, are ineffective parents because they are raising a child without the presence and influence of a father figure, which theorists, he maintains, argue is vital to the psychosocial development of children, male and female.

Parenting is an area that has so many unknown factors, influences, and outcomes. Two-parent, high-income families sometimes have children who grow up with emotional and/or behavioral problems. Single parents can raise healthy, well-adjusted children. Some heterosexual couples raise children effectively, and some do not; some lesbian or gay couples raise children effectively, and some do not.

Although there is much research exploring correlations between economic health, number of parents, and other factors, literature reviewing the connections between a parent's sexual orientation and her or his ability to parent remains inconclusive. There are studies maintaining that children need to be raised by a married, heterosexual couple, and there are studies asserting that a same-sex couple can do just as effective a job.

There is also insufficient information about homosexuality itself and the effects that having a lesbian, gay, or bisexual parent may or may not have on a child. The lack of information and plethora of misinformation breed fear. In at least two countries, depending on the official(s) involved in screening for the adoption, the prospective parents may be required to provide proof that they are heterosexual. When people are afraid, they want to protect—in this case, people who do not understand the basis of sexual orientation feel they need to protect children. In doing so, they sometimes make decisions that are not always in the best interest of the child. For example, in 1996, a divorced heterosexual couple living in Florida was battling over custody of their 11-year-old daughter. The male partner had recently completed an eight-year prison sentence for the murder of his first wife and had married his third. His ex-wife, however, had since met and partnered with a woman. A judge determined that the man and his new wife would provide a more appropriate home for the child than the child's mother because she was in a relationship with another woman. In the end, the judge believed that the child would do best in a home with a mother and a father, even though the father was convicted of second-degree murder and accused of sexually molesting his daughter from his first marriage.

How do you feel about this? If you feel that heterosexual couples are more appropriate parents than same-sex couples, how would the fact that one of the heterosexual partners had committed a capital crime affect your opinion?

Sometimes we argue for what we think "should be" in a given situation. A challenge arises when comparing the "should be" to the "is"—what we think is best as opposed to the reality. If you feel that heterosexual married couples make the best parents, what should be done with those same-sex couples who are providing a loving, stable home for their children? Would it be best to leave the child where she or he is, or do you think the child would be better off removed from her or his existing family structure and placed with a heterosexual couple? Clearly, this is a discussion and debate that will continue as more and more same-sex couples not only adopt but also have biological children of their own.

YES

Joan Biskupic

Same-Sex Couples Redefining Family Law in USA

Donna Colley and Margaux Towne-Colley, a lesbian couple bringing up a son in Omaha, face an ongoing dilemma.

They could stay in Nebraska, where Colley has a satisfying job as a lawyer, the couple own a home and are close to their neighbors. It's also where state law does not allow both women to be legal parents to Grayson, a blond, blue-eyed toddler who was delivered by Towne-Colley after she was artificially inseminated with sperm from an anonymous donor.

That leaves the couple with another option: Leave Nebraska and build a new life in one of about a dozen states that recognize same-sex couples as parents.

Such legal status isn't just symbolic. Because Colley can't be a legal parent to 16-month-old Grayson under Nebraska law, the child would not be entitled to government benefits if Colley were to become disabled or die. The boy would not be guaranteed support payments from Colley if the two women were to split up. And if Towne-Colley were to die, Colley wouldn't automatically receive custody of the boy.

Legal analysts say the choice they face is typical of the forces that are transforming family law across America. Gay and lesbian couples increasingly are going to court seeking to adopt children, acquire rights as parents, take on shared last names, and secure a range of benefits similar to those enjoyed by heterosexual couples.

Nearly three years after Vermont approved civil unions for homosexual couples, the evolving acceptance of such couples nationwide is reflected in recent court decisions in which judges have looked not only at biology when determining who is a "parent," but at the roles people play in households. Many judges are saying sexual orientation shouldn't matter in deciding what makes a family. A few conservative groups are fighting the tide, without much success.

Recent cases in Pennsylvania and Delaware symbolize the new age in family law, and judges' increasing flexibility in defining parental roles. Courts in those states ordered lesbians to pay child support for children they had been rearing with their partners before the couples split up.

"People are recognizing that these non-traditional families are here to stay, and courts are finding ways to support the children," says Susan Becker, professor at the Cleveland-Marshall College of Law at Cleveland State University.

But as Colley and Towne-Colley's situation suggests, the rules aren't the same for everyone.

State laws—and local attitudes—vary widely when it comes to adoption, child support, domestic partnerships, and other issues that affect same-sex couples. Courts, laws, and government policies in conservative states in America's heartland and in the South generally are less tolerant of efforts to give gay and lesbian couples the same rights as heterosexuals:

- Nebraska's Supreme Court last year refused to allow a lesbian to formally adopt the boy whom she and her partner (the birth mother) are rearing. Such "second parent" adoptions, which allow a second adult to assume responsibility for a child without the biological parent losing any rights, are legal for gay and lesbian couples in California, Connecticut, Delaware, Illinois, Massachusetts, New Jersey, New York, Pennsylvania, Vermont, and the District of Columbia. In a dozen other states, some local courts have backed such arrangements.
- Four states—Texas, Oklahoma, Kansas, and Missouri—still ban sex between consenting homosexual adults, although the laws are rarely enforced. The U.S. Supreme Court on March 26 will consider a challenge to Texas' law.
- Eight states and about three dozen cities and counties—mostly on the East and West coasts—now provide benefits for the partners of their gay and lesbian public employees, gay-rights advocates say.

No group tracks all cases involving gay and lesbian family issues. But those on both sides of the debate over whether gay and lesbian parents should be granted more rights agree that homosexuals' increasing aggressiveness on family issues has won them gains in courts and beyond.

"In the past, when gay and lesbian couples tried to adopt, they really couldn't identify themselves as gay," says Michele Zavos, a Washington, D.C., lawyer who specializes in gay family law. "Now, they can, either when going through a second-parent adoption or with an agency." . . .

Gay-rights advocates say it's all a reflection of the rising profile of gay men and lesbians in politics, the workplace, and everyday life. "People know now that gay and lesbian relationships are not exceptional," says Patricia Logue, a lawyer in Chicago for the Lambda Legal Defense and Education Fund. "Now, we're seeing what the political winds will bear in each state."

"I Am a Stranger to My Child"

Same-sex couples and their families have become hot topics for TV shows, movies, and media reports in recent years. The increasing openness of same-sex couples, fueled by the successes of the gay-rights movement, has made it seem as though there has been an explosion of such families.

But firm numbers are difficult to come by. The U.S. Census Bureau did not collect figures on same-sex couples until 2000, so there are no reliable statistics on the growth in such households. The 2000 Census found 1.2 million people living in households with unrelated adults of the same sex, but analysts say that figure is low because it was derived from a part of the Census form that some people ignored.

Similarly, estimates of children of gay or lesbian parents vary widely. Judges have cited various reports that put the number of children living with at least one gay or lesbian parent at 6 million to 12 million.

"The sheer number of support groups, magazines, and Web sites for gay and lesbian parents suggests that the number is significant," says Denver lawyer Kim Willoughby, who specializes in issues regarding same-sex couples.

Advances in reproductive technology, including artificial insemination, egg donation, and in-vitro fertilization, have given gay men and lesbians ways to become parents beyond adoption.

Although it has become easier for same-sex couples to work with private adoption agencies, they sometimes do not disclose their sexual orientation, making reliable statistics about such adoptions difficult. Gay men or lesbians who adopt foreign children typically have one partner adopt as an individual and the other partner initiate a second-parent adoption later.

After Towne-Colley, 38, got pregnant two years ago, she and Colley, 43, planned to return briefly to Vermont, where they had a civil union ceremony in 2000. (Towne added Colley's name to hers that year.) They wanted Grayson to be born there because the state would allow both women to be listed as parents on his birth certificate. But they were still in Nebraska in October 2001, when Grayson was born nine weeks early.

Working around Nebraska law, the couple drafted wills, a parenting agreement, and other papers that spell out their responsibilities for Grayson. "We are trying to do everything we can to tie ourselves together legally and bind me to our son," says Colley, whose salary and benefits provide for the family.

Still, Colley says, "under the law, I am a stranger to my child." For now, she and Towne-Colley are staying in Nebraska and not challenging its parenting laws. They are mindful of last year's state Supreme Court decision against a lesbian couple and say they don't want to risk an adverse ruling.

Amy Miller, a lawyer for the ACLU of Nebraska, represented the lesbian couple whose case went to Nebraska's high court. The court said state law forbids a second adult from adopting a child unless the birth mother (in this case, one of the partners) gives up her rights to the child.

Miller says her unidentified clients wanted to make sure that if the birth mother died, their 3-year-old son, Luke, could receive Social Security and other benefits tied to her partner. After they lost in court, they moved to Portland, Ore. Thanks to a second-parent adoption there, Miller said, they both are Luke's legal parents.

In Cincinnati, Cheryl, 41, and Jennifer, 36, are rearing a 2-year-old boy who is the product of an egg harvested from Cheryl, fertilized by sperm from an anonymous donor, and implanted in Jennifer.

The couple, who agreed to be interviewed if only their first names were used, say they might seek shared parental rights. But they know that Ohio courts often reject such efforts. They say moving out of state is not an option. "This is just as much our state as anyone else's," Cheryl says.

Focusing on "Functional" Parents

Ohio has been a battleground for the new generation of family law cases. The state Supreme Court has handed victories to those on both sides of the issue.

During the past year, the court endorsed shared last names for gay and lesbian couples but rejected second-parent adoptions for homosexuals. In Cleveland Heights, voters gave health benefits to gay and lesbian partners of city employees. An effort to reverse the move through a referendum failed. . . .

But Duke University law dean Katharine Bartlett says judges have struggled with nontraditional families since divorce rates jumped three decades ago. "Courts aren't trying to contribute to the demise of traditional families. But they recognize the reality of families today and 'functional' parents."

That was evident in a Pennsylvania case in December. The state Superior Court affirmed a trial judge's order that a lesbian should pay support for five children she had been bringing up with her ex-partner. That case followed one in Delaware in which a judge ordered a woman to pay support for a son that her former partner had through in-vitro fertilization.

But providing for children isn't always the overriding factor in such cases. Last year in Idaho, a local magistrate denied a gay man, Theron McGriff, custody of his two children from a marriage to a woman. The magistrate said McGriff, 38, couldn't visit them if he continued to live with another man. Idaho's Supreme Court agreed to hear McGriff's appeal.

"Sexual orientation should be irrelevant," says Shannon Minter, McGriff's attorney "Unless you're living under a rock, you know the way people live has changed."

Timothy J. Dailey  **NO**

State of the States: Update on Homosexual Adoption in the U.S.

The legal status of homosexual adoption varies from state to state, and is constantly changing due to court decisions and new state laws addressing the issue. Further complicating the issue are gay activist organizations that present misleading accounts of court rulings and laws reflecting unfavorably on homosexual parenting.

States That Specifically Prohibit Gay Adoption

Three states, Florida, Mississippi, and Utah, have passed statutes specifically prohibiting homosexual adoption. The advocates of gay adoption downplay the Utah statute, asserting that it was not intended to prevent adoption by homosexuals. Liz Winfeld, writing in the *Denver Post,* discusses claims that the Utah law was aimed squarely at homosexuals: "Not true. Utah disallows any unmarried person from adopting regardless of gender or orientation."[1] . . .

In fact, the Utah law was enacted specifically to close loopholes in Utah adoption laws that were being taken advantage of by homosexual couples seeking to adopt children. . . .

The ensuing fight led to the legislature passing a statute barring homosexual adoptions. . . .

States That Specifically Permit Gay Adoption

USA Today reports that seven states, including California, Connecticut, Illinois, Massachusetts, New Jersey, New York, Vermont, and the District of Columbia permit homosexuals to adopt.[2] However, at present, the inclusion of California on this list is inaccurate.

States That Permit Second-Parent Adoption

Homosexual couples have adopted children through "second-parent" adoption policies in at least twenty states. There is no evidence that homosexuals in the remaining states are permitted to adopt children, a fact admitted by the gay activist Human Rights Campaign (HRC): "In the remaining 24 states, our research has not revealed any second-parent adoptions."[3]

At least one state has reversed its policy of permitting second-parent adoptions. In November 2000, the Superior Court of Pennsylvania ruled that same-sex couples cannot adopt children.[4] In addition, a court decision in California has reversed that state's policy of permitting homosexuals to adopt children. On October 25, 2001, the 4th District Court of Appeal (San Diego) ruled that there was no legal authority under California law permitting second-parent adoptions.[5] . . .

Homosexual Households in the United States

There are widely varying and unsubstantiated claims about the numbers of children being raised in gay and lesbian households. . . .

- The U.S. Census Bureau reports that there are 601,209 (304,148 male homosexual and 297,061 lesbian) same-sex unmarried partner households, for a total of 1,202,418 individuals, in the United States.[6] If 1 million children were living in households headed by homosexual couples, this would mean that, on average, *every* homosexual household has at least one child.
- However, a survey in *Demography* indicates that 95 percent of partnered male homosexual and 78 percent of partnered lesbian households do *not* have children.[7] This would mean that the 1 million children presumed to be living in homosexual households would be divided among the 15,000 (5 percent of 304,148) male homosexual and 65,000 (22 percent of 297,061) lesbian households that actually have children. This would result in an astounding 12.5 children per gay and lesbian family.

The cases highlighted by the media to generate sympathy for homosexual adoption typically feature "two-parent" homosexual households. Of course, some children are also being raised by a natural parent who identifies himself or herself as homosexual and lives alone. Nevertheless, the hypothetical calculations above give some indication of how absurdly inflated most of the estimates are concerning the number of children being raised by homosexuals. Far from being the proven success that some claim, homosexual parenting remains a relatively rare phenomenon.

Implications for Homosexual Parenting

Demands that homosexuals be accorded the right to . . . adopt children fit into the gay agenda by minimizing the differences between homosexual and heterosexual behavior in order to make homosexuality look as normal as possible. However, as already shown, only a small minority of gay and lesbian households have children. Beyond that, the evidence also indicates that comparatively few homosexuals choose to establish households together—the type of setting that is a prerequisite for the rearing of children. Consider the following:

- HRC claims that the U.S. population of gays and lesbians is 10,456,405, or 5 percent of the total U.S. population over 18 years of age.[8] The best available data supports a much lower estimate for those who engage in same-sex sexual relations.[9] However, assuming the higher estimate for the purposes of argument, this would indicate that *only 8.6 percent* of homosexuals (1,202,418 out of 10,456,405) choose to live in a household with a person of the same sex.

- HRC asserts that "30 percent of gay and lesbian people are living in a committed relationship in the same residence."[10] Assuming HRC's own figures, that would mean over 3 million gays and lesbians are living in such households, which, as shown above, is a wildly inflated estimate over the census figures. It is worth noting that the HRC claim amounts to a tacit admission that 70 percent of gays and lesbians choose not to live in committed relationships and establish households together.

- HRC claims that the numbers of gay and lesbian households were "undercounted" by the census. However, if true, it would represent an unprecedented, massive undercount of 260 percent on the part of the U.S. Census Bureau.

The census figures indicate that only a small minority of gays and lesbians have made the lifestyle choice that is considered a fundamental requisite in any consideration regarding adoption, and only a small percentage of those households actually have children. The evidence thus does not support the claim that significant numbers of homosexuals desire to provide a stable family setting for children.

The Nature of Homosexual "Committed Relationships"

Gay activists admit that the ultimate goal of the drive to legitimize homosexual marriage and adoption is to change the essential character of marriage, removing precisely the aspects of fidelity and chastity that promote stability in the home. They pursue their goal heedless of the fact that such households are unsuitable for the raising of children:

- Paula Ettelbrick, former legal director of the Lambda Legal Defense and Education Fund, has stated, "Being queer is more than setting up house, sleeping with a person of the same gender, and seeking state approval for doing so. . . . Being queer means pushing the parameters of sex, sexuality, and family, and in the process transforming the very fabric of society."[11]
- According to homosexual writer and activist Michelangelo Signorile, the goal of homosexuals is to redefine the term *monogamy*.

For these men, the term "monogamy" simply doesn't necessarily mean sexual exclusivity. . . . The term "open relationship" has for a great many gay men come to have one specific definition: A relationship in which the partners have sex on the outside often, put away their resentment and jealousy, and discuss their outside sex with each other, or share sex partners.[12]

- The views of Signorile and Ettelbrick regarding marriage are widespread in the homosexual community. According to the *Mendola Report*, a mere 26 percent of homosexuals believe that commitment is most important in a marriage relationship.[13] . . .

Even those who support the concept of homosexual "families" admit to their unsuitability for children:

- In their study in *Family Relations*, L. Koepke et al. observed, "Even individuals who believe that same-sex relationships are a legitimate choice for adults may feel that children will suffer from being reared in such families."[14]
- Pro-homosexual researchers J. J. Bigner and R. B. Jacobson describe the homosexual father as "socioculturally unique," trying to take on "two apparently opposing roles: that of a father (with all its usual connotations) and that of a homosexual man." They describe the homosexual father as "both structurally and psychologically at social odds with his interest in keeping one foot in both worlds: parenting and homosexuality."[15]

In truth, the two roles are fundamentally incompatible. The instability, susceptibility to disease, and domestic violence that is disproportionate in homosexual relationships would normally render such households unfit to be granted custody of children. However, in the current social imperative to grant legitimacy to the practice of homosexuality in every conceivable area of life, such considerations are often ignored.

But children are not guinea pigs to be used in social experiments in redefining the institutions of marriage and family. They are vulnerable individuals with vital emotional and developmental needs. The great harm done by denying them both a mother and a father in a committed marriage will not easily be reversed, and society will pay a grievous price for its ill-advised adventurism.

Notes

1. Liz Winfeld, "In a Family Way," *Denver Post*, November 28, 2001.
2. Marilyn Elias, "Doctors Back Gay "Co-Parents," *USA Today*, February 3, 2002.
3. "Chapter 4: Second-Parent Adoption," in *The Family* (Human Rights Campaign, 2002). . . .
4. Ibid.
5. Bob Egelko, "Court Clarifies Decision on Adoptions," *San Francisco Chronicle*, November 22, 2001. The decision is under review by the California Supreme Court.
6. "PCT 14: Unmarried-Partner Households by Sex of Partners" (U.S. Census Bureau: Census 2000 Summary File 1).
7. Dan Black et al., "Demographics of the Gay and Lesbian Population in the United States: Evidence from Available Systematic Data Sources," *Demography* 37 (May 2000): 150.

8. David M. Smith and Gary J. Gates, "Gay and Lesbian Families in the United States: Same-Sex Unmarried Partner Households," *Human Rights Campaign* (August 22, 2001): 2.

9. Dan Black et al., "Demographics of the Gay and Lesbian Population," "4.7 percent of men in the combined samples have had at least one same-sex experience since age 18, but only 2.5 percent of men have engaged in exclusively same-sex sex over the year preceding the survey. Similarly, 3.5 percent of women have had at least one same-sex sexual experience, but only 1.4 percent have had exclusively same-sex sex over the year preceding the survey." (p. 141.)

10. Ibid.

11. Paula Ettelbrick, quoted in William B. Rubenstein, "Since When Is Marriage a Path to Liberation?" *Lesbians, Gay Men, and the Law* (New York: The New Press, 1993), pp. 398, 400.

12. Michelangelo Signorile, *Life Outside* (New York: HarperCollins, 1997), p. 213.

13. Mary Mendola, *The Mendola Report* (New York: Crown, 1980), p. 53.

14. L. Koepke et al., "Relationship Quality in a Sample of Lesbian Couples with Children and Child-free Lesbian Couples," *Family Relations* 41 (1992): 228.

15. Bigner and Jacobson, "Adult Responses to Child Behavior and Attitudes Toward Fathering," Frederick W. Bozett, ed., *Homosexuality and the Family* (New York: Harrington Park Press, 1989), pp. 174, 175.

EXPLORING THE ISSUE

Should Lesbian and Gay Individuals Be Able to Adopt Children?

Critical Thinking and Reflection

- What are some arguments made by each side with which you agree or disagree?
- What are the strengths and weaknesses of the two positions made in this issue?
- Pick the side with which you most agree. What are some additional arguments you would make to strengthen the case for or against lesbian and gay adoption?
- Think more broadly of the issue of lesbian and gay adoption. What are the characteristics of good parenting? What role does the biological sex and sexual orientation play in your definition?

Is There Common Ground?

This particular issue becomes more challenging for finding common ground. Is there a middle position? Could it involved allowing lesbian and gay couples to act as foster parents, but not adoptive parents? However, what happens when a gay couple raises a child in foster care for eight years, and then the child is available for adoption? Does the state take the child away from the gay couple in which he was raised?

Regardless, we know that some people who are gay or lesbian marry someone of the opposite sex and later come to terms with their sexual orientation. If they already have children from that marriage, then we already have children who may be raised entirely or at least partially by same-sex-headed households. Without engaging in the topic of adoption, we can already examine the impact that same-sex couples have when raising children. What sort of childhood does that create? Are the experiences significantly different from children raised by heterosexual parents?

Additional Resources

Human Rights Campaign:

                              http://www.hrc.org

Lambda Legal:

                              http://www.lambdalegal.org/

American Family Association:

                              http://www.afa.net

Focus on the Family:

                              http://www.focusonthefamily.com/

ISSUE 14

Are Teenagers Too Young to Become Parents?

YES: The National Campaign to Prevent Teen and Unplanned Pregnancy, from *One in Three: The Case for Wanted and Welcomed Pregnancy* (May 2007)

NO: Simon Duncan, Claire Alexander, and Rosalind Edwards, from "What's the Problem with Teenage Parents?" *Teenage Parenthood: What's the Problem?* (2010)

Learning Outcomes

As a result of this issue, readers will be able to:

- Identify critical research about the state of and consequences of teenage parenting.
- Compare and contrast the major research cited and analysis used in examining teenage parenthood.
- Evaluate the impact of teen parenthood on teens themselves, as well as on the larger American society.

ISSUE SUMMARY

YES: The National Campaign to Prevent Teen and Unplanned Pregnancy is dedicated to reducing teenage pregnancy. Their research argues that teens face significant consequences if they have unplanned pregnancy.

NO: Simon Duncan, Claire Alexander, and Rosaline Edwards have written a chapter in a book about teen pregnancy and parenting. This chapter, which takes a global perspective by looking at another Western society, England, argues that teenage pregnancy and parenting is not a problem.

Most people agree that it is important to reduce teenage pregnancy and parenthood. Teens involved in a pregnancy often did not plan that pregnancy. Indeed, about half of all pregnancies in the United States are unplanned—about 3 million each year.

Since the Clinton administration, there has been ongoing debate about the federal government's role in funding programs to reduce teen pregnancy: whether the best way to keep teenagers from having children is to teach them about contraception and abstinence, or only teach them about abstinence so that they fear the consequences of having sex. Although there is debate about whether abstinence-only or comprehensive sexuality education is the best approach, the goals tend to be the same: keep teenagers from pregnancy and parenthood.

In the United States, 30 percent of girls will become pregnant at least once by the age of 20. Many will terminate their pregnancies while others will decide to become parents. Sometimes fathers remain involved; often teen mothers are left as single parents, perhaps with support from their parent(s), guardian(s), and/or caretaker(s).

This issue will focus on adult views of teenage parenthood. However, it is important to take some time to read the perspective of teenage parents themselves. On Pregnancystories.net, teens have posted some of the following stories about their young pregnancy and parenthood:

15 and pregnant—well im 15 and two weeks pregnant. I told my boyfriend at the time and he was happy but as soon as his parents found out they said he was too young to be a dad. . . . Im looking forward to having my baby and iv got all the support i need. To all the girls who am pregnant and dont have a man . . . dont let him get you down cuz they aint worth it.

Abi

my perfect accident—hey everyone my name is johanna, i am 18 years old and i have a 5 month old baby. when i was about 4 months off my 17th birthday me and one of my close guy friends started doing a friends with benefits sort of thing, at first it was great but then we let our emotions become involved and i fell in love with him. we decided to end it and he got a girlfriend pretty much straight away which hurt me. soon after i found out that i was pregnant and i told him, but he didnt believe me i had to confirm it with the doctor before anything happened. he was far from happy with it and started saying that it was all my fault i was a whore and a bitch, eventually his girlfriend broke up with him because of it. he still to this day hates me but i dont care i now have a beautiful 5 month old baby boy dominic jason, who is my world! my mum is so over the moon with everything and im happy to be a single mum, i now realize he did me a favor, i couldve never been with him after that or exposed dominic to that!

johanna

single mommy—Hi my name is Alex, I am 19 and i have a 1 year old daughter. it all started when I was 17 i got pregnant to my boyfriend of 2 years johnny, i was shocked and scared at first but eventually told him and everyone, we decided to keep the baby and be young parents, but as my pregnancy went on johnny started to push away, and eventually when I was 26 weeks he got a football scholarship to college, we talked about it and he wasnt ready to become a father, so he left for college a week later, i was devastated but i had my daughter to think of, i have birth to Lilliana Jayde 4 weeks after i turned 18, i am now 19 and lilliana is 13 and a half months old, we are very happy she is my world, i regularly send johnny pictures we keep in touch he still wants to know that lilliana is okay but she has never met him. But im happy i have a wonderful job, and im renting a nice 3 bedroom house, i have great friends and family.

What do you think about these narratives of teens who are currently or will soon be parents? Their perspective seems fairly positive. Do you think that their experience will meet their expectations? Are they providing a realistic view or an overly rosy views? In your view, are their expectations rationale? Are they in denial? Can you see a difference in the support network that some teens have versus others? What impact will that have?

Although there are a great deal of publications about keeping teens from having sex, there is a lack of consensus on this issue—as seen from these teen voices. This Yes selection contains an research from the National Campaign to Prevent Teen and Unplanned Pregnancy, a mainstream American publication, stating that teens are too young to have children.

The opposing viewpoint comes from Europe, and it does so for a number of reasons. First, Europe is not having the same debate about *whether* teens should have sex at all, a topic which has proven highly controversial in the United States (e.g., see the U.S. debate about abstinence-only education versus comprehensive sexuality education). Second, England and much of Western Europe have a more extensive social safety net program than is typically found in the United States. Third, in examining family and personal relationships, it is sometimes valuable to take a global perspective. What does that culture have in common with ours? What is different? What is it about their perspective or approach that you find compelling? What is it about their perspective or approach that you find wrong or even damaging?

We also know that teens in the United States have a much higher rate of pregnancy than they do in England and Western Europe. Research tells us that there is not a significant difference in teenage sexual behavior between the countries. So what causes this difference? Is it an institutional issue of privilege and resources? In the United States, we have a higher proportion of poor citizens per capita than in Western Europe. Or is it a question of education? In the United States, children often receive little if any sexuality education, and many only learn about abstinence. In Western Europe, it is not regarded as controversial to teach children about contraception if they are at an age at which they may become sexually active.

Regardless of the difference in pregnancy rates, this issue provides readers with the opportunity to take a closer look at different views on whether this is a problem.

One in Three: The Case for Wanted and Welcomed Pregnancy

Defining the Problem

The nation has made extraordinary progress in preventing early pregnancy and childbearing. The teen pregnancy rate declined 36 percent between 1991 and 2002 (the most recent data available) and the teen birth rate has declined by one-third. In fact, few social problems have improved as dramatically as has this one.

When the National Campaign to Prevent Teen Pregnancy began in 1996, we challenged the nation to reduce the teen pregnancy rate in the United States by one-third over a 10-year period. Ten years later, demographic projections suggest that the nation may well have achieved this goal. Even so, it is still the case that one-third of teen girls become pregnant before they are 20, and the rate of teen pregnancy in the United States remains far higher than in other comparable countries. Mindful of the continuing problem, in 2006 we challenged the nation to reduce the rate of teen pregnancy by *another* one-third over the next 10 years.

But when the progress among teens is looked at within the context of pregnancy and childbearing in America more generally, it is increasingly apparent that although teens are moving in the right direction, their older brothers and sisters, friends, relatives, and neighbors are not.

A new analysis of existing data by the National Campaign indicates that about one in three pregnancies in America are unwanted. In this analysis, unwanted pregnancies include (1) pregnancies that end in abortion (about 1.3 million), (2) births resulting from pregnancies that women *themselves* say they did not want at the time of conception or *ever* in the future (about 567,000); and (3) a smaller number of miscarriages that were also of unwanted pregnancies (179,000). In other words, just over 2 million of the 6.4 million pregnancies in America in 2001 (the most recent data available) were unwanted.

Moreover, between 1994 and 2001, the *rate* of unwanted pregnancy in the United States increased slightly (4 percent) from 31.9 to 33.2 unwanted pregnancies per 1,000 women aged 15–44. In fact, the rate of unwanted pregnancy increased among women in every age group with the exception of teens.

An unwanted pregnancy is not to be confused with a pregnancy that may have come at an inconvenient or awkward time; in fact, some women will say, for example, that their third child was a pleasant surprise, and sometimes pregnancy comes a bit sooner than a couple might wish. The children born months later from these mistimed pregnancies are often welcomed into stable and nurturing families.

But some pregnancies are more than unexpected or mistimed; they are greeted by women with anguish—sometimes even alarm—especially when they occur at a time in a woman's life when she is not prepared to raise a child—or, in many instances, *another* child. She may not have adequate personal or financial supports in place or have other serious problems or challenges. It is these pregnancies that are of particular concern, as detailed later in this monograph.

Of the 2 million unwanted pregnancies estimated to have occurred in 2001:

- More than half (54 percent) occurred to women in their twenties (1,092,000 pregnancies): about one third (32 percent) were to women aged 20–24 (651,000 pregnancies); more than one in five (22 percent) were to women aged 25–30 (441,000 pregnancies).
- About three in ten (28 percent) were to women aged 30–44 (577,000 pregnancies).
- About two in ten (18 percent) occurred to teens aged 15–19 (366,000 pregnancies).
- In addition, almost three fourths (72 percent) of unwanted pregnancies are to unmarried women (1,475,000 pregnancies), and just over a quarter (28 percent) of unwanted pregnancies occur to married women (565,000 pregnancies).

What the National Campaign Plans to Do

In response to these important statistics, the National Campaign to Prevent Teen Pregnancy is expanding its mission. We will continue to work on preventing teen pregnancy. And we will now *also* focus on reducing the high level of unwanted pregnancy in the United States among young adults in their twenties where the majority of such pregnancies occur. This expansion is made possible by the William and Flora Hewlett Foundation, which has made a ten-year commitment to preventing unwanted pregnancy and reducing the need for abortion in America.

In opening this new front, the National Campaign will use the experience and knowledge we have gained in our work with teens to encourage young adults to bring more intentionality and planning to their pregnancies. We will continue in a common sense, bipartisan, and research-based fashion using many of the same strategies that have contributed to the nation's progress in reducing teen pregnancy over the past 10 years. In this new work with young adults, we will encourage personal responsibility among women and men and responsible public policies as well. We will:

- work with opinion leaders, policymakers, and program leaders at the national and state levels;

- support public information and education about a wide range of topics;
- encourage careful, consistent use of family planning by all who are sexually active and not seeking pregnancy;
- encourage responsible, healthy relationships among young adults (which can include refraining from sexual activity in some circumstances) to help them achieve their future family and career goals;
- engage the entertainment media, faith communities, parents, and others;
- emphasize the role of men in pregnancy prevention and planning; and
- support practical, evidence-based polices that advance our mission.

Helping Americans reduce their high levels of unwanted pregnancy is a complex challenge, of course, and it will require intense attention and ongoing action from many sectors. Although the National Campaign has many ideas about what to do, there is much we need to learn about underlying causes and possible remedies. Accordingly, over the next several months, the National Campaign will be continuing to learn from a wide variety of experts, policymakers, those on the front lines, and young adults themselves about unwanted pregnancy and what might be done to improve the situation. This outreach has already begun and will be intensifying in the upcoming months.

Taking strong steps to increase the proportion of pregnancies that are fully wanted and welcomed is long overdue. It is worth repeating: one in three pregnancies—over *2 million* each year—are unwanted. We think the country can do far better.

Why Preventing Unwanted Pregnancy Matters

Reducing unwanted pregnancy will bring significant benefits to women, men, children, families, and society in general.

Increasing the proportion of pregnancies that are wanted and welcomed will help ensure healthier pregnancies, healthier babies, and enhanced child development.

New guidelines about preconception care from the Centers for Disease Control and Prevention underscore how planning for pregnancy and being at optimal health before pregnancy can help to dramatically improve a woman's chance of having a healthy pregnancy and baby. Unfortunately, women who experience an unwanted pregnancy often do not have the opportunity to engage in such preconception care.

Even when taking into account the existing social and economic factors, women experiencing an unwanted pregnancy are less likely to obtain prenatal care and their babies are at increased risk of both low birthweight and of being born prematurely, both of which increase the risk of many serious problems including infant mortality. These mothers are also less likely to breastfeed their infants.

Children born from unwanted pregnancies also face a range of developmental risks as well. For example, these children report poorer physical and mental health compared to those children born as the result of an intended pregnancy. They also have relationships with their mothers that are less close during childhood (and possibly into adulthood) when compared to peers who were born as the result of an intended pregnancy.

A new analysis from Child Trends indicates that, after controlling for numerous background factors, children two years old who were born as the result of an unwanted pregnancy have significantly lower cognitive test scores when compared to children born as the result of an intended pregnancy. These cognitive test scores include direct assessment of such skills as listening, vocabulary, exploring, problem solving, memory, and communication, as well as a child's overall mental ability relative to other children in his or her age group.

Increasing the proportion of pregnancies that are wanted and welcomed will help reduce both out-of-wedlock births and child poverty.

Over two decades of social science research makes clear that children fare better when their parents are older, have completed at least high school, are in stable and committed relationships—marriage, in particular—and are ready to take on the complex challenges of being parents. But many children born as the result of unwanted pregnancies are not welcomed into such families.

The majority of children from an unwanted pregnancy are born to women who are either single or cohabiting. This is important because children who are raised in single-parent families face a number of challenges. For example, when compared to similar children who grow up with two parents, children in one-parent families are twice as likely to drop out of high school, 2.5 times as likely to become teen mothers, 1.4 times as likely to be both out of school and out of work, and five times more likely to be poor. Even after adjusting for a variety of relevant social and economic differences, children in single-parent homes have lower grade-point averages, lower college aspirations, and poorer school attendance records. As adults, they also have higher rates of divorce.

Moreover, an analysis of data from 1970 to 1996 by National Campaign President Isabel Sawhill shows that virtually all of the increase in child poverty over that period was related to the growth of single-parent families. In the 1970s, some of this increase was the result of rising divorce rates, but since the early 1980s, virtually all of the increase has been driven by the increased numbers of never-married mothers.

All such data suggest that reducing unwanted pregnancy will increase the proportion of children born into circumstances that better support their growth and development. For example, the National Campaign estimates that preventing unwanted pregnancy has the potential to reduce non-marital childbearing by 26 percent.

Increasing the proportion of pregnancies that are wanted and welcomed will reduce the need for abortion.

Although there are many deeply felt and strongly held beliefs nationwide about the proper place of abortion in American life, virtually all of us see value in lessening the need for abortion and would prefer that fewer women have to confront an unwanted pregnancy in the first place. Through primary prevention—that is helping couples avoid unwanted pregnancy—the 1.3 million abortions in America each year can be dramatically decreased.

Increasing the proportion of pregnancies that are wanted and welcomed will help reduce disparities.

Disparities in unwanted pregnancy are on the rise. A woman below the poverty line is now nearly four times as likely as a woman at or above 200 percent of poverty to have an unintended pregnancy—a complex measure that includes *both* unwanted and mistimed pregnancy. Reflecting this trend, the abortion rate for low-income women increased 22 percent between 1994 and 2000. Still, 40 percent of all unintended pregnancies are to women at or above 200 percent of poverty.

Increasing the proportion of pregnancies that are wanted and welcomed will help women and men better plan their future.

That an unwanted pregnancy can derail the future plans of individuals is self-evident. For example, an unexpected, unwanted pregnancy can interrupt a young person's education and diminish future job prospects—a scenario that is becoming ever more serious with the increasing demand for a well-educated workforce. Reducing the high level of unwanted pregnancy in this country will unquestionably help many teens and adults achieve economic security and more stable relationships, which benefits not only them but also their children and society.

What the American Public Knows and Believes

Public opinion surveys conducted on behalf of the National Campaign by two widely respected communications firms, the Glover Park Group and Public Strategies Inc., make clear that there is broad and deep public support for the goal of reducing the number of unwanted pregnancies. In fact, over two-thirds (69 percent) of the American public believes it is important to reduce the number of unwanted pregnancies in the United States.

The public also supports several ways to encourage more young adults to increase the proportion of pregnancies that are fully wanted and welcomed by both partners:

- 87 percent support strengthening a culture of *personal responsibility* regarding sex, getting pregnant, and bringing children into the world, as well as strengthening the norm of always practicing family planning when a couple is not ready to have a child.
- 82 percent support *responsible policies* that will increase the use of contraception, particularly by those who cannot afford it and by those at greatest risk for having an unwanted pregnancy.

- 90 percent of the public support the idea of providing *more education* to teens, parents, and young adults in their 20s and 30s that encourages them to take sex, pregnancy, and family formation seriously; stresses personal responsibility and respectful relationships; and includes extensive information about contraception.

In this same survey, the most commonly cited reason for reducing unwanted pregnancy was to improve the quality of life for children:

- 24 percent of adults say that the single most important reason for reducing teen and unwanted pregnancy is because children who grow up wanted have a better future.
- 20 percent say it is because more children are likely to grow up living with both a father and a mother.

More generally, the vast majority of Americans believe that young people should complete their education, have the means to raise a child, and be married before becoming pregnant:

- 88 percent of the American public believes that children generally do better when they are raised in two-parent, married families.
- 97 percent believe it is important to have the means to take care of a child without outside assistance before becoming a parent.
- 96 percent believe that finishing one's education before becoming a parent is important.
- 90 percent believe that being married before becoming pregnant is important.

Despite these widely shared sentiments, the *magnitude* of the unwanted pregnancy problem in the United States—and which groups are most at risk—are not well understood. In particular, very few Americans realize that teens are only a small part of the problem. For example:

- Even though less than 20 percent of all abortions are to teens, 4 out of 5 Americans think that the percentage is higher (often much higher).
- 77 percent of Americans assume that teens have the highest number of unplanned pregnancies; in fact, young adults do.
- Only 15 percent of the public knows that unmarried teens are *more likely* than unmarried women in their 20s to have used an effective method of contraception the last time they had sex.

Teens Still Matter a Lot

This monograph makes the case that adults, not just teenagers, are having difficulty in overall pregnancy planning. Even so, there are two primary reasons why the nation should continue to focus on teen pregnancy given all its serious consequences.

Despite a one-third decline in teen pregnancy and birth rates since the early 1990s, the teen pregnancy rate in the United States is *still* the highest among comparable countries. One in three teens becomes pregnant at least once by age 20. For some subgroups, the news is even more sobering. For example, 51 percent of Latina teens become pregnant by the time they leave their teen years. There is also some evidence to suggest that the progress the nation has made in preventing teen pregnancy and childbearing has begun to slow or, in some cases, to reverse—all of which suggests that the nation's efforts going forward will need to be more intense and creative.

A crisp focus on preventing teen pregnancy and childbearing is also important because the knowledge, attitudes, and behavioral patterns that develop in adolescence strongly affect behavior in the years that follow. In other words, the teen years are a critical place to start to prevent unwanted pregnancy among women of all ages. In our work with teenagers, the National Campaign will continue to encourage teens to delay sexual activity—their best choice—and to practice family planning if they are sexually active.

A Final Note

Unwanted pregnancy among young adults is a complex problem, and getting people to change their behavior is a difficult proposition at best. Even so, we believe this nation can do far better and are optimistic about the chances for success. When the National Campaign began a decade ago, there was a sense that teen pregnancy was an intractable problem and the organization's goal of reducing the teen pregnancy rate by one-third was greeted with great skepticism. Ten years later, the situation has improved dramatically. This progress suggests that *adults* can do a better job, too, and that a higher proportion of all pregnancies can be wanted and welcomed.

If the National Campaign's efforts and those of others lead to less unwanted pregnancy, more young adults will be deliberate, serious, and intentional about pregnancy, childbearing, and family formation. In so doing, more children will be welcomed into the world by parents who are ready to provide them with the love, care, and nurture we want for every child in this country. More children will grow up in two-parent, married families or other fully supportive and stable circumstances; there will be less poverty, a lighter tax burden, less stress on families, and stronger communities. And there will be far less need for abortion.

Simon Duncan, Claire Alexander,
and Rosalind Edwards

 **NO**

What's the Problem with Teenage Parents?

[W]hy is there such an invested need in presenting an unremittingly negative image of young parents, and what does this say about the values placed on family and the role of paid work in twenty-first-century Britain? How—and why—have policy makers and news makers got the story about teenage parents so wrong?

New Labour and Teenage Parenting: An Economic or Moral Agenda?

2010 marks the year by which New Labour pledged to halve the number of pregnancies for under-eighteen-year-olds in the UK. The government's ten year Teenage Pregnancy Strategy was launched in 1999 in a report from the Social Exclusion Unit (SEU), then at the heart of government in Cabinet Office and itself resulting from a putative 'underclass unit' set up by Peter Mandelson, then Minister without Portfolio, in 1997. The report, which has set the framework for government policy since then, saw teenage pregnancy as a major social and economic problem, where Britain did much worse than other west European countries. Or as Tony Blair, then Prime Minister, put it, in his forward to the Social Exclusion Unit report:

> Some of these teenagers, and some of their children, live happy and fulfilled lives. But far too many do not. Teenage mothers are less likely to finish their education, less likely to find a good job, and more likely to end up both as single parents and bringing up their children in poverty. The children themselves run a much greater risk of poor health, and have a much higher chance of becoming teenage mothers themselves. Our failure to tackle this problem has cost the teenagers, their children and the country dear.

The SEU report identified the causes of this problem as low expectations and ignorance among teenagers, and mixed messages from the media. While the SEU report made clear a strong relationship between teenage pregnancy and social disadvantage, this association was downplayed either as cause or remedy, rather young parenting was seen to strongly reinforce disadvantage. And the way out was through a dual goal of prevention and direction—to reduce the number of under-eighteen pregnancies by half, and increase the number of teenage parents entering education, training, or employment to sixty per cent.

The heady political symbolism and mobilisation created by the media's moral panic reinforced the need for government to be seen to tackle what was already identified as a problem for 'teenagers, their children and the country.' All this was underlined by contrasting national teenage birth rates or, as Tony Blair put it in his forward to the SEU's 1999 document, Britain's 'shameful record.' British rates remained among the highest in the 28 OECD developed countries (30 per 1000 in 1998, compared to 10 or less in Germany, France, Scandinavia and the Netherlands). Only the USA at 52.1, and more marginally Canada and New Zealand, had higher rates. This comparative failure has an important policy impact, as suggested by the highlighting of international comparisons in most government and policy reports. For while the UK seemed to be 'stuck,' as the SEU put it, the experience of western Europe implied that teenage pregnancy and parenting, perceived as a difficult social problem, was nonetheless amenable to policy solution. Underlying this comparison is an issue around economic, as well as social, competition—how can Britain compete with an inadequate workforce, where teenage pregnancy supposedly restricts educational achievement and employment participation.

This international comparative lesson was emphasised by the appreciation that local rates also vary widely across Britain; it is not just young women who are poorer that are more likely to become pregnant, and least likely to use abortion to resolve pregnancy—they also live in poorer areas. In contrast, some richer areas in Britain have teenage abortion and pregnancy rates more like supposed European exemplars such as The Netherlands. The 'problem' of teenage pregnancy was ripe for intervention by a reforming new government.

Hence the New Labour government rolled out its teenage pregnancy strategy from 1999 onwards, originally under the direction of a Ministerial Task Force, and co-ordinated by the Teenage Pregnancy Unit (TPU). Starting in 2001, each top tier local authority had an agreed teenage pregnancy strategy to reach local 2010 targets around the desired national average. Each local strategy was led by a Teenage Pregnancy Coordinator, working with a Teenage Pregnancy Partnership Board, and supported by a Local Implementation Grant. These local Strategies were supported and performance managed by a Regional Teenage Pregnancy Coordinator, based in the regional government office. Local indicators, such as levels of conceptions in targeted age groups, availability and use of services, and health outcomes, were devised to help monitor progress towards achieving these targets. In line with government objectives for 'joined-up' approaches to service and policy development, work locally was intended to proceed in conjunction with other national government initiatives such as Sure Start, Sure Start Plus and the Children's Fund, and other national government departments were expected actively to support the strategy. In this way the TPU would hopefully reach the two main targets, as set by the Social Exclusion Unit—to halve the under—eighteen teenage conception rate by 2010 and to substantially increase the participation of teenage parents in education, training or employment.

This is an impressive machinery. But the 'low expectations' explanation—which points towards tackling social disadvantage—seems to have been neglected. Rather, policy in practice focused on the 'ignorance' explanation—British youth were seen as deficient in their sexual health knowledge, poor users of contraception, shy about sex, and wary about accessing services. Perhaps this focus was the more appealing when current policy thinking tends to stress individual behaviour and motivations, rather than structural influences on behaviour, like social disadvantage. Certainly, on a relatively low budget (the initial TPU budget was only £60 million) it might have been here that the policy implementers hoped for 'quick wins,' when taking on social disadvantage would cost a lot more and take a lot longer. Policy then ended up pathologising teenage pregnancy and childrearing, when it was seen to arise from 'inappropriate motivations, ignorance and sexual embarrassment,' rather than supporting the positive features of parenting.

How has this approach endured the experience of implementation? The Department for Communities, Schools, and Families report *Teenage Parents: the next steps* was to give new guidance to local authorities and primary care trusts given the previous eight years experience. The report recognises failures in reaching the desired targets—the reduction rate in teenage births was only 11.8% over the period, rather than approaching the desired 50% by 2010; similarly only about 30% of teenage mothers were in employment, education and training (EET), rather than 60%. Hence the need for a 'refreshed strategy' as the report's introduction puts it. There was also a whole battery of research produced since the SEU's original 1999 report, which as a whole pointed to a substantial gap between policy and experience, indicating both that the outcomes for teenage parents were not as dire as assumed and that young parenting encapsulated many positive features as well as problems. This includes research reviewed, or directly commissioned, by the TPU itself. But despite recognition of 'What teenage mothers and young fathers say' in the new 2007 report (in its chapter four), the existing two-track approach remained. Teenage parenting was as a problem in and of itself and should be cut, and the further need was to integrate remaining young parents into a productive workforce. 'Refreshed' was more about changing the implementation channels from specialised services into mainstream midwifery and health visiting services, Children's Centres, and Youth Support Services.

The report bases the essential continuation of the two-track approach on its enumeration of the disadvantaged characteristics of teenage mothers, and the poor outcomes they—and their children—experience, using a whole range of social and economic indicators. There are a number of key features that can be identified in this policy portrait of teenage parenthood, and that echo the media and political representations discussed above. First there is the clear gendering of this discourse, with the focus being primarily on young mothers, while young fathers play a very secondary role. This links into an assumed conflation between young motherhood (where many will live with partners or grandparents, and others will have 'live apart together' relationships') and single motherhood. Second, there is the insistence on the negative consequences of teenage pregnancy on both the mother and child, in which health, emotional and economic 'wellbeing' are taken as the key problem areas (and largely seen as interchangeable). Third, there is the emphasis on prevention of pregnancy rather than support for teenage parents—and in the 2007 report, rather chilling, concern to prevent further pregnancies for young mothers (for some young mothers, especially those with partners, would like to reach a desired family size). Fourth, is the conflation of socio-economic deprivation with teenage pregnancy, the implication being that teenage pregnancy is a cause of poverty. The report asserts that these poor outcomes are partially independent of wider factors of social deprivation and rather points to 'the lifestyles and behaviour of teenage mothers' as contributory factors. Fifth, there is the 'classing' of the issue, with teenage pregnancy linked to specific socio-economic groupings, and their associated problems, in particular the low levels of labour market participation. Sixth, there is the insistence on education, training and paid employment as the sole legitimate pathway to social inclusion and to ameliorating the negative effects of young parenthood.

Hence Beverley Hughes, then Minister for Children, Young People, and Families, wrote in her forward to the 2007 report that:

> Children born to teenage mothers are more likely to live in deprived areas, do less well at school, and disengage from learning early—all of which are risk factors for teenage pregnancy and other poor outcomes.

Equally, one could write that teenage mothers commonly show resilience and motivation, and become more socially connected and purposeful, where pregnancy usually marks a turning point for the better, become more likely to take up education and employment, and do no worse—and often better—than their social peers once pre-existing disadvantage is allowed for. This contrast is the terrain of this book.

The Myth of the Teenage Pregnancy Epidemic

The perceived social threat from teenage parenting is buttressed by a negative public consensus around teenage conception and pregnancy itself. This consensus assumes that teenage pregnancy is increasing rapidly, that this increase is particularly marked among younger teenagers, that all teenage pregnancies are unplanned, that all these unplanned conceptions are unwanted, and that new teenage mothers are inevitably also single mothers without stable relationships with partners. All these assumptions are unfounded, but all serve to bolster the negative evaluation of subsequent teenage parenting, and hence the nature of the policy response.

Newspaper headlines frequently announce 'soaring' teenage birth rates, creating an 'epidemic' of births to teenagers. Indeed as many as 81% of respondents to a 2008 Ipsos MORI poll thought that teenage pregnancy was increasing, while about a quarter of the 16–24 age group thought that 40% of 15–17 year-old

Table 1

Live Births and Birth Rates for Women Under 20, 1951–2008

	Numbers of live births	Birth rate per 1000 women aged 15–19
1951	29,111	21.3
1956	37,938	27.3
1961	59,786	37.3
1966	66,746	47.9
1971	82,641	50.6
1976	54,500	29.8
1981	60,800	30.9
1986	57,406	30.1
1991	52,396	33.1
1996	44,667	30.0
2001	44,189	28.0
2004	45,028	26.9
2005	44,830	26.3
2006	45,509	26.6
2007	44,805	26.0
2008	44,683	see note

Sources: ONS Birth Statistics, Health Statistics Quarterly.

Note: 2008 birth rate not available at time of press.

girls became parents each year. In fact there have been substantial declines in both birth rates and absolute numbers of births to teenagers since the 1960s and early 1970s (see Table 1). By 2007 only 11.4% of conceptions were to women aged under 20, with an even smaller share of births—6.4%. In addition few teenage mothers are under 16, only around 6% in 2006, accounting for just 0.9% of all births in Britain by 2007, while around 80% of teenage mothers were 18 or 19 years-old. Overall, teenage birth rates are now at around the same level as in the 1950s, that supposed 'golden age' of family.

What *is* different is that in the 1950s and 1960s, the majority of teenage parents married—although many seem to have been hastily enforced 'shot-gun marriages,' notorious for high rates of dysfunctionality and breakdown. In addition, probably around 20% of the children were adopted shortly after birth. In contrast, by the 2001 census only 9% of teenage parents were married; although around 30% cohabited; in addition, around another quarter jointly registered the birth with the father at another address—which suggests some continuing parental relationship on the 'living apart together' (or LAT) model. There are now very few adoptions of teenage mothers' children. These trends away from marriage, and towards unmarried cohabitation and 'living apart together' reflect those for the population as a whole, especially among younger age groups. Thus in 2006, around 0.5% of all 18–24 year-olds in Britain were married, with 12% cohabiting, while as many as 35% were in 'living apart together' partner relationships.

Whatever the level of teenage pregnancy, it is assumed in the public and media discourse that all teenage pregnancies are unplanned, that all unplanned conceptions are unwanted, and that most result from ignorance if not wilful immorality. Certainly the Social Exclusion Unit's framework 1999 report identified 'ignorance'—the 'lack of accurate knowledge about contraception, STIs (sexually transmitted infections), what to expect in relationships and what it means to be a parent' as major cause of teenage pregnancy. This is repeated in succeeding policy and guidance documents. But there is little support for the assumption that teenage parents are particularly ignorant about sex, contraception, and parenting, that low levels of knowledge 'cause' teenage pregnancy, or that increased knowledge reduces pregnancy. It is hard to find young mothers who become pregnant due to ignorance about sex and contraception. Similarly, a meta-analysis of preventative strategies focusing on sex education, and improved access to advice and contraceptive services, concluded that this did not reduce unintended pregnancies among young women aged between 11–18.

Indeed, a significant minority of teenage mothers, and fathers, positively plan for pregnancy. Some are hoping for birthing success after an earlier miscarriage, others in this group, especially those with partners, plan for subsequent children so as to complete their desired family size and hence 'build' a family. Many other teenage parents are 'positively ambivalent' towards childbirth—that is, they do not actually plan it but would quite like a baby and do not use contraception for that reason. For most teenage parents, pregnancy may well be 'unplanned,' but then so are many, if not most, pregnancies for all women—the very idea of 'planning pregnancy' is something of a grey area to say the least. Few teenage mothers, it seems, regret early childbirth, as many of the succeeding chapters show. As with other women 'unplanned' pregnancy does not necessarily mean 'unwanted' pregnancy for teenage parents. Or, as Germaine Greer put it: 'We have 39,000 unwanted pregnancies a year unwanted by the Government that is. No one is speaking for the mums.'

This set of policy and public assumptions is the starting point for Pam Alldred and Miriam David in their examination on the role and importance of education in young mothers' lives, and on their gendered expectations regarding parenthood. For their research shows how the values and priorities expressed by young mothers do not fit comfortably within the model presented in the Teenage Pregnancy Strategy (TPS), nor with many of the values assumed in, or explicitly asserted by, the TPS. In particular, the chapter questions the assumptions that early mothering is undesirable or aberrant; that education or training in the child's early years is desirable or even accessible to young mothers; and that either 'parenting' or 'studying' can be assumed to be gender-neutral activities. The logic the authors find at work in the young women's lives in their study seems to reflect the dominant values in their community and this logic questions the link between teenage pregnancy and social exclusion asserted in government policy. Similarly; in chapter three, Jan Macvarish and Jenny Billings discuss how the teenage mothers in their study, living in Kent, made moral and thoughtful decisions about contraception, proceeding with their pregnancy, and engagement with health and welfare services. Rather than suffering 'broken' family circumstances, teenage parents were often embedded in networks of support, and were optimistic that parenthood would shift them onto a positive life trajectory.

Statistical Outcomes—Social Disadvantage Versus Teenage Mothering

The influential UNICEF report *Teenage Births in Rich Nations* claims that:

> giving birth as a teenager is believed to be bad for the young mother because the statistics suggest that she is much more likely to drop out of school, to have low or no qualifications, to be unemployed or low paid, to grow up without a father, to become a victim of neglect and abuse, to do less well at school, to become involved in crime, use drugs and alcohol.

But in fact the statistics show nothing of the sort—if we deal with the errors committed by statements like these. For the statement does not compare like with like in reaching its 'much more likely' attribution of statistical causation; ascribing causal effects to teenage motherhood is pretty meaningless if we compare teenage mothers with all mothers, rather than those of a similar background. Rather, if we wish to measure the statistical effect of teenage motherhood (and then go on to ascribe a social effect, which is not necessarily the same thing), we need to control for variation in other variables, so that we do compare like with like. In more formal terms, statistical analysis needs to control for 'selection effects:' This is a variant of the correlation problem so beloved in statistical textbooks. Variable X may be highly correlated with 'dependent' variable Y, but this does not mean that X causes Y; rather both may be caused by an unacknowledged variable A. In this case, becoming a young mother may not cause the poor outcomes—in terms of education, employment, and income—experienced by many teenage mothers; rather, both young motherhood, and poor outcomes, may be caused by pre-pregnancy social disadvantage. In this sense, social disadvantage may 'select' particular young women, and men, to become teenage parents, and this disadvantage will continue post pregnancy. Teenage parenting may therefore be a part of social disadvantage, rather than its cause. But if statistical studies do not control for these selection effects, then they will not be able to recognise this.

In fact, there has been a tradition of statistical studies which do try to take account of these selection effects. Some researchers devised 'natural experiments' where selection effects would be better controlled, such as comparisons between cousins whose mothers were sisters, between sisters, or between twin sisters (only one of whom was a teenage mother), and between teenage mothers and other women who had conceived as a teenager but miscarried (who presumably would have gone on to become mothers). This type of research began in the USA, and found that the social outcome effects of mother's age at birth were very small, or as Saul Hoffman put it in his systematic review of the US research 'often essentially zero.' Indeed, by their mid/late twenties, teenage mothers in the USA did better than miscarrying teenagers with regard to employment and income and this meant, ironically, that government spending would have increased if they had not become young mothers.

The UK-based studies available at the time the 1999 SEU report was produced did not take this 'natural experiment' approach to controlling selection effects, and instead relied on more general statistical controls of social background, like educational level, socio-economic status, housing type, and so on. Although they also concluded that much of the adverse social conditions linked with teenage parenting were associated with pre-pregnancy social disadvantage, this is perhaps why they nevertheless came to more ambivalent conclusions about the social effect of teenage pregnancy in itself. Since the publication of the SEU report, however, a number of British studies have taken up the 'natural experiment' approach, with the same results as in the USA. John Ermisch and David Pevalin, using the British Cohort Study to assess differences between miscarrying and successful teenage pregnancies, found that teen birth has little impact upon qualifications, employment or earnings by thirty years of age. While teenage mothers' partners were more likely to be poorly qualified or unemployed, and this then impacted on the mothers,' and their children's, standard of living, this is also akin to a selection effect. In itself, age of birth has little effect. A complementary study using British Household Panel data to follow teenage mothers over time came to similar conclusions, as does a study by Denise Hawkes on twins, where only one became a teenage mother. Finally, Karen Robson and Richard Berthoud used the Labour Force Survey to assess the link between high rates of poverty and high rates of teenage fertility among minority ethnic groups, particularly for the extreme case of Pakistanis and Bangladeshis where both variables are particularly high. They concluded that teen birth has little effect on future poverty, and does not lead to any further disadvantage beyond that experienced by the ethnic group as a whole.

In chapter four, Denise Hawkes follows this work in providing a wide-ranging statistical review of the life experiences and circumstances of teenage mothers and their children in Britain, compared with other mothers, based on the Millennium Cohort Study. She uses three indicative sets of statistical analyses to examine: (1) life course experience for mothers prior to the birth of the first child, (2) the early life circumstances of children at nine-months, and (3) health, cognitive, and behavioural outcomes for children at ages three and five. The first set of analyses, confirming earlier statistical studies, shows that teenage motherhood is really a symptom of a disadvantaged life course rather than the cause of it. The second set shows that those children with teenage mothers are indeed born into families experiencing multiple disadvantages. However, it is not the mother's age at first birth which is the main driver of these disadvantages—rather, it is the prior disadvantages experienced by the young mothers during their own childhoods. Again, this finding substantiates earlier research. The final set of statistical analyses takes comparison into a new area, and show that having a teenage mother does not significantly affect the chances of a pre-school child experiencing poor health, and makes little difference to how children score on cognitive tests. There is some difference for a few behavioural indices, but this largely disappears once prior life disadvantage is accounted for.

Hawkes notes that the starting point for most policy interventions around teenage parenthood is that the root of the problem is that the mother is a teenager—but her statistical analyses find that being a teenage mother does not in itself lead to poorer outcomes either for the mothers themselves or their children. Rather teenage motherhood often signals a life of exposure, for both mothers and children, to a range of social and economic disadvantages. She concludes that these results suggest a shift in government policy away from incidence of teenage motherhood itself, and a refocusing on the social and economic causes of teenage motherhood. What is more this sort of policy would be sensible because the factors associated with becoming a teenage mother appear to be the same factors as those influencing the life chances of their children.

Perhaps there can never be an accurate statistical measurement of the 'effect' of teenage motherhood, in the sense of finding some ultimate truth. Nonetheless, this statistical research tradition shows that—in these outcome terms—teenage childbearing in itself can be seen as only a minor social problem. It is not the teenage bit which is particularly important in these terms, but rather it is social and economic disadvantage which produce poor outcomes. In so far as teenage mothers are over-represented among the disadvantaged, this is because of their 'selection' through pre-existing disadvantage. A policy focus on being a teenage mother can only approach this wider problem of social disadvantage obliquely. Or as Hoffmann concluded for the USA, this sort of statistical study 'no longer supports the notion that teenage childbearing is a devastating event' and 'casts considerable doubt on the received wisdom about the consequences of teenage childbearing.'

Qualitative Accounts of Agency—Young Parents' Values and Experiences

What about the mothers and fathers themselves? A tradition of small-scale qualitative research focuses on their actual understandings and experiences of becoming a parent. In this way, qualitative research can help explain just why the statistical studies find that age of pregnancy has little effect on social outcomes, and may actually make things better. While Hilary Graham and Elizabeth McDermott see quantitative and qualitative research as contradictory (the former seeing teenage motherhood as a route to social exclusion, the latter as an act of social inclusion), this contradiction perhaps relates more to the way these results have been framed, interpreted and used within opposing discourses, rather than to the findings themselves. Instead, we can profitably see quantitative and qualitative studies as complementary in providing, on the one hand, extensive evidence about overall social patterns and, on the other, intensive evidence on the social processes that create these patterns.

What these qualitative studies find is that many mothers express positive attitudes to motherhood, and describe how motherhood has made them feel stronger, more competent, more connected to family and society, and more responsible. Resilience in the face of constraints and stigma, based on a belief in the moral worth of being a mother, is one overriding theme. For some, this has given the impetus to change direction, or build on existing resources, so as to take up education, training, and employment. There has been less research on young fathers, but what there has been tends to contradict the 'feckless' assumption. Like teenage mothers, most of the fathers are already socially disadvantaged, and it does not appear that fathering will in itself make this any worse. But, also like teen mothers, most express positive feelings about the child and want to be good fathers. Most contributed maintenance in some way, and many were actively involved in childcare (this varies by age, with the youngest least likely to be involved). And, like teenage mothers, there is some evidence that successful fathering could be a positive turning point in young men's lives. In fact, it was an invisibility to professionals, as well as housing problems, which often excluded them from the parenting they desired. Again, like teen mothers, young fathers may be less of a social threat, more of a social possibility.

That teenage motherhood has a positive side is an enduring finding over time in this research tradition. Nearly two decades ago, the study by Ann Phoenix of teenage mothers in London, in the mid-1980s, found that most of the mothers and their children were faring well. Most (and their male partners) had already done badly in the educational and employment systems, and it did not seem that early motherhood had caused this or that deferring motherhood would have made much difference. Rather, if anything, motherhood was something of a turning point which 'spurred some women on' into education and employment. Contributions to this edited collection testify that, two decades later, this more positive picture remains pertinent.

While Phoenix's research prefigures the statistical 'natural experiments,' it remains unacknowledged in that tradition, and does not feature in the SEU 1999 framework report. The positive side to research findings about teenage mothering seems to be regularly disregarded in the more official literature, even when government commissions the research. Recent examples include TPU commissioned research on teenage mothers in rural and seaside 'hotspots', and on teenage mothers and education. The former noted how for some young women, motherhood: 'increased their self-esteem and enhanced their lives, providing a sense of security and stability in lives characterised by transience, detachment and low economic aspirations', while the TPU's own evidence showed that having a child provides motivation for young mothers to aspire to new educational and employment goals.

That teenage parenting can have many positive sides is a theme that reappears in most of the chapters in this book. In chapter five, Eleanor Formby, Julia Hirst, and Jenny Owen provide a compelling illustration across three generational cohorts of teenage parents from Sheffield and Doncaster. Having a baby as a teenager did not necessarily predict adversity, and the problems experienced arose more from the particular social and economic circumstances the mothers and fathers found themselves in, rather than the age at which pregnancy occurred. For mothers, difficulties in accessing appropriate housing was a major problem, while fathers recounted their sense of exclusion or marginalisation from the processes of antenatal care, childbirth, and postnatal care. While the mothers and fathers in the sample had not planned pregnancy, all recounted their pleasure at having a baby and never regretted the decision to continue with the pregnancy. Parents across all generations and social classes spoke of their parenting in positive terms, even if early parenthood for the mothers (but not the fathers) was accompanied by a sense of 'loss' of teenage life. All made explicit references to the positive 'turning-point' offered by pregnancy: the opportunity to make new plans, including the beginnings of a strong family unit or renewed efforts to gain qualifications and secure more certain futures. Despite the pleasure and pride that all participants described, stigma was also a feature of parenting that each generation, but mostly mothers, highlighted. Hence, living in a community where young parents were not unusual was cited as hugely influential, contrasting to the isolation experienced by some older and middle generation mothers who lived in middle-class communities where young parenthood was less visible. This theme is continued in chapter six by Ann McNulty. Exploring three generations of related young mothers down the generations in particular families, in the north-east of England, she challenges ideas about intergenerational transmission of low aspirations, and shows how each generation of young mothers in a family wanted to achieve, and wanted their daughters to achieve, in education and employment. Unmet expectations in relation to career options were more a matter of the (often declining) economic circumstances in their localities, rather than any culture of low aspiration. The chapter also notes the marked shift, over recent decades, towards a negative conceptualisation of young motherhood.

This positive theme is replicated in other national contexts. Lee Smith-Battle's research in the USA is paradigmatic. She followed a small, diverse group of teenage mothers over 8 years, finding that many described mothering as a powerful catalyst for becoming more mature, and for redirecting their lives in positive ways. Mothering often 'anchors the self, fosters a sense of purpose and meaning, reweaves connections, and provides a new sense of future.' Indeed, two of the themes identified in a meta-synthesis of US qualitative studies of teenage mothers undertaken during the 1990s are 'Motherhood as positively transforming' and 'Baby as stabilising influence.'

In this way, qualitative research can explain the patterns found by extensive statistical studies; they suggest just why teenage parenting does not produce particularly poor outcomes, and can sometimes make things better for young people. In addition, the qualitative research can go further in explaining the processes involved in teenage parenting just because it allows more attention to context and diversity—usually stripped out by extensive studies in their concentration on average measurement. This is not just a qualification to the statistical results, whereby teenage parents' experiences can be shown to vary significantly in different social groups and geographical places. For this also takes us to a vital 'missing link, and a key to understanding the agency of teenage parents—the life worlds in which they live. Becoming a teenage mother, and it seems a father, can make reasonable sense in the particular life worlds inhabited by some groups of young women and men. Recently, Rachel Thomson has conceptualised this as the 'economy of values' particular to different communities, and earlier Ann Phoenix found that early motherhood was common, and normally uncensured, in the social networks inhabited by the working-class teenage mothers in her 1980's London sample. BatttleSmith shows much the same for the USA; early motherhood often made sense in terms of local constitutions of opportunity, constraint, and social practice.

In chapter seven, we discuss our own research findings, from a small sample in Bradford, that teenage parents saw themselves unexceptionally as 'just a mother or a father' like any other. They were motivated to achieve well in education and employment so as to provide a stable future for their children, while at the same time they lived in communities where family and parenting was placed centrally as a form of local inclusion and social participation. The case of the two Asian mothers, who were married, is an indicative example. In this way, ethnicity, as well as class, shaped expectations around motherhood. The young mothers and fathers in the sample spoke of their positive experience and the ways in which having children had given them a sense of responsibility and adult status. The teenage mothers in the study were little different from many other mothers who morally and socially prioritise motherhood, not employment. It is not that the young mothers rejected education and employment; rather, self-esteem and identity are centred round motherhood; paid work was important more as a secondary and supportive part of life. While they faced many struggles, these were often linked to problems of wider social disadvantage, and they themselves strongly challenged the idea that these were related to their position as *young* parents. They resisted being characterised solely as a teenage mother or father and saw themselves as having multiple roles and identities, as individuals, partners, workers, students.

In chapter eight, Jenny Owen and colleagues develop this theme with respect to ethnicity. Drawing on a study of teenage mothers in Bradford, Sheffield, and three London boroughs, they examine in depth the transition to motherhood by young minority ethnic mothers. This reveals the strengths that these mothers draw on to deal with double-faceted prejudice—based on age and race/ethnicity—and their determination to make something of their own and their children's lives. However, at the same time many of the experiences of these young mothers are 'strikingly unremarkable': like older mothers, they are proud of their children; they aim to put them first; and they encounter familiar dilemmas in reconciling 'care' commitments with making a living and reaching accommodations with partners and other family members. This adds further weight to the general argument that 'teenage parents' should not be described as a homogenous group somehow separate from other mothers.

Conclusions: Experience v Policy?

The evidence substantiated in the chapters which follow shows that teenage childbirth does not often result from ignorance or low expectations, it is rarely a catastrophe for young women, and that teenage parenting does not particularly cause poor outcomes for mothers and their children. Expectations of motherhood can be high and parenting can be a positive experience for many young men and women. Furthermore, becoming a teenage parent can make good sense in the particular life worlds inhabited by some groups of young women and men. Policies about teenage parenting, however, assume the opposite. Unfortunately, this also means that policy will be misdirected in its aims, use inappropriate instruments, and may be unhelpful to many teenage parents.

This brings us to the last question posed by the 'problem' of teenage parenting. Why then, is there such a yawning gulf between policy assumptions and the experiences of its subjects? And why does policy seem so resistant to evidence? This is the subject of our concluding chapter nine; the way forward, we claim, necessitates a 'smashing' of the policy making mould maintained by the 'epistemic community' existing around teenage parenting. We refer here to a network of professionals and policymakers with a shared set of normative, analytical and causal beliefs, with an agreed, shared and self-reinforcing knowledge base, and a common set of interests. Parameters of preferred policy models and narratives of cause and effect are set, to the exclusion of other ideas and information, even if those other data are more representative of everyday reality. The impetus is to retain these dominant and agreed conceptions in developing (further) policies, protecting them not only from critical scrutiny but even from recognising the existence of challenging alternative scenarios. Researchers working outside of these favoured models, with messages at odds with current policy directions, are unlikely to be heard or, if heard, considered relevant.

In this way, a monochrome, negative, stereotype of teenage parents and parenting has become embedded in policy, bolstered by shared assumptions about social participation and the nature of social mobility, and by neo-liberal ideas about individual choice and rationality. Ideas about what is 'rational' are integrally linked to what is held to be socially acceptable, which in turn is regarded as a universal 'common sense' applicable in all contexts, rather than being rooted in the specific perspectives of a particular classed and gendered group of people who have the ability to judge others and place them as outside of rationality. In the case of teenage mothers and fathers, they are envisaged as ignorant, immoral or both because they have deviated from the cost-benefit calculative, future-oriented planned pathway of life. As other chapters show, this thinking is at odds with the complex reality of young mothers' and fathers' understandings and motivations, and yet is unequivocally accepted as an accurate portrayal. And all this, we suggest, is underlain by idealisations of children and childhood, where teenage parents, and mothers especially, are regarded as taking on the 'adult' responsibilities of parenthood before they have undergone the necessary sloughing off of the immaturity of childhood.

They are (almost) children who have disrupted the regulation represented by the boundaries of adulthood and childhood, embodying the breakdown of social order and the nation's moral turpitude.

The question remains of how to move on. On the basis of the evidence presented in this book, we suggest there needs to be a refocus on the value of parenthood in itself, both socially and for individuals. For teenage parents, this might focus on the positive experience of becoming a mother and father, and on young parents' own resilience and strengths. Education and employment for young parents should be recognised as a components of parenting (which would also include 'full-time' mothering at home), rather than as a return to individualised rational economic planning where children are seen as an obstacle. Policy may also be better directed at improving employment for young people as a whole in declining labour markets, and regenerating disadvantaged neighbourhoods, rather than targeting teenage parenting in itself. Teenage parenting might then be approached as a way through and out of disadvantage, given its positive potential, rather than a confirmation of it. It could be seen as more opportunity than catastrophe. Certainly stigmatising policies directed at the assumed ignorance and inadequacy of teenagers will be inappropriate.

EXPLORING THE ISSUE

Are Teenagers Too Young to Become Parents?

Critical Thinking and Reflection

- What are some arguments made by each side with which you agree or disagree?
- What are the strengths and weaknesses of the two positions made in this issue?
- Compare and contrast the competing arguments made about teenage parenthood. What conclusions do you reach about the different research cited?
- Think more broadly about the amount of teen parenthood. If it is a problem, what is the cause of this problem? If it is not a problem, should society be concerned in any way with the ways in which we educate and prepare teens for sexual activity, as well as the potential for parenthood?

Is There Common Ground?

Virtually everyone will agree that the outcome that they want is for (a) teens to make decisions about their sexual behavior that are consistent with their long-term goals and (b) children of teen parents to be raised with opportunities to achieve their American dream. What needs to be done to ensure that? Do we need to take a look at how we prepare teens with sexuality education? Should the approach we take be abstinence-only education? Should it be comprehensive sexuality education? What role does it play to help teens identify their long-term goals? When teens have children, what sort of role does family and society play in providing that young child with a social safety net? Is that solely the responsibility of the teen parent(s)? Or is there a larger societal responsibility at play?

Additional Resources

Bilingual site for teenage parents:

http://www.teenageparent.org/

American Academy of Pediatrics:

http://www.healthychildren.org/English/ages-stages/teen/dating-sex/pages/
Teen-Parents.aspx?nfstatus=401&nftoken=00000000-0000-0000-0000-
000000000000&nfstatusdescription=ERROR%3a+No+local+token

TeenPregnancy.com provides advice:

http://www.teenpregnancy.com/

About.com on teen pregnancy:

http://pregnancy.about.com/od/teenpregnancy/a/Teen-Pregnancy.htm

Internet References . . .

American Association of Sex Educators, Counselors, and Therapists

The American Association of Sex Educators, Counselors, and Therapists is a not-for-profit, interdisciplinary professional organization whose members share an interest in promoting understanding of human sexuality and healthy sexual behavior.

http://www.aasect.org

American Association for Marriage and Family Therapy

The American Association for Marriage and Family Therapy (AAMFT) is the professional association for the field of marriage and family therapy. The AAMFT facilitates research, theory development, and education, and develops standards for graduate education and training, clinical supervision, professional ethics, and the clinical practice of marriage and family therapy. Their Web site also features a search engine for finding a licensed marriage/family therapist.

http://www.aamft.org

The Rape, Abuse, and Incest National Network

The Rape, Abuse, and Incest National Network is the nation's largest anti–sexual assault organization, operating the National Sexual Assault Hotline, offering educational information and resources and advocating for effective policies to reduce the incidence of sexual assault.

http://www.rainn.org

Men Can Stop Rape

Men Can Stop Rape (formerly Men's Rape Prevention Project) works to empower male youth and the institutions that serve them to work as allies with women in preventing rape and other forms of "men's violence." Through awareness-to-action education and community organizing, the organization seeks to promote gender equity and build men's capacity to be strong without being violent.

http://www.mencanstoprape.org

The American Red Cross

The American Red Cross, founded in 1881 by Clara Barton, is the nation's "premier emergency response organization." In addition to domestic disaster relief, the Red Cross offers services in the following areas: community services that help the needy; support and comfort for military members and their families; the collection, processing, and distribution of lifesaving blood and blood products; educational programs that promote health and safety; and international relief and development programs.

http://www.redcross.org

Twenty-First-Century Family and Relationship Issues

***W**ith technology today, relationships develop through the Internet and sexting. With reality television, anyone can become a star if the camera shines on them. When shifting gears to law and relationships, statutory rape laws have become gender-neutral. In the midst of all of this, a small but increasingly visible minority are rejecting monogamy. These issues account for changing concepts of what constitutes agreed upon rules for families and relationships. This section examines six important questions about twenty-first-century families and relationships:*

- Is Cybersex "Cheating"?
- Is Internet Pornography Harmful to Teenagers?
- Are Statutory Rape Laws Effective at Protecting Minors?
- Do Reality Television Shows Have a Negative Influence on Teenage Pregnancy and Parenting?
- Should There Be Harsh Penalties for Teens Sexting?
- Are Open Relationships Healthy?

ISSUE 15

Is Cybersex "Cheating"?

YES: Susan A. Milstein, from "Virtual Liaisons: Cybersex Is Cheating," written for *Taking Sides: Family and Personal Relationships* (2009)

NO: Crystal Bedley, from "Virtual Reality: Cybersex Is Not Cheating," written for *Taking Sides: Family and Personal Relationships* (2009)

Learning Outcomes

As a result of this issue, readers will be able to:

- Identify the major arguments made for and against whether cybersex is cheating.
- Compare and contrast the competing arguments made for and against cybsersex as cheating in this issue.
- Evaluate the implications of cybersex on the impact this has on dating, marriage, and other intimate relationships.

ISSUE SUMMARY

YES: Susan Milstein is a certified health education specialist and a certified sexuality educator. She is an associate professor in the Department of Health Enhancement at Montgomery College in Maryland, as well as the lead consultant for Milstein Health Consulting. Milstein contends that while it is diffcult to create a universal definition of cheating, the majority of people feel that cybersex outside of a primary relationship is cheating.

NO: Crystal Bedley argues that the anonymous nature of cybersex means that it is not cheating.

What is your definition of infidelity? Does it include flirting? Phone sex? Sexting? If you are in a committed relationship, does your significant other have the same definition? Too often, couples fail to have this conversation. In the event that this conversation occurs, they may find that they have significantly different definitions of what is monogamy as well as what is infidelity.

This divergence in definitions can lead to significant conflict within a relationship. The differences may very well be vast without even raising the topic of cybersex.

Infidelity is a common occurrence in American society. Most people know more than one person who has been unfaithful. National headlines are full of famous Americans who had been unfaithful to their spouses: Eliot Spitzer, John Edwards, A-Rod, Tiger Woods, and Peter Cook, Christie Brinkley's former husband. All of these cases involved real life, in-person affairs.

However, cybersex is creating new types of headlines among the powerful. A conservative Congressman from Florida was caught sending sexually explicit text messages to teenage pages working in Washington, DC. A couple of years later, a liberal Congressman from New York was caught sending similar photos, but these were to young women on Twitter. For both men, the scandal destroyed their political careers. While this case did not involve the question of whether this was cheating, it raised a national dialogue regarding the expected norms related to virtual sex.

Infidelity dates as far back in human history as marriage. Sometimes infidelity is sanctioned by society or the spouse, but it is typically forbidden. Infidelity can lead to marital breakups, creating great stress and instability in people's lives. It is highly unlikely for in-person infidelity to guarantee anonymity.

Cyberspace has fundamentally altered the landscape for meeting others, particularly for anonymous sexual encounters. Now without leaving one's home, with minimal risk of meeting someone one knows, a person can have written, spoken, or streaming video cybersex with different people at any time. Indeed, one can log on at any time and find a significant number of people looking to meet someone.

In fact, there is not even a need to be yourself. Online, people change their hair color, height, weight, eye color, sexual history, age, race, and gender. It is possible to have cybersex with a level of anonymity that cannot be realized in person. One can live out their sexual fantasies without fear of rejection from someone they care about, or even know who they are. With the opportunity for sexually explicit virtual meetings, the personal risk of being identified recedes.

Cybersex has created a new dimension, a potential form of twenty-first-century infidelity, depending on one's definition of infidelity. This is new terrain that presents a unique set of challenges. The lines of what is cheating may be difficult to draw with new technology. Even if you determine that certain scenarios are off limits, temptation to stray is virtually omnipresent when in the privacy of your own residence.

Before reading this issue, write down your definition of infidelity. Include a definition of what types of cybersex, if any, you regard as being unfaithful. Does anything on your list surprise you? While reading, examine the ways in which the authors' assessment compares and contrasts with your values. What are some ways in which your beliefs were supported? What are some of the ways in which they were challenged? In addition, what are the generational differences, if any, of views of cybersex and infidelity?

Have you ever hid something from your significant other that you feared would make him or her jealous? Maybe texting an ex? Visiting a strip club? Going out to a platonic dinner with someone you find attractive? While none of these incidents are physical sexual encounters with another person, many people will conceal these encounters out of fear that their significant other will regard them as being unfaithful in their relationship. Each incident described has some degree of emotional or physical interaction. In contrast, cybersex can be nonphysical and anonymous. Facing reduced risks for exposure and regular access to virtual sexual encounters, cybersex creates a new set of boundaries to be negotiated in a relationship.

Cybersex potentially changes the ways in which trust is extended within a relationship. While access to anonymous sexual encounters may be a threatening prospect to many, there is a fundamental question which needs to be asked and evaluated that has not changed despite the virtual world of sexual relations: What is a healthy relationship?

Write down what you consider to be the most important qualities of a healthy relationship. Then rank how important the different qualities are. This should provide a larger perspective related to cybersex and infidelity. Whether the Internet exists or not, the qualities of healthy relationships should remain constant.

Once you have identified your views about sexual infidelity and cybersex, are you ready to talk about your criteria with a significant other? How might you respond to answers that may differ from yours? Specifically, weigh whether or not you can negotiate if you have decidedly different values related to cybersex and infidelity. How much are you willing to compromise your beliefs? What are your expectations related to how your significant other will compromise his or her beliefs?

If you are in a relationship that lacks equality or fails to communicate respectfully, you may find that this conversation is difficult to have. If you are in a relationship of equality and mutual respect, this conversation is far easier, provided that you and your partner feel comfortable having frank conversations about sexuality. Keep in mind that it is normal to struggle when having frank conversations about sexuality. It might be a good idea to acknowledge that at the start of such a conversation and not to be too hard on yourself if the conversation is challenging.

Melanie Davis, an expert on communicating about sexuality within families and relationships, advises that a person do the following in starting this conversation: "The first thing is for the person who wants to bring up the conversation to define the purpose of the conversation. It is just curiosity, or is there some sort of fear? Or is there a need to disclose something? That can help you get into the right frame of mind. If you think your partner is cheating on you, it might come across as accusing the person, and that is never an effective way to start a conversation. The other thing to consider is where you're going to have the conversation. It is probably not a conversation you want to have in the middle of a crowded restaurant. If you fear what will be disclosed, you might want to have the conversation in the presence of a counselor or a therapist who can help guide the conversation."

Davis adds, "Sometimes you just want to test the waters conversationally. A good way to do that is to remark about a TV show or an article that you read, something that can get you to that topic of conversation in a neutral way."

Once these conversations begin, you may find that they are likely to get easier, provided you have a cooperative and supportive partner. If these conversations cannot occur, it may not be surprising if people get hurt when they lack a full understanding of each other's boundaries and their rationale behind them.

YES

Susan A. Milstein

Virtual Liaisons: Cybersex Is Cheating

Consider the following behaviors: flirting with a coworker, engaging in intimate phone calls or sending love letters to someone other than your partner, looking at sexually explicit images while masturbating, having a one-night stand. Would any of these behaviors be cheating?

You may have answered "yes" to none, some, or all of these behaviors, whereas your partner's answers may have been very different. For this reason, defining cheating can be difficult. Many couples may never take the time to sit down and discuss what behaviors they consider to be cheating but feel betrayed nonetheless when certain lines are crossed. The lines of what is considered cheating may become even more blurred when the actions in question take place online.

Enter the world of cybersex.

What Is Cybersex?

There is no single definition of cybersex. It is a broad term that may be used to encompass a variety of behaviors, including different methods of communication that happen online like love letter e-mails or instant messages. Sex, Etc. (http://www.sexetc.org/) defines cybersex as "Sexual encounters that take place entirely via the Internet." This would include going on a virtual "date" in a chat room that may involve one or both people masturbating in real life. These dates may happen simply by typing on a keyboard, or they may include the use of webcams and microphones.

Meeting for cybersex can take place in a multitude of places, including chat rooms, inside online games like World of Warcaft, or inside the virtual world of Second Life. Thanks to webcams, Skype, and Googlechat, you don't necessarily need a specific site like a chat room to meet—you just need the time, the technology, and another person. The definition of cybersex will continue to evolve as technology changes, and for some, the new definition will include the use of teledildonics.

For some people, the use of teledildonics with a person other than a significant other crosses yet another boundary in the world of cybersex and infidelity.

So, What Is Cheating?

Many of us associate sexual infidelity with the word "cheating." It involves having sexual contact with someone other than your partner. How much sexual contact is required for it to be cheating will vary from one person's definition to another. It may extend beyond sexual intercourse to include oral sex or kissing, but regardless of how much contact is involved, most of us usually think of something physical when we think of cheating. But, there's more to it than that. Online or offline, cheating on a significant other may involve physical acts, which is called sexual infidelity, or it may involve emotional infidelity (Whisman & Wagers, 2005).

Emotional infidelity occurs when someone is spending time with, giving attention to, or falling in love with someone other than their partner (Shackelford, LeBlanc, and Drass, 2000; Whitty and Quigley, 2008). Regardless of whether it is emotional or sexual infidelity, violating the bounds of one's relationship can lead to anger, jealousy, hurt, resentment, and potentially the ending of the relationship.

Subotnik and Harris (2005) describe four different types of affairs one might see in offline relationships. The first type is the serial affair, where there are a string of one-night stands or affairs that lack both an emotional connection and commitment. The second type of affair is the fling, which can be seen in one-night stands. The other two types of affairs are the romantic love affair and the long-term affair. These two affairs are similar in that there is a deep emotional component to each. One thing that differentiates these two affairs is the amount of time that is invested in each. All of these types of affairs can be carried out online through cybersex, and like offline affairs, they can have a tremendous negative impact on relationships.

Then there's the emotional affair, or what Glass and Staeheli (2003) describe as the "extramarital emotional involvement" (p. 35). This emotional involvement consists of three components: emotional intimacy, secrecy, and sexual chemistry. All three of these components may happen during cybersex, whether it's a one-time "date" in a chat room or an affair which is taking place solely online.

As with offline affairs, relationships where cybersex has occurred face many challenges. The affair may lead to conflict and a decision to separate or divorce as a result of the online cheating (Docan-Morgan and Docan, 2007; Schneider, 2000; Young, Griffin-Shelley, Cooper, O'Mara, and Buchanan, 2000). The partner who was cheated on may feel a host of emotions, including betrayal, abandonment, and shame (Schneider, 2000). Part of the healing process for the partner who was cheated on through cybersex involves learning to cope with what happened and trying to find closure (Maheu and Subotnik, 2001).

Cybersex and Cheating

Research is showing that people do believe that cybersex is cheating and that it can have a negative impact on relationships. One study found that 33 percent of respondents felt that cybersex of any kind was cheating. If certain circumstances occurred, for instance, the use of webcams, or having cybersex repeatedly with the same person, then the number increased to 58 percent (McKenna, Green, and Smith, 2001).

One researcher, Monica Whitty, has completed a number of studies looking at which specific cybersex behaviors people believe constitute infidelity. What she has not been able to do is come up with one list of cybersex behaviors that everyone agrees is cheating. But this is to be expected. If you look back at the behaviors at the beginning of this article, you'll see why one list of "cheating behaviors" will probably never exist for cybersex or for offline behaviors. What her research has shown is that there are many who believe that cybersex is infidelity and that it can have just as much of a negative impact on a relationship as cheating that is done offline (Whitty, 2003, 2005).

The research previously mentioned was done using respondents' opinions based on hypothetical situations. It would be easy to say that what someone says in a hypothetical situation may be different from what that person would say if faced with the same situation in real life. This may be true in that people who have found out that their partners had been engaging in cybersex might be more likely to say that they feel like they were cheated on.

When looking at studies that involved people who had direct experience with cybersex, you can see the negative impact that it has on people and their relationships. One study found that the offline partners of those engaging in cybersex reported feeling hurt, abandoned, and betrayed (Schneider, 2000). In another study, one-quarter of the people surveyed who were engaging in cybersex admitted that it had affected their primary relationship (Underwood and Findlay, 2004).

Given the findings of these studies, it should come as no surprise that therapists are seeing the impact of cybersex among their clients. In one study, a majority of marriage and family therapists reported having clients where cybersex was a problem, and 16 percent of the therapists reported that cybersex was the primary reason why the couple was in therapy (Goldberg, Peterson, Rosen, and Sara, 2008). And this is just the beginning, as the number of people affected seems to be increasing. In the two years prior to the survey, more than half of the therapists said their cybersex caseload had increased (Goldberg, Peterson, Rosen, and Sara, 2008).

Cybersex Is Cheating

We know that people who are involved in committed relationships are having cybersex. In a survey done in 1998, almost 85 percent of people who reported that they were engaging in online sexual activity were either married or in a committed relationship (Maheu and Subotnik, 2001).

We also know that cybersex is viewed by many as cheating and that it can have the same long-term negative impact on relationships that offline infidelity has.

So what's the bottom line? If what one person is doing is going outside the bounds of his or her relationship, then it's cheating, and it doesn't matter if it's in a hotel room or a chat room.

References

T. Docan-Morgan and C. A. Docan, "Internet Infidelity: Double Standards and the Differing Views of Women and Men," *Communication Quarterly* (vol. 55, no. 3, 2007).

S. P. Glass and J. C. Staeheli, *"Not 'Just Friends.' Rebuilding Trust and Recovering Your Sanity after Infidelity* (New York: Free Press, 2003).

P. D. Goldberg, B. D. Peterson, K. H. Rosen, and M. L. Sara, "Cybersex: The Impact of a Contemporary Problem on the Practices of Marriage and Family Therapists," *Journal of Marital and Family Therapy* (vol. 34, no. 4, 2008).

M. M. Maheu, and R. B. Subotnik, *Infidelity in the Internet. Virtual Relationships and Real Betrayal* (Naperville, IL: Sourcebooks, Inc., 2001).

K. Y. A. McKenna, A. S. Green, and P. K. Smith, "Demarginalizing the Sexual Self," *The Journal of Sex Research* (vol. 38, no. 4, 2001).

J. P. Schneider, "Effects of Cybersex Addiction on the Family: Results of a Survey," *Sexual Addiction & Compulsivity* (vol. 7, 2000).

Sex, Etc., "Cyber Sex" (n.d.). Retrieved March 15, 2009, from http://www.sexetc.org/glossary/1148.

T. K. Shackelford, G. J. LeBlanc, and E. Drass, "Emotional Reactions to Infidelity," *Cognition & Emotion* (vol. 14, no. 5, 2000).

R. B. Subotnik and G. G. Harris, *"Surviving Infidelity. Making Decisions, Recovering from the Pain* (Avon, MA: Adams Media, 2005).

H. Underwood and B. Findlay, "Internet Relationships and Their Impact on Primary Relationships," *Behaviour Change* (vol. 21, no. 2, 2004).

M. A. Whisman and T. P. Wagers, "Assessing Relationship Betrayals," *Journal of Clinical Psychology* (vol. 61, no. 11, 2005).

M. T. Whitty, "Pushing the Wrong Buttons: Men's and Women's Attitudes toward Online and Offline Infidelity," *CyberPsychology and Behavior* (vol. 6, no. 6, 2003).

——— "The Realness of Cybercheating. Men's and Women's Representations of Unfaithful Internet Relationships," *Social Science Computer Review* (vol. 23, no. 1, 2005).

M. T. Whitty and L-L. Quigley, "Emotional and Sexual Infidelity Offline and in Cyberspace," *Journal of Marriage and Family Therapy* (vol. 34, no. 4, 2008).

K. S. Young, E. Griffin-Shelley, A. Cooper, J. O'Mara, and J. Buchanan, "Online Infidelity: A New Dimension in Couple Relationships with Implications for Evaluation and Treatment," *Sexual Addiction & Compulsivity* (vol. 7, 2000).

Crystal Bedley  **NO**

Virtual Reality: Cybersex Is Not Cheating

As the Internet continues to expand and evolve, so do the possibilities for engaging in sexual encounters online. From chat rooms, to social networking sites, to virtual boy/girlfriends, new technologies are shaping the ways in which desires can be explored and indulged. Couples must navigate these new technologies to determine the role(s) that virtual encounters may or may not play in their relationships. Some people might enjoy engaging in cybersex, whereas their partners may not; some couples may enjoy engaging in cybersex together, whereas others may not. To understand whether a particular cybersex act is a form of cheating, therefore, one must take into account the nature of the relationship. Ultimately, whether cybersex is a form of cheating depends largely on both the interpersonal dynamics of the couple *and* the intentions and perceptions of the cybersex participant.

The term "interpersonal dynamics" refers to the nature of the relationship between the two romantic partners. More specifically, interpersonal dynamics shape how partners come to agree or disagree about the meanings of particular acts (e.g., whether cybersex is a form of cheating). Importantly, the ways in which couples negotiate their relationships, especially when each partner has different expectations, shape how both partners will interpret particular behaviors. For example, few people would argue that, if both partners agree to participate in cybersex together, that their shared action is a form of cheating. Moreover, if one partner communicates to the other partner that she or he would like to engage in cybersex and the other partner consents, then most would agree that the partners are being faithful to one another. Each of these examples demonstrates how the interpersonal dynamics of the couple determine whether cybersex is cheating. The ways partners choose to communicate with one another and the decisions they reach are critical for understanding whether cybersex is cheating or an expression of sexual desires. If both partners share an understanding of cybersex as an expression of sexual desire that does not constitute cheating, then it is clear that cybersex is not cheating. By the same token, if both partners believe the act of cybersex is cheating, then there is no reason to draw a different conclusion.

In contrast, if a partner deceives the other partner in order to engage in cybersex, one could argue that in this context, cybersex is an act of infidelity. Because relationships are built on mutual trust (among other factors), deception not only serves to destabilize the relationship but also becomes the framework for interpreting the cybersex act as an act of cheating. Importantly, recent research suggests that deception and emotional unavailability are primary reasons why partners view cybersex as equivalent to adultery (Schneider, 2003). In these cases, it is clearer that cybersex is an act of infidelity.

Although there are a variety of ways to engage in cybersex, when it comes to interpreting cybersex as cheating, traditionally the virtual form of the sex act is often inconsequential, trumped by the emotional toll paid by the partners involved in the relationship. Consider the following example:

> Shannon and Kendall are in a long-term committed relationship. Neither partner has been physically or emotionally intimate with anyone outside of the relationship. One day, Kendall decides to participate in a mutual masturbation session with an anonymous person he meets in a chat room. Minutes later, Shannon walks into Kendall's office and witnesses the masturbation session. Devastated by what she sees, Shannon feels that Kendall has cheated. From Shannon's perspective, Kendall's online session is a form of cheating because of the sexual intimacy Kendall shared with the other person. From Kendall's perspective, Shannon is overreacting. Kendall believes that because cybersex does not involve physical contact, it is not cheating. So, Kendall views the cybersex act as a way of exploring one's fantasies in a safe environment.

This scenario illustrates the notion that the same act (in this case, the act of participating in a mutual masturbation session) can be interpreted in different and sometimes conflicting ways. For this reason, I argue that the individual perceptions of each partner are important to understanding whether cybersex should be considered cheating. The expression "individual perceptions" refers to the beliefs and/or attitudes of a person, which shape how the individual will interpret a particular behavior. Unlike interpersonal dynamics, which involve a negotiated agreement (or disagreement) about the meanings attributed to particular acts, individual perceptions are those beliefs held by each individual about the meanings attributed to particular acts, *regardless* of the beliefs of one's partner. To clarify the distinction between individual perceptions and interpersonal dynamics using the current example, it is clear that Kendall's individual perception is that the cybersex act is not a form of cheating, whereas Shannon's perception is that it is cheating. The interpersonal dynamics of the couple can be described as a disagreement over the cybersex act because each partner's perceptions are at odds with the other's.

Because partners can have differing perceptions of the same act, it is critical to also consider each partner's perception of cybersex to understand whether the cybersex is a form of infidelity. On the one hand, let's assume that Shannon is not emotionally hurt by the act of masturbation alone, but rather is hurt that Kendall transgressed upon an important moral boundary in their relationship; namely, that partners are to remain sexually faithful to one another. On the other hand, Kendall does not see cybersex as cheating because the cybersex was used only to facilitate masturbation. Because masturbation has never been considered an act of cheating throughout the course of their relationship, Kendall believes that cybersex is merely another form of masturbation. Therefore, Kendall's perception of cybersex as masturbation reinforces the belief that Kendall is remaining sexually faithful to Shannon. Undoubtedly, Shannon and Kendall have differing views about the same act. If Shannon and Kendall cannot come to an agreement about whether or not the online mutual masturbation session was indeed an act of cheating, then whose perception helps us to best understand whether this act of cybersex is a form of cheating?

Traditionally, the perceptions of the partner not involved in the act of cybersex determine whether the act is considered cheating. In other words, if the partner not involved in the act of cybersex believes cybersex is cheating, then it is cheating.

But why should the perceptions of the partner prevail over the perceptions of the cybersex participant? The short answer is that they should not. Instead, whether an act of cybersex is cheating depends primarily not only on the intentions of the person who engages in cybersex but also on how this person perceives the cybersex act. I am arguing that rather than privilege the perceptions of the person not directly involved in the cybersex act, one must focus instead on the cybersex participant. Specifically, it is important to take into account both the intentions *and* perceptions of the cybersex participant in order to determine whether an act of cybersex is a form of infidelity.

To demonstrate the significance of one's intention in relation to the cybersex act, it is helpful to think about the following contrasting examples. In the first example, the cybersex participant intends to seek sexual and/or emotional pleasure from a person who is outside the participant's relationship. The person may feel guilty for engaging in cybersex because she believes that she is being unfaithful given the nature of the cybersex encounter (e.g., cybersex acts that foster emotional and/or sexual intimacy). In this case, because the cybersex participant's intentions and perceptions of her behavior are adulterous, then this act should be interpreted as cheating. Even if a cybersex encounter does not begin with adulterous intentions, if the cybersex participant's intentions and/or perceptions of the act change during the course of the encounter, then the act could still be considered cheating. For many cybersex participants, however, this is not the reality of their experience. To state this point differently, many people who engage in cybersex do not engage in cybersex in order to cheat on their partners. Because people often do not engage in cybersex to harm their relationship, it is important to consider other intention/perception understandings of the cybersex act.

Now consider the case of a person who engages in cybersex with the sole intention of having an orgasm. It is important to point out that this person is not engaging in deceptive behavior in order to take part in the cybersex act. In this case, the cybersex participant is not looking to create an emotional connection with another person but instead is seeking out a stimulating aid for the purpose of masturbating. This person could choose to watch a pornographic movie, for instance, but instead chooses a chat room for arousal. In fact, an in-depth interview study of cybersex participants found that these participants often "equated participation in chat rooms with watching a movie or reading a novel" (Mileham, 2007, p. 16). Therefore, not only does the person involved in the cybersex act intend to engage in masturbation (a sexual act that is not generally considered to be a form of cheating), his perception of the experience is the same. Specifically, the cybersex participant perceives the cybersex act as an act of masturbation, not infidelity. From this perspective, I argue that the cybersex participant did not cheat on his partner because he did not intend to cheat, nor did he perceive the act as cheating.

For those who still remain skeptical as to whether cybersex is cheating, it is critical to understand the implications of this position. If someone believes that, although the cybersex participant thinks he is simply masturbating, he is actually cheating on his partner, then where can we draw the distinction between other forms of masturbation and cheating? Is the person who masturbates to a racy magazine cheating on her partner? Moreover, how do we make sense of situations where a person's mind wanders during sex? Is one cheating if he thinks of someone other than his partner during sex? Clearly, neither of these cases seems to constitute cheating. Skeptics must be aware that if the intentions and the perceptions of the cybersex participant are overlooked, then a variety of sex acts should also be considered alternative forms of cheating. Yet, if these masturbatory acts were all considered cheating, many of us would have to acknowledge that we've cheated on our partners!

By privileging the perceived "victim's" individual perceptions of the cybersex act above the intentions and perceptions of the cybersex participant, one is more likely to conclude that cybersex is cheating. It has been my aim to question this traditional bias to suggest that many of the acts typically considered cheating are vastly more complicated. By highlighting the intentions and perceptions of the cybersex participant, it becomes clear that many cybersex acts are not necessarily acts of infidelity. Often, cybersex is used to sexually enrich the lives of those who take part, which can ultimately benefit a relationship rather than destroy it.

References

B. L. A. Mileham, "Online Infidelity in Internet Chat Rooms: An Ethnographic Exploration," *Computers in Human Behavior* (vol. 23, 2007), 11–13.

J. Schneider, "The Impact of Compulsive Cybersex Behaviours on the Family," *Sexual and Relationship Therapy* (vol. 18, no. 3, 2003), 329–354.

EXPLORING THE ISSUE

Is Cybersex "Cheating"?

Critical Thinking and Reflection

- What are some arguments made by each side with which you agree or disagree?
- What are the strengths and weaknesses of the two positions made in this chapter? Pick the side with which you most agree.
- What are some additional arguments you would make to strengthen the case for or against cybersex constituting cheating?
- Think more broadly of the issue of cybersex. What are some of the ways in which it is or can be unhealthy? What are some of the ways in which it is or can be healthy?

Is There Common Ground?

The truth is that couples may often disagree in many ways over what constitutes cheating. There is a long list of questions that will elicit different answers from individuals. Is kissing someone else cheating? Does talking with your ex constitute cheating? How about dinner with your ex? Getting a lap dance from at a strip club? Getting a lap dance at a party? Looking at pornography? A lack of understanding of your partner's definition of monogamy can lead to serious problems in a relationship. Refer to the advice of Melanie Davis in the Introduction to this section and work on communicating openly and honestly within relationships.

Additional Resources

The following Web sites examine the question as to whether cybersex is cheating:

http://marriage.families.com/blog/is-cybersex-cheating#

http://www.lovematters.info/cybersex-cheating-does-it-count

http://www.ivillage.com/cybersex-really-cheating-0/4-n-282345

ISSUE 16

Is Internet Pornography Harmful to Teenagers?

YES: Wayne Grinwis, from "Is Pornography Harmful to Teenagers? Yes!" revised from *Taking Sides: Family and Personal Relationships* (2009)

NO: Justin A. Sitron, from "Why Porn Is Not Harmful to Teens," revised from *Taking Sides: Family and Personal Relationships* (2009)

Learning Outcomes

As a result of this issue, readers will be able to:

- Identify critical research about the impact of pornography on teens.
- Compare and contrast interpretations of research in determining how to help teens develop in a way that is consistent with being sexually healthy.
- Evaluate the unique role of the Internet and pornography on teens.

ISSUE SUMMARY

YES: Wayne Grinwis has been a sexual health educator for Planned Parenthood for 15 years. He is also adjunct professor in the Department of Health at West Chester University. Grinwis credits Andrea Daniels for help with this article. Grinwis argues that pornography is all right for adults, but for teenagers, it can create unrealistic expectations about sex, provide a negative and inaccurate sexuality education, and increase sexual violence against women.

NO: Justin Sitron is an assistant professor of education at Widener University. Sitron argues that pornography has no negative impact on teenagers and, in fact, has potential benefits. Sitron contends that Internet pornography can be helpful in providing teens an opportunity to see real bodies, a chance to learn about sex from seeing rather than doing, and an open door for communication with parents.

T he First Amendment to the U.S. Constitution states, "Congress shall make no laws . . . abridging the freedom of speech." While this amendment is written as an absolute, there are limitations to speech that are known as unprotected speech, including libel, slander, seditious speech, and obscenity. It is the latter form of unprotected speech that is the focus of this issue, as obscenity is often used as synonymous with pornography. For many children, the Internet has allowed greater access to pornography than ever before.

In the United States, federal censorship of obscene materials began with the Tariff Act of 1842. While prosecutions were initially limited, the American middle class grew following the Civil War. Many social reformers believed that America too often failed to apply proper moral values, thus leading to social problems. Anti-vice societies were formed and worked to create laws regarding labor, prison reform, temperance, welfare, and obscenity. By 1873, America had a federal anti-obscenity law, often referred to as the Comstock Law.

During this time, anti-obscenity laws were designed to protect three groups who were considered to be particularly vulnerable, which included women, the lower classes, and children. Today, women and the so-called lower classes are not considered groups that deserve legal protections, though the primary audience for pornographic pictures and films today is men.

A challenge that has existed regarding censorship has been to determine specifically what is obscenity. In 1973, The Supreme Court of the United States provided the following standard for evaluating whether materials are pornographic in the case of *Miller v. California*:

1. That the average person, applying contemporary standards, would find a work, taken as a whole, appeals to the prurient interest;
2. Whether the work depicts or describes, in a patently offensive way, sexual conduct specifically defined to be offensive and "hard core" by the applicable state law;
3. That the work, taken as a whole, lacks serious literary, artistic, political, or scientific value.

Therefore, there exists a legal standard of how to define pornography and legal precedent that pornography is regarded as unprotected speech. In addition, there is legal precedent that children do not have the right to have access to pornography. As a result, the federal government sought to create new censorship policies in the face of children's access to pornography online.

Congress passed and President Clinton signed into law both the Communications Decency Act of 1996 and the Child Online Protection Act of 1998. Each of these laws was struck down by the Supreme Court. The Supreme Court did not challenge the fact that pornography can be censored for children. However, there was no mechanism to limit children's access to online pornography without also limiting adult access to pornography. When censoring unprotected speech, in this case children's access to pornography, laws cannot be so broad that they also censor protected speech, in this case adults' access to pornography.

With limited means for government censorship, controlling access to pornography becomes almost entirely the domain of parents and children. The access to sexually explicit materials that exists is unprecedented in human history. Children today have more access to sexually produced materials than ever before. Previously, parents were urged to leave their computer in a common, public space in their house. Today, however, few families buy desktop computers, opting instead for a portable laptop which can be privately used more easily. In fact, many children access the Internet whenever they want, wherever they want, via their iPhone or another portable device.

This issue examines the debate over the impact of pornography on teenagers. The conclusions that one reaches should have significant implications in what teenagers should be taught by their parents about pornography.

Pornography is one of the most controversial issues addressed in this volume. What are some of the ways in which these articles reinforced your value system? What are some of the ways in which these articles challenged your value system? How did it feel when your value system was challenged?

In some sections of this issue, Grinwis and Sitron addressed the same issue but cited different research, therefore reaching different conclusions. For example, Grinwis stated that pornography can lead to sexual violence, in part by citing research published by the National Online Resource Center on Violence Against Women. In contrast, Sitron argued that the research is divided but that a meta-analysis published in the *Annual Review of Sex Research* found no association between pornography and "high levels of sexual aggression." What are some ways that you can examine these resources to determine which research you think is accurate?

Students may find important research topics raised in this issue. That can include topics that were specifically examined in this issue as well as other issues not specifically examined. What are some related topics that are important to address?

For example, Sitron's article cites the significant amount of amateur pornography uploaded onto the Internet when he addresses the diversity of body images available online. A separate issue to consider, particularly for young people, are issues of consent for uploading photographs and video online. One significant technological difference for teenagers today as compared to generations past involves the degree of access to photo and video cameras. Some questions that can be considered are the following:

- What are some of the ways, if any, that teenagers today feel pressure to photograph and record themselves hooking up?
- How does seeing amateur pornography online influence discussions or actual behavior with teenagers about recording themselves when hooking up?
- How can teenagers ensure that their pictures or video will never be posted online without their consent?
- Have teenagers had experiences being recorded without first giving consent?
- Does consent to be recorded mean that there is consent to show the footage to others?

- Sometimes amateur footage is seen by millions of people. How might seeing amateur pornography featuring people one meets in their everyday lives possibly affect their college admissions? College scholarships? Job prospects? Familial relationships?
- In short, what are the rights of people featured in amateur pornography available online?

Beyond these questions, middle school and high school students need to know that some teenagers are being prosecuted for creating child pornography when recording themselves engaged in sexual activities before they have reached the age of 18. Crimes that teenagers are charged with can range from public indecency to the creation of child pornography, possession of child pornography, and distribution of child pornography. Some of these young people have been convicted of felonies, sentenced to long prison terms, and will be required to register as sex offenders after their release.

Today, teenagers have not just access to pornography but also the ability to create pornography with greater ease than ever before. While it is important to research the impact of viewing pornography on teenagers, it is also necessary to conduct more research to better understand the ways in which the creation of amateur pornography may be affecting the young people involved.

YES

Wayne Grinwis

Is Pornography Harmful to Teenagers?

There are some who would argue that pornography has no acceptable audience or any valid place, even for entertainment purposes, in a healthy relationship. In this mindset, pornography might even be considered harmful and its effects wide-reaching enough to encapsulate every age group who may be attracted to the lure of a little adult fantasy. High school students, grandparents, Baby Boomers, Gen Xers—all would fall victim to its inappropriate ideals if we were to place a general label of "harmful"—a sort of "Mr. Yuck" sticker for grown-ups, if you will—onto pornography. I am unable to do such a thing. In the right setting and with the right frame of mind, pornography can be a pleasurable addition to an adult individual's or couple's sexual life.

When speaking of teenagers, however, the term *harmful* may well apply. Without the proper maturity and level of experience, navigating through the very adult world of relationships and sex, most teens simply do not possess the necessary tools needed for their first foray into fantasy, and many of the themes found in a good deal of easily accessible pornography may actually be harmful to their adolescent development.

Access to Pornography

Before we can examine pornography's harmful effects on teenagers, we must first discuss the specifics of what pornography actually is. Former Supreme Court Justice Potter Stewart said, in discussing a potential definition of pornography, "I know it when I see it" (*Jacobellis v. Ohio,* 1964). That statement, albeit somewhat glib, brings to mind a serious thought: In the high-tech, ever-evolving cyber-realm that young people today inhabit, they are inundated with more varied forms of pornography than ever before, stumbling upon sites that they probably shouldn't and gaining access to those deemed "adult-only" by easily tiptoeing around safeguards as flimsy as a few keystrokes and the honor system.

In the past, teens had to seek out pornography by obtaining and viewing magazines (*Playboy* and *Hustler* are among the more tame periodicals), locating old VHS films or DVDs not hidden quite carefully enough in their own homes, or watching soft-core versions of these films on cable (good 'ol' "Skinemax"—

an informal reference to occasional late-night viewing opportunities on Cinemax—has long been a favorite). However, tech-savvy young people have more opportunities than ever before to satisfy their sensual cravings. In recent years, pornographic-like activity has been added to some video games (*Grand Theft Auto,* one of the most popular video games among this demographic, is rife with sexual content), and then, of course, there is the ever-pervasive Internet, which, to many teens, is just as tangible a home as the concrete structures they inhabit with their family members. Although the one-time estimate that over 80 percent of Internet sites are pornographic was proven false (Godwin, 2003), recent estimates are that 12 percent of all Web sites are porn and that a quarter of all search engine requests are for porn (Ropelato, 2003). Even if someone were trying to avoid this type of explicit sexual material, it would only be the über-diligent who would succeed in avoiding pornography on the Internet, and it is important to note that not all teenage exposure to pornography is intentional; contact may be unintended—stumbled upon when receiving emails advertising porn sites or even through the simple act of employing an Internet search (Bryan, 2009). For those who do take the time to seek out pornography, their fingers don't have far to travel on their computer keyboards. From things as basic as still pictures to home videos of sexual encounters, from monthly subscription services to "fetish" sites, thousands upon thousands of hours of porn can easily be found online.

It is true that most adult sites stipulate that a viewer must be "18 to enter;" however, age is often established by a simple mouse click stating that the visitor is, indeed, the required age or by asking the visitor to enter in his or her birthdate. Young people can handle the simple math of subtracting a few years from the date on which they were born in order to appear age-appropriate for viewing.

Now that we have determined the ease with which pornography can be viewed and before we begin to examine the harmful effects of pornography on teenagers, we must first establish the gender of which we speak. Do we mean male teens or female? The simple answer is both. Although teens actively seeking out and viewing pornography are predominantly male, girls are also affected by the messages boys receive.

But all of this—the pervasive and easily accessible nature of pornography—is not in and of itself proof positive of its harmful nature when speaking in terms of teens. We must now begin to dig deeper to unearth the negative effects that exposure to an adult-oriented fantasy world has upon adolescent development by examining pornography's fostering of unrealistic expectations when it comes to sexual encounters and body image, its role as an unqualified sexuality educator, and its bent toward violence.

Unrealistic Expectations

How many times has this happened to you? You're in your office making copies, perhaps scantily clad and probably glistening a little from the heat of the copier, and in walks a very attractive member of the opposite sex, who immediately begins complimenting your body and undressing you. Moments later, you are in the throes of passion, with the copier working overtime capturing fantasy, flipbook-worthy images of all that is happening on it.

This has never happened to you? Then clearly you are not living in the world of pornography.

Most teenagers lack the abstract processing skills that advise them that the incidents and images displayed in pornography are not representative of most adults' sex lives. Teens exposed to what the pornography industry and, indeed, its consumers ordain as "sexy" or "passionate" or "hot," and who lack the aforementioned skills, eventually begin to think that the sexual acts displayed are necessary to have the desired adjectives listed above become attributes of their own lives.

This is especially true when it comes to body image. Average people, who are endowed in a very average way, are not typically stars of the pornographic industry, or at least not pre–surgical alteration. As teenagers watch pornography, they cannot help but make comparisons to the unrealistic images they see and, consequently, may begin to find themselves and perhaps their own partners less attractive. As if being a teenager and dealing with hormonal changes and body image insecurities weren't difficult enough, now teenagers are comparing pornographic superstars to their own developing young bodies and those of their partners.

However, it is not body image alone that suffers through the consumption of pornography. Often a teen's view of the sex act itself becomes skewed in an unrealistic and unhealthy way, especially when pornography becomes the educator through which he or she learns about sex.

Pornography as Education

Where do young people actually learn to have sex? Comprehensive sexuality education, although widely favored in this country (despite the current trend of abstinence-only education), doesn't include demonstrations or lessons on how to engage in the act of having sex. Likewise, most parents surely don't advise their children on the virtues and techniques of making love. When people lose their virginity, one hopes the experience will happen with a partner whom they are able to feel comfortable with and who will accept their genuine selves. In an ideal situation, one inexperienced partner should be able to say to the other: "I don't really know what I'm doing!" However, sad truth though it may be, that is not usually the case. Many times, people lose their virginity with someone they've just met, or when they've been drinking or using drugs, or with someone they care about but with whom they aren't completely intimate—in other words, not someone with whom they can allow themselves to be completely vulnerable. That leaves pornography as the most viable sexual education tool.

We've already established that pornography sets up unrealistic expectations, and that most certainly poses a problem when people are modeling their sex life after knowledge—albeit knowledge that has no basis in reality—gleaned from pornography and when they lack any other alternative. But consider the advantages film has over real life. What appears to the viewer as a

15-minute sexual encounter may have taken eight hours to film, incorporated multiple camera angles to find the best view of the bodies, and required extensive editing in order to make it work—all advantages that the fantasy world of pornography has over typical sexual experiences.

This leads us to our last concern: Besides the unrealistic expectations created by viewing and utilizing pornography, even inadvertently, as an educational tool, the simple, yet serious fact is that pornography can contribute to greater acceptance of sexual violence. This is because much of pornography is based around images and incidents that are degrading toward women, exhibit misogynistic attitudes, and largely focus on the pleasure of the male as its utmost goal.

Sexual Violence

Pornography is rarely about love, intimacy, tenderness, and affection. It is about sex. People don't view pornography to feel closer to themselves or their partner emotionally. They view it for the purpose of arousal and, often, use it as an impetus for masturbation or intercourse. As previously stated, viewers of pornography are predominantly male, and because of this and of its aforementioned purpose, pornography often objectifies women—props who become a means to an end, with an end most likely translating into male orgasm.

In much of the pornographic world, women are there to serve men and to be dominated by them, the ideas of sexual arousal and power becoming intertwined in a way that can be processed cognitively by an adult, but not by a teenager whose emotions and hormones so often overrule any rational thought (Peter and Valkenburg, 2007). Think of the underlying meaning of a porn staple, "the money shot," where the male subject in a pornographic film ejaculates onto his partner, expressing his regard for her with an action devoid of any feeling or affection. If this doesn't model the idea that women are objects, then what does?

The fact is, young men who view pornography are more likely to have negative perceptions of women and be more accepting of violence toward them (Jensen and Okrina, 2004). This is not to say that all men who view pornography will engage in an act of sexual assault, but viewing pornography certainly contributes to a misogynistic culture, a culture where men feel entitled to view and treat women as sexual objects, and in that type of culture, men are more inclined to take advantage of women and, indeed, have an easier time justifying sexual violence.

Although adult men may have the internal processing skills to understand that what they see in porn is not an accurate portrayal of how men should treat women, teenage boys often have not developed that capacity. When they continually see a man belittle a woman in pornography—either emotionally or physically—they view that attitude as acceptable. This is especially true if young men view porn with their friends, as the pack mentality increases the support for this notion—further proof that no good can come of inappropriate sexual content coupled with immaturity.

Conclusion

A healthy sexual appetite is normal and can be expressed in myriad ways. For adults, viewing pornography with a partner can be a fun and "inspiring" experience, but it requires maturity to keep it in the proper context.

Though youth has its advantages, it also has its limitations. Young men and women who are just beginning to develop as sexual beings should take care to learn from examples of loving, mature, and healthy relationships. Pornography does not provide the proper model for any of these and is more likely to prove harmful to teens than advantageous in any way. A healthy sex life is not teeming with unrealistic expectations or fraught with an underlying sense of violence or disrespect. Teenagers whose sexual education is informed through the dark, sensual world of pornography are sure to come to the opposite conclusion, and their relationships will only suffer because of it.

References

C. Bryan, "Adolescence, Pornography, and Harm," *Trends and Issues in Crime and Criminal Justice* (vol. 368, 2009).

M. Godwin, *Cyber Rights: Defending Free Speech in the Digital Age* (Cambridge, MA: MIT Press, 2003).

Jacobellis v. Ohio, 378 U.S. 184, 197 (1964).

R. Jensen and D. Okrina, *Pornography and Sexual Violence* (2004). Retrieved March 14, 2009, from National Online Resource Center on Violence Against Women, http://new.vawnet.org/Assoc_Files_VAWnet/AR_PornAndSV.pdf.

J. Peter and P. M. Valkenburg, "Adolescents' Exposure to a Sexualized Media Environment and Their Notions of Women as Sex Objects," *Sex Roles* (vol. 56, 2007).

J. Ropelato, *Internet Pornography Statistics* (2003). Retrieved March 22, 2009, from Top Ten Reviews, http://www.internet-filter-review.toptenreviews.com/internet-pornography-statistics.html.

Justin A. Sitron

 **NO**

Why Porn Is Not Harmful to Teens

The question about whether pornography is harmful is something that has been on the minds of researchers, parents, and others for decades (Malamuth, Addison, and Koss, 2000). Since the invention of the Internet, the question has become more and more popular, as access to pornography has become as easy as pressing the keys on a keyboard and clicking a mouse. While years ago most people had to go to a bookstore, video store, or adult sex shop to access pornography, now one does not even need to leave one's home or even pay for it. With much more explicit cable television programming and the advent of the Internet, accessing pornography for teens is as easy as finding out the answers to a question on their geography homework (and, the teens might say, infinitely more interesting!). Some researchers even have shown that some youth who access porn do so unintentionally (Sabina, Wolak, and Finkelhor, 2008; Ybarra and Mitchell, 2005).

The question about whether pornography is harmful, dangerous, or leads to aggressive sexual behavior has been studied in adults with varying results (e.g., Fukui and Westmore, 1994; Kutchinsky, 1991). Quite simply, some researchers have found that it makes men more aggressive, whereas others find that it does not. Malamuth, Addison, and Koss (2000) conclude in their meta-analysis of such studies that ". . . for the majority of American men, pornography exposure (even at the highest levels assessed here) is not associated with high levels of sexual aggression" (p. 85). So why the big concern about teens having access to porn?

While in recent years there is growing interest in the effects of online pornography on youth, there has been little research done to date (Sabina, Wolak, and Finkelhor, 2008). In maintaining my position that porn is not harmful to people—teen and adult alike—I need to describe the context in which pornography exists. By and large, the opposing viewpoint—that pornography is harmful to teens—comes from a place of fear; fear of sex and sexual pleasure that has been a part of American society since before the word "American" even existed (Klein, 2006).

The sexual value system that prevails in the United States sees sex as St. Augustine of Hippo saw it after his conversion from a period of lust and sexual promiscuity to a Christian man of high morals—sexual behaviors are only appropriate between a man and a woman, within the confines of marriage, and for procreative purposes. This same value system is one that leaves out something that has become a part of American mainstream media in recent years with sex therapists and relationship counselors on America's talk shows, like *Oprah, Tyra Banks,* and *Dr. Phil,* among others, as well as the nightly news: sexual pleasure. Sexual pleasure is a part of pornography, whether it is something that filmmakers aim to represent on the screen or it is being experienced by pornography's viewers. It is a part of sexual expression and sexual behaviors. If it were not, our culture would not be spending as much time discussing it—and certainly nowhere nearly as much money on it—as it does.

In a society that values sex for reproduction rather than for sexual pleasure and an individual's right to ecstasy and self-fulfillment, the very idea that our teenagers might be experiencing pleasure or witnessing others doing so incites an even more pronounced fear. Certainly, these fearful individuals speculate, indulgent pleasure can only have one outcome—danger or harm. Therefore, the idea of consuming pornography is reserved for the lowest members of society—criminals, perverts, sex maniacs, and so on. Those who aim for achieving the greater good by being successful in our careers, raising families, and experiencing a sense of spiritual satisfaction wouldn't allow ourselves to stoop to self-satisfying physical pleasure. It is far too much of a distraction, and therefore not valued.

Varying media, when relating stories about the Internet, frequently discuss either the wealth of information that it offers or the dangers of its use. Sutter (2000) connects the statements I make above with a recurring fear of humanity since its very first scholars: "The furor over Internet pornography follows the classic pattern of moral panic throughout the ages. From Plato's concerns regarding the 'dramatic poets' effects on the young to the 1980s 'video nasties' scare, to screen violence and internet pornography in the 1990s and beyond: the contexts change but the arguments are consistent" (p. 338). So, I ask that we reconsider the question and begin to explore the panic from a new angle: an angle that begs us to ask what the harmful effects of the panic itself may be.

The panic in which our society engages around the harmfulness of pornography, as I mentioned before, is about the assumption that sexual pleasure is harmful and therefore something from which teens must be protected. Consider this short scenario:

> A parent and 10-year-old child are sitting around the living room, and perhaps the child is sitting on the floor playing with a toy while the parent is flipping through prime-time television. After flipping through the channels, the parent decides on a favorite love story. Although the story itself is over the child's head, the child is otherwise occupied. As the story progresses, the child begins to watch and ends up captivated until the parent switches the channel, which sparks protest in the child because the story was so engaging. The parent's response is, "Go back to playing with your toys, I want to watch something else." What sparked the change of channel? The two main characters engaged in a kiss that transformed into the removal of clothing and rolling in the sheets. No nudity. No words between the characters of any kind, just a romantic ballad in the background and two people beginning to kiss passionately and remove clothing.

Although the child in the story objects to the channel being changed, the parent does nothing to engage the child in a discussion about why the channel was changed or what was going on in the story before the flick of the remote. The message that is entirely implicit in this situation is that kissing and the touching of naked bodies between two adults is not something a child should see. If something suitable for prime-time television is too harmful for children, the mainstream thinking would certainly hold that pornography is harmful as well, if not more so.

I disagree. I posit here that there are benefits to teens watching pornography: (1) Internet pornography offers teens an opportunity to see real bodies; (2) pornography offers an opportunity for teens to learn by watching rather than by doing; and (3) pornography opens doors for communication.

Internet Pornography Offers Teens an Opportunity to See Real Bodies

The days of pornography being only accessible in commercially produced formats (DVD, VHS, film, etc.) are gone. Such content has been described by researchers as being responsible for promoting artificial and unrealistic body types in women and men alike. Certainly, this is not a phenomenon left to the pornography industry alone; producers of mainstream film, television, and video all contribute to the perpetuation of unrealistic body types as more beautiful than that of the average viewer. Why, then, should pornography be held to a higher standard than any other type of media?

On the Internet, there is a multitude of sites where Internet users can generate their own original video content and post it on Web sites for others to see. A visitor to sites like XTube.com and Bigbeautifulwomen.com can see a variety of different film clips that include a diversity of body types, sexual orientations, gender, body hair levels, and sexual behaviors ranging from the most mainstream to fetishes. Such a site can build a sense of self-esteem for individuals who might never have seen other people whose nude bodies are like their own.

Pornography Offers an Opportunity for Teens to Learn by Watching Rather Than by Doing

Howard Gardner's (1983) theory of multiple intelligences, which articulates the varying ways in which people express their learning styles, has had a great impact on the ways in which educators approach teaching students. Two of the intelligence styles are kinesthetic, which learns best by physically doing and/or handling something, and visual, which prefers seeing. Teens who match either of these two learning styles may be able to use pornography as a substitute for actual sexual behaviors. Although the kinesthetic learners might be motivated naturally to engage in sex, they may find watching it or masturbating while watching it to be a learning experience. They can understand what they do and don't find arousing; they can learn about their own bodies and what feels and does not feel good. Pornography, and any sexually explicit material for that matter, can actually serve as an excellent teaching tool. Considering that no one has ever gotten pregnant or acquired a sexually transmitted infection from masturbation, one might go so far as to argue that teens who view porn might be able to maintain a decision to remain abstinent longer than teens who do not.

In addition to pornography serving as a tool for varied learning styles, it also serves as a medium through which to portray sexual behaviors. There are few educational venues for teens to see sex in this way. Sexuality, as it is taught in schools, is taught very much separate from the rest of the human body, often even in a different set of classes from other body parts and their functions. Sexual health and reproduction are usually a stand-alone unit in a health class or biology class. The focus of such education is on how the parts work, what their purpose is (procreation), and how to avoid disease. So, although the body parts (uterus, vagina, ovaries, penis, testicles, prostate, etc.) are explained, and often their functions described, all of it is done as if they are detached organs from the rest of the body and without discussion of pleasure.

From a learning standpoint, adolescents and teens are concrete learners—they must have very specific, straightforward examples to support teaching in order for that teaching to resonate. Talking hypothetically about sexual behaviors is often much more challenging for a teenager to understand than seeing an actual representation of it. Pornography provides teens with that representation.

Pornography Opens Doors for Communication

Finally, pornography offers us, as adults, an opportunity to engage young people in conversations about sexuality. If we engage in conversations with young people about sexuality, sexual bodies, and sexual pleasure, we provide teens with valuable lessons. Pornography as a medium, therefore, becomes neutral, neither good nor bad. It is merely another teachable moment for educators and parents alike.

Realistically speaking, the context in which pornography is viewed is the complicated and potentially troubling component. Sure, some pornography depicts stereotypical sexual behaviors, unrealistic body types, and even behaviors that some perceive to be violent or degrading, but this all presents just as many challenges for teens as it does for adults. Viewing pornography, if not done critically and with discussion, may leave the viewer with misconceived notions of sexual behavior and pleasure. The problems with pornography are cultural and social and can be further understood and framed appropriately with teens only if adults are willing to engage teens in a discussion—a discussion that may even include watching pornography together. Adults sometimes expect that they can control their children's lives, their exposure to the world, and their behaviors. The reality is that while many parents take action to censor their children's Internet access, friends, and media viewing, children who aim to find pornography will always be able to do so. In addition, as mentioned earlier, even children who do not aim to find or view pornography sometimes come upon it unwittingly. The irony of the situation is that enough studies have been done to demonstrate that adolescents and children are sexual, whether alone or with someone else, and even without engaging in sexual behavior, they have fantasies and think about it. As most adults who work with children and teens will tell you, when adults are not present, sex is something teens talk about.

If adults and children don't discuss sex and sexuality, then where are the models for adults to discuss it as well? Pornography, whether viewed in secret, in groups, or with adults present, opens the door for young people to talk about sex and their feelings about it and to find out what important adults in their lives think about it. Pornography presents an opportunity to raise many questions, if the questions are allowed to be asked. Openly discussing sexuality can bring a lot of potential benefits to teens as they age. To consider the ramifications of a culture where sex is taboo, one only needs to read through a chapter in a text on the treatment of sexual dysfunctions. So many of the problems that adults face with the expression of their sexuality have their roots in their lives as children, teenagers, and young adults—times in their lives when sex was not discussed openly, positively, or in constructive ways. Rather than predispose our teens to a future with sexual dysfunction and a fear of finding support around their sexuality, why not begin conversations about sex when young people naturally want to have them?

If our answer to the question posed as the title of this section—Is viewing pornography harmful to teens?—is "yes," we begin on a misguided, thorny path of protecting children and teens from pornography, sexual pleasure, and sex in general by shutting and locking the doors to learning and communication. On the other hand, if the answer is "no," doors open to begin a dialogue about pornography, its use, misuse, benefits, and detriments, and an invaluable conversation can begin between adults and children about healthy sexual expression.

References

A. Fukui and B. Westmore, "To See or Not to See: The Debate over Pornography and Its Relationship to Sexual Aggression," *Australian and New Zealand Journal of Psychiatry* (vol. 28, 1994).

M. Klein, *America's War on Sex* (New York: Praeger Publishers: 2006).

B. Kutchinsky, "Pornography and Rape: Theory and Practice? Evidence from Crime Data in Four Countries Where Pornography Is Easily Accessible," *International Journal of Law and Psychiatry* (vol. 14, 1991).

N. M. Malamuth, T. Addison, and M. Koss, "Pornography and Sexual Aggression: Are There Reliable Effects and Can We Understand Them?" *Annual Review of Sex Research* (vol. 11, 2000).

C. Sabina, J. Wolak, and D. Finkelhor, "The Nature and Dynamics of Internet Pornography Exposure for Youth," *CyberPsychology & Behavior* (vol. 11, 2008).

G. Sutter, "'Nothing New Under the Sun': Old Fears and New Media," *International Journal of Law and Information Technology* (vol. 8, 2000).

M. L. Ybarra and K. J. Mitchell, "Exposure to Internet Pornography Among Children and Adolescents: A National Survey," *CyberPsychology & Behavior* (vol. 8, 2005).

EXPLORING THE ISSUE

Is Internet Pornography Harmful to Teenagers?

Critical Thinking and Reflection

- What are some arguments made by each side with which you agree or disagree?
- What are the strengths and weaknesses of the two positions made in this issue? Compare and contrast the competing arguments made about the impact of Internet pornography on teens. What conclusions do you reach about the different research cited?
- Think more broadly about the amount of privacy that teens have to view pornography. Also, consider the wide access that they have to cell phones that record video. How might this combination affect their own sexual behaviors, the recording of the own sexual behaviors, and sending/posting video recordings of their sexual behaviors?

Is There Common Ground?

While the authors may disagree over the impact of pornography, they both would probably agree about the potential dangers of recording and posting teens' own sexual behaviors. We have seen some cases of teens committing suicide after sexually explicit video of them has been posted online. What are some things that can occur to create a generation of more sexually literate teenagers who make decisions that are consistent with their long-term goals? What responsibilities do families have to teach their children about creating sexually explicit videos? What responsibilities do schools have to teach children about creating sexually explicit videos?

Additional Resources

C. Bryan, "Adolescence, Pornography, and Harm," *Trends and Issues in Crime and Criminal Justice* (vol. 368, 2009).

M. Godwin, *Cyber Rights: Defending Free Speech in the Digital Age* (Cambridge, MA: MIT Press, 2003). *Jacobellis v. Ohio*, 378 U.S. 184, 197 (1964).

R. Jensen and D. Okrina, *Pornography and Sexual Violence* (2004). Retrieved March 14, 2009. Accessible online at National Online Resource Center on Violence Against Women, http://new.vawnet.org/Assoc_Files_VAWnet/AR_PornAndSV.pdf.

L. Margolies, *Teens and Internet Pornography* (2010). Psych Central. Retrieved September 4, 2011. Accessible online at http://psychcentral.com/lib/2010/teens-and-internet-pornography.

Optenet. (2010). More than one third of Web pages are pornographic [Press release]. Retrieved September 10, 2010. Accessible online at http://www.optenet.com/en-us/new.asp?id=270.

J. Peter and P. M. Valkenburg, "Adolescents' Exposure to a Sexualized Media Environment and Their Notions of Women as Sex Objects," *Sex Roles* (vol. 56, 2007).

ISSUE 17

Are Statutory Rape Laws Effective at Protecting Minors?

YES: Sherry F. Colb, from "The Pros and Cons of Statutory Rape Laws," CNN.com (February 11, 2004)

NO: Marc Tunzi, from "Curbside Consultation: Isn't This Statutory Rape?" *American Family Physician* (May 2002)

Learning Outcomes

As a result of this issue, readers will be able to:

- Identify the major arguments made regarding diverse views for statutory rape laws.
- Compare and contrast the competing arguments made for and against statutory rape laws in this issue.
- Evaluate the impact statutory rape laws have on issues such as adolescent sexual behavior, spreading of sexually transmitted infections, and teenage pregnancy.

ISSUE SUMMARY

YES: Sherry F. Colb, columnist and law professor, uses a case study involving a statutory rape case to raise concerns about whether rape and assault cases would be prosecuted sufficiently without statutory rape laws. Although not perfect, statutory rape laws can be assets in such rape cases as when the older partner denies the rape occurred or denies responsibility for a resulting pregnancy or infection.

NO: Marc Tunzi, a family physician, believes that statutory rape laws are ineffective because people can get around them too easily. These laws, he argues, require that an otherwise healthy relationship between two people of different ages be criminalized solely because there is some kind of sexual activity involved. As a result, medical and other licensed professionals do not want to break up these relationships that, in their professional opinion, are not problematic based on just the age difference between the two partners.

The term "rape" refers to forced sexual contact between two people that usually involves the insertion of a penis or inanimate object into another person's vagina, anus, or mouth. Rape is against the law in every state in the United States and usually results in heavy penalties on the rapist.

Statutory rape laws say that sexual behavior between two people where one individual is below a certain age is against the law even if there was no force involved. These laws, which were originally created to protect adolescent girls from predatory adult males, are different in every state. The age at which a person is considered legally able to engage in sexual behavior, called the "age of consent," is different in every state, too. Most state laws are no longer restricted to a female victim and male perpetrator; they now apply to couples of any gender combination, including same-sex relationships. Yet some cases receive far more attention than others. For example, the media has carried news of former school teacher Mary Kay Letourneau, an adult who was convicted of statutory rape for having a sexual relationship with an adolescent student. Even though the two claimed then (and maintain now) that they were in love, the law said that this relationship was illegal, and Ms. Letourneau went to prison.

People who support statutory rape laws argue that in any relationship where there is a significant age difference, the older of the two people has an inherent power advantage over the younger. Even if the younger partner agrees to have sex, statutory rape law supporters argue, that person was not old enough to make a well-thought-out decision—and may have been coerced emotionally, even if not physically. What an older partner has can be very seductive—power, money, a job, a car, and more. These tangible things, they argue, play a powerful role in a younger person's decision-making process. In addition, it is quite flattering for a 14-year-old to have a 24-year-old person interested in her or him. One wonders, however, what a 24-year-old could possibly have in common, developmentally and experientially, with a 14-year-old. Statutory rape laws are designed, in part, to keep these types of unequal relationships from becoming sexual in nature.

Others disagree, saying that statutory rape laws are ineffective, judgmental, patronizing, and sexist. Opponents to statutory rape laws argue that adolescents and teenagers are able to make their own decisions about their sexual behavior, even if their partner is older. Opponents maintain that relationships are about much more than sexual behavior, and that if a relationship is otherwise healthy and loving, penalizing the couple for their age difference does more to ruin lives than save them. There are young men, they argue, who have gone to jail because the parents of their younger partners learned that they were having sex and wanted to punish them. As a result, these young men have a jail sentence on their records forever, solely because of an age difference.

What do you think about statutory rape laws? Do they protect, or do they discriminate? Do you think that an adult has more power than a teenager just because she or he is older? If so, is this power strong enough that the adolescent or teen could not say whether she or he wanted to have sex with that adult? What are some of the inherent problems with a significant age difference in a relationship? What are some of the positive things that can happen from two people of different ages having a relationship?

In the following selections, Sherry F. Colb takes the side of the victim, arguing that statutory rape laws, although inherently imperfect, do much more good than harm. For the number of young adolescents who claim they were forced to have sex (particularly by a known assailant), when the situation is often a simple matter of believing one person over the other, statutory rape laws give young rape victims a voice. Dr. Marc Tunzi raises the concern that other health professionals have: how statutory rape laws affect health professionals' guarantee of confidentiality and informed consent to their patients. These laws, he argues, are discriminatory against young men (because these cases most commonly involve an older male partner and a younger female partner), condescending to young women, and sometimes culturally disrespectful if there is a value that early sexual relationships are appropriate within the couple's particular cultural group.

The combination of age and sexuality is a sensitive subject in many cultures and societies. In the United States, we have many double standards about the age difference between sexual and romantic partners and the gender of the people involved in the relationship. An older man with a much younger woman is much more commonplace than an older woman with a much younger man. An adult male pursuing a teenage girl is seen as a predator, while an adult female doing the same is seen as much less threatening. Even in some court cases, judges have dismissed charges in cases where the older partner was female and the younger one male. It is as if the law does not see an adolescent girl as being able to consent, but a younger male is simply "coming of age" by being sexual with an older partner. In our mainstream society's eyes, an adolescent girl has lost something by being sexual so young; she has shown poor judgment and has been taken advantage of by this terrible older male. An adolescent male in the same situation with an adult woman, however, is often seen as having gained from the relationship—respect and experience. Are these assumptions prejudicial to boys? To girls?

There is an episode of *South Park* in which one of the characters finds his younger brother, who is in kindergarten, in bed with his female teacher. The character goes to the police to report that there is a teacher at school having sex with a child at school. The police are concerned, then they learn that the child is male and the teacher is female. At that point, they respond with, "Nice"; and "She's hot."

While this exchange is meant to be funny, what does it reveal about our society's larger views about whether or not someone is a victim of statutory rape?

There are far too many unhealthy and abusive relationships. People bring different things to their relationships, including different levels of power. In some cases, age brings power with it; in others, money and experience, race or ethnicity, or physical ability—the examples can continue almost endlessly. The questions that remain are these: In what way can people have healthy, respectful, equal relationships given the inherent power differences that are there? To what extent can and should personal relationships be governed by law?

YES

Sherry F. Colb

The Pros and Cons of Statutory Rape Laws

A 10-Year Sentence for Marcus Dwayne Dixon

Recently, the Georgia Supreme Court heard arguments in *Dixon v. State*. The case involves the conviction of Marcus Dwayne Dixon for statutory rape and aggravated child molestation. (Dixon was acquitted of rape and several other charges.)

Statutory rape is sex between an adult and a minor, while aggravated child molestation also involves an injury. At the time of his offense, Dixon was an 18-year-old high school football player who had sex with a 15-year-old female classmate. The aggravated child molestation statute mandates a ten-year minimum sentence, and Dixon challenges the harshness of the resulting penalty.

The case has attracted claims of racism, because the victim was a white girl and the convict an outstanding African-American student with a football scholarship to Vanderbilt.

One provocative underlying (though unstated) question that has contributed to the notoriety of this case is whether the law can legitimately send teenagers to prison for having sex with other teenagers, in the absence of force. Because every state has a statutory rape law in some form, this case presents a challenge to a long and continuing tradition of criminal laws that confine men for what could be consensual sex with minors who are close to the age of majority.

Such liability is controversial in a number of ways, but it also has some benefits that are often overlooked by critics, thus leaving us with a difficult dilemma that admits of no easy answers.

Statutory rape laws have a checkered past. A primary purpose was to guard the virginity of young maidens against seduction by unscrupulous cads. To give up one's "virtue" to a man who was unwilling to pay with his hand in marriage was foolish and presumptively a product of youthful, poor judgment.

Such laws had more to do with preserving female virginity than with the force and violence that define rape. One sign of this is the fact that a man could (and in some states still can) defend himself against statutory rape charges by proving that his victim was already sexually experienced prior to their encounter (and thus not subject to being corrupted by the defendant).

Justifications for Statutory Rape Laws

Despite their unsavory beginnings, however, some feminists have favored these laws as well. Progressive women supported such statutes mainly as measures to help combat the sexual abuse of young girls.

Though a statutory rape charge would not require proof of force or coercion, feminists observed, young girls were (and may continue to be) especially vulnerable to being raped by the adults in their lives. In one study, for example, 74 percent of women who had intercourse before age 14 and 60 percent of those who had sex before age 15 report having had a forced sexual experience.

In addition, prosecutors attempting to prove rape in court have historically faced significant burdens, such as corroboration requirements premised on the complaining witness's presumptive lack of credibility.

For many years, legal thinkers like 18th-century British jurist Sir Matthew Hale were convinced that rape "is an accusation easily to be made and hard to be proved, and harder to be defended by the party accused, though never so innocent." Thus, rape law did not provide a reliable or efficacious vehicle for addressing most sexual violence, and it continues to be of limited utility for acquaintance rapes. . . .

For this reason too, feminists may have viewed statutory rape laws as a godsend. As long as there was sexual intercourse and an under-age victim, the jury could convict. And more importantly, that possibility itself might deter real sexual abuse.

Is Statutory Rape Just Rape Without Proof of One Element?

Viewing statutory rape laws as salutary in this way does raise a serious problem, however. In *In Re Winship,* the U.S. Supreme Court required that prosecutors prove every element of a crime beyond a reasonable doubt before a conviction can be constitutionally valid. Removing the "force" element of rape and leaving only intercourse and age might seem to amount, from some perspectives, to a presumption that the force element of rape is established, without the prosecutor's having to prove it and without the defense even having the option of affirmatively disproving it.

Such a presumption allows for the possibility that a fully consensual sexual encounter will be prosecuted and punished as rape. Some might understandably believe that this unfairly subjects essentially innocent men to unduly harsh treatment, simply in the name of deterring other, unrelated men from engaging in very different and far more culpable sorts of conduct.

Responses to Concerns About Prosecuting Consensual Sex

There are two potential responses to this concern. First, at some level, we might have doubts about the competence of a minor to "consent," in a meaningful way, to sexual activity. Because of her youth, the minor might not fully appreciate the full physical and emotional implications of her decision (including the possibility of offspring for which she will likely have little means of support).

Of course, many adults might also fall into this category, and the decision to treat intercourse as distinctive in this way may simply represent a revival of the old view that maidens should be protected from the corruption of their virtue. Why, otherwise, should girls who are sexually attracted to men be considered the men's victims rather than participants in arguably unwise and socially costly, but mutually gratifying, activity?

Another response to the concern about innocent men is more in keeping with feminist concerns. It is that when sexual activity with a minor is truly consensual, the activity is unlikely, at least in modern times, to be prosecuted. In other words, to the extent that statutory rape is truly a consensual and therefore victimless crime in a particular case, it is highly unlikely to generate a criminal action.

In the Dixon case, for example, the 15-year-old victim claimed that the defendant "tracked her down in a classroom trailer that she was cleaning as part of her duties in an after-school job, asked if she was a virgin, grabbed her arms, unbuttoned her pants, and raped her on a table." This description renders the statutory rape and aggravated child molestation prosecution something other than the state targeting consensual activity for unduly harsh punishment.

Though Dixon was acquitted on the rape charge, that fact does not rule out the possibility of sexual assault. It means only that the jury was not convinced beyond a reasonable doubt that Dixon forced the 15-year-old girl to have sex against her will.

The normative question, then, becomes this: Is the likelihood that consensual sex will be punished by imprisonment sufficient to override the benefits of statutory rape legislation in facilitating the fight against actual sexual abuse of young adults?

Is Convicting in the Absence of Force Unacceptable?

One reaction to this question is that even the theoretical possibility of convicting in a case of consensual sex is unacceptable and unconstitutional. Prosecutors and juries, on this reasoning, should not have the option of finding a person guilty in the absence of force, regardless of how unlikely they are to exercise that option. Consensual sex is not criminal, period.

The assumptions underlying this reaction, however, though understandable, are at odds with other areas of the criminal law. Consider drug laws. Possession of a large quantity of narcotics is regularly treated as a far more serious offense than possession of a smaller quantity. One reason is that the first is viewed as possession with the intent to distribute (that is, drug dealing), while the second is thought to be consistent with personal use. Since legislators and others view dealing as much more harmful than mere possession, the penalties are accordingly more severe.

Yet possession of a large quantity of drugs, though highly suggestive, is not necessarily accompanied by an intent to distribute. A person might, for example, possess large amounts of drugs to avoid having to risk apprehension, or sources drying out, through repeated purchases.

Suppose the drug statute did require proof of intent to distribute. If so, then the judge would, on request, have to instruct the jury that the bare fact of quantity alone is enough for a conviction only if the jury draws the inference, beyond a reasonable doubt, that the defendant intended distribution. Without such a finding of intent, the jury would have to acquit.

With the statute providing instead that quantity is the sole element, however, intent becomes legally irrelevant. As a result, even a prosecutor and jury who know that the defendant is simply saving up for an anticipated heroin shortage rather than planning to deal drugs can convict the defendant of the more serious felony without giving rise to any grounds for appeal.

By crafting a statute without an "intent to distribute" element, in other words, legislators target distribution without requiring its proof (or even allowing for its disproof). One might characterize this as an end run around the constitutional requisite of proving every element of guilt beyond a reasonable doubt.

The same "end run" accusation can be leveled against statutory rape laws. Young girls may represent a substantial portion of rape victims, perhaps because they are vulnerable and have not yet become sufficiently suspicious of the people around them. In most cases, moreover, a truly consensual encounter with a minor will probably not be brought to a prosecutor's attention or trigger the prosecutorial will to punish.

As with drug possession laws, then, the omission of a requirement that would pose proof problems might generally serve the interests of justice, despite appearances to the contrary.

Consensual Sex with Minors Is Not a Fundamental Right

What permits legislatures the discretion to enact such laws, ultimately, is the fact that (like drug possession), consensual sex with minors is not a constitutionally protected activity. Even if it is victimless, sex with a minor may be criminalized and punished severely without resort to a force requirement. Indeed, it once was punished routinely in this way because of misogynist concerns about preserving female purity.

In modern times, though, when consensual sex among teenagers is generally understood to be both common and profoundly different from the crime of rape, there might still be a role for statutory rape laws in protecting young girls from actual rapists, through deterrence and through the real possibility of retribution.

Racism Raised in the Dixon Case

A remaining concern is the worry about racism specifically, and discrimination more generally, that arises whenever officials are vested with a large amount of discretion. In Dixon's case, one witness testified that the victim said that the sexual intercourse in question was consensual but that she claimed it was rape to avoid the wrath of her violent, racist father. This testimony may have given rise to reasonable doubt in the jury on the rape charges.

In easing the burden of proof at trial by eliminating the requirement of proving force, then, the law does permit unscrupulous prosecutors and complainants to bring charges on the basis of what is truly victimless behavior.

One does wonder, though, why a girl would tell a violent and racist father about a sexual encounter with a black man in the first place, rather than simply keeping the information from him, if the encounter were actually consensual.

Are Statutory Rape Laws Worth Their Cost?

In short, the crime of statutory rape may have originated from repressive and misogynist conceptions of sexuality. Nonetheless, it has (and may always have had) redeeming characteristics, even from an enlightened perspective that takes into account the realities of prosecuting rape and of women's equality. It makes it easier, for example, to prosecute and thus to deter real rapists who count on jury skepticism about acquaintance rape allegations.

Still, reducing burdens of proof relies a great deal on trust—in victims and in prosecutors—that the omitted element will truly be present when cases come to trial. If and when that trust is misplaced, . . . a grave injustice can result.

 **NO**

Curbside Consultation: Isn't This Statutory Rape?

Case Scenario

Several pregnant teenagers in my practice are underage and have boyfriends older than 18. Isn't this statutory rape? Some of these patients are immigrants who prefer to keep a low profile, not calling the attention of local authorities to themselves or their boyfriends. In most cases, the sex is consensual, and the teens involved don't particularly care about legal fine points. However, I do, because I have often seen older boyfriends disappear, becoming "deadbeat dads." If I reported these young men, maybe they would be forced to fulfill their obligations. On the other hand, reporting them might disrupt a potentially viable relationship. What is my obligation?

Commentary

"Isn't this statutory rape?" our colleague asks. The answer is . . . "maybe." Statutory rape laws were first enacted to protect minors from older predators. States differ considerably in the legal definition of statutory rape.[1] For example, in California, where my practice is located, the age of consent for lawful sexual relationships is 18. If the age difference between the adult and the minor victim is more than three years, the charge is a felony; if three years or less, it is a misdemeanor. In Hawaii, the age of consent is 14. In other states, the age of consent ranges from 15 to 18 years, and many states have associated provisions that specify the level of offense depending on age differences and other factors.

Consideration of the legal fine points of statutory rape requires knowledge of specific state laws. Most states require that health care providers report injuries related to criminal violence regardless of the age of the victim, and four states (California, Colorado, Kentucky, and Rhode Island) require health professionals to report domestic violence.[2] While reporting violent injuries is a well-accepted practice, there continues to be controversy about domestic violence laws (for example, what if the victim doesn't want the abuse reported?). Most experts, however, believe that unreported domestic violence simply breeds more violence and that it should be reported in most cases.

Whether statutory rape is considered violence may depend on the consent of the minor involved. From a strictly legal standpoint, minors are unable

From *American Family Physician*, May 1, 2002. Copyright © 2002 by American Academy of Family Physicians. Reprinted by permission.

to give consent, which is exactly the reason statutory rape laws exist. However, in the majority of statutory rape cases, minors have given consent (legally or not) to having sex, limiting any potential criminal charge to that of domestic violence rather than the more serious charge of child abuse.

In fact, whether health care professionals are required to report consensual statutory rape to authorities really depends on whether the specific state considers it a type of child sexual abuse, which is reportable in all states. Unfortunately, laws on mandatory statutory rape reporting are confusing and often do not appear to be enforced even where they exist.[3–5] California child abuse law requires health practitioners and other child-related professionals to report statutory rape only when the adult is 21 years or older and the minor is younger than 16 years.[6] California law also specifically states that "the pregnancy of a minor does not, in and of itself, constitute a reasonable suspicion of child abuse."[6]

Many people believe that enforcing statutory rape laws will decrease the teen pregnancy rate and the number of young families needing public support because of "deadbeat dads." In fact, part of the 1996 federal welfare reform law specifically directed state and local governments to develop and enforce strict measures against statutory rape for those very reasons. California's response was a multimillion-dollar vertical prosecution program that allows the same prosecutor and investigator to remain on a case from beginning to end, while other states have developed their own programs.[4]

Even though more statutory rape convictions have resulted from these efforts, there is no real evidence that any of the programs have been the effective deterrents that Congress intended. In fact, there are still a lot of 16- and 17-year-olds on my hospital's labor and delivery unit. What these laws may have influenced is the unwillingness of pregnant teens to seek early prenatal care. While knowledge of statutory rape laws does not appear to prevent adult–minor relationships from occurring, fear of these laws may keep some young women from seeking prenatal care as a means of protecting their boyfriends from incarceration or deportation. Many professionals who work with pregnant adolescents are beginning to collect evidence supporting this concern.[1,4]

Another issue for family physicians is that statutory rape laws seem to conflict with the law as it applies to our practice and our understanding of informed consent for adolescents in other situations. Many teens have the capacity to participate in their own health care decision-making, even regarding serious and terminal illnesses. For example, teens are specifically able to consent for contraception, STD treatment, and pregnancy care in nearly all cases. The only illegality may be actually having sex.

The problem is that not all teens and situations are the same. Some teens are much more mature than others of the same age and are as able to consent to sexual activity just as an 18- to 20-year-old could. At the same time, I think all of us would question a relationship between even the most mature 15-year-old and a 25- or 30-year-old. My own experience is that many teens of 16 and 17 know the emotions and consequences of having intercourse just as well as many teens of 18 and 19. In some of my Latina patients, becoming sexually active at a young age seems culturally acceptable and, at times, even encouraged within their culture. I, however, discourage it quite strongly. The question is whether enforcing laws against it is the right approach.

What is the right thing for a family physician to do when caring for a patient who has been involved in statutory rape (as defined by state law)? Not all young men are "deadbeat dads"—many work and are as responsible and dedicated to their partners and children as older men with older partners. Removing a source of financial and emotional support by incarcerating a young man in this situation would probably not help the young woman and her baby; in fact, it might possibly harm them.

If criminal violence has been involved, it must be reported to authorities. If domestic violence has been involved and the victim is a minor, I would report it as a case of child abuse even if the state does not have a mandatory domestic violence reporting law. If it is not violence, given the fact that mandatory statutory rape reporting laws are confusing and not necessarily enforced, I believe that a physician should report only after carefully considering several factors.

How mature is the minor? Is he or she in school and responsible in other matters? Does the minor have the capacity to consent to intercourse? Is she or he using contraception? Does the minor understand the consequences of pregnancy?

Is the couple's relationship truly consensual? What is the couple's age difference? Are they 16 and 36 (an older predator), or are they 16 and 19? Is the adult partner using physical or other power to take advantage of the minor?

If the patient is a pregnant minor, is her adult male partner emotionally and financially responsible and supportive? Is this a potential family in the making, or has the man already abandoned the patient?

Family physicians will probably not report most cases to authorities, believing instead that building patient trust and making appropriate referrals to social services and other allied health professionals are the right things to do for the patient and family involved.

References

1. Donovan P. Can statutory rape laws be effective in preventing adolescent pregnancy? Family Planning Perspectives 1997; 29:30–4, 40.

2. Rodriguez MA, McLoughlin E, Nah G, Campbell JC. Mandatory reporting of domestic violence injuries to the police. JAMA 2001; 286:580–583.

3. Madison AB, Feldman-Winter L, Finkel M, McAbee GN. Commentary: Consensual adolescent sexual activity with adult partners—conflict between confidentiality and physician reporting requirements under child abuse laws. Pediatrics 2001; 107(2). . . .

4. Oliveri R. Statutory rape law and enforcement in the wake of welfare reform. Stanford Law Review 2000; 52:463–508.

5. Leiter RA, ed. National survey of state laws. 2d ed. Detroit-Gale, 1999; 313–30.

6. California Penal Code section 261.5 (Unlawful sexual intercourse with a minor) and California Penal Code sections 11165.1 and 11166 (Child Abuse and Neglect Reporting Act).

EXPLORING THE ISSUE

Are Statutory Rape Laws Effective at Protecting Minors?

Critical Thinking and Reflection

- What are some arguments made by each side with which you agree or disagree?
- What are the strengths and weaknesses of the two positions made in this issue? Pick the side with which you most agree. What are some additional arguments you would make to strengthen the case for or against statutory rape laws?
- Think more broadly of the issue of statutory rape laws. What is required to give consent to sexual behavior, and what age or ages are clearly fair criteria in making sex illegal?

Is There Common Ground?

Both authors in this issue would not want someone to engage in sex with someone with which they have not consented. However, drawing this line is difficult. While age is one criteria for consent, what are some others? How mature should a person be (which is not always tied directly to age)? How much should a person know about sexually transmitted infections and their prevention? How much should a person know about pregnancy prevention? How should a person evaluate whether they are ready to have sex?

Additional Resources

California Penal Code section 261.5 (Unlawful sexual intercourse with a minor) and California Penal Code sections 11165.1 and 11166 (Child Abuse and Neglect Reporting Act).

P. Donovan, "Can Statutory Rape Laws be Effective in Preventing Adolescent Pregnancy?" *Family Planning Perspectives* (vol. 29, 1997: 30–34, 40).

M. A. Rodriguez, E. McLoughlin, G. Nah, and J. C. Campbell, "Mandatory Reporting of Domestic Violence Injuries to the Police," *JAMA* (vol. 286, 2001: 580–83).

A. B. Madison, L. Feldman-Winter, M. Finkel, and G. N. McAbee, "Commentary: Consensual Adolescent Sexual Activity with Adult Partners—Conflict Between Confidentiality and Physician Reporting Requirements Under Child Abuse Laws," *Pediatrics* (vol. 107, no. 2, 2001).

R. A. Leiter, ed., *National Survey of State Laws,* 2nd ed. (Detroit-Gale, 1999, pp. 313–30).

R. Oliveri, "Statutory Rape Law and Enforcement in the Wake of Welfare Reform," *Stanford Law Review* (vol. 52, 2000: 463–508).

ISSUE 18

Do Reality Television Shows Have a Negative Influence on Teenage Pregnancy and Parenting?

YES: Jessica Isner, Annie Koval, and Lisa Paul, from "True-Life Teen Moms, Experts Say MTV's 'Reality' Off the Mark," *NWI Parent* (March 9, 2011)

NO: The National Campaign to Prevent Teen and Unplanned Pregnancy, from "Evaluating the Impact of MTV's *16 and Pregnant* on Teen Viewers' Attitudes About Teen Pregnancy," *Science Says* (October 2010)

Learning Outcomes

As a result of this issue, readers will be able to:

- Identify critical research about the impact of reality television on teenage parenting.
- Compare and contrast the major research cited and analysis used in examining the impact of reality television on teenage pregnancy and parenting.
- Evaluate the impact of reality television on the larger spirit of teen behavior and decision making.

ISSUE SUMMARY

YES: Jessiva Isner, Annie Koval, and Lisa Paul wrote this article for *NWI Parent*, which advertises that their publication provides "Real Solutions for Real Families." The authors are concerned that MTV's episodes related to teenage parenthood fail to capture accurately the true challenges of teenage parenthood.

NO: The National Campaign to Prevent Teen and Unplanned Pregnancy is dedicated to reducing teenage pregnancy. Their research reveals that teenagers who watch *16 and Pregnant* are more likely to express a negative view about the ways in which parenthood affects a teen's life.

Some people claim that the first reality show was *Candid Camera,* a show that dates back to the late 1940s, and was intended to catch people in mildly embarrassing situations. Allen Funt said that *Candid Camera* "caught people in the act of being themselves." A modern-day version of that would be *America's Funniest Home Videos.* On both shows, participants might be mildly embarrassed at having been caught getting frustrated in an encounter, but it did not result in the kind of shame that would be experienced by the participants in some of today's reality television shows.

A show from the 1950s, *Queen for a Day,* had housewives talk about how difficult their lives were with all of their children. Whoever had the worst life won a wide variety of cleaning products and appliances intended to save her time and make her life easier. Other shows exist today that intend to make viewers feel better for helping someone whose life is in a difficult position. *Extreme Makeover Home Edition* captures this very concept.

However, reality television began to change. Robert Thompson, director of the Center for the Study of Popular Television at Syracuse University, explains that reality television is "a new way of telling a story which [is] half fiction—the producers and creators set up a universe, they give it rules, they make a setting, they cast it according to specific guidelines as to who they think are going to provide good pyrotechnics. But then they bring in non-actors with no scripts and allow this kind of improvisation like a jazz piece to occur."

Reality television took on increasing popularity when MTV debuted *The Real World* during the 1990s. Less than a decade later, competitive reality television would emerge in a genre significantly different from *Star Search.* Huge ratings were realized by a reality television show, *Survivor. Survivor* had viewers transfixed over contestants catching and eating rats, treachery toward best friends, illicit romance, and attempts to capture the $1,000,000 prize.

The success of *Survivor* would have major implications for television programming. All of a sudden, all you needed was a film crew and production costs. There was no negotiating with stars about what they should get paid. There were people who just wanted to be on television, who just wanted a chance to win the big monetary prize, or who thought that they could turn their reality-show appearance into wider fame.

Indeed, some have done just that. From *Jersey Shore,* Snooki and the Situation are reported to earn $10,000–$30,000 per episode. Snooki is reported to earn an additional $20,000 per appearance to attend events or speak in public. The Situation is reported to earn millions of dollars per year.

Reality television, by some estimates, makes up 17 percent of the programming on television. Research about the most successful reality television series shows that they have three elements: curiosity, family, and social contact. Additional popular themes for viewers of reality television include romance, idealism, and honor. Think of the reality shows that you have watched. Are these characteristics present in the shows that you have watched most?

If you were to write a reality show to be popular based on these criteria what topic might it be about? Would that topic be merely entertaining, or would it have a positive impact on society? In what ways might there be a conflict with giving viewers what they want and creating a show that reinforces good and positive messages?

There was a time when people had to achieve something in order to become famous. They had to exceed at athletics, acting, singing, or playing an instrument. Or at least they had a lucky break, with the right person seeing them perform, leading to stardom.

Today, that is no longer required. A few people achieve stardom merely by the reality television camera turning its lens their way. In some cases, fame is achieved for what is commonly regarded as wrong, or even outrageous, behavior.

If we live in a society that tends to have a negative view of teenage pregnancy and parenthood, what level of interest would there be in television shows that highlight teenage pregnancy? Let's revisit the characteristics that researchers say viewers most want in reality television. Would a television show about teenage mothers have the most desired characteristics of reality television? Curiosity? Yes, for those who do not personally know teen parents. Family? Absolutely. Social contact? Clearly. Romance? There is room for that—or the absence of it—in these episodes. Idealism? Without question. Honor? Certainly.

Many people believe that reality television tends to be morally wrong. Indeed, just think about what was considered objectionable when *Survivor* first aired. Today, reality television often becomes increasingly controversial, with stars who stand out, often due to their outrageous behavior.

So television shows about teenage parents meet all the criteria that research shows the public wants in reality television. Now that we know the market exists, the next question to ask is, what is the impact that such shows have on teenage sexual decision making and behavior?

Some child development experts say that the adolescent brain is not properly wired for putting reality television into context. Others say that it is like any other form of media: Most children put it in the proper context, while just some do not.

Of course, if they are copying mannerisms, such as being rude to a friend, that is unkind, but not as life-changing as pregnancy and parenthood.

If you watch reality television, what shows have they been? What impact have these shows had on you? Have they influenced your behavior for the better? For the worse? Have the changed your awareness about certain issues? Have any reality shows encouraged you to make bad decisions? Have they encouraged you to make good decisions?

The articles in this issue make competing arguments about the influence of shows about teenage parenting and pregnancy. One article is a compelling opinion piece, while the other contains thoughtfully conducted research.

YES

Jessica Isner,
Annie Koval, and Lisa Paul

True-Life Teen Moms, Expert Say MTV's "Reality" Off the Mark

Once upon a time splits her time between being a mom and going to school.

Once upon a time, Kelsey Kruse was an average high school sophomore in Yorkville.

She was a good Catholic, a good student, and she was dating a star athlete in the senior class. Technically, she wasn't allowed to date until she was 16, but that wasn't a problem—until she got pregnant.

Now a 19-year-old student and mother of two-year-old Halle, Kruse vividly recalls what it was like to be a pregnant teenager. And she can promise it was nothing like MTV portrays it on shows such as "Teen Mom" and "16 & Pregnant."

Kruse feels as though MTV stars like Amber Portwood and Jenelle Evans do not offer a realistic glimpse of young motherhood. Unfortunately, these shows have become so prominent on today's pop culture spectrum that Kruse worries they could be leading young high school students to believe that teen pregnancy is far more glamorous—and easy—than it actually is.

"These girls are living the life right now—they're being paid to get pregnant and have kids," she said. "To a teenage girl, that sounds pretty cool: I'm just going to get pregnant, go on one of these shows, and I'm going to be famous."

Kruse fears that the overexposure of teen pregnancy in the media could subtly encourage high school girls to get pregnant long before they are ready.

"It influences teens when [they] see their favorite celebrity out partying and drinking," she said. "When you see them shopping somewhere, you want to shop there. Celebrities being pregnant is no different from them doing those other things."

Teens today consume more media and are more tech savvy than ever, said Julie Dobrow, director of communications and media studies at Tufts University in Medford, MA.

"Media are an important source of information for teens about some topics," she said. "Particularly, things like sex—which are not taught well in school—are difficult for many to speak about with their parents and are embarrassing for them to talk about at all."

Whether teens are talking about it at home, pregnancy seems to be inescapable in the media. In recent years, young motherhood has become a pop culture trend, and this has not been lost on teens, said Emilie Zaslow, assistant professor of communication studies at Pace University in New York City.

"Generally, the research shows that there is not a direct link between media and behavior," she said, "but there is strong evidence that media does have an influence on attitudes and values, and how we see the world."

Some experts said that teens have the wherewithal to be critical of the media and make their own decisions, regardless of what they consume.

In other words, teens are not easily manipulated, suggested Eitan Schwarz, an adolescent and pediatric psychiatrist in Skokie.

"Media isn't a cause and effect—it's an indirect thing," he said. "Media doesn't cause anything. On the other hand, media tends to amplify things."

Schwarz suggested teenagers with low self-esteem could be more susceptible to the media's messages concerning pregnancy.

"Some of these girls want to have a baby because they want someone to love them—they are looking for love—and they are wanting it from the baby," he said. "Many times, these girls don't really have a lot to give because they want stuff for themselves—and that's not an equation that works for the baby or for mothers, either."

Still, there has been no conclusive evidence regarding the ways in which teens are influenced by specific television programming. National Campaign to Prevent Teen and Unplanned Pregnancy conducted a survey that found 82 percent of teens mentioned MTV's "Teen Mom" as a deterrent for teen pregnancy.

But 21-year-old student Matt Bridge, the father of Kruse's child, said society glorifies teen pregnancy, even if it doesn't necessarily encourage it.

"It portrays it like, 'Hey, if you get pregnant, your life is going to be a golden road because we're going to reward you for it,'" he said. "It seems like you get rewarded these days for being a teen and getting pregnant, when really it's not a good thing—if you don't get lucky and you're not one out of a million to get on that show."

Some organizations are seizing this opportunity to change the ways in which teenagers learn about safe sex, said Shireen Schrock, the community education director for Planned Parenthood of Illinois. TV shows and movies provide parents with the opportunity to have an open dialogue with their kids about sex.

"We are trying to use that to encourage parents, on an ongoing basis, to look for those teachable moments where they can have conversations about sexuality," she said. "Those TV shows and movies have actually really opened up those teachable moments and those conversations, which is a good thing."

But Zaslow suggested this type of discussion should begin in classrooms because media education is limited in our country, compared with the United Kingdom and Canada.

"The United States has some of the worst media education," she said. "And it is because we are the biggest producers of media—[producers] have a large strong hold."

Being able to determine fact versus fiction in terms of media messages is integral to adolescent decision-making.

"We want to work with young people about developing a filter for some of those media messages because we know that there are lots of different messages in the media about teen pregnancy," Schrock said. "We would like to use those TV shows as a way to help teens talk about real life and get them to really start thinking about how it would affect their own life in applying it."

To start, Kruse encouraged using education to defeat age-old stereotypes of teen mothers, many of which are perpetuated on TV.

"Just because you got pregnant at a young age, you can still go to college," Kruse said. "You can still have a good career, you can still have a good life for yourself.

Getting pregnant at a young age doesn't mean your life's over."

Evaluating the Impact of MTV's *16 and Pregnant* on Teen Viewers' Attitudes About Teen Pregnancy

Media Use

- American children ages 11–14 spend approximately 8 hours and 40 minutes with media every day—more than 5 hours are spent watching television.
- Teens age 15–18 spend nearly 8 hours with media every day—4 hours and 22 minutes are spent watching television.

Teens' Perspectives

New polling data, from a nationally representative survey commissioned by The National Campaign, asked teens their opinions on media and teen pregnancy and their views about *16 and Pregnant*. Findings from young people ages 12–19 include:

- Six in ten teens have watched at least some of *16 and Pregnant*.
- Among those teens who have watched the show, 82% think that the show helps teens better understand the challenges of teen pregnancy and parenthood, compared to 15% who believe that it glamorizes teen pregnancy.
- In addition, the clear majority of teen boys (67%) and girls (79%) agree with the statement, "When a TV show or character I like deals with teen pregnancy, it makes me think more about my own risk (of becoming pregnant/causing a pregnancy) and how to avoid it."

Introduction

Concerns exist about the sexual content in popular media and the influence these images and messages might have on young people's sexual behavior. Sexual content in the media has increased over the past several decades, and research has found that the sexual content in media can influence teens, attitudes about sex and contraception, and may also influence their sexual behavior. In fact, research has documented an association between exposure to sexual content on television and teen pregnancy.

Little research, however, has been conducted to better understand how media might also have positive effects by, for example, decreasing risky sexual behavior and promoting healthier decisions among teens. Given that teens' use of media has increased over the past decade, and that the amount of sexual content in the media has also increased, it is reasonable to explore whether media might be used to help prevent teen pregnancy.

This *Science Says* presents results from an evaluation study designed to learn more about how watching and discussing episodes of the popular MTV documentary-style reality show *16 and Pregnant* influences teens, perceptions of getting pregnant, and becoming a parent at a young age. The document also includes new public opinion data that shed light on teens, perceptions of *16 and Pregnant,* in particular, and their views about how media might influence teens, decisions about sex more generally. Complete results from this new public opinion survey of both teens and adults will be available soon in a Campaign report entitled "With One Voice 2010."

About the Evaluation

The National Campaign worked with innovation, Research, and Training, Inc. (iRT) to learn more about teens, perceptions of the show *16 and Pregnant*, and whether or not watching and discussing the show affected their attitudes about teen pregnancy. In partnership with the Boys & Girls Clubs of America (see more information below), 18 clubs in one southern state participated in this research study. The clubs were randomly assigned to either see the episodes (treatment = nine clubs) or not (control = nine clubs). All participants obtained parental consent and completed questionnaires at baseline and again a week later. Teens in the treatment groups viewed three episodes of the first season of *16 and Pregnant* (the "Maci," "Amber," and "Ebony" episodes). Boys & Girls Club members watched one episode per day and the episodes were shown in different orders at different clubs. A group leader led a discussion of the shows with the teens each day. Control group teens did not view or discuss the episodes at the clubs, but did complete the pre- and post-test questionnaires.

A total of 162 teens participated and completed both the pre- and post-test questionnaires (78 from the control group and 84 from the treatment group). The average age of the participants was 13.5 years, ranging from 10 to 19 years. . . . Most participants were female (62%), and three-quarters (75%) were African American. Nearly three-quarters of all participants (73%) received reduced or free lunch at school. About one-third (34%) of the participants reported having had sex.

Television Shows vs. Prevention Programs

Television and other media alone do not cause—and cannot prevent—teen pregnancy. However, entertainment media can reach millions of teens with important messages about teen pregnancy. It is important to note that there is a critical distinction between this evaluation—which attempts to understand teens, views about teen pregnancy as a result of watching and discussing

MTV's *16 and Pregnant*—versus an impact evaluation of a prevention program whose sole purpose is to reduce teen pregnancy. While evidence-based teen pregnancy prevention programs are guided by specific behavioral theories and have the explicit goal of changing behavior to reduce risk of teen pregnancy, television shows such as *16 and Pregnant* are created for entertainment with the goal of attracting viewers and keeping them engaged.

Key Findings

- *16 and Pregnant* got teens talking and thinking about teen pregnancy. The majority of teens who watched and discussed the show in a group also later talked to a friend about the show. More than one-third—40%—talked to a parent afterward and about one-third spoke to a sibling or girlfriend/boyfriend. Clearly, this show is an excellent conversation-starter for teens.
- The more teens talked about the show, the less likely they were to think that teen pregnancy and teen parenthood are commonplace, or to agree with the statement, "Most teens want to get pregnant." Parents and practitioners should be encouraged to talk about this show (and others like it) to the teens in their lives to help ensure that these young people know what the adults in their lives think about these shows and their messages.
- The teens in this study enjoyed watching and discussing the *16 and Pregnant* episodes and thought that the show was realistic. Neither the boys nor girls who watched the episodes wanted to imitate the teens in the episodes they watched. In fact, nearly all teens (93%) who watched the show agreed (53% strongly agreed) with the statement: "I learned that teen parenthood is harder than I imagined from these episodes." Although some have claimed that the show "glamorizes" teen pregnancy, the findings from this evaluation and the polling data noted above show that teens do not share that view.

Other Findings

A number of other findings emerged from this study. Analysis of the pre- and post-test questionnaires determined that regardless of whether or not they watched the episodes, girls had more realistic expectations than boys did about teen parenthood. In particular, many girls felt that becoming a teen parent would make it hard for them to finish high school, to attend college, and to achieve future career goals. Research shows that fewer than four in ten mothers who have a child before they turn 18 earn a high school diploma by age 22. Overall, girls disagreed more strongly than boys with the notion that becoming a teen parent would help to get their lives on track. Teen boys were less likely than the girls to believe that teen parenthood would have a negative impact on their educational or career goals.

In addition, teens who saw and discussed the episodes reported that they enjoyed watching and talking about the show and that they learned something new from doing so. The more they liked it, the more likely they were to have negative views about teen pregnancy.

Teens were eager to recommend the show to others; 89% of participants agreed (56% of those strongly agreed) with the statement: "I think all teenagers should watch a show like this." Many said they would recommend that friends participate in the discussion, too.

Cautionary Note

A few findings from the evaluation suggest that viewing *16 and Pregnant* could have an undesirable effect on some viewers. More specifically, teens who watched and discussed the episodes were more likely to believe that teens do want to get pregnant, compared to those in the group who did not watch or discuss the episodes. Note that discussing the episodes later with a friend seemed to moderate this finding somewhat. Also, among teens who had never had sex, those who viewed and discussed the episodes were more likely than those who had not to believe that most teens want to get pregnant, and that if they were to get pregnant or cause a pregnancy, that they "will be with the baby's mother/father forever."

In addition, regardless of whether they watched and discussed the episodes or not, sexually experienced teens were more likely than those teens who had not had sex to think that if they became a teen parent, their parents would help them raise the baby. Sexually experienced teens were also more likely to believe that people would view them as more mature if they had a child as a teen.

What It All Means

These types of shows reach a large number of teens and can be used in a positive way. The results of this project clearly support the idea that teens are interested in watching and discussing reality television shows about teen pregnancy, and that messages about the realities of teen pregnancy and parenting in these shows can influence teens, attitudes about the challenges of teen parenthood. Given the popularity of these shows, their messages clearly reach a large number of teens. For all these reasons, adults who work with teens should consider viewing and discussing episodes of such shows in their activities or programs that are designed to help reduce teen pregnancy and/or foster positive youth development more broadly.

Parents should use these shows to help them talk to their teens about sex, love, and relationships. According to the new polling data noted above, three-quarters of teens and adults agree that stories and events in TV shows and other media can be a good way to start conversations about sex, love, and relationships. This project provides further evidence to suggest that documentary-style shows, presented in ways that are appealing and interesting to teens, can be a useful way to start these conversations. Parents should be encouraged to watch these shows with their teens and use the story lines to openly discuss the challenges typically brought on by too-early pregnancy and parenthood.

If teens express positive views about teen pregnancy, talk to them about the benefits of waiting to start a family. Some teens might see pregnancy and parenthood as something that would make them seem more mature, would help them get their life on track, or would be a way to keep a boyfriend/ girlfriend. It is crucial for parents and other adults to acknowledge that parenthood can be positive and rewarding, but that babies need and deserve adult parents, and that getting an education and having a stable, long-term partner can help them become good parents.

Groups such as Boys & Girls Clubs of America (BGCA) can play a valuable role in efforts to reduce teen pregnancy. The evaluation study summarized here shows that groups like the BGCA can be valuable leaders in preventing teen pregnancy because they work with many young people who are at high risk of teen pregnancy. Many of the BGCA facilitators enjoyed the sessions described here, although it is also true that some felt unprepared to lead the discussions. Training group discussion leaders could help to ensure that they feel comfortable in discussing the risks and problems associated with teen pregnancy and parenthood, and in dispelling the idea that teen pregnancy happens to most teen girls (it does not) or that early parenthood is a good way to get a teen's life on track. There is value in enlisting the help of health educators and experts in health communications who are well versed in adolescent development and youth culture particularly for community partners who may not be familiar with current media or with the topic of teen pregnancy.

EXPLORING THE ISSUE

Do Reality Television Shows Have a Negative Influence on Teenage Pregnancy and Parenting?

Critical Thinking and Reflection

- What are some arguments made by each side with which you agree or disagree?
- What are the strengths and weaknesses of the two positions made in this issue? Compare and contrast the competing arguments made about reality television's impact on teens. What conclusions do you reach about the different narratives and research?
- Think more broadly about the amount of reality television and teen parenthood. What is the impact in the end on how teenagers think about their long-term goals and behaviors?

Is There Common Ground?

While programming constantly changes, it is safe to assume that reality television, due to its low production costs, will remain a popular choice for television programmers. We may not all agree on the impact of such shows, but most would agree that we want children to be literate, aware, and thoughtful of the media that they are consuming. Chances are that much of the programming will become increasingly outrageous. What are adults doing to help children and adolescents navigate those messages? Should we teach critical media literacy in schools? In the home? How do we help children and adolescents put these shows into their proper perspective?

Additional Resources

"Why America Loves Reality TV" from *Psychology Today:* http://www.psychologytoday .com/articles/200109/why-america-loves-reality-tv

Reality TV World: http://www.realitytvworld.com/

The Case for Reality TV: http://www.theatlantic.com/magazine/archive/2007/05/the-case-for-reality-tv/5791/

The New Yorker: "Reality Television and American Culture": http://www.newyorker .com/arts/critics/atlarge/2011/05/09/110509crat_atlarge_sanneh

ISSUE 19

Should There Be Harsh Penalties for Teens Sexting?

YES: Lisa E. Soronen, Nicole Vitale, and Karen A. Haase, from "Sexting at School: Lessons Learned the Hard Way," National School Boards Association, *Inquiry & Analysis* (February 2010)

NO: Julie Hilden, from "How Should Teens' 'Sexting'—The Sending of Revealing Photos—Be Regulated?" Findlaw.com (April 28, 2009)

Learning Outcomes

As a result of this issue, readers will be able to:

- Identify arguments made for and against taking teen sexting seriously.
- Compare and contrast the major arguments cited and analysis used in examining penalties for teen sexting.
- Evaluate the ways in which teen sexting affects the lives of teens who participate.

ISSUE SUMMARY

YES: Lisa E. Soronen, Nicole Vitale, and Karen A. Haase are writing on legal issues for the National School Boards Association. This article encourages administrators to hand over cell phone sexting cases to the appropriate law enforcement agencies.

NO: Julie Hilden is a graduate of Harvard College and Yale Law School. A former clerk for Supreme Court Justice Stephen Breyer, she has more recently appeared on *Good Morning America,* Court TV, CNN, and NPR. Hilden argues that harsh penalties are extreme and unjust.

Sexting—the slang term for the use of a cell phone or other similar electronic device to distribute pictures or video of sexually explicit images. It can also refer to text messages of a sexually charged nature.

We know that teens participate in a significant amount of interaction electronically. In 2010, the average American teen, ages 13–17, sent 3,339 texts per month. This can be difficult for adults to understand, as they only send and receive approximately 10 text messages per day. As a result, a decidedly different level of communication occurs among teens while sending text messages.

Why do teens sext? Are the reasons similar? How often does it occur?

According to the National Campaign to Prevent Teen and Unplanned Pregnancy, this is how many teens ages 13–19 are engaging in sending or posting nude or seminude pictures or videos of themselves:

20 percent of teens overall

18 percent of teen boys

22 percent of teen girls

11 percent of young teen girls (ages 13–16)

How many teens are sending or posting sexually suggestive messages?

39 percent of all teens.

36 percent of teen girls.

40 percent of teen boys.

48 percent of teens say they have received such messages.

What accounts for the differences that we see in gender? Why are some teens not engaging in such behavior? Lack of technology? Personal morals? Lack of a trusted person to send such messages to? Once someone presses Send, these images can go anywhere, but who are the pictures, photos, and videos initially being sent to?

71 percent of girls and 67 percent of guys who have sent such images have directed them to their boyfriend or girlfriend.

21 percent of girls and 39 percent of boys have sent them to someone they wanted to hook up with or date.

15 percent have sent them to someone they only met online.

Do they understand the risks? They appear to. Over 70 percent of teens know that sending and posting such photos, videos, or messages "can have serious negative consequences."

Of course the biggest fear that most people have is that a person will share these images with others. How often does that occur?

44 percent of boys and girls say it is common for sexually explicit text messages to be shared with others.

36 percent of girls and 39 percent of boys say it is common for nude or seminude photos to be shared.

Does sexting affect their lives? Many say that it does. For example, 22 percent of teens say that they are more forward and aggressive via electronic communication than in real life; and 38 percent say it makes dating or hooking up more likely. In fact, 29 percent say that sending such messages means you are "expected" to date or hook up.

If that is the impact, what is the motivation? Over 60 percent say it is to be "fun or flirtatious." Over half of girls who send sexually explicit messages or photos were giving their significant other a "sexy present." Almost half sent them in response to something they had received. Even 40 percent of girls say that they sent such messages as a joke. One-third of girls do so to "feel sexy."

What about pressure from their peers? Fifty-one percent of girls say they send such messages due to pressure from a guy. Only 18 percent of teen boys report that pressure from a female. Close to one out of four teens post sexually explicit messages, photos, or videos as a result of being pressured by their friends.

If sexting is so common, what are some helpful guidelines to keep in mind when doing so? According to the National Campaign to Prevent Teen and Unplanned Pregnancy, these five steps should occur before pressing the Send button:

1. **Don't assume that anything you send or post will remain private.** Your messages and images will get passed around, even if you think they won't.
2. **There is no changing your mind in cyberspace—anything you send or post will never truly go away.** Something that seems fun and flirty on a whim will never really die. Potential employers, college recruiters, teachers, coaches, and parents, friends, enemies, strangers, and others may be able to find your past posts, even after you have deleted them.
3. **Don't give in to the pressure to do something that makes you uncomfortable, even in cyberspace.** Peer pressure is major motivation for sexting—a very bad motivation.
4. **Consider the recipient's reaction.** Not everyone will take the messages as you intend. For example, 40 percent of teen girls have sent a sexually explicit message as a joke, but 29 percent of boys take it as a sign that she wants to hook up or date.
5. **Nothing is truly anonymous.** Even if you think you are anonymous online, it may be easier to find you than you realize. Many people learn this the hard way when they think what they are doing will occur without their true identity ever being revealed.

It is not just teens. According to the American Association of Retired Persons (AARP), sexting is up among senior citizens. Relationship coach Susan Blake explains that seniors engage in sexting because they "want sexual activity. They want to flirt. It makes them feel healthy and young."

One senior citizen says that she likes to send sexually explicit messages because she feels that she has a "naughty secret. If you're sitting in a restaurant waiting for your food, you can just talk dirty to someone, and no one knows what you're doing. I would rather talk on the phone. But I'm also comfortable with hiding behind texting if I want to say something dirty."

However, senior citizens are not being charged with harsh penalties in response to their sexting. Teenagers, however, are sometimes finding that their lives will never be the same. Will harsh laws and a punishing adult reaction reduce the degree to which teens send sexually explicit messages? If not, what will?

In this issue, one side argues that schools need a harsh reaction to protect themselves. The opposing view is that we are being far too tough on teens with our treatment of them over sexting. See which argument you find most compelling.

YES

**Lisa E. Soronen, Nicole Vitale,
and Karen A. Haase**

Sexting at School: Lessons Learned the Hard Way

A 16-year-old boy asks his 15-year-old girlfriend to send him a naked photo of herself. She does so via text message, thinking that the photo will remain private and will show him how much she cares about him. Three weeks later, the couple breaks up, and her boyfriend forwards the text message to his friends, who quickly spread the image throughout the school. The girl is teased for months afterward, her grades plummet, and the formerly sunny teen refuses to go to school or to socialize with other students.

As many school attorneys and administrators know, this case is far from isolated. "Sexting," the practice by which teens forward sexually explicit images of themselves or their peers via text messaging, has become increasingly common nationwide. According to a frequently cited survey from the National Campaign to Prevent Teen and Unplanned Pregnancy, one in five teens have sent or posted nude or seminude photos of themselves online or via text message. Twenty-two percent of teens have received a nude or semi-nude photo of someone else. The study found that while most of the images are exchanged between boyfriends or girlfriends, 15 percent of teens have forwarded images to someone they only know online.

The potential detrimental effects that sexting can have on students are vast. Educators, child psychologists, and prosecutors agree that most teens do not understand the implications that sexting may have on their futures. While sexting often originates as a private exchange between a teen and his or her love interest, relationships can quickly deteriorate. Before long, the seemingly private images can be distributed throughout the school. These incidents can be highly embarrassing for students and, in some extreme cases, can have deadly consequences. At least two female students have committed suicide after the sexually explicit photos of themselves sent to a boy were disseminated to classmates. As discussed below, criminal prosecution—including being required to register as a sex offender—is another possible long-term negative consequence of sexting.

This article discusses a number of legal and practical issues related to sexting in schools. Specifically, this article discusses searching cell phones, what steps administrators can and should take upon discovering sexting, anti-sexting policies, and preventing sexting through education.

Searching Cell Phones

School administrators typically find out about sexting through the rumor mill. Of course, the only way administrators can determine if sexting actually has happened and who is involved is to ask students or to "see for themselves." In the ideal world, students will readily admit to being involved in sexting upon being questioned by administrators. In the real world, administrators may feel they need to search cell phones as part of a sexting investigation. Depending on the facts, searching a student's cell phone without a warrant may violate the Fourth Amendment. Likewise, it is at least arguable that searching open text messages on a cell phone without consent violates the Stored Communications Act. To avoid Fourth Amendment and Stored Communications Act issues, school administrators may always seek consent of a student and his or her parents before searching a cell phone as part of a sexting investigation.

Fourth Amendment Concerns

The U.S. Supreme Court held in *New Jersey v. T.L.O.* that school officials may search students as long as the search is reasonable; that is, the search must be justified at its inception and reasonable in scope. According to the Court:

> Under ordinary circumstances, a search of a student by a teacher or other school official will be "justified at its inception" when there are reasonable grounds for suspecting that the search will turn up evidence that the student has violated or is violating either the law or the rules of the school. Such a search will be permissible in its scope when the measures adopted are reasonably related to the objectives of the search and not excessively intrusive in light of the age and sex of the student and the nature of the infraction.

In no reported cases to date has a student challenged administrators searching his or her cell phone in a sexting investigation. However, in *Klump v. Nazareth Area School District*, a federal district court denied a school district's motion to dismiss on the basis of qualified immunity in a case involving a search of a student's cell phone. A teacher confiscated Christopher Klump's cell phone because he displayed the phone in violation of a school policy that prohibited the display or use of cell phones during school hours. The teacher and the assistant principal called other students in Christopher's phone directory to see if they were also violating district policy and accessed his text messages and voicemail.

Christopher asserted that these actions constituted an unreasonable search in violation of his Fourth Amendment rights. The court found that confiscation of the cell phone was justified because Christopher was caught violating the district's policy prohibiting the use or display of cell phones during school hours. However, the search of the cell phone violated Christopher's Fourth Amendment rights because: "They had no reason to suspect at the outset that such a search would reveal that Christopher Klump himself was violating another school policy; rather, they hoped to utilize his phone as a tool to catch other students, violations." The search of the cell phone, therefore, was not reasonable in scope.

It is not too difficult to imagine a fact pattern involving sexting where a school district could argue persuasively that an administrator's search of a student's text messages and pictures was justified at its inception and reasonable in scope. For example, let's say Christopher Klump showed an administrator an inappropriate picture a classmate texted him. As part of an investigation, the administrator should determine whether the named classmate actually sent Christopher the picture. It would seem a search of the classmate's text messages sent to Christopher Klump would be justified at its inception and reasonable in scope. Likewise, simply asking the classmate to present his cell phone to the administrator and calling the number in Christopher's phone associated with the text probably would be all the proof an administrator would need.

School administrators can take a few steps to make it more likely that searches of cell phones in sexting investigations pass Fourth Amendment muster. First, as described in the paragraph above, in some instances administrators can rely on information provided by technology—rather than just rumors—to determine whose phone to search and where to look. Second, while common sense indicates that sexting is a violation of school rules, explicitly prohibiting it in a school district policy or a student code of conduct will make it clear. Third, providing notice in the school district's cell phone policy that the administration may search cell phones if it has reasonable suspicion that a search will reveal that school rules have been violated, may also support a district's argument that a search was reasonable.

If school administrators ask school resource officers (SROs) to search a student's cell phone, the more demanding probable cause standard may apply. Likewise, if school administrators ask the police to search the student's phone, the probable cause standard likely will apply to the search.

In some instances, administrators may need to search to find a cell phone; for example, let's say Christopher's classmate in the example above denies having a cell phone at school. The time Christopher received the text message or a call to the student's parents about whether he generally brings a cell phone to school may cast doubt on the student's claim that his phone is not with him. If administrators search for the phone, they should consider T.L.O.'s requirement that the search be permissible in scope when determining where to look.

Stored Communications Act Concerns

In *Klump v. Nazareth Area School District*, Christopher Klump also argued that the school district violated Pennsylvania's version of the federal Stored Communications Act (SCA) by accessing his text messages, phone numbers, and call records. It is a violation of the federal SCA (which is very similar to Pennsylvania's statute) to: "(1) intentionally access without authorization a facility through which an electronic communication service is provided; or (2) intentionally exceed an authorization to access that facility; and thereby obtain, alter, or prevent authorized access to a wire or electronic communication while it is in electronic storage in such system."

The district court concluded that a call log and phone number directory are not "communications" under the statute, so searching them did not violate Pennsylvania's SCA. However, concluding that Christopher's "voice mail at least would have been stored by his cell phone provider and not in the cell phone itself," the court did not dismiss the unlawful access claims related to the voicemail or text messages.

While not argued in this case, under the federal SCA courts have held that open emails of which a recipient maintains a copy do not meet the definition of "electronic storage."

"Electronic storage" is defined as: "(A) any temporary, intermediate storage of a wire or electronic communication incidental to the electronic transmission thereof; and (B) any storage of such communication by an electronic communication service for purposes of backup protection of such communication." An open email is not in "temporary, intermediate storage"; instead, it is in "post-transmission storage." Open emails that users store on an Internet Service Provider's (ISP) system are not backup copies; backup copies are made by ISPs to protect the email from technical problems before it is transmitted.

Under this rationale, Christopher's opened text messages contained on his phone would not be in "electronic storage." Instead, they would be in post-transmission storage and are not "backups" maintained by his cell phone company to protect its system integrity. In other words, had the court analyzed this case by applying the definition of "electronic storage," it likely would have concluded Christopher's open text messages did not fall under the SCA.

The federal SCA allows users to authorize access to communications otherwise protected by the statute. To avoid possibly violating the SCA school districts may seek authorization from the student and his or her parents before searching a student's cell phone. If consent is denied, the federal SCA allows the government to compel the content of electronic communications from providers of "electronic communication service" and "remote computing service," which includes cell phone companies, after obtaining a search warrant, subpoena, etc.

Sexting Has Been Discovered . . . Now What?

When sexting arises in the school setting, it can have broad practical and legal implications. When school administrators discover sexting, they should consider at least the following: (1) telling the parents of all the students involved; (2) reporting the sexting to the police; (3) reporting the sexting as suspected abuse or neglect; (4) minimizing exposure to child pornography charges; (5) whether, who, and how to discipline the students involved; and (6) preventing the harassment and bullying of students involved in sexting. The rather dramatic story of a Virginia assistant principal charged with possession of child pornography and failure to report suspected child abuse after he asked a student to send him a seminude picture in the student's cell phone as part of a sexting investigation, illustrates what can happen when a school administrator fails to take the steps listed above.

Assistant principal Ting-Yi Oei explained that after he viewed an inappropriate picture contained in a student's cell phone, he showed the picture to the principal, who instructed him to transfer it to Oei's computer "in case we needed it later." Oei did not know how to do this, so the teen texted the picture to Oei's cell phone and told Oei how to forward it to his work email address. Oei could not identify the person in the photograph, concluded it was probably not a student at the school, told the principal what happened, and assumed the matter was closed.

Two weeks later, the boy caught with the photo was suspended for pulling down a girl's pants in class. Oei told the boy's mother about the sexting when he told her about the suspension. She was outraged that he had not informed her of the picture earlier and complained to the police. They conducted an investigation, and Oei showed them the photograph on his cell phone after he could not find it on his computer.

A month later, Oei was charged with failure to report suspected child abuse. The commonwealth (district) attorney dropped that charge but later charged him with possession of child pornography. The circuit court dismissed the child pornography charge finding that the picture—which at worst maybe showed a nipple—did not meet the definition of "sexually explicit visual material," pursuant to Virginia's child pornography statute.

Tell the Parents of All Students Involved

School administrators should notify parents promptly upon discovering that their child is the subject of, is in possession of, or has sent inappropriate pictures for many reasons. First, contacting parents immediately should demonstrate that the pictures were viewed for investigative purposes only, dissuading parents from pursuing child pornography charges. Second, as the Ting-Yi Oei incident illustrates, some parents want to know about sexting as soon as possible. Any concern regarding a parent's potential overreaction is outweighed by the district's duty to act in place of the parents while their children are at school. Parents should be told of this dangerous behavior, and administrators should follow abuse and neglect reporting statutes if they fear a parent's reaction might be violent.

Tell the Police

State law or school district policy may require school districts to report to the police certain crimes that have happened on school grounds. It may come as a surprise to school administrators that sexting in some states in some instances may be a crime. In fact, students in a number of states have been charged criminally and convicted of violating child pornography laws by sexting. For example, students likely could be prosecuted for sexting under Ohio's Illegal Use of Minor in Nudity-oriented Material or Performance statute, which prohibits "[p]hotograph[ing] any minor . . . in a state of nudity, or creat[ing], direct[ing], produc[ing], or transfer[ing] any material or performance that shows the minor in a state of nudity. . . ." Under the Ohio statute, it appears that both the girlfriend and the boyfriend from the example at the beginning of this article could be convicted. The girlfriend photographed herself nude and transferred the picture; the boyfriend further transferred the picture. The Ohio Legislature is considering adopting a statute specifically aimed at minors sexting.

Prosecutors across the country have taken various approaches to sexting. Parties who have been charged include the "victim," the recipient, and the disseminator. Prosecutors in some instances may not charge anyone at all or may recommend that those charged participate in a diversion program. Few reported cases discuss whether, and under what circumstances, students can be criminally prosecuted for sexting. . . . In this case, a school district discovered sexting and informed the district attorney. The parents of the girls depicted in the photographs successfully challenged the district attorney's threat to criminally prosecute them unless they participated in an education and counseling program. This case has been appealed to the Third Circuit.

District attorneys have been heavily criticized for prosecuting children engaged in sexting—particularly when the result is the child prosecuted being required to register as a sex offender. As one district attorney points out, child pornography laws were intended to prosecute child sexual predators, not minors who may not even know what child pornography is. Miller is a great example of backlash against district attorneys prosecuting sexting cases.

To respond to myriad concerns raised by sexting, in 2009, lawmakers in at least 11 states have introduced legislation addressing the issue, according to the National Conference of State Legislatures. At least two other states— Kentucky and Virginia—are expected to consider legislation in 2010. . . . To summarize, a number of states have adopted (Vermont, North Dakota) or proposed (Ohio, Pennsylvania) legislation that specifically addresses sexting as a crime separate from child pornography with lesser penalties. Other states have created (Nebraska) or proposed to create (New York) an affirmative defense to child pornography statutes for sexting in some circumstances. Two states have proposed to create (New Jersey, Pennsylvania) educational diversionary programs for students charged or convicted of sexting. Two other states (Colorado, Oregon) have amended their Internet sexual exploitation of a minor statutes to include texting. Finally, two states have proposed to educate students about sexting (New York, New Jersey).

Given that sexting is a new phenomenon and that most child pornography statutes were adopted before cell phones were widely used and sexting was a national problem, school attorneys in most instances will not be able to determine definitely whether a crime has been committed. For this reason, school districts are well-advised to inform the police of sexting so that they can conduct a criminal investigation. However, any school administrator who knows the facts of *Miller v. Skumanick* as described by the district court—where the district attorney threaten to charge the girls depicted in the photographs with felonies that could result in a long prison term, a permanent record, and registration as sex offenders—would think twice before telling the police about sexting. School administrators should not assume all district attorneys will prosecute all sexting cases or that school administrators will be unable to influence the district attorney. Sexting is a new crime. For this reason, many district attorneys likely would welcome input from school district officials on how to handle these cases. Particularly if the district is going to discipline the students involved, the district attorney may be amenable to not charging the students criminally depending on facts of the case.

It is always a good idea for school district officials to try to foster cooperation with local police and the prosecutors. The best time to approach the district attorney's office about this issue is before sexting occurs on campus and before a district attorney has had the chance to decide that prosecuting sexting cases will be the new "tough on crime" tactic. Likewise, part of building a good relationship with the district attorney's office may be asking for input on how the district should punish sexting and inviting the district attorney to participate in the district's sexting education and prevention efforts.

Report Sexting as Suspected Child Abuse and Neglect

A sexted image may constitute child abuse or neglect, depending on the state's definition of these terms and what is exactly depicted in the photograph. All states have child abuse and neglect reporting statutes which apply to school districts. Most, if not all, statutes include in the definition of child abuse and neglect sexual crimes against a child. For example, Virginia's definition of an abused or neglected child include one: "[w]hose parents or other person responsible for his care commits or allows to be committed any act of sexual exploitation or any sexual act upon a child in violation of the law." Virginia's Department of Social Services states that child abuse occurs when a parent: "[c]ommits or allows to be committed any illegal sexual act upon a child including incest, rape, fondling, indecent exposure, prostitution, or allows a child to be used in any sexually explicit visual material."

Ting-Yi Oei admitted that he did not think about the sexting incident in terms of whether it violated Virginia's child abuse and neglect reporting statute. It is unlikely Oei could have been successfully prosecuted under this statute for at least three reasons. First, he did not know the identity of the girl, though her identity was determined later. Second, he did not know she was only 16. Third, the circuit court ruled in Oei's possession of child pornography case that the picture was not "sexually explicit visual material." Had Oei known the girl's identity and age, and had the picture been more revealing, Oei likely would have had a reporting obligation under Virginia law.

In short, depending on the state's definition of abuse and neglect and depending on the visual depiction in the sexted photograph, school districts may have an obligation to report sexting under child abuse and neglect reporting statutes.

Minimize Exposure to Child Pornography Charges

School administrators should take steps to avoid being accused of possession of child pornography by prosecutors or disgruntled parents. This may simply involve turning over confiscated evidence of sexting to the police immediately.

In fact, Oei may have avoided being charged altogether had he taken possession of the boy's phone and turned it over to the police promptly, like the school officials in Miller, instead of receiving and maintaining the photo on his own phone.

School administrators should also take steps to avoid charges of disseminating child pornography. As described later in this article, a lawsuit has been filed against a Washington state school district which rather cryptically accuses school officials of showing sexted photographs of a student to "other adults" in violation of Washington's dissemination of child pornography statute. The district denies doing so in its answer. Regardless of what actually happened in this case, it illustrates that a school administrator who discovers sexting should not share the images with other school employees much less non-employees.

The Utah legislature, likely in response to the Ting-Yi Oei incident, has passed a law to ensure that school employees and others cannot be liable "when reporting or preserving data" in a child pornography investigation. . . .

Discipline the Students Involved

As the case described below illustrates, school districts should consider disciplining all students involved in the sexting—the student featured in the image, students who received the image (unless they deleted it immediately), and students who disseminated the image—equally if possible.

The parents of a Washington state high school student are suing the school district for violating Washington's sexual equality statute for only punishing their daughter in a sexting incident. The parents admit in their complaint that their daughter took a naked picture of herself which was circulated among other students. The school district suspended her for one year from the cheer squad for violating the athletic code. Her parents alleged that the school district violated Washington's sexual equality statute by punishing only her and not the football players who possessed and viewed the picture of her. The school district responded that it did not discipline the football players because it did not know who sent, received, or forwarded the pictures. The daughter refused to tell the district because she did not "want to get anyone in trouble."

Whether the sexual equality claim is successful, plaintiffs do have a fair point that the boys who received and did not immediately delete the photograph of their daughter—or, worse yet, forwarded it—also should have received punishment. While a court likely will not be sympathetic to the daughter's refusal to inform the district of the football players who received and forwarded the picture of her, it likewise might not be sympathetic to the school district's failure to investigate further without her help.

Preventing Bullying and Harassment

Eighteen-year-old Jessica Logan committed suicide after being bullied and harassed after her ex-boyfriend forwarded to other students nude photos she took of herself and sent to him. Her parents are suing the school district, who was aware of the sexting, claiming that the district did not do enough to stop her from being harassed. Whether their claim against the district will be successful, it illustrates that districts should take measures to prevent harassment before and following a sexting incident.

Preventing bullying and harassment at school generally is a difficult task. At minimum, those involved in a sexting incident should be specifically instructed not to harass the "victims" of sexting. Likewise, before a sexting incident occurs, parents and school staff should be informed that sexting may occur, discipline will result, and harassment is prohibited. If an incident occurs, these messages might have to be reiterated. Finally, if harassment or bullying related to a sexting incident occurs, the district's anti-harassment/bullying policy should be followed and harassers should be disciplined.

Anti-sexting Policies

Adopting anti-sexting policies may be one approach school districts can take to prevent sexting. Obviously, no anti-sexting policy will stop sexting altogether, no matter how carefully written or widely circulated. However, an anti-sexting policy will put students and their parents on notice that sexting is unacceptable and has serious consequences.

School districts may take a variety of policy approaches to prevent sexting. Districts may revise existing policies addressing acceptable use, student codes of conduct, cell phones, harassment and bullying, or other similar subject areas, to prohibit sexting. School districts may ban cell phone use during school or cell phone possession at school altogether to prevent sexting. Some boards may decide that they need a separate policy addressing sexting.

Districts adopting a comprehensive anti-sexting policy should consider including the following elements. First, an anti-sexting policy should clearly state that the mere possession of sexually explicit digital pictures on any device is prohibited regardless of whether the state's child pornography law is violated. Second, the policy should state that all involved in sexting, unless they deleted images right away, will be punished. For example, student handbook language should prohibit "sending, sharing, viewing, or possessing pictures, text messages, emails, or other material of a sexual nature in electronic or any other form on a computer, cell phone, or other electronic device." Third, the policy should inform students that their parents and the police may be contacted and sexting may be reported as suspected child abuse or neglect. Fourth, the policy should put students on notice that administrators may search their cell phones if they have reasonable suspicion a student has been involved in sexting. Fifth, the consequences for sexting should be clearly stated but should include discretionary wording that allows administrators to adjust punishments up or down as appropriate. Finally, the policy should prohibit harassment and bullying related to sexting incidents and should punish nonconforming behavior.

Education as Prevention

Education professionals—including school lawyers—should make parents, staff, and students aware of the existence of and dangers of sexting. School districts should consider a variety of actions to raise awareness of and increase education about sexting. Districts may partner with other community organizations or public offices to provide staff trainings on bullying, cyber-bullying, and computer/Internet safety, including sexting and safety on social networking sites. This can include in-school assemblies for students, professional development for staff, training for school board members, distribution of school rules and policies through student handbooks, newsletters/correspondence to the community, meeting with parent groups, and resources on the school webpage and public forums.

Any education around sexting can and should be aimed at the whole community when possible. This means including students, board members, and staff as well as parents and community members. While the majority of recent press has involved middle and high school students, education regarding computer/Internet/technology safety should include younger children as appropriate. A variety of websites and documents provide information about sexting for students, parents, and educators.

Conclusion

The world of social interaction through new technologies is evolving at break-neck speed. Because young people are trendsetters—particularly when technology is involved—schools are affected by these changes. Disturbing, new technology trends like sexting have significant legal implications for school districts that may not be immediately obvious even to an experienced school administrator or school lawyer. However, sexting has been a growing problem long enough to give us the Ting-Yi Oei incident, Washington state case, and the Jessica Logan case, all of which are full of lessons learned about sexting. School attorneys must pass these lessons learned on to their clients.

How Should Teens' "Sexting"— The Sending of Revealing Photos—Be Regulated?

Recently, the *Wall Street Journal* and its law blog reported on a Pennsylvania controversy over "sexting"—the practice of sending nude or semi-nude photos of oneself or others via cell phone. After some "sexted" photos were confiscated from students at a high school, the local District Attorney threatened to file broad child-pornography charges if the teens were not willing to enroll in a five-week compulsory educational program covering topics such as "what it means to be a girl in today's society." (This topic is telling; sexting controversies often seem to be connected to adults' discomfort with girls' expression of their sexuality. It seems likely, too, that discomfort with gay teens' sexuality will eventually lead to a sexting controversy as well.)

The ACLU rightly responded with a lawsuit. Because First Amendment rights were at issue, the suit could properly be filed prior to charges being brought, in order to address the ongoing "chilling effect" on speech of the threat of prosecution hanging overhead. A federal judge has temporarily enjoined the D.A. from filing charges, with a hearing to occur in June.

These particular charges are ill-grounded in law, as the ACLU has pointed out. The photos at issue show teen girls in their bras or, in one case, topless. In contrast, child-pornography laws typically cover lascivious displays of the genitals and/or sexual activity. Thus, this is likely to be an easy case—as the judge's initial ruling, granting an injunction in the ACLU's favor in part because of its high likelihood of success on the merits, indicates.

This is not the first time that old laws have proven to be a bad fit with recent technology. But it's an especially worrying example of a general problem, because both criminal charges and First Amendment rights are at issue.

In this [article], I will consider how the law should respond when much harder cases regarding sexting come along, as they inevitably will. These cases would involve photos of underage teens having sex, displaying their genitals in a lascivious way, or both. Accordingly, these cases could validly form the basis for child-pornography charges. But should they always trigger charges? Or should the law be adjusted to take into account the factual nuances of the case?

From *Findlaw.com*, April 28, 2009. Copyright © 2009 by Julie Hilden. Reprinted by permission of the author.

Should There Be "Romeo and Juliet" and Age-Specific Exceptions for Sexting?

There is no question that if an adult traffics in photos that fit the child-pornography laws—that is, photos that include a lascivious display of an underage person's genitals, or show an underage person having sex—it is a very serious crime, as well as despicable behavior. Indeed, the Supreme Court recently issued an opinion allowing the prosecution of even those traffickers who offer virtual child pornography (involving no real children) but believe it is real—as I discussed in a prior column.

But what if teenagers take the photographs and do the trafficking, and the subjects and recipients of the photos are exclusively the teenagers themselves? Should the crime—and the penalties—be the same?

My answer is a strong "No." We should craft new laws specifically for sexting before old laws—designed for graver and much more morally bankrupt, dangerous, and exploitative contexts—are applied to sexting, and serious injustice results.

One good model for the regulation of teens' sexting might be the statutory rape laws—which sometimes offer a so-called "Romeo and Juliet" exception when the two parties to an act of sex are close in age (say, 18 and 16, or 17 and 15). If a 16-year-old "sexts" a photo of himself or herself at an 18-year-old high school classmate's invitation, surely that is far less disturbing than if the 16-year-old does so at the invitation of a 40-year-old adult.

Such exceptions might accord well with our sense of when sexting is really disturbing, and appropriately deemed a crime, and when it is better addressed (if at all) with non-criminal remedies such as school suspension, parental punishments, and the like. Notably, the ACLU, in the Pennsylvania case, has suggested that "sexting," in some cases, is not innocuous and may perhaps be penalized—but not through the criminal law.

The Tricky Issues of Consent That Sexting Raises, Especially with Respect to Forwarding

"Romeo and Juliet" exceptions in the sexting context probably will do more good than harm, in practice. But they will also have costs, if they are applied as bright-line rules.

That's because sexting is, in a way, more complicated than statutory rape. Statutory rape, by definition, comes out of a consensual act of sex; if it didn't, it would just be rape. The argument is that the young person's consent is not valid due to his or her immaturity, not that consent was not given. Thus, defining a crime as statutory rape moots out the consent issue. But often, the nature of sexting is intertwined with issues of consent and lack of consent that cannot be so easily put aside.

For instance, a 16-year-old sophomore girl might "sext" a nude photo she has taken of herself to her 18-year-old senior boyfriend, yet not intend that he share it with his 18-year-old friends. In my view, the girl's sexting the photo to the boyfriend would and should be immune from prosecution under a Romeo and Juliet exception—but one might argue that his forwarding of the photo to his same-age friends should not be immune (especially, but perhaps not only, if the girl did not consent to the forwarding). In other words, with respect to sexting, a pure age-based Romeo and Juliet exception, one that renders consent irrelevant, could be a refuge for scoundrels.

This example shows a strong tension between simple, bright-line age-based safe harbors for sexting, and a nuanced inquiry into whether the original "sexter" consented to forwarding. And there may be another nuance as well: Based on my admittedly limited knowledge as a member of Generation X and a viewer of the documentary *American Teen* (which covers a sexting story, among others), it seems to me that sexting in high school may be intimately bound up with issues of popularity, insecurity, and humiliation. And that explosive mix could lead to important and tricky issues regarding consent, particularly consent to forwarding.

For instance, a teen might authorize forwarding, but then later falsely claim that he or she did not consent, if the forwarding was accompanied by the forwarder's humiliating commentary on his or her body or if such commentary by recipients led to humiliation at school. Parental disapproval—or ignorance—of teen relationships could lead to lying, too. In addition, a good-looking teen could deem it cooler to pretend that he or she was not, in fact, the driving force ensuring that a particularly flattering and explicit photo of him or her had ended up being "sexted" to the whole school but was "shocked, shocked to discover" that this had occurred.

In sum, I suspect that there is a whole complex anthropology here that it will be difficult for adults to fully understand. High-school communities might have unspoken "default rules," such as: "You can forward, but only with the photographer's—or subject's—okay." Or, "You can forward, but only to our clique, not to outsiders."

It's worth considering here that the worst sexting abuses, among teenagers, might lead to a civil claim for intentional infliction of emotional distress, or to expulsion from school. In light of these possible remedies, as well as the chance that parents will take action, it's possible that Romeo and Juliet exceptions, although not ideal, might be good enough.

Such exceptions would still allow authorities to crack down on the 18-year-old senior who takes and "sexts" a photo of a 13-year-old eighth-grader, and who truly is engaging in child pornography. Yet these exceptions would also avoid imposing stiff criminal penalties on more-or-less same-age kids for what is, in essence, ugly immaturity, not crime. Alternatively, a compromise solution would create low-level misdemeanor offenses relating to sexting—offenses that would ensure that teenagers, who are often impulsive, could not ruin their lives with a single, ill-considered forward.

EXPLORING THE ISSUE

Should There Be Harsh Penalties for Teens Sexting?

Critical Thinking and Reflection

- What are some arguments made by each side with which you agree or disagree?
- What are the strengths and weaknesses of the two positions made in this issue?
- Compare and contrast the competing arguments made about harsh responses to sexting. Think more broadly about teens' sexting. Is it healthy or unhealthy? Natural or dangerous? What are the larger implications of sexting behaviors? What conclusions do you reach about the different arguments cited?

Is There Common Ground?

No one wants to see teens feel humiliated as a result of sexting messages being shared, or even made public. Is the answer harsh penalties or education? Our laws are still evolving regarding how to respond to teen sexting. However, that shouldn't stop us from better educating children about digital citizenship. Are children receiving a proper education in this regard? Is this the job of schools? Parents? Places of worship? Can parents do a better job being aware of who their children are communicating with? Are there proper limits on electronic communication for children as they develop their digital citizenship skills? Should parents monitor what their children are posting? Do children know what their parents' expectations are of them online?

Additional Resources

Psychology Today on teens' sexting:

> http://www.psychologytoday.com/blog/teen-angst/201103/sexting-teens

ABC News and "Sexting Teens Going Too Far":

> http://abcnews.go.com/Technology/WorldNews/sexting-teens/story?id=6456834

Pew Internet and American Life Project and teens' sexting research:

> http://www.pewinternet.org/Reports/2009/Teens-and-Sexting.aspx

Safeteens.com provides sexting tips:

> http://www.safeteens.com/teen-sexting-tips/

ISSUE 20

Are Open Relationships Healthy?

YES: **Donald Dyson**, from "Seeing Relationships Through a Wider Lens: Open Relationships as a Healthy Option," written for *Taking Sides: Family and Personal Relationships* (2009)

NO: **Stanley Kurtz**, from "Here Come the Brides: Plural Marriage Is Waiting in the Wings," *The Weekly Standard* (December 26, 2005)

Learning Outcomes

As a result of this issue, readers will be able to:

- Identify the major arguments made for and against open relationships.
- Compare and contrast the competing arguments made for and against open relationships in this issue.
- Evaluate the implications of open relationships on the stability of marriage and the larger fabric of American society.

ISSUE SUMMARY

YES: Donald Dyson is assistant professor of human sexuality education at Widener University and the national co-chair of the conference for the American Association of Sexuality Educators, Counselors, and Therapists. Dyson argues that there are essential qualities of a healthy relationship and that an open relationship can be successful.

NO: Stanley Kurtz, a writer and senior fellow at the Ethics and Public Policy Center, argues that allowing same-sex marriage will create a slippery slope, eventually leading to plural marriages. Kurtz contends that such marriages prove destructive to the institution of marriage itself.

During the nineteenth century, the U.S. Congress outlawed polygamy. Although all citizens of the United States were affected by this, the intent was to target members of the Church of Latter-Day Saints, otherwise known as Mormons. In fact, in order for Utah to join the union, the state first had to adopt anti-polygamy laws.

In the late 1870s, George Reynolds, a Mormon resident of Utah, was arrested for having multiple wives. He was convicted and sentenced to two years in prison and was fined $200. Reynolds challenged his conviction, and the case, *Reynolds v. United States,* reached the Supreme Court of the United States.

The Court ruled to uphold anti-polygamy and anti-bigamy laws, stating: "Polygamy has always been odious among the northern and western nations of Europe, and, until the establishment of the Mormon Church, was almost exclusively a feature of the life of Asiatic and of African people."

The bizarre, and frankly racist, choice of words in the Supreme Court opinion seemingly blames people of color, who were largely banned from the Mormon Church at that time, for white, Mormon polygamy. Aside from this language, this decision provides case law in addition to already existing statutory law stating that there is no right to plural marriages.

Although polygamy is illegal in the United States today, sex outside of a primary relationship—including sex outside marriage—occurs to a significant degree. Over the course of a heterosexual marriage, an estimated 24 percent of husbands and 18 percent of wives have sex outside marriage. The temptation to have sex outside marriage is clearly significant, and the practice is fairly common. These statistics reflect the frequency of sex outside marriage *without* the permission of one's spouse.

The difference between infidelity and an open relationship is that in an open relationship, sex occurs outside the marriage or relationship with the consent of one's partner or spouse. Open relationships have been referred to as wife swapping, swinging, and "the lifestyle." "Wife swapping" is perhaps the most misappropriated phrase. First, it implies that all open relationships are inherently heterosexual. Second, it indicates that men possess the power and that women are commodities being traded.

Heterosexual women in open relationships are often in high demand. Women in such relationships often find that they have a significant amount of power. In fact, in some relationships, the man might push to experiment with swinging, only to find that he does not care for it after seeing how sought-after his partner is by other men.

It is a challenge to find open relationships represented positively in television or film. A number of major American cities have swingers clubs that typically cater to heterosexual couples and single women. Due to the stigma associated with open relationships, most people within them work to conceal this from friends, family, and acquaintances.

Although open relationships exist, the majority of Americans believe that sex outside marriage is morally wrong and destructive. These individuals typically regard sexual intimacy and emotional intimacy as inseparable. They will often voice concerns that open relationships are bound to threaten the stability of a person's marriage or committed relationship.

When reading these articles, give some thought to historical factors that influence sexual morality today. Examine how your value system affects your reaction to these articles.

Sometimes the concept of open relationships is addressed in a cursory way by the popular media:

- On one episode of the sitcom *King of Queens,* Doug and Carrie, a married couple featured in the show, both agree that they can have sex outside their marriage with their dream person if the opportunity arises. They have to tell each other who that person is. Carrie shares first, disclosing a famous celebrity. Doug agrees to her choice, then shares his choice: a woman he works with. Amid laughter, Carrie refuses to accept his choice.
- On an episode of the cable series *Entourage,* Vincent Chase, a fictional Hollywood star, meets a woman in public and has sex with her in a nearby hotel room. He asks her whether they can see each other again. She explains she is engaged and can only do this once. She and her fiance both have a list of famous people they are allowed to have sex with.

Despite these examples from popular television shows, monogamy is treated as such a universal value that a significant number of readers may have never heard of polyamory or open relationships before reading this issue. What are some of the reasons that people are hesitant to discuss alternatives to monogamy? What is the impact, positive or negative, of this silence on individual relationships?

Aside from the diverse views of polyamory espoused by Dyson and Kurtz, this issue exposes fundamentally different philosophies. Dyson argues that open relationships can be positive. The argument portrays the impact of open relationships as self-contained to the individuals involved rather than assuming that such an arrangement will have a single, universal impact on all relationships. In contrast, Kurtz contends that any redefinition of marriage will be the start of a slippery slope that will ultimately affect everyone by causing the institution of marriage itself to disintegrate.

What do their views reveal about their position on the Political Ideology Continuum examined in the Introduction to this book? How do your views on this topic compare and contrast with other relationship issues raised in this book? The truth is that many people in open relationships are traditionally conservative, and many people committed to lifetime monogamy are quite liberal.

Regardless of the conclusion that you reach, this issue should help readers understand that one cannot make an assumption that relationship monogamy is a universal value. It is well advised for the reader to talk with a significant other at some point about his or her views on monogamy and relationships.

YES

Donald Dyson

Seeing Relationships Through a Wider Lens: Open Relationships as a Healthy Option

Introduction: The Current Cultural Context for Relationships

There are many ways in which human beings have learned to organize their daily relationships. People sometimes have family with whom they are very close; they have layers of social circles in which they operate, have friends, good friends, and intimate friends (some of whom may also be lovers). People have lovers and spouses; they have husbands and wives; they have partners and playmates. Each of these relationships involves a unique level of intimacy, the level of which is usually determined by the unique natures of the individuals involved.

Often, when people think of ideal relationship structures, they initially think of the types of relationships with which they are most familiar, or to which they have been most exposed. In Western cultures such as the United States, that relationship structure is most often a heterosexual, monogamous, married couple. In fact, so strong is the bias toward this one type of relationship structure, the questions of multiple partners or alternatives to monogamy are rarely discussed or considered.

Pile on top of this unquestioned assumption the cultural and clinical bias we see attached to sexual activity outside a monogamous pair bond. When one even considers sex with someone other than a primary partner, immediately the words "infidelity" and "cheating" spring to mind. Connected to those words are the culturally constructed ways in which people are supposed to respond to such things: anger, jealousy, hurt, rage. Indeed, such behaviors have many iconic images attached to them, including throwing a partner's belongings onto the front yard or cutting the partner's face out of pictures from a photo album.

Almost never does one instantly consider the possibility that the couple has agreed to a relationship style different from the monogamous monopoly. In the Clinton/Lewinsky scandal of the 1990s, in which Hillary Clinton was seen by some as a devoted wife who "stood by her man," and by others as a weak woman who should have divorced her husband for cheating on her—few considered the possibility that then-President Clinton and his wife might have had a different relationship style. Instead, people wondered why Mrs. Clinton remained with her spouse and conjectured that the president must have been

An original essay written for this volume. Copyright © 2009 by Donald A. Dyson, Ph.D. Reprinted by permission.

a sex addict of some sort. This type of knee-jerk reaction clearly illustrates the monogamist (assuming that everyone is or should be monogamous) cultural bias in which we now live.

Add to this the prevailing cultural myth of "The One." This myth creates the expectation that somewhere, out there in the wide world, there is just one special person (think of the idea of a "soulmate") that is waiting for each of us. That person will meet all of our emotional, physical, intellectual, social, and sexual needs. That person will be the "yin" to our "yang." That one special person will become a person's "better half." That one individual, somewhere out there in the world, will "complete" another person. With every Disney movie supporting this romanticized ideal, how can we, as a culture, *not* believe that such a "One" exists?

Consider, then, where this leaves us. We are culturally programmed to consider only traditional, pair-bonded relationships that without question include sexual monogamy. We are taught that the proper definition of sex outside a committed relationship is cheating and it should be punished, or at least pathologized. We are brainwashed with the myth of "The One"; taught to believe that we must find that person within the billions of people in the wide world. In essence, people today are taught from early childhood to hold the highest of standards for potential partners, believing that this special person must be everything to them. Is it any wonder that the divorce statistics for traditional marriage relationships are so high?

One Possible Scenario: Consider This

The author's first experience with a couple who had an open relationship was in meeting a heterosexual married couple in their 60s. After a 30-year relationship, when they were in their 50s, the wife in the couple was diagnosed with a degenerative illness—one they were told would result in a loss of sensation in her sexual organs. In addition, the medicine that she took to slow the progression would result in a decrease in her interest in sex. Given this inevitability, the couple looked for viable alternatives. Neither wanted to end their marriage; they were both still very much in love. They also continued to enjoy an active sex life, which was very important to both of them.

How could they resolve their dilemma? Was the wife to ask the husband to give up sex entirely for the rest of his life? Was the husband to foreswear sexual activity of any kind out of a grand gesture for his wife—a promise that would have been ripe for building resentment and bitterness?

This couple chose to open their relationship. The result was wonderful for both of them. They continued to be happy for 10 years after, and may still be enjoying the love they have nurtured for decades.

Alternatives: What Options Exist?

In reality, there are many "lifestyles" that people have adopted and adapted over time to suit their intimacy needs. In his 1985 work, Dr. William R. Stayton identified 17 different types of relationships. These included traditional monogamy, serial monogamy, singlehood, single parenthood, child-free marriage, polyamory, polyfidelity, open marriage, group marriage, swinging, synergamy, communal living, cohabitation/trial marriage, family clusters, secret affairs, celibate monogamy, and lifelong celibacy/chastity.

Of those 17, polyamory, polyfidelity, open marriage, group marriage, swinging, synergamy, family clusters, and secret affairs are relevant to this discussion. Briefly:

- "Polyamory" is a general term often used to describe all forms of multi-partner relating.
- Polyfidelity is a form of group relationship where all the members agree to be faithful within their group and commit to exist as a family.
- Open marriage is when the primary couple agrees to engage in sexual activities with others outside the dyad. In these situations, couples usually make agreements that dictate the nature of relationships and sexual activities that would be deemed acceptable outside the primary relationship.
- Group marriage usually includes three or more people who agree to "marry" each other.
- Swinging is often a couple's experience and includes the practice of having sexual relationships with others, sometimes in groups, and is founded upon responsible, consensual sexual relating.
- Synergamy is when one or both people involved in a couple have an additional intimate relationship outside that pair. This arrangement often includes the establishment of more than one household and the full involvement of the individual in more than one family system.
- Family clusters include multiple family systems that are interdependent in social, relational, financial, and sometimes sexual functioning.

Secret affairs are relevant here because it is this type of "open relationship" that is most practiced in our current cultural milieu. Current statistics estimate that between 45 and 50 percent of married women and between 50 and 60 percent of married men engage in extramarital sex at some point during their relationships (Atwood and Schwartz, 2002). Although this type of relationship is the most common, it is also the most damaging. It is estimated that 60 to 65 percent of divorces result from secret affairs. In addition, the betrayal of trust, the lack of communication, and the resulting deceptions are often considered to be the most harmful outcomes of these experiences.

The Argument: Why Are Open Relationships Healthy?

With all of these options giving context to the argument, it must be acknowledged that no matter the specifics of the lifestyle or relationship choice, it is the practice of a relationship that makes any of them healthy or unhealthy. It is the behavior of the people involved that has the greatest effect on the relative healthiness of any given relationship style.

Whether checking dating and relationship Web sites, looking through marriage encounter brochures, perusing the outlines of pre-cana marriage classes, or flipping through the pages of *The Complete Idiot's Guide to a Healthy Relationship* (Kuriansky, 2001), each source includes three basic requirements for healthy and long-lasting relationships: trust, honesty, and communication. Although some sources include additional components, the universality of these three is striking.

Let us consider these three in reverse order, beginning with communication. The skills of good communication are the stuff of workshops, lesson plans, relationship and marriage seminars, and countless books and articles. These skills include using direct language, "I" statements, and active listening, among others. What is critically important here, though, is that these skills are not dependent on the type of relationship in which they are used. The same skills work effectively in conversations with one's parents, one's coworkers, and with one's sexual and relationship partners.

Good communication in open relationships is no different from good communication in monogamous ones. Instead, because of the many complexities inherent in dyadic communication, including significant others, those complexities increase exponentially. As a result of this explosion, open relationships might offer individuals increased opportunities for intimacy, as well as challenges to honing their communication skills.

Add to these multiple complexities the sensitive nature of the topics about which the individuals involved are communicating. Conversations are occurring about intimacy needs, sexual desires and fantasies, and personal preferences, as well as limitations, jealousy, attraction, and so much more. Many couples never brave these waters. For people involved in open relationships, they are necessary and sometimes daily conversations.

This level of communication leads directly into the next aspect of healthy relationships: honesty. As individuals broach subjects such as sexual desires, jealousies, and possibilities, the need for and reliance upon honesty increases. In the context of loving relationships, people can begin to express not only the ways that they feel fulfilled by a partner, but also the wants and needs that they are experiencing that are not being met by their primary partner. They can be honest about their sexual and emotional attractions to others. These are topics that are often avoided by other couples for fear of hurting one another or for fear of reprisals for having these types of feelings.

In this way, the honesty required within open relationships can be a very healthy benefit to the relationship overall. Secret keeping and lying take energy. So does honest communication . . .

Finally, the practice of open and honest communication requires a significant degree of vulnerability. As individuals express their wants and needs, their often secret desires and attractions, and their jealousy or fears of loss, the resulting vulnerability is incredibly acute. When this vulnerability is met with equal honesty and care, and when good communication is present and practiced, the result is a significant increase in trust and intimacy between the partners.

Trust, or the reliance upon the strength, integrity, ability, and surety of a person, is certainly a cornerstone of healthy relationships. It is usually built, bit by bit, within the shared experiences of vulnerability and care experienced by people within their relationships. In the context of open relationships, this trust is discussed, explored, and tested in ways that many in monogamous relationships never openly experience. As people practice honesty in their relationships, discuss sexual boundaries and limitations, acknowledge and explore their own desires, and allow their partners to do the same, that trust can increase, and the bonds between people can become stronger.

Summary

No type of relationship, in and of itself, is inherently or unequivocally healthy or unhealthy. It is the practice of relationships that give them their subjective qualification. Healthy relationships require effective, open communication; honesty; and trust. Open relationships can, indeed, be characterized by all of those things, thus characterizing them as healthy.

In addition, open relationships may offer some specific benefits. They can release individuals and relationships from the unspoken specter of monogamy. That is not to say that couples who discuss alternative relationship structures and choose monogamy are less healthy or self-aware. Instead, it demonstrates that the discussion and intentional choices related to monogamy are opportunities for growth and increased intimacy.

Open relationships also have the power to allow individuals to be less "perfect" within their relationships and more human in their strengths and shortcomings. The pressure to be someone's "everything" and the resulting disappointment and resentment when that individual falls short of those expectations have surely been the demise of many potentially wonderful relationships. Exploring options for individuals to have their wants and needs met outside a dyadic relationship might well be the healthiest thing within a given relationship.

As people express their intimacy needs, their sexual fantasies, and their desires, they practice honesty in ways that many others never do. This exploration and reflection allow individuals to build increased levels of sexual awareness and self-awareness that have the potential to benefit not only themselves, but also all of their current and future partners.

And finally, open relationships by necessity include the constant practice of good communication skills. The opportunities to practice talking about all aspects of the relationship increase skills that are easily transferable to other situations. Healthy and honest communication is a benefit to every relationship. Open relationships are not a paradigm to be compared and contrasted with traditional monogamous ones. Instead, they are a paradigm all their own and should be measured against standards for good relationships, not monogamy.

For more information about open relationships, consider *Loving More: The Polyfidelity Primer,* by Ryam Nearing (PEP Publishing, 1992) or *The Ethical Slut,* by Dossie Easton and Catherine A. Liszt (Greenery Press, 1998).

References

J. D. Atwood and L. Schwartz, "Cyber-Sex: The New Affair Treatment Considerations," *Journal of Couple and Relationship Therapy* (vol. 1, no. 3, 2002).

J. Kuriansky, *The Complete Idiot's Guide to Healthy Relationships,* 2d ed. (Fort Smith, AZ: Alpha Books, 2001).

W. R. Stayton, "Alternative Lifestyles: Marital Options," in D. C. Goldberg and P. J. Fink, eds., *Contemporary Marriage: Special Issues in Couples Therapy* (Homewood, IL: Dorsey, 1985).

Here Come the Brides: Plural Marriage Is Waiting in the Wings

On September 23, 2005, the 46-year-old Victor de Bruijn and his 31-year-old wife of eight years, Bianca, presented themselves to a notary public in the small Dutch border town of Roosendaal. And they brought a friend. Dressed in wedding clothes, Victor and Bianca de Bruijn were formally united with a bridally bedecked Mirjam Geven, a recently divorced 35-year-old whom they'd met several years previously through an Internet chatroom. As the notary validated a *samenlevingscontract,* or "cohabitation contract," the three exchanged rings, held a wedding feast, and departed for their honeymoon.

When Mirjam Geven first met Victor and Bianca de Bruijn, she was married. Yet after several meetings between Mirjam, her then-husband, and the De Bruijns, Mirjam left her spouse and moved in with Victor and Bianca. The threesome bought a bigger bed, while Mirjam and her husband divorced. Although neither Mirjam nor Bianca had had a prior relationship with a woman, each had believed for years that she was bisexual. Victor, who describes himself as "100 percent heterosexual," attributes the trio's success to his wives' bisexuality, which he says has the effect of preventing jealousy.

The De Bruijns' triple union caused a sensation in the Netherlands, drawing coverage from television, radio, and the press. With TV cameras and reporters crowding in, the wedding celebration turned into something of a media circus. Halfway through the festivities, the trio had to appoint one of their guests as a press liaison. The local paper ran several stories on the triple marriage, one devoted entirely to the media madhouse.

News of the Dutch three-way wedding filtered into the United States through a September 26 report by Paul Belien, on his Brussels Journal website. The story spread through the conservative side of the Internet like wildfire, raising a chorus of "I told you so's" from bloggers who'd long warned of a slippery slope from gay marriage to polygamy.

Meanwhile, gay marriage advocates scrambled to put out the fire. M.V. Lee Badgett, an economist at the University of Massachusetts, Amherst, and research director of the Institute for Gay and Lesbian Strategic Studies, told a sympathetic website, "This [Brussels Journal] article is ridiculous. Don't be fooled—Dutch law does not allow polygamy." Badgett suggested that Paul Belien had deliberately mistranslated the Dutch word for "cohabitation contract" as "civil union," or even "marriage," so as to leave the false impression that the triple union had more legal weight than it did. Prominent gay-marriage advocate Evan Wolfson, executive director of Freedom to Marry, offered up a detailed legal account of Dutch cohabitation contracts, treating them as a matter of minor significance, in no way comparable to state-recognized registered partnerships.

In short, while the Dutch triple wedding set the conservative blogosphere ablaze with warnings, same-sex marriage advocates dismissed the story as a silly stunt with absolutely no implications for the gay marriage debate. And how did America's mainstream media adjudicate the radically different responses of same-sex marriage advocates and opponents to events in the Netherlands? By ignoring the entire affair.

Yet there is a story here. And it's bigger than even those chortling conservative websites claim. While Victor, Bianca, and Mirjam are joined by a private cohabitation contract rather than a state-registered partnership or a full-fledged marriage, their union has already made serious legal, political, and cultural waves in the Netherlands. To observers on both sides of the Dutch gay marriage debate, the De Bruijns' triple wedding is an unmistakable step down the road to legalized group marriage.

More important, the De Bruijn wedding reveals a heretofore hidden dimension of the gay marriage phenomenon. The De Bruijns' triple marriage is a bisexual marriage. And, increasingly, bisexuality is emerging as a reason why legalized gay marriage is likely to result in legalized group marriage. If every sexual orientation has a right to construct its own form of marriage, then more changes are surely due. For what gay marriage is to homosexuality, group marriage is to bisexuality. The De Bruijn trio is the tip-off to the fact that a connection between bisexuality and the drive for multipartner marriage has been developing for some time.

As American gay-marriage advocates were quick to point out, the cohabitation contract that joined Victor, Bianca, and Mirjam carries fewer legal implications and less status than either a registered partnership or a marriage—and Dutch trios are still barred from the latter two forms of union. Yet the use of a cohabitation contract for a triple wedding is a step in the direction of group marriage. The conservative and religious Dutch paper *Reformatorisch Dagblad* reports that this was the first known occurrence in the Netherlands of a cohabitation contract between a married couple and their common girlfriend. . . .

So the use of cohabitation contracts was an important step along the road to same-sex marriage in the Netherlands. And the link between gay marriage and the De Bruijns' triple contract was immediately recognized by the Dutch. The story in *Reformatorisch Dagblad* quoted J.W.A. van Dommelen, an attorney opposed to the De Bruijn union, who warned that the path from same-sex cohabitation contracts to same-sex marriage was about to be retraced in the matter of group marriage.

Van Dommelen also noted that legal complications would flow from the overlap between a two-party marriage and a three-party cohabitation contract. The rights and obligations that exist in Dutch marriages and Dutch cohabitation contracts are not identical, and it's unclear which arrangement would take precedence in case of a conflict. "The structure is completely gone," said Van Dommelen, as he called on the Dutch minister of justice to set up a working group to reconcile the conflicting claims of dual marriages and multipartner cohabitation contracts. Of course, simply by harmonizing the conflicting claims of dual marriages and triple cohabitation contracts, that working group would be taking yet another "small step" along the road to legal recognition for group marriage in the Netherlands.

The slippery-slope implications of the triple cohabitation contract were immediately evident to the SGP, a small religious party that played a leading role in the failed battle to preserve the traditional definition of marriage in the Netherlands. SGP member of parliament Kees van der Staaij noted the substantial overlap between marriage rights and the rights embodied in cohabitation contracts. Calling the triple cohabitation contract a back-door route to legalized polygamy, Van der Staaij sent a series of formal queries to Justice Minister Piet Hein Donner, asking him to dissolve the De Bruijn contract and to bar more than two persons from entering into cohabitation contracts in the future.

The justice minister's answers to these queries represent yet another small step—actually several small steps—toward legal and cultural recognition for group marriage in the Netherlands. To begin with, Donner reaffirmed the legality of multipartner cohabitation contracts and pointedly refused to consider any attempt to ban such contracts in the future. Donner also went so far as to assert that contracts regulating multipartner cohabitation can fulfill "a useful regulating function" (also translatable as "a useful structuring role"). In other words, Donner has articulated the rudiments of a "conservative case for group marriage."

The SGP responded angrily to Donner's declarations. In the eyes of this small religious party, Donner had effectively introduced a form of legal group marriage to the Netherlands. A party spokesman warned of an impending legal mess—especially if the De Bruijn trio, or others like them, have children. The SGP plans to raise its objections again when parliament considers the justice department's budget.

It's not surprising that the first English-language report was a bit unclear as to the precise legal status and significance of the triple Dutch union. The Dutch themselves are confused about it. One of the articles from which Paul Belien drew his original report is careful to distinguish between formal marriage and the cohabitation contract actually signed by Victor, Bianca, and Mirjam. Yet the very same article says that Victor now "officially" has "two wives."

Even Dutch liberals acknowledge the implications of the De Bruijn wedding. Jan Martens, a reporter and opinion columnist for *BN/DeStem*, the local paper in Roosendaal, wrote an opinion piece mocking opposition to group marriage by religious parties like the SGP. Noting the substantial overlap between cohabitation contracts and marriage, Martens said he agreed with the SGP that the De Bruijn triple union amounts to a "short-cut to polygamy." Yet Martens emphasized that he "couldn't care less if you have two, three, four, or sixty-nine wives or husbands."

Minority religious parties and their newspapers excepted, this mixture of approval and indifference seems to be the mainstream Dutch reaction so far.

Not only has Justice Minister Donner articulated the beginnings of a conservative case for group marriage, but Green Party spokesman Femke Halsema, a key backer of gay marriage, has affirmed her party's support for the recognition of multipartner unions. The public has not been inclined to protest these developments, and the De Bruijn trio have been welcomed by their neighbors. . . .

When it comes to marriage, culture shapes law. (It's a two-way street, of course. Law also influences culture.) After all, Dutch same-sex marriage advocates still celebrate the foundational role of symbolic gay marriage registries in the early 1990s. Although these had absolutely no legal status, the publicity and sympathy they generated are now widely recognized as keys to the success of the Dutch campaign for legal same-sex unions and ultimately marriage. How odd, then, that American gay-marriage advocates should respond to the triple Dutch wedding with hair-splitting legal discourses, while ignoring the Dutch media frenzy and subsequent signs of cultural acceptance—for a union with far more legal substance than Holland's first symbolic gay marriages. Despite the denials of gay-marriage advocates, in both legal and cultural terms, Victor, Bianca, and Mirjam's triple union is a serious move toward legalized group marriage in the Netherlands.

Given the stir in Holland, it's remarkable that not a single American mainstream media outlet carried a story on the triple Dutch wedding. Of course the media were all over the Dutch gay marriage story when they thought the experiment had been a success. In late 2003 and early 2004, in the wake of the Supreme Court's *Lawrence v. Texas* decision, which ruled sodomy laws unconstitutional, and looming gay marriage in Massachusetts, several American papers carried reports from the Netherlands. The common theme was that Holland had experienced no ill effects from gay marriage, and that the issue was no longer contentious. . . .

Although the triple Dutch union has been loosely styled "polygamy," it's actually a sterling example of polyamory. Polyamorists practice "responsible nonmonogamy"—open, loving, and stable relationships among more than two people (see "Beyond Gay Marriage: The Road to Polyamory," *The Weekly Standard*, August 4/August 11, 2003). Polygamous marriages among fundamentalist Mormons or Muslims don't depend on a blending of heterosexuality and bisexuality. Yet that combination perfectly embodies the spirit of polyamory. And polyamorists don't limit themselves to unions of one man and several women. One woman and two men, full-fledged group marriage, a stable couple openly engaging in additional shifting or stable relationships—indeed, almost any combination of partner-number and sexual orientation is possible in a polyamorous sexual grouping.

Polyamorists would call the De Bruijn union a "triad." In a polyamorous triad, all three partners are sexually connected. This contrasts with a three-person "V," in which only one of the partners (called the "hinge" or "pivot") has a sexual relationship with the other two. So the bisexuality of Bianca and Mirjam classifies the De Bruijn union as a polyamorous bisexual triad. In another sense, the De Bruijn marriage is also a gay marriage. The Bianca-Mirjam component of the union is gay, and legalized gay marriage in Holland has clearly helped make the idea of a legally recognized bisexual triad thinkable. . . .

The germ of an organized effort to legalize polyamory in the United States can be found in the Unitarian Church. Although few realize it, the Unitarian Church, headquartered in Boston, played a critical role in the legalization of same-sex marriage in Massachusetts. Julie and Hillary Goodridge, lead plaintiffs in *Goodridge v. Department of Public Health,* were married at the headquarters of the Unitarian Universalists in a ceremony presided over by the Reverend William G. Sinkford, president of the Unitarian Universalist Association. Hillary Goodridge is program director of the Unitarian Universalist Funding Program. And Unitarian churches in Massachusetts played a key role in the struggle over gay marriage, with sermons, activism, and eventually with marriage ceremonies for same-sex couples. Choosing a strongly church-affiliated couple like the Goodridges as lead plaintiffs was an important part of the winning strategy in the *Goodridge* case.

It's a matter of interest, therefore, that an organization to promote public acceptance of polyamory has been formed in association with the Unitarian Church. Unitarian Universalists for Polyamory Awareness (UUPA) was established in the summer of 1999. At the time, the news media in Boston carried reports from neighboring Vermont, where the soon-to-be-famous civil unions case was about to be decided. And the echo effect of the gay marriage battle on the polyamory movement goes back even further. The first informal Unitarian polyamory discussion group gathered in Hawaii in 1994, in the wake of the first state supreme court decision favorable to same-sex marriage in the United States.

"Our vision," says UUPA's website, "is for Unitarian Universalism to become the first poly-welcoming mainstream religious denomination." Those familiar with Unitarianism's role in the legalization of gay marriage understand the legal-political strategy implicit in that statement. UUPA's political goals are spelled out by Harlan White, a physician and leading UUPA activist, on the society's website. Invoking the trial of April Divilbiss, the first American polyamorist to confront the courts, White says, "We are concerned that we may become the center of the next great social justice firestorm in America."

White maintains that American polyamorists are growing in number. An exact count is impossible, since polyamory is still surrounded by secrecy. Polyamorists depend on the Internet to connect. Even so, says White, "attendance at conferences is up, email lists and websites are proliferating, and poly support groups are growing in number and size." As for the Unitarian polyamorists, their email list has several hundred subscribers, and the group has put on well-attended workshops at Unitarian General Assemblies since 2002. And although the number of open polyamorists is limited, some Unitarian ministers already perform "joining ceremonies" for polyamorous families. . . .

Shortly after the second article appeared, UUA president Sinkford circulated a statement among Unitarians acknowledging that press interest in Unitarian polyamory had "generated a great deal of anxiety" among the church's leadership. "Many of us are concerned that such press coverage might impair our ability to witness effectively for our core justice commitments." Sinkford appeared to be expressing a concern that had been stated more baldly in the original *Chronicle* article. According to the *Chronicle,* many of the students and faculty at the Unitarians' key west-coast seminary, Starr King School for the Ministry, in Berkeley, see the polyamory movement as a threat to the struggle for same-sex marriage.

In other words, Unitarians understand that moving too swiftly or openly to legitimize polyamory could validate the slippery-slope argument against same-sex marriage. So with news coverage prematurely blowing the cover off the Unitarians' long-term plan to legalize polyamory, President Sinkford took steps to hold UUPA at arm's length. Sinkford issued a public "clarification" that distanced the church from any formal endorsement of polyamory, yet also left room for the UUPA to remain a "related organization." . . .

The other fascinating angle in the *San Francisco Chronicle*'s coverage of the Unitarian polyamorists was the prominence of bisexuality. Most members of UUPA are either bisexual or heterosexual. One polyamorist minister who had recently come out to his congregation as a bisexual treated polyamory and bisexuality synonymously. "Our denomination has been welcoming to gays and lesbians and transgendered people," he said. "Bisexuals have not received the recognition they deserve." In other words, anything less than formal church recognition of polyamory is discrimination against bisexuals.

Two developing lines of legal argument may someday bring about state recognition for polyamorous marriage: the argument from polyamory, and the argument from bisexuality. In a 2004 law review article, Elizabeth F. Emens, of the University of Chicago Law School, offers the argument from polyamory (see "Monogamy's Law: Compulsory Monogamy and Polyamorous Existence," *New York University Review of Law & Social Change*). Polyamory is more than the mere practice of multiple sexual partnership, says Emens. Polyamory is also a disposition, broadly analogous to the disposition toward homosexuality. Insofar as laws of marriage, partnership, or housing discriminate against polyamorous partnerships, maintains Emens, they place unfair burdens on people with "poly" dispositions. Emens takes her cue here from the polyamorists themselves, who talk about their "poly" inclinations the way gays talk about homosexuality. For example, polyamorists debate whether to keep their poly dispositions "in the closet" or to "come out."

Emens's case for a poly disposition was inspired by the radical lesbian thinker Adrienne Rich, who famously put forward a "continuum model" of lesbianism. Rich argued that all women, lesbian-identified or not, are in some sense lesbians. If women could just discover where they fall on the "lesbian continuum," then even those women who remain heterosexually identified would abandon any prejudice against homosexuality.

Following Rich, Emens argues that all of us have a bit of "poly" inside. By discovering and accepting our own desires for multiple sexual partners, then even those who remain monogamous would abandon their prejudice against polyamorists. Of course, some people fall at the extreme ends of these continuums. Some folks are intensely monogamous, for example. But by the same token, others are intensely polyamorous. Whether for biological or cultural reasons, says Emens, some folks simply cannot live happily without multiple simultaneous sexual partners. And for those people, Emens argues, our current system of marriage is every bit as unjust as it is for homosexuals. . . .

The second legal strategy available to the polyamorists is the argument from bisexuality. No need here to validate anything as novel-sounding as a "polyamorous disposition." A case for polyamory can easily be built on the more venerable orientation of bisexuality. While no legal scholar has offered such a case, the groundwork is being laid by Kenji Yoshino, a professor at Yale Law School and deputy dean for intellectual life.

Yoshino's 2000 *Stanford Law Review* article "The Epistemic Contract of Bisexual Erasure" has a bewildering title but a fascinating thesis. Yoshino argues that bisexuality is far more prevalent than is usually recognized. The relative invisibility of bisexuality, says Yoshino, can be attributed to the mutual interest of heterosexuals and homosexuals in minimizing its significance. But according to Yoshino, the bisexuality movement is on the rise and bound to become more visible, with potentially major consequences for the law and politics of sexual orientation.

Defining bisexuality as a "more than incidental desire" for partners of both sexes, Yoshino examines the best available academic studies on sexual orientation and finds that each of them estimates the number of bisexuals as equivalent to, or greater than, the number of homosexuals. Up to now, the number of people who actively think of themselves as bisexuals has been much smaller than the number who've shown a "more than incidental" desire for partners of both sexes. But that, argues Yoshino, is because both heterosexuals and homosexuals have an interest in convincing bisexuals that they've got to make an all-or-nothing choice between heterosexuality and homosexuality.

Heterosexuals, for example, have an interest in preserving norms of monogamy, and bisexuality "destabilizes" norms of monogamy. Homosexuals, notes Yoshino, have an interest in defending the notion of an immutable homosexual orientation, since that is often the key to persuading a court that they have suffered discrimination. And homosexuals, adds Yoshino, have an interest in maximizing the number of people in their movement. For all these reasons and more, Yoshino argues, the cultural space in which bisexuals might embrace and acknowledge their own sexual identity has been minimized. Yoshino goes on to highlight the considerable evidence for the recent emergence of bisexuality as a movement, and predicts that in our current cultural climate—and given the numerical potential—bisexuality activism will continue to grow.

In addition to establishing the numerical and political significance of bisexuality, Yoshino lays down an argument that could easily be deployed to legalize polyamory: "To the extent that bisexuals are not permitted to express their dual desires, they might fairly characterize themselves as harmed." Yet Yoshino does not lay out a bisexual defense of polyamory. Instead Yoshino attacks—rightly— the stereotype that treats all bisexuals as nonmonogamous. Yet the same research that establishes the monogamous preferences of many bisexuals also confirms that bisexuals tend toward nonmonogamy at substantially higher rates than homosexuals. (See Paula C. Rust, "Monogamy and Polyamory: Relationship Issues for Bisexuals," in Firestein, ed., *Bisexuality: The Psychology and Politics of an Invisible Minority*.) That fact could easily be turned by a bisexuality rights movement into an argument for legalized polyamory. . . .

In 2004, the *Journal of Bisexuality* published a special double issue on polyamory, also released as the book *Plural Loves: Designs for Bi and Poly Living*. It's clear from *Plural Loves* that the polyamory movement now serves as the de facto political arm of the bisexual liberation struggle. As one contributor notes, "the large number of bi people in the poly movement provides evidence that bisexuality is one of the major driving forces behind polyamory. In other words, polyamory was created and spread partly to satisfy the need for bisexual relationship structures. . . . [T]he majority of poly activists are also bisexual. . . . Poly activism is bi activism. . . . The bi/poly dynamic has the potential to move both communities towards a point of culture-wide visibility, which is a necessary step on the road to acceptance."

Clearly, visibility and acceptance are on the rise. This past summer, the *Baltimore Sun* featured a long, friendly article on the polyamorists' national conference, held in Maryland. In September, the *New York Times* ran a long personal account of (heterosexual) polyamory in the Sunday Styles section. But the real uptick in public bisexuality/polyamory began with the October 2005 release in New York of the documentary *Three of Hearts: A Postmodern Family*.

Three of Hearts is the story of the real-life 13-year relationship of two men and a woman. Together for several years in a gay relationship, two bisexual-leaning men meet a woman and create a threesome that produces two children, one by each man. Although the woman marries one of the men, the entire threesome has a commitment ceremony. The movie records the trio's eventual breakup, yet the film's website notes their ongoing commitment to the view that "family is anything we want to create." . . .

Of course, many argue that true bisexuality does not exist. In this view—held by a variety of people, from some psychiatrists to certain pro-gay-marriage activists—everyone is either heterosexual or homosexual. From this perspective, so-called bisexuals are either in confused transition from heterosexuality to homosexuality, or simply lying about their supposedly dual sexual inclinations. Alternatively, it's sometimes said that while female bisexuality does exist, male bisexuality does not. A recent and controversial study reported on by the *New York Times* in July 2005 claimed to show that truly bisexual attraction in men might not exist.

Whatever view we take of these medical/psychiatric/philosophical controversies, it is a fact that a bi/poly rights movement exists and is growing. Whether Koen Brand and Bianca and Mirjam de Bruijn are "authentic" bisexuals or "just fooling themselves," they are clearly capable of sustaining polyamorous bisexual V's and triads for long enough to make serious political demands. *Three of Hearts* raises questions about whether the two men in the triangle are bisexual or simply confused gays. But with two children, a 13-year relationship, and at one time at least a clear desire for legal-ceremonial confirmation, the *Three of Hearts* trio is a harbinger of demands for legal group marriage. Public interest in the De Bruijn triangle has already raised the visibility and acceptance of polyamorous bisexuality in the Netherlands. For legal-political purposes, acceptance is what matters. And given Yoshino's numerical analysis, the growth potential for self-identifying bisexuals is substantial.

Americans today respond to gay and bisexual friends and family members in a variety of ways. Despite stereotypical accusations of "homophobia," the traditionally religious generally offer a mixture of compassion and concern. Many other Americans, conservative and liberal alike, are happy to extend friendship, understanding, and acceptance to gay and bisexual relatives and acquaintances. This heightened social tolerance is a good thing. Yet somehow the idea has taken hold that tolerance for sexual minorities requires a radical remake of the institution of marriage. That is a mistake.

The fundamental purpose of marriage is to encourage mothers and fathers to stay bound as a family for the sake of their children. Our liberalized modern marriage system is far from perfect, and certainly doesn't always succeed in keeping parents together while their children are young. Yet often it does. Unfortunately, once we radically redefine marriage in an effort to solve the problems of adults, the institution is destined to be shattered by a cacophony of grown-up demands.

The De Bruijn trio, Koen Brand, the Unitarian Universalists for Polyamory Awareness, the legal arguments of Elizabeth Emens and Kenji Yoshino, and the bisexual/polyamory movement in general have been launched into action by the successes of the campaign for gay marriage. In a sense, though, these innovators have jumped too soon. They've shown us today—well before same-sex marriage has triumphed nationwide—what would emerge in its aftermath.

Liberals may now put behind-the-scenes pressure on the Dutch government to keep the lid on legalized polyamory for as long as the matter of gay marriage is still unsettled. The Unitarian polyamorists, already conflicted about how much recognition to demand while the gay marriage battle is unresolved, may be driven further underground. But let there be no mistake about what will happen should same-sex marriage be fully legalized in the United States. At that point, if bisexual activists haven't already launched a serious campaign for legalized polyamory, they will go public. It took four years after the full legalization of gay marriage in the Netherlands for the first polyamory test case to emerge. With a far larger and more organized polyamory movement in America, it might not take even that long after the nationalization of gay marriage in the United States.

It's easy to imagine that, in a world where gay marriage was common and fully accepted, a serious campaign to legalize polyamorous unions would succeed—especially a campaign spearheaded by an organized bisexual-rights movement. Yet win or lose, the culture of marriage will be battered for years by the debate. Just as we're now continually reminded that not all married couples have children, we'll someday be endlessly told that not all marriages are monogamous (nor all monogamists married). For a second time, the fuzziness and imperfection found in every real-world social institution will be contorted into a rationale for reforming marriage out of existence.

EXPLORING THE ISSUE

Are Open Relationships Healthy?

Critical Thinking and Reflection

- What are some arguments made by each side with which you agree or disagree?
- What are the strengths and weaknesses of the two positions made in this issue? Pick the side with which you most agree. What are some additional arguments you would make to strengthen the case for or against open relationships? Think more broadly of the issue of open relationships. What sort of attitudes exist about open relationships? How will this affect those who choose to participate? How might it affect other couples in which there is strong disagreement over whether open relationships are healthy?

Is There Common Ground?

What is your response to Dyson's argument that the impact depends on the individual relationship? What is your response to Kurtz's argument that same-sex marriage will lead to polyamory? Is the progression as inevitable as he contends? What are some other factors that influence your views related to monogamy and polyamory?

This issue specifically asks whether open relationships are healthy. Is there a universal definition for what is emotionally healthy regarding sexual partners? Specifically, is monogamy a universal value that should be practiced in all relationships? Is polyamory a universal value that should be practiced in all relationships? What, if anything, would you regard as a standard relationship model that all couples should aspire to? Is sex outside marriage cheating if your spouse approves of it? Most importantly in seeking common ground, what kind of communication is necessary to ensure that people are being honest about their feelings?

Additional Resources

Polyamory Forum:

> http://www.polyamory.com/forum/

Xeromag presents Polyamory 101:

> http://www.xeromag.com/fvpoly.html

The Daily Beast reports on polyamory:

> http://www.thedailybeast.com/newsweek/2009/07/28/only-you-and-you-and-you.html

Alternatives to Marriage Project presents polyamory:

> http://www.unmarried.org/polyamory.html

Contributors to This Volume

EDITOR

DR. DAVID M. HALL, a distinguished corporate diversity trainer and educator, is the author of *Allies at Work: Creating a Lesbian, Gay, Bisexual, and Transgender Inclusive Work Environment* and the editor of *Taking Sides: Family and Personal Relationships*, a college text. He is the creator of *BullyShiled*, a bullying prevention mobile application for the iPhone and Droid. Dr. Hall is the recipient of teaching and humanitarian awards at the national, state, and local level. Those awards include the Gay, Lesbian, and Straight Education Network Educator of the Year Runner-Up Award, Teacher as Hero Award from the National Liberty Museum, Outstanding Alumnus from Widener University, and Outstanding Pennsylvanian from the Pennsylvania Jaycees. Dr. Hall's long list of clients includes JP Morgan Chase, Merck, the U.S. Department of Energy, PSE&G, The Hershey Company, Blue Cross Blue Shield of Florida, Safeway, The University of Pennsylvania, and many others.

AUTHORS

CLAIRE ALEXANDER is a co-author of *Teenage Parenthood: What's the Problem?* Dr. Alexander is a reader in the Department of Sociology at the London School of Economics.

CRYSTAL BEDLEY has taught Introduction to Sociology, Deviance, and Research Methods at Rutgers University. Her current research focuses on the construction and maintenance of multiracial identities.

RACHEL L. BERGERON is an assistant clinical professor of psychiatry at the Yale University School of Medicine.

JOAN BISKUPIC is the Supreme Court correspondent for *USA Today*. She has also served as the Supreme Court reporter for *The Washington Post* and the legal affairs writer for *Congressional Quarterly*. The author of several reference books, she recently completed a biography of retired Justice Sandra Day O'Connor.

WILLIAM BRENNAN is regarded as one of the greatest intellectual leaders of the twentieth-century Supreme Court. He was regarded for writing extraordinarily forward-thinking opinions, especially regarding civil rights and civil liberties.

JEANNE BROOKS-GUNN is Virginia and Leonard Marx Professor of Child Development and Education at Teachers College, Columbia University. As a developmental psychologist, Brooks-Gunn serves as consultant to and trainer of in-house researchers, faculty, and students in areas of child development. He is a member of the National Advisory Committee of the Institute for Research on Poverty, an advisory board member of Substance Abuse and Sex of the National Center on Addiction and Substance Abuse, and a senior faculty affiliate of the Joint Center on Poverty Research, Northwestern University/University of Chicago.

WARREN BURGER was the Chief Justice of the Supreme Court during a time in which it was slowly moving in a more conservative direction. He was an instrumental voice in many cases before the Supreme Court that had a more conservative outcome.

SARAH WERTHAN BUTTENWIESER has published articles in numerous magazines, including *Brain Child, Bitch,* and *New England Watershed*. She has been a regular contributor to *Mothers Movement Online, Literary Mama,* and *Mamazine*.

ALLAN C. CARLSON is president of the Howard Center for Family, Religion & Society and Distinguished Fellow in Family Policy Studies at the Family Research Council in Washington, D.C.

SHERRY F. COLB is a professor at Rutgers Law School in Newark, New Jersey, where she has taught courses in criminal procedure, evidence, mental health law, and feminist legal studies. She has published articles in a variety of law reviews, covering such areas as Fourth Amendment privacy,

Fourteenth Amendment liberty from physical confinement, and the role of personal character in criminal culpability.

TIMOTHY J. DAILEY is a senior research fellow at the Center for Marriage and Family Studies at the Family Research Council (FRC), where he specializes in "issues threatening the institutions of marriage and the family." His experience includes college-level instruction both at home and abroad, including several years in Israel teaching the historical, geographical, and archaeological background of the Bible.

NORMAN DANIELS is a professor and American philosopher, ethicist, and bioethicist at Harvard.

TONY DOKOUPIL is a staff writer at *Newsweek* and *The Daily Beast*. Dokoupil writes about different issues affecting national life, often related to diversity.

SIMON DUNCAN is a co-author of *Teenage Parenthood: What's the Problem?* Duncan is a professor of comparative social policy at the University of Bradford.

DONALD A. DYSON is a professor at Widener University, Center for Social Work Education. He is also a researcher for the New Jersey Department of Health and Senior Services.

ROSALIND EDWARDS is a co-author of *Teenage Parenthood: What's the Problem*? Edwards is a professor at London South Bank University.

MARK GOOD is a professor of counselor education at West Chester University and the president of Opn-Wyd, a diversity and communication company.

EZRA E. H. GRIFFITH is the deputy chair for clinical affairs and professor of psychiatry and African American studies in the psychiatry department at the Yale University School of Medicine.

WAYNE GRINWIS has been a sexual health educator for Planned Parenthood for 15 years. He is also an adjunct professor in the Department of Health at West Chester University of Pennsylvania.

KAREN A. HAASE co-authored "Sexting at School: Lessons Learned the Hard Way." Haase is an attorney with the law firm Harding and Shultz in Lincoln, Nebraska.

WEN-JUI HAN is an associate professor at the Columbia University School of Social Work, where she focuses on such topics as social welfare policy, with an emphasis on children and families; the effects of maternal employment and child care on children's cognitive and behavior outcomes; the impact of welfare reform and child care subsidies on families; work schedules and child care use of low-income and welfare families; and child care issues facing immigrant families.

JULIE HILDEN is a graduate of Harvard College and Yale Law School. A former clerk for Supreme Court Justice Stephen Breyer, she has more recently appeared on *Good Morning America*, Court TV, CNN, and NPR.

STEVEN F. HUBACHEK is the Counsel of Record for the Federal Defenders of San Diego, Inc.

JESSICA ISNER co-authored "Do Reality Television Shows Have a Negative Influence on Teenage Pregnancy and Parenting?" for *NWI Parent*.

CHRIS JEUB is a writer and president of Training Minds Ministries and is a former public school teacher. Chris and his wife have 11 children, all of whom he and his wife have home-schooled.

CALVIN P. JOHNSON, ESQ., is the former Chief Public Defender of the Fifth Judicial District. He started the first full-time public defender office in out-state Minnesota. He is a member of the Minnesota Bar Association and National Association of Criminal Defense Lawyers.

NEAL KUMAR KATYAL represented Salim Ahmed Hamdan, the driver for Osama bin Laden, in a successful U.S. Supreme Court case challenging the president's authority to create military commissions without legislative authority, the HYPERLINK "http://legaltimes.typepad.com/blt/2009/01/katyal-tapped-as-political-deputy-in-solicitor-generals-office.html"BLT reported Saturday. In a New Yorker article, Katyal suggested that a new federal court should be created to try terrorism suspects at Guantanamo Bay.

ANTHONY KENNEDY is an Associate Justice of the U.S. Supreme Court. He received his LL.B. from Harvard Law School in 1961 and worked for law firms in San Francisco and Sacremento, California, until he was nominated by President Gerald Ford to the U.S. Court of Appeals for the Ninth Circuit in 1975. He was nominated by President Ronald Reagan to the Supreme Court in 1988.

ANNIE KOVAL co-authored "Do Reality Television Shows Have a Negative Influence on Teenage Pregnancy and Parenting?" for *NWI Parent*.

STANLEY KURTZ is a contributing editor to the *National Review Online* and a fellow at the Hoover Institution. His writings have also appeared in *Policy Review, The Wall Street Journal,* and *Commentary*. He received his Ph.D. in social anthropology from Harvard University and later taught at Harvard, and he was also a Dewey Prize lecturer in psychology at the University of Chicago.

MARY B. MAHOWALD is a professor at the Pritzker School of Medicine at the University of Chicago. She is the author of *Women and Children and Health Care: An Unequal Majority; Disability, Difference, Discrimination: Perspectives on Justice in Bioethics and Public Policy;* and *Genes, Women, Equality*.

PAUL T. MERO is president of the Sutherland Institute and a trustee of the ALS Foundation.

SUSAN A. MILSTEIN received her Ed.D. in human sexuality education from Widener University and is a certified health education specialist in the Department of Health Enhancement, exercise science and physical education at Montgomery College. Professor Milstein was named "Emerging Professional" in the field of sexology by the Society for the Scientific Study of Sexuality at the 50th-anniversary national conference. She has also appeared as a guest speaker on NPR's Bryant Park Project, in their spot "The Tough Task of Teaching Sex Ed."

CAROLE MOORE is a freelance writer for *Scholastic Family Matters* and other publications.

SANDRA DAY O'CONNOR was the first woman appointed to the United States Supreme Court. For much of her time on the court, she was the justice most likely to wind up in the majority opinion. A graduate of Stanford Law School, O'Connor was an Arizona state senator and state judge, O'Connor was appointed to the Supreme Court by Ronald Reagan in 1981.

LISA PAUL co-authored "Do Reality Television Shows Have a Negative Influence on Teenage Pregnancy and Parenting?" for *NWI Parent*.

JOHN A. ROBERTSON is the Vinson and Elkins Chair at the University of Texas School of Law at Austin. He served as a professor at the University of Wisconsin Law School and as the Russell Sage Fellow in Law and Social Science at Harvard Law School. He is the author of two books about bioethics, *The Rights of the Critically Ill* and *Children of Choice: Freedom and the New Reproductive Technologies*. He currently serves as the chair of the Ethics Committee of the American Society for Reproductive Medicine.

JOHN R. RODENBERG is the District Court judge. He has served that term since 2000. Prior to his appointment on the bench, he was an attorney with Berens, Rodenberg & O'Connor, a family law practice and also served as part-time Assistant Brown County Attorney. Judge Rodenberg is a 2010 recipient of the Rosalie E. Wahl Judicial Award of excellence from the MSBA Public Law Section.

JENNIFER RUSSELL ESQ., is an attorney at SeniorLAW Center and addresses the legal concerns of senior relatives.

ANTONIN SCALIA is an Associate Justice of the U.S. Supreme Court. He taught law at the University of Virginia, the American Enterprise Institute, Georgetown University, and the University of Chicago before being nominated to the U.S. Court of Appeals by President Ronald Reagan in 1982. He served in that capacity until he was nominated by Reagan to the Supreme Court in 1986.

JUSTIN A. SITRON is an assistant professor of education at Widener University. He is also a certified sex educator and specialist in cross-cultural sexuality. He has presented at conferences of international and national organizations in cross-cultural sensitivity and sexuality issues.

LISA E. SORONEN co-authored "Sexting at School: Lessons Learned the Hard Way." Soronen is the senior attorney for the National School Boards Association.

PETER SPRIGG is the director of the Center for Marriage and Family Studies at the Family Research Council (FRC), having been senior director of culture studies for two years prior to his appointment. He oversees FRC's efforts to analyze and influence our culture as it relates to "marriage and family structure; education; human sexuality and the homosexual agenda; religion in public life; and the arts and entertainment." He also serves as executive editor of the monthly e-mail newsletter *Culture Facts*.

JANE JOHNSON STRUCK served as the Editor at Large of Today's Christian Woman magazine for over 8 years, and has served as a contributing editor and author for Charisma and Sphere magazine for several years. You can find Jane blogging on the Internet.

THE HUMAN RIGHTS CAMPAIGN (HRC) is the country's largest gay and lesbian organization, providing a national voice on gay and lesbian issues. HRC effectively lobbies Congress, mobilizes grass-roots action in diverse communities, invests strategically to elect a fair-minded Congress, and increases public understanding through innovative education and communication strategies.

THE NATIONAL CAMPAIGN TO PREVENT TEEN AND UNPLANNED PREGNANCY is dedicated to reducing teenage pregnancy.

ANGELA THOMAS is the co-author of *My Single-Mom Life*, published by Thomas Nealson. Thomas, a mother of four, possesses a Masters degree from the Dallas Theological Seminary.

DAVID TREVASKIS, ESQ., is a distinguished national speaker who works as Director of Pro Bono Services for the Pennsylvania Bar Association.

MARC TUNZI is director of the Family Practice Residency Program at Natividad Medical Center, Salinas, California, and associate clinical professor of family and community medicine at the University of California, San Francisco, School of Medicine. He received his medical degree from the University of California, San Diego, School of Medicine.

THOMAS M. VANDER VEN is an associate professor in the sociology department at Ohio University, specializing in the areas of crime and delinquency; work, family, and crime; criminological theory; and the sociology of social problems.

NICOLE VITALE co-authored the article "Sexting at School: Lessons Learned the Hard Way." Vitale assisted in this article as an intern with the National School Boards Association.

JANE WALDFOGEL is professor of social work and public affairs at the Columbia University School of Social Work, and a research associate at the Centre for Analysis of Social Exclusion at the London School of Economics. Dr. Waldfogel currently is a member of the National Academy of Science's Committee on Family and Work Policies and the author of *The Future of Child Protection: How to Break the Cycle of Abuse and Neglect* (Harvard University Press, 1998).